FAMINE AND FOOD SUPPLY
IN THE GRAECO-ROMAN WORLD

RESPONSES TO RISK AND CRISIS

FAMINE AND FOOD SUPPLY
IN THE GRAECO-ROMAN WORLD

RESPONSES TO RISK AND CRISIS

PETER GARNSEY

Reader in Ancient History and
Fellow of Jesus College, Cambridge

CAMBRIDGE
UNIVERSITY PRESS

Published by the Press Syndicate of the University of Cambridge
The Pitt Building, Trumpington Street, Cambridge CB2 1RP
40 West 20th Street, New York, NY 10011–4211 USA
10 Stamford Road, Oakleigh, Melbourne 3166, Australia

First published 1988
First paperback edition 1989
Reprinted 1993

British Library cataloguing in publication data
Garnsey, Peter
Famine and food supply in the Graeco-Roman world:
responses to risk and crisis.
1. Famine – Mediterranean Region
I. Title
363.8   HC244.5.Z9F3

Library of Congress cataloguing in publication data
Garnsey, Peter
Famine and food supply in the Graeco-Roman world:
responses to risk and crisis/Peter Garnsey.
p.   cm.
Bibliography.
Includes index.
1. Food supply – Greece – History. 2. Food supply – Rome – History.
3. Famines – Greece – History. 4. Famines – Rome – History.
I. Title.
HD9015.G82G37 1988
338.1'9'38 – dc19   87-16737

ISBN 0 521 35198 7 hard covers
ISBN 0 521 37585 1 paperback

Transferred to digital printing 1999

CONTENTS

Contents

TABLES AND FIGURES

TABLES

FIGURES

TO MY PARENTS

PREFACE

Ancient historical studies have traditionally followed the literary sources in their preoccupation with wars and international relations, political events and institutions, and the careers and personalities of powerful and charismatic individuals. However, the first concern of the vast majority of the inhabitants of the Mediterranean in ancient times was not whether Alexander the Great would reach the Ocean that surrounded the inhabited world, or whether Julius Caesar was justified in crossing the Rubicon, but food: how to feed themselves and their dependants.

Famine is a major preoccupation of geographers, anthropologists, economists and historians of periods other than antiquity. While interest has been kindled by contemporary events, it is also recognised that the study of famine leads to a deeper understanding of the dynamics of particular societies.

Historians of antiquity have by and large neglected the topic. There is room for a study that will assess the ability of the peoples of the ancient Mediterranean to produce and distribute essential foods in a setting marked by climatic variability, traditional farming methods, a rudimentary transport system and a significant level of urbanisation.

Food crisis is a consequence of the breakdown of the system of production, distribution and consumption of essential foodstuffs. An analysis of the origins and impact of famine would involve one in an investigation of the whole material basis of Graeco-Roman civilisation. Discussion of these matters must be postponed for the present. This book is limited in focus; it concerns the responses of both urban and rural dwellers to food crises, actual or anticipated.

Three introductory chapters on the definition, frequency and severity of food crisis (in Part I) preface a general discussion of the mechanisms for coping with the risk and actuality of food crisis (in Part II). An exhaustive catalogue of food crises has not been attempted. I have chosen to present instead criteria for the evaluation and com-

parison of individual crises and an account of the strategies open to and
adopted by residents of both city and countryside. My aim in these
sections and in the work as a whole has been to produce an interpreta-
tive account of food crisis in antiquity based on a qualitative analysis of
the evidence.

An essential first step is to understand the meaning of 'famine'.
'Famine' is normally used by translators, commentators and historians
as a blanket term to refer to any food crisis mentioned in the ancient
sources. In this book famine is defined as a catastrophic food crisis,
which is responsible for a dramatic rise in mortality rates in a given
population. Starting from this definition, I establish that famines were
rare and that food crises less serious than famines, which I call food
shortages, were common. The famine/shortage distinction is important; it both enables us to make a realistic assessment of the scale of the
problem, and confirms that significant public responses to the risk and
presence of food crises were possible and are potentially recoverable
from the ancient sources. Man was helpless in the face of famine,
epidemic disease or earthquake. Apart from propitiating the gods,
there was very little he could do about any of these natural disasters.
But if the typical food crisis was a shortage not a famine, and if
situations of shortage which did not amount to famine were frequent
and unpredictable occurrences, then it makes sense to ask what
practical steps were taken to ward them off or reduce their impact.

Food supply was a recurring problem for rural and urban dwellers
alike. In addition to the constraints imposed by the eternal facts of
climate and geography, the existing technology and the primitive
development of agricultural knowledge, peasant farmers had to
compete for the food they produced with the populations of cities to
which they were politically and economically subject. Their survival
depended upon their success in practising risk-minimising production
strategies, and building up a safety net of social and economic
relationships with kinsmen, neighbours, villagers and patrons.

Urban centres included consumers, often in very considerable
numbers, who did not make any contribution to agricultural production. Cities were in part wealth-creating, but their survival
depended crucially on their capacity to exploit a rural territory. As
urban populations developed and grew too large for their agrarian
base, they had either to siphon off surplus consumers or develop
exchange or trading relationships. One therefore looks for and expects
to find a network of institutions designed to monitor or administer
long-term trade and to ensure the distribution of imported (and
locally produced) goods among the citizenry. The results of such an

investigation are striking. Instead of an elaborate structure of protective mechanisms designed to buffer ordinary consumers against food shortage, we find that civic governments produced a variety of rudimentary, ad hoc measures. The key role in the resolution and alleviation of food crises was performed by local men of wealth, who, on the one hand, controlled food production and distribution, and, on the other, dominated local government.

Among ancient states, Athens and Rome deviate from the general practice of minimal government intervention in the provision of access to food supplies. But this was not the case at all times. Athens only built up an impressive structure of laws and institutions to secure the food supply in the fourth century BC, while Rome developed a regular food supply system from the turn of the third century BC and operated monthly distributions of grain from 123 BC; the grain was not handed out gratis to most citizens until 58 BC. The rest of the book (Parts III and IV) is taken up with a systematic account of food supply and food crisis in Athens and Rome, at once the best documented and the least typical of ancient states. The experience of Athens is examined from roughly the beginning of the sixth century BC, the age of Solon, to the suppression of democracy by the Macedonians in 322 BC, and that of Rome from the beginnings of the Republic, traditionally 509 BC, to the end of the Principate, around the middle of the third century AD.

The studies of Athens and Rome run along roughly parallel lines, in that both are built around the historical development of institutionalised responses to the food supply problem. However, in the case of Athens, I begin with an assessment of the productive potential of the rural hinterland, Attica, while in the case of Rome, I end with an examination of the effect of the demands of the imperial power on the subject peoples (Chapters 6 and 15, respectively). Chapter 6 is not a full investigation of climate and agriculture in Attica (which is best pursued elsewhere), but a re-evaluation of the evidence for Attic cereal production and the import of cereals into Athens. There is reason to believe that scholars have seriously underestimated the agricultural potential of Attica and the contribution of domestic production to Athens' food needs, and in consequence dated Athens' dependence on foreign grain too early and misinterpreted the available evidence for Athenian foreign policy in the archaic period in the light of their mistaken assumptions. In the case of Rome, there is the challenge of bringing to bear on a traditional problem, the nature of Roman rule, a considerable body of evidence that has not been collected and addressed before: namely, the data relating to the supply, distribution and shortage of food in the cities of the empire. An old debate is moved onto new terrain: the question at issue is the impact of the demands of the imperial power on the living standards and survival chances of the mass of subject communities and households.

In writing this book I have received information, advice and encouragement from friends, colleagues and students on all sides. Paul Cartledge, Tim Cornell, Michael Crawford, Mogens Hansen, Michael Jameson, David Lewis, Paul Millett, Ian Morris, Dominic Rathbone, Dorothy Thompson, Frank Walbank and Gregory Woolf have read all or part of this book in draft and enabled me to make numerous improvements. I have benefited from discussions with Tom Gallant, who also gave me valuable assistance in data analysis. I am grateful to Christopher Hope for allowing me to draw on his mathematical and computer skills, to Paul Roesch and his colleagues in Lyon for introducing me to the epigraphic material from the Hellenistic age, and to Peter Brown for encouraging me to move beyond the canonical texts and to 'rummage in the rubbish-bins of history'. Finally, I acknowledge funding from the Economic and Social Research Council for the initial stages of a parallel project on the agroclimatology of the Mediterranean, which has influenced the writing of the early chapters of this book.

Cambridge   P.G.
May 1987

ABBREVIATIONS

Most of the abbreviations are those of *L'Année Philologique*. In addition the following may be unfamiliar to some readers.

Abbott and Johnson	F. F. Abbott and A. C. Johnson, *Municipal Administration in the Roman Empire*, Princeton, 1926
AE	*L'Année Epigraphique*
Austin	M. M. Austin, *The Hellenistic World from Alexander to the Roman Conquest*, Cambridge, 1981
BAR	*British Archaeological Reports*
BGU	*Ägyptische Urkunden aus den Staatlichen Museen zu Berlin, Griechische Urkunden*, 1895–
CIG	*Corpus Inscriptionum Graecarum*
CIL	*Corpus Inscriptionum Latinarum*
CMG	*Corpus Medicorum Graecorum*
C. Ord. Ptol.	M. T. Lenger, *Corpus des ordonnances des Ptolemées*, 2nd edn, Brussels, 1980
CSEL	*Corpus Scriptorum Ecclesiasticorum Latinorum*
FE	*Forschungen in Ephesos*
FGH	F. Jacoby, *Die Fragmente der griechischen Historiker*, Berlin, 1923–
FIRA²	*Fontes Iuris Romani Anteiustiniani*, 2nd edn, 1940–3
Fornara	C. W. Fornara, *Archaic Times to the End of the Peloponnesian War: Translated Documents of Greece and Rome*, Vol. 1, 2nd edn, Cambridge, 1983
Harding	P. Harding, *From the End of the Peloponnesian War to the Battle of Ipsus: Translated Documents of Greece and Rome*, Vol. 2, Cambridge, 1985
IG	*Inscriptiones Graecae*
IGR	*Inscriptiones Graecae ad Res Romanas pertinentes*
ILAlg.	*Inscriptions latines de l'Algérie*
ILLRP	*Inscriptiones Latinae Liberae Rei Publicae*
ILS	*Inscriptiones Latinae Selectae*
LBW	P. Le Bas and W. H. Waddington, *Voyage archéologique en Grèce et en Asie Mineure 1843–1844* ... 6 vols., Paris, 1853–70

Abbreviations

Meiggs and Lewis	R. Meiggs and D. Lewis, *A Selection of Greek Historical Inscriptions*, Oxford, 1958
Nouveau Choix	*Nouveau Choix d'inscriptions grecques: textes, traductions, commentaire*, L'Institut Fernand-Courby, Paris, 1971
OGIS	*Orientis Graeci Inscriptiones Selectae*
P. Erl.	*Die Papyri der Universitätsbibliothek Erlangen*, 1942
P. Lond.	*Greek Papyri in the British Museum*, 1893–1917
P. Oxy.	*The Oxyrhynchus Papyri*, 1898–
PSI	*Pubblicazioni della società italiana per la ricerca dei Papiri greci in Egitto*, 1912–
SEG	*Supplementum Epigraphicum Graecum*
SHA	*Scriptores Historiae Augustae*
*Syll.*³	*Sylloge Inscriptionum Graecarum*, 3rd edn
TAM	*Tituli Asiae Minoris*
Tod II	M. N. Tod, *A Selection of Greek Historical Inscriptions*, Vol. 2, Oxford, 1948
Wilcken, *Chr.*	L. Mitteis and U. Wilcken, *Grundzüge und Chrestomathie der Papyruskunde*, Leipzig, 1912

MEASURES, WEIGHTS AND COINS

1 Greek medimnos of wheat = 6 Roman modii = 51.7 litres = 40 kg = 127,400 kcals.

1 hectare = 4 Roman iugera = 11 Greek plethra.

1 Attic talent = 6,000 drachmas = 36,000 obols.

1 Roman denarius (= 1 Attic drachma) = 4 sestertii = 16 asses.

MAPS

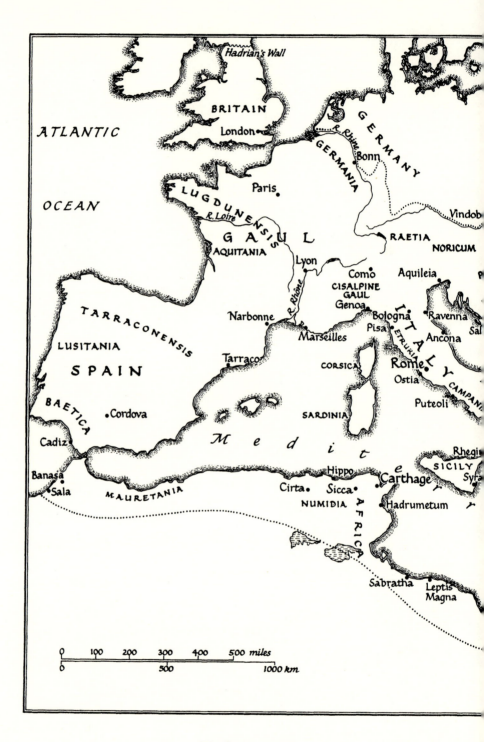

1　The Roman world

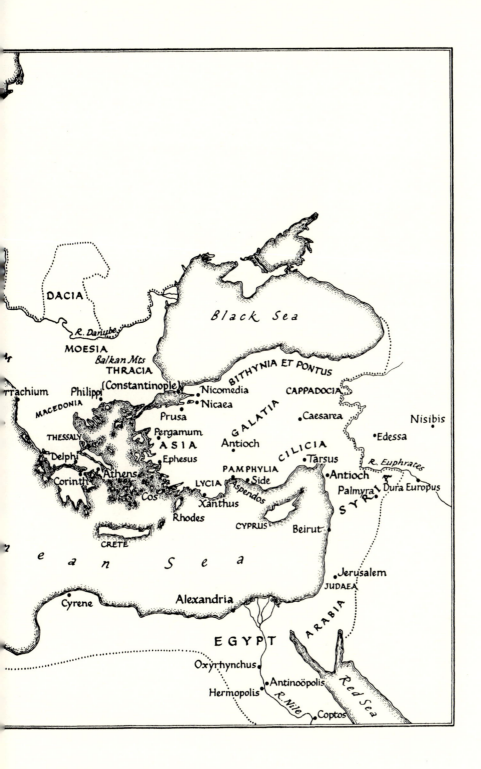

DACIA

Black Sea

R. Danube

MOESIA

Balkan Mts
THRACIA

BITHYNIA ET PONTUS

rrachium   Philippi   (Constantinople)   Nicomedia   CAPPADOCIA

MACEDONIA   Nicaea   Nisibis

                        Prusa   GALATIA   Caesarea

THESSALY   Pergamum   Edessa

                        ASIA   Antioch   CILICIA   R. Euphrates

Delphi   Ephesus   Tarsus

Corinth   Athens   PAMPHYLIA   Side   Antioch

                LYCIA   Aspendos   Palmyra   Dura Europus

        Cos   Xanthus   SYRIA

                Rhodes   CYPRUS   Beirut

        CRETE

e   a   n   S   e   a   Jerusalem

                                                JUDAEA

Cyrene   Alexandria   ARABIA

                        Oxyrhynchus   Red Sea

                        Antinoöpolis

                Hermopolis   R. Nile

                                Coptos

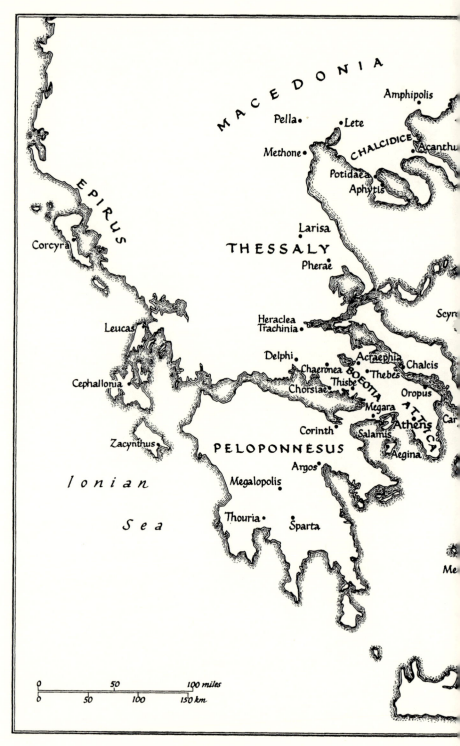

2 The Greek world

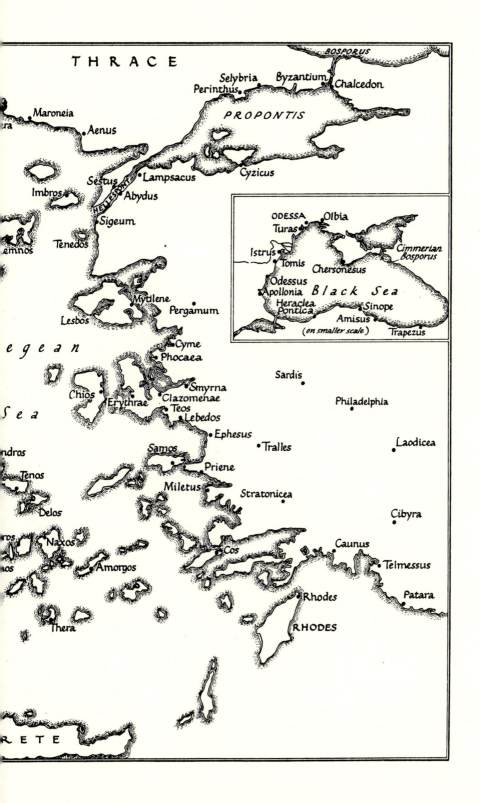

THRACE

Maroneia

Aenus

BOSPORUS

Selybria
Perinthus
Byzantium
Chalcedon

PROPONTIS

Sestus •Lampsacus
Cyzicus
Imbros
Abydus
HELLESPONT
Sigeum

Tenedos

emnos

ODESSA Olbia
Turas
Istrus
Tomis
Chersonesus
Odessus
Apollonia *Black Sea*
Heraclea
Pontica Sinope
Amisus
(on smaller scale) Trapezus
Cimmerian
Bosporus

Mytlene
Pergamum
Lesbos

e g e a n

•Cyme
•Phocaea

Sardis

Philadelphia

Chios
Erythrae
Clazomenae
•Teos
•Smyrna
Lebedos

S e a

Ephesus

Laodicea

ndros

Samos
•Tralles

Tenos

Priene

Miletus

Stratonicea

Cibyra

Delos

Naxos
Cos

Caunus

ros

•Telmessus

Amorgos

os

Thera

Rhodes

Patara

RHODES

RETE

S e a

PART I
THE INCIDENCE AND SEVERITY OF FOOD CRISIS

1

FAMINE AND SHORTAGE

The Chronicle of Ps.–Joshua the Stylite, Chapter 38. The year 811 [AD 499–500]. In the month of Adar [March] of this year the locusts came upon us out of the ground, so that, because of their number, we imagined that not only had the eggs that were in the ground been hatched to our harm, but that the very air was vomiting them against us, and that they were descending from the sky upon us. When they were only able to crawl, they devoured and consumed all the Arab territory and all that of Rasain and Tella and Edessa. But after they were able to fly, the stretch of their radii was from the border of Assyria to the Western sea [the Mediterranean] and they went northwards as far as the boundary of the Ortaye. They ate up and desolated these districts and utterly consumed everything that was in them ... Presently, in the month of Nisan [April], there began to be a dearth of grain and of everything else, and four modii of wheat were sold for a dinar. In the months of Khaziran [June] and Tammuz [July] the inhabitants of these districts were reduced to all sorts of shifts to live. They sowed millet for their own use, but it was not enough for them, because it did not thrive. Before the year came to an end, misery from hunger had reduced the people to beggary, so that they sold their property for half its worth, horses and oxen and sheep and pigs. And because the locusts had devoured all the crop, and left neither pasture nor food for man or beast, many forsook their native places and removed to other districts of the north and west. And the sick who were in the villages, as well as the old men and boys and women and infants, and those who were tortured by hunger, being unable to walk far and go to distant places, entered into the cities to get a livelihood by begging; and thus many villages and hamlets were left destitute of inhabitants. They did not however escape punishment ...; for the pestilence came upon them in the places to which they went, and even overtook those who entered into Edessa; about which I shall tell presently to the best of my ability, though no one, I think, could describe it as it really was.

Chapter 39. Now, however, I am going to write to you about the dearth, as you asked me ... Wheat was sold at this time at the rate of four modii for a dinar and barley at six modii. Chickpeas were five hundred numia a kab; beans, four hundred numia a kab; and lentils, three hundred and sixty numia a kab; but meat was not as

[1] W. Wright, *The Chronicle of Joshua the Stylite* (Cambridge, 1882).

3

yet dear. As time went on, however, the dearth became greater, and the pain of hunger afflicted the people more and more. Everything that was not edible was cheap, such as clothes and household utensils and furniture, for these things were sold for a half or a third of their value, and did not suffice for the maintenance of their owners, because of the great dearth of bread. At this time our father Mar Peter set out to visit the emperor in order to request him to remit the tax. The governor, however, laid hold of the landed proprietors, and used great violence on them and extorted it from them, so that, before the bishop could persuade the emperor, the governor had sent the money to the capital. When the emperor saw that the money had arrived, he did not like to remit it; but in order not to send our father away empty, he remitted two folles to the villagers . . . whilst he freed the citizens from the obligation of drawing water for the Greek soldiery.

Chapter 40. The governor himself too set out to visit the emperor, girt with his sword, and left Eusebius to hold his post and govern the city. When this Eusebius saw that the bakers were not sufficient to make bread for the market, because of the multitude of country people, of whom the city was full, and because of the poor who had no bread in their houses, he gave an order that everyone who chose might make bread and sell it in the market. And there came Jewish women, to whom he gave wheat from the public granary, and they made bread for the market. But even so, the poor were in straits, because they had not money wherewith to buy bread; and they wandered about the streets and porticoes and courtyards to beg a morsel of bread, but there was no one in whose house bread was in superfluity. And when one of them had begged [a few] pence, but was unable to buy bread therewith, he used to purchase therewith a turnip or a cabbage or a mallow and eat it raw. And for this reason there was a scarcity of vegetables, and a lack of everything in the city and villages, so that the people actually dared to enter the holy places and for sheer hunger to eat the consecrated bread as if it had been common bread. Others cut pieces off corpses, that ought not to be eaten, and cooked and ate them . . .

Chapter 41. The year 812 [AD 500–1]. In this year, after the vintage, wine was sold at the rate of six measures for a dinar, and a kab of raisins for three hundred numia. The famine was sore in the villages and in the city; for those who were left in the villages were eating bitter-vetches; and others were frying the withered fallen grapes and eating them, though even of them there was not enough to satisfy them. And those who were in the city were wandering about the streets, picking up the stalks and leaves of vegetables, all filthy with mud, and eating them. They were sleeping in the porticoes and streets, and wailing by night and day from the pangs of hunger; and their bodies wasted away, and they were in a sad plight, and became like jackals because of the leanness of their bodies. The whole city was full of them, and they began to die in the porticoes and in the streets.

Chapter 42. After the governor Demosthenes had gone up to the emperor, he informed him of this calamity; and the emperor gave him no small sum of money to distribute among the poor. And when he came back from his presence to Edessa, he sealed many of them on their necks with leaden seals, and gave each of them a pound of bread a day. Still, however, they were not able to live, because they were tortured by the pangs of hunger, which wasted them away. The pestilence became worse about this time, namely the month of the latter Teshri [November]; and still

4

more in the month of the first Kanun [December], when there began to be frost and ice, because they were passing the nights in the porticoes and streets, and the sleep of death came upon them during their natural sleep. Children and babes were crying in every street. Of some the mothers were dead; others their mothers had left, and had run away from them when they asked for something to eat, because they had nothing to give them. Dead bodies were lying exposed in every street, and the citizens were not able to bury them, because, while they were carrying out the first that had died, the moment they returned they found others. By the care of Mar Nonnus, the lodging house keeper, the brethren used afterwards to go about the city, and to collect these dead bodies ... The stewards of the [Great] Church, the priest Mar Tewath-il and Mar Stratonicus ... established an infirmary among the buildings attached to the [Great] Church of Edessa. Those who were very ill used to go and lie down there; and many dead bodies were found in the infirmary, which they buried along with those at the lodging house.

Chapter 43. The governor blocked up the gates of the colonnades attached to the winter bath, and laid down in it straw and mats, and they used to sleep there, but it was not sufficient for them. When the grandees of the city saw this, they too established infirmaries, and many went in and found shelter in them. The Greek soldiers too set up places in which the sick slept, and charged themselves with their expenses. They died by a painful and melancholy death; and though many of them were buried every day, the number still went on increasing. For a report had gone forth throughout the province of Edessa, that the Edessenes took good care of those who were in want; and for this reason a countless multitude of people entered the city. The bath too that was under the Church of the Apostles beside the Great Gate was full of sick, and many dead bodies were carried forth from it every day ... And when the graves of the lodging house and the Church were full, the governor went forth and opened the old graves that were beside the Church of Mar Knoa, which had been constructed by the ancients with great pains, and they filled them. Then they opened others, and they were not sufficient for them; and at last they opened any old grave, no matter what, and filled it. For more than a hundred bodies were carried out every day from the lodging house and many a day a hundred and twenty, and up to a hundred and thirty, from the beginning of the latter Teshri [November] till the end of Adar [March] ... In the month of Shebat [February] too the dearth was very great, and the pestilence increased. Wheat was sold at the rate of thirteen kabs for a dinar, and barley eighteen kabs. A pound of meat was a hundred numia, and a pound of fowl three hundred numia, and an egg forty numia. In short there was a dearth of everything edible.

Chapter 44. There were public prayers in the month of Adar [March] on account of the pestilence, that it might be restrained from the strangers ... In the month of Nisan [April] the pestilence began among the people of the city and many biers were carried out in one day, but no one could tell their number. And not only in Edessa was this sword of the pestilence, but also from Antioch as far as Nisibis the people were destroyed and tortured in the same way by famine and pestilence. Many of the rich died, but not of hunger; and many of the grandees too died in this year. In the months of Khaziran [June] and Tammuz [July], after the harvest, we thought that we might now be relieved from dearth. However our expectations were

5

not fulfilled as we thought, but the wheat of the new harvest was sold as dear as five modii for a dinar.

Chapter 45. The year 813 [AD 501–2]. After these afflictions of locusts and famine and pestilence about which I have written to you, a little respite was granted us by the mercy of God.

Were scenes such as those witnessed by Ps.-Joshua the Stylite a regular feature of ancient Mediterranean society, urban or rural? How frequent was famine? Ps.-Joshua and the abbot Sergius who commissioned the *Chronicle* both appear to have regarded the famine at Edessa as a singular event. The plague of locusts of the year preceding and the disappointing wheat crop of the year that followed are treated as minor disorders, and can be taken as more representative.

A brief working definition of famine might run as follows:

Famine is a critical shortage of essential foodstuffs leading through hunger to starvation and a substantially increased mortality rate in a community or region.

Famine is to be distinguished from shortage, a milder form of subsistence crisis, defined as:

A short-term reduction in the amount of available foodstuffs, as indicated by rising prices, popular discontent, hunger, in the worst cases bordering on starvation.

Food crises are not always serious. Famine is a catastrophe. It is a categorical error, committed frequently in the literature, to describe every food crisis as a famine.

The boundary between famine and shortage is indistinct. An authority on modern famine has written: 'Criteria do not exist to measure the degree of hunger, emaciation or elevation of death rate serving to differentiate famine from shortage.'[2] In view of this judgement, it would be idle for students of antiquity to imagine that they can employ the famine/shortage distinction with a high level of precision. In the long run, however, the idea of a spectrum or continuum of food crises holds out more promise than the famine/shortage dichotomy. Each food crisis occupies a place on a continuum leading from mild shortage to disastrous famine.

The proposition for which I will argue is that famines were rare, but that subsistence crises falling short of famine were common. The undertaking is ambitious. It involves making both quantitative and qualitative judgements on the basis of evidence that on the face of it is deficient. How is the question 'how many' to be answered when there is no prospect of compiling anything approaching a comprehensive list of subsistence crises? How can we say 'of what kind' recorded crises were,

[2] Bennett (1968). On defining famine, see e.g. Sen (1981), 39–40; Dando (1980), 57ff.

6

how can they be located on the famine/shortage continuum, given that there is no 'famine narrative' from antiquity which can rival the *Chronicle* of Ps.-Joshua in length and detail? Are we condemned therefore to produce a mere catalogue of attested food crises which never rises above the level of description?[3]

[3] See now Garnsey (1992).

2

THE FREQUENCY OF FOOD CRISIS

PROXY-DATA

Historians of all periods before the recent past have uniformly lacked both long series of data on harvest-size in the case of staple crops, and direct quantitative data on climate, the main factor affecting agricultural performance. However, ingenious use has been made of food prices and real wages as indices of shortage or abundance, and of wine yields, harvest dates and tree rings as pointers to climatic fluctuations. Ancient historians have been unable to turn to such substitute data, though the work of dendroclimatologists will before long significantly advance our knowledge of the climate of antiquity.[1]

However, the broad pattern of food crisis in antiquity can be recovered if such ancient evidence as exists for food crisis is combined with modern data on climate and agricultural yield. The latter data can be used as substitute or proxy-data in the absence of detailed records of climate for any period of history which experienced substantially similar climatic conditions.

Classical antiquity is generally thought to have been one such time.[2] This supposition receives some general support from the literary sources, which present quite unsystematically a picture of a recognisably 'Mediterranean' climate, and from scientific analyses of glacier and tree-line fluctuations and pollen deposits. It is true that scholars have disagreed about the precise pattern of secular climatic change.

[1] Appleby (1979); Schofield (1985); Bryson and Padoch (1980); Pfister (1980); Le Roy Ladurie and Baulant (1980). For dendroclimatological studies in progress, see Kuniholm and Striker (1983). The methodology outlined below (cf. Garnsey, Gallant and Rathbone (1984)) is being developed in the context of a study of the agroclimatology of the Mediterranean by P. Garnsey and T. Gallant (in progress). (Tables 1–3 were produced by T. Gallant on the basis of data collected for this study.) Climatic matters that receive only brief discussion here will be treated in detail in that work.

[2] See e.g. Wagstaff (1981); Wagstaff and Gamble, in Renfrew and Wagstaff (1982), 95ff.; Denton and Karlen (1973); Greig and Turner (1974); Vita-Finzi (1969) with Bintliff (1982). General studies of Mediterranean geography include Semple (1932); Walker (1962); Birot and Dresch (1964); Smith (1979).

8

But if one's interest is in conjuring up the day-to-day, year-to-year conditions of agricultural production largely at a subsistence level, these matters are of less significance than two other points about the ancient climate which are suggested by the modern meteorological data: regional diversity and interannual variability.

First, the climate of the Mediterranean is (and has always been) exceptionally diverse from region to region, a point not lost on Aristotle:

Sometimes it happens that droughts or rain occur over a large area, sometimes over a part; often the country as a whole receives the seasonal rains or more, while in some sections of the area there is drought; sometimes it is the opposite, and the area generally has either slight rainfall or even conditions of drought, while in a given section the share of water is abundant.[3]

A cursory glance at rainfall and temperature charts reveals that the so-called 'typical' Mediterranean climate (briefly, winter rain and mild temperatures followed by summer heat and drought) is not enjoyed uniformly throughout the region. In fact, the mosaic of rainfall distribution is too complicated to be captured by a regular rainfall map. Sudden and frequent variations in vegetation, from humid to arid, are a striking feature of islands and peninsulas, reflecting a complex precipitation pattern as well as the physical properties of the soil, altitude and other microenvironmental factors. Classifications such as that of Le Houérou identifying no fewer than 64 climatic sub-types in the Mediterranean basin as a whole make no allowance for the occurrence of countless microclimates in circumscribed locations.

Secondly, a high level of interannual variability of climate has been a constant feature of the Mediterranean region since the Great Ice Age, even if the precise shape it has taken has differed from period to period. In particular, rainfall is very erratic, unevenly distributed between seasons, and often in short supply, especially in the southern and eastern sectors of the Mediterranean. Therefore harvest fluctuations are and were regular and crop failures inevitable, though not precisely predictable, throughout the region. As Rabbi Eleazar b. Perata, who flourished in the first half of the second century AD, wrote:

From the day the Temple was destroyed the rains have become irregular in the world. There is a year which has abundant rains, and there is a year with but little rain. There is a year in which the rains come down in their proper season and a

---

[3] Aristotle, *Meteorol*, 2.4; Le Houérou (1977); cf. Brichambaut and Wallen (1963) (12 main climatic regions in the Near East). For the olive as marker of different climatic zones, see Walker (1962), 38ff.

year in which they come out of season ... In the period of the Second Temple the rains came on time and as a result the crops were of far better quality.[4]

Crop failure is neither a sufficient nor a necessary condition of food crisis, but it does underlie many such crises. For the most part a crop fails because of insufficient or excessive rainfall at the critical period of plant growth. In the Mediterranean the growth period comprises the months from October to May. Figures on the probability of crop failure in a given area can be arrived at through the analysis of rainfall statistics for the crucial months in the light of scientifically determined plant thresholds: these are, approximately, 300 mm for wheat and 200–250 mm for barley.[5]

The points for and against the use of modern data as a guide to past conditions are obvious. The quality of the data that can be assembled for climate and yield is clearly superior to anything that can be arrived at by indirect means. On the other hand, the data can be employed only to construct a model of climate, climatic and harvest variability, and no model can precisely reproduce reality.

Case-studies

To illustrate the way in which the data can be utilised for our purposes I choose Attica (that is, the homeland of Athens), Odessa on the northern Black Sea coast, Thessaly and Samos. Athens notoriously was a net importer of cereals from the fifth century BC (many would say from the early sixth century). The northern Black Sea region and Thessaly are normally regarded as net exporters. Samos was probably more typical of Greek cities in veering between a 'normal' modest surplus and sporadic shortfall.

An analysis of precipitation from October to May in Attica (1931–60) produces the following results. The percentage probability of a failure of the wheat crop was 28%, of the barley crop 5.5%; that is, wheat failed more than 1 year in 4, barley about 1 year in 20. (The probability of a failure of dry legumes was 71%, which gives a failure rate of almost 3 years in 4.)

If conditions prevailing in antiquity were in general comparable (the precise figures are not transferable), then we can see that there is no question but that the staple crops in Attica must have been very vulnerable. How frequently Athenians suffered from shortages as

---

[4] *Bavli Taanit* 19b; see the English translation in Epstein (1938), 96. Mariolopoulos (1962); Wigley and Farmer (1982); Gallant (1982a), ch. 1.

[5] Plant moisture thresholds: Arnon (1972), II, 4, 74. The threshold for dry legumes is 350–400 mm.

distinct from crop failure would have depended upon their ability to bring in, store and distribute the foodstuffs which they required, and their willingness to eat barley, the cereal which grew best in Attica. To answer these questions it would be necessary to fall back on the ancient evidence for Athenian political history, foreign relations, food supply and diet.

As it happens, the internal history of Athens is reasonably well documented. The same cannot be said of Thessaly and the Greek colonial territory on the northern Black Sea coast. Both are usually seen as grain-exporters, unlike Athens, though there is sporadic inscriptional evidence for food crisis.

If the modern climate data for Thessaly can serve as a guide to the situation in antiquity, the likelihood of a failure or severe reduction in the harvest was actually marginally less in Attica than in the plain of Larisa, the area of Thessaly best suited in most respects to cereal production. The wheat crop will fail as in Attica more than 1 year in 4 and the barley crop 1 year in 10. (Dry legumes will fail slightly less often than in Attica, more than 4 years in 10.) Moreover, yields tend to co-vary across Thessaly; that is to say, the major crops tend to fail, and succeed, together (see Table 1). This means that in times of drought the Thessalians had to go a considerable distance for supplies, while in a good year they had at their disposal a sizeable surplus for extra-regional exchange. In perhaps 328 BC Larisa received from Cyrene the equivalent of 75,000 Attic medimnoi (around 39,375 hl) of wheat; about two centuries later, the whole of Thessaly sent 80,625 Attic medimnoi (around 42,325 hl) of wheat to Rome late in the year.[6]

The next example is indirectly relevant to Athens. The modern city of Odessa lies in the north of the Black Sea region, in an area colonised by the Greeks in the archaic age. Callatis, Tomis, Tyras, Olbia and the cities of the Tauric Chersonese lie in this region and enjoy a similar climate. The data show that in 46 out of 100 years in modern times the wheat crop will have been seriously deficient. In other words, almost every other year Odessa and the surrounding region has needed to import wheat or draw on stocks held over from a recent good season. If local inhabitants were prepared to accept a substitute for wheat, they could in principle have fallen back on foods made from barley or another relatively drought- or frost-resistant grain. Barley will have failed only 15–16 years in 100 – that is, once every 6–7 years. These figures suggest that if the Greek cities did export large quanti-

---

[6] *SEG* IX 2+ = Tod II 196; Garnsey, Gallant and Rathbone (1984).

Table 1. *Thessaly (1911, 1926–36,[a] 1955–6, 1959–80): interannual variability of the major cereal and leguminous crops. Partial correlation coefficients, controlling for time.*

Nomos of Trikkala

	Wheat	Barley	Broad beans	Chickpeas	Lentils
Wheat	—	0.7071	0.3216	0.4079	0.2002
Barley	0.7071	—	0.4718	0.4395	0.3422
Broad beans	0.3216	0.4718	—	0.3518	0.3756
Chickpeas	0.4079	0.4395	0.3158	—	0.6450
Lentils	0.2002	0.3422	0.3756	0.6450	—

Nomos of Karditsa

	Wheat	Barley	Broad beans	Chickpeas	Lentils
Wheat	—	0.8764	0.3393	0.6464	0.2350
Barley	0.8764	—	0.5244	0.5279	0.2001
Broad beans	0.3393	0.5244	—	0.4971	0.0270
Chickpeas	0.6464	0.5279	0.4971	—	0.1050
Lentils	0.2350	0.2001	0.0270	0.1050	—

Nomos of Larisa

	Wheat	Barley	Broad beans	Chickpeas	Lentils
Wheat	—	0.8638	0.1359	0.3934	0.5585
Barley	0.8638	—	0.3102	0.2482	0.5159
Broad beans	0.1359	0.3102	—	0.1586	0.3385
Chickpeas	0.3934	0.2482	0.1586	—	0.2019
Lentils	0.5585	0.5159	0.3385	0.2019	—

Nomos of Magnesia

	Wheat	Barley	Broad beans	Chickpeas	Lentils
Wheat	—	0.7633	0.1121	0.1303	0.4071
Barley	0.7633	—	0.3514	0.3930	0.5655
Broad beans	0.1121	0.3514	—	0.6429	0.4742
Chickpeas	0.1303	0.3930	0.6419	—	0.5872
Lentils	0.4071	0.5655	0.4742	0.5872	—

[a] This date-span does not apply to the data for Karditsa and Magnesia.
This table is reproduced by courtesy of the Roman Society.

ties of wheat on a regular basis to the cities in the Aegean, it was not wheat produced locally, in their own territories.

There are implications also for the inhabitants of the Black Sea cities and their territories as consumers. Cities of the Odessa region, specific-

Table 2. *Samos (1926–36, 1955–6, 1963–80): interannual variability of the major cereal and leguminous crops. Partial correlation coefficients, controlling for time*

	Wheat	Barley	Kidney beans	Broad beans	Chickpeas	Lentils
Wheat	—	0.7965	0.1356	0.1444	0.2899	0.3700
Barley	0.7965	—	−0.0874	−0.1037	0.1562	0.4401
Kidney beans	0.1356	−0.0874	—	0.4296	0.4845	−0.4244
Broad beans	0.1444	−0.1037	0.4269	—	0.5162	−0.0803
Chickpeas	0.2899	0.1564	0.4845	0.5162	—	−0.0507
Lentils	0.3700	0.4401	−0.4244	−0.0803	−0.0507	—

ally Tomis, Olbia and Istros, can be shown to have suffered sporadically from food crisis during the Hellenistic period (roughly, from the third to the first century BC). For example, at about the turn of the third century BC the wealthy Protogenes intervened on three occasions in Olbia when grain was short. Although no continuous history of these cities can be written, it appears that in the Hellenistic age, at least, the system of food supply frequently broke down under the combined impact of sporadic tribal incursions and normal climatic irregularities.[7]

Finally, on Samos, the main subsistence crops, wheat and barley, fail once every two years on average, and usually together. Crop failure is associated with excessive rather than insufficient rainfall on Samos, which receives more than double the rainfall of Athens, Larisa or Odessa in the winter months. Climatic irregularities form an essential part of the explanation of the island's easily documented susceptibility to food crisis in the Hellenistic period (see Table 2).

Examples could be multiplied: vulnerability to crop failure can in principle be measured in respect of any location for which satisfactory data are available.

To sum up: the use of modern agroclimatological data as substitutes for the precise quantitative evidence from antiquity that we lack makes possible the assessment of an area's susceptibility to food crisis and of its vulnerability in comparison with other areas. The chances of taking the analysis further in any particular instance depend on the quality of the available information relating to the social, economic and political context. Food crisis can be inflicted on a community by human activity, with or without the aid of nature. The frequency and severity of subsistence crises will vary with the incidence of imperialism, war,

[7] E.g. *Syll.*[3] 731 (Tomis); *Nouveau Choix* no. 6 (Istros); *Syll.*[3] 495 (Olbia).

piracy, civil strife, and the extent of the economic and non-economic exploitation of producers and consumers by the powerful.

THE ANCIENT EVIDENCE

Historians, whatever their interests, normally sidestep the problem of the inadequacy of the primary sources by focusing on the best-known ancient communities, especially classical Athens and Rome. This is a legitimate procedure, as long as it is recognised that the sources for Athens and Rome are themselves neither complete nor unproblematic, and that Athens and Rome were the least typical of ancient states.

Both classical Athens and Rome experienced periods when food crises were frequent. In Rome between 509 and 384 BC at least one year in nine, and between 123 and 50 BC about one year in five, were affected by shortages in consequence of war, civil disorder, disease and climatic irregularities. In addition, the food supply of Rome was frequently disrupted during the Punic Wars of the third century BC, the civil wars of 49–31 BC and perhaps surprisingly the Principate of Augustus (27 BC – AD 14). Classical and Hellenistic Athens from the fourth century BC on was extremely susceptible to food crisis, especially in the period of Macedonian domination ushered in by the battle of Chaeronea in 338 BC. In contrast, few food crises occurred while Athens was dominant in the Aegean for much of the fifth century BC. Similarly, with the exception of the periods already signalled, food crisis was relatively uncommon in the city of Rome in the 800 or so years of the Republic and Principate. The generalisation that suggests itself is that the relatively crisis-free periods in Athenian and Roman history were those in which successful imperialism abroad was combined with stable government at home.

Outside Athens and Rome the data are more sparse, consisting in the main of isolated literary and epigraphical texts. But such evidence can be enlightening, when for example reference is made directly or indirectly to recurring crises. Boulagoras, a rich citizen of Samos, intervened on three separate occasions around the middle of the third century BC in times of grain shortage. Protogenes and Moschion were active as frequently in their cities of Olbia and Priene, respectively. The inscription for Polycritus of Erythrae gives a detailed description of his service to the city in two distinct food crises, but also refers to frequent comparable acts of generosity 'in response to which the people often honoured him in the past and put up a stele in the market place recording those honours awarded him'. In the period of the Principate, recurring food crises can be deduced from the multiple benefactions of leading citizens of cities such as Perge, Apamea, Epidaurus and Megalopolis.[8] Away from the urban environment of the Graeco-Roman city, drought is referred to in Rabbinic literature from the second to the fourth century so frequently that one can be misled into believing that rainfall was abnormally low in the period in question.[9] The rain-making prowess of Palestinian or Babylonian Rabbis is on display in a series of often charming tales, such as the following:

> R. Hama b. Hanina ordained a fast but no rain fell. People said to him: 'When R. Joshua b. Levi ordained a fast, rain did fall.' He replied: 'I am I, and he is the son of Levi. Go and ask him that he may come and pray for us and let us concentrate on our prayer, perhaps the whole community will be contrite in heart and rain will fall.' They prayed and no rain fell. He then asked them: 'Are you content that rain should fall on our account?' They replied: 'Yes.' He then exclaimed: 'Heaven, heaven, cover thy face.' But it did not cover its face. He then added: 'How brazen is the face of heaven.' It then became covered and rain fell.

The evidence is not merely anecdotal. The Mishnaic tractate *Taanit* is full of drought-breaking prescriptions. It is laid down, for example, that prayers for rain should begin on the third of Marheshvan (November), and that in the continued absence of rain over the ensuing fortnight public fasting should take place on Mondays and Thursdays until the drought was over.[10]

In the world of the Graeco-Roman city the alleviation of food crises by private benefactors was so regular as to be an institutionalised feature of the society. The same people also accepted appointment, sometimes singly, sometimes with others, as officials with special responsibility for the grain supply, *sitonai* or grain commissioners, *sitophulakes* or grain wardens, or some other such name. Officials of this type are found in so many cities of the Greek East in the Hellenistic and Roman periods that they may be taken as a standing feature. Where the office was hereditary or was held for life, as for example in Sparta, then the implications for the community in question are manifest and grim.[11]

In some cities, the grain commissioners had access to a permanent grain fund – another sign of permanent anxiety about the food supply in the communities concerned. An inscription from the turn of the third century BC records the recent establishment of a special grain-purchase

[8] *SEG* II 366 = Austin 113; *Syll.*³ 495 = Austin 97; *Inschr. Priene* 108; *Inschr. Erythrai-Klazomenai* 28; *IGR* III 796; IV 785; *IG* IV 944; V.2 515.

[9] Sperber (1974), in his none the less useful discussion, succumbs to the temptation, without undertaking the necessary comparative study. For a survey of biblical and other evidence, see Patai (1939).

[10] *Taanit* 25a, cf. Epstein (1938), 131.

[11] On the *sitones*, see briefly Jones (1940), 217–18; *IG* v.1 526; 551 (Sparta).

fund on Samos and gives details of its management. The launching of this fund by public subscription may be taken as proof that the island still suffered periodically from food crisis half a century after the active career of Boulagoras. It would be interesting to know how far the Samians, in organising the fund and the grain distributions that it paid for, were building on existing institutions and practice; and for how long the fund and the elaborate machinery for administering it were maintained. The Samian fund appears to have been quite unusual in providing for distribution of grain gratis to all citizens in all years, good or bad, until the grain ran out.[12] Normally, the purpose of a standing grain fund was to ensure that emergency grain could be quickly purchased for resale in the market, though it was always open to a generous grain commissioner or private benefactor to subsidise the consumer.

A clause in the grain fund inscription indicates that the Samians debated the food supply every year in the assembly in the month of Artemision, that is, in the spring, when the size of the harvest would have been roughly calculable (ll. 31–7). This practice could certainly have both predated the institution of the grain fund and survived its demise. It recalls the Athenian custom (attested for the 330s at least) of debating the food supply each prytany in the main assembly meeting, and is a sure sign of a permanent anxiety over the food supply. I do not think it likely that Samians and Athenians were alone in monitoring the food supply of their cities in this way.[13]

The conclusion is that the situation in the vast majority of communities of the Mediterranean was broadly similar to that of Rome in the fifth century BC and Athens in the fourth and following centuries. That is to say, inasmuch as communities lacked the capacity to exploit other peoples, or did not enjoy stability of government over long periods of time, they were endemically vulnerable to food crisis through a combination of human and natural causes.

---

[12] *Syll.*³ 976 = Austin 116. On the effectiveness of the Samian scheme, see p. 81 below. For the *sitonikon*, see e.g. *IGR* III 1421–2, IV 580, *IG* III 645, IV 2, IX.2 1029 cf. 1093; *Digest* 50.8.2.2–5.

[13] *Ath. pol.* 43.4.

3

THE INFREQUENCY OF FAMINE

Subsistence crises were common in antiquity. How frequently did they assume the proportions of famine?

Vulnerability to *repeated* crop failure may be estimated on the basis of the modern data. This has relevance to the question of the severity of food crises, in so far as crop failure underlies most food crises: a succession of bad harvests will produce a much more serious shortage than a single bad harvest.

Table 3 shows that harvest failure is considerably more likely to occur in one year than in two years in succession. Thus, where drought is an important precipitating cause of food crisis, genuine famines are much rarer than mere shortages. The same general picture would emerge (with countless variations) if the analysis were extended to other areas of the Mediterranean.

How much further the matter is taken depends on what is made of the ancient evidence. Here a piece-by-piece examination of particular food crises will yield a poor return. In the words of Marc Bloch, 'the

Table 3. *Percentage probability of crop failure in Larisa,*
Athens and Odessa

	1 year	2 successive years
Larisa		
Wheat	28.5	8.1
Barley	9.7	0.9
Athens		
Wheat	28.0	7.8
Barley	5.5	0.3
Odessa		
Wheat	46.0	21.1
Barley	15.6	2.4

knowledge of fragments, studied by turns, each for its own sake, will never produce the knowledge of the whole; it will not even produce that of the fragments themselves'.[1] The way forward is to extract from the content, and perhaps the language, of the 'famine narratives' criteria by which crises may be characterised and differentiated, and to grade individual crises in the light of these criteria.

THE LANGUAGE OF FOOD CRISIS

The following terms are merely a selection from the rich vocabulary of food crisis: in Greek, *limos/limottein, sitodeia, spanis, aporia, aphoria, endeia, kairos*; in Latin, *fames, inopia, penuria, caritas, annona* (*cara, gravis*).

A survey of the literary sources shows that a writer's choice of words is not necessarily a good index of the intensity of a particular food crisis.

The various words and expressions divide according to the aspect of the crisis to which they are referring: the impact on the consumer, the state of the food supply, the level of prices. *Limos* and *fames* denote hunger. A larger group of words are translatable as food shortage, the direct and immediate cause of hunger. *Caritas, annona cara* and other such terms present one aspect of a subsistence crisis, the high price of food. *Kairos* is a generalised word for crisis. In short, there is no single hierarchy of terms.

This is reflected in linguistic usage. It is exceptional for a source to make contrasts between terms. *Caritas*, high prices, occasionally confronts *fames*, hunger, as in Cicero's discussion of the crisis of 57 BC in Rome: 'This then was the situation; high prices in the present (*praesens caritas*) and the prospect of hunger (*futura fames*).' However, earlier in the same passage Cicero has failed to set off *inopia* (shortage) against *fames* (hunger): 'When the state of the food supply (*annona*) was worsening so that we began to fear not mere high prices but actually shortage and hunger, the mob flocked to the temple of Concord, whither the consul Metellus was summoning the senate.'

The historians share Cicero's lack of concern for terminological precision. In Polybius' history, subsistence crises that accompany sieges are referred to apparently indiscriminately as *limos* or *endeia* (shortage). In one such passage dealing with the siege of Agrigentum by the Romans in the course of the First Punic War, Polybius remarks that the Carthaginian general, Hanno, decided to risk battle, having received intelligence from the commander within the city that 'the people could not withstand hunger, and many were deserting to the enemy because of the shortage'. Again, in Cassius Dio's description of

[1] Bloch (1954), 155.

the crisis beginning in Rome in AD 6, words for hunger (*limos*) and shortage (*sitodeia*) occur side by side: 'Now the masses, distressed by hunger and the tax and their losses in the fire, were ill at ease ... The city was in commotion over these things until the shortage ceased.' *Limos* is the preferred word of both Cassius Dio and Appian in their descriptions of the prolonged subsistence crisis of 41–36 BC in Rome. However, Appian at the outset of his narrative of these events employs *aporia* (shortage) as a variant.[2]

Finally, *limos* and *fames* can mean, perhaps essentially do mean, 'life-threatening hunger'. But they also have a broad sense which takes in the whole area of meaning from hunger to death by starvation, and starvation of few as well as of many. It would therefore be ill-advised to infer merely from their occurrence that a particular shortage was of famine proportions. Even the addition of a supporting adjective with the sense of 'serious' does not solve the problem, for this practice is not followed systematically and consistently.

To sum up: the language of food crisis in the literary sources is of limited use in enabling us to discriminate even broadly the severity of individual food crises. There is a presumption that words for high prices and hunger point to different grades of crisis. But beyond this it is difficult to go. In particular, there is imprecision at the 'famine end' of the spectrum: it cannot be assumed that *fames* or *limos* are always employed in the narrow sense of famine as opposed to hunger.

The inscriptions, the other main source of evidence for subsistence crises, do not offer the terminological exactitude that is lacking in the literary sources. There is the additional striking fact that they systematically avoid the terms for hunger or starvation. *Fames* is used once in rather singular circumstances. A Roman governor, Antistius Rusticus, issued a decree in AD 92 or 93 in connection with a food crisis in Antioch in Pisidia in south-west Asia Minor.[3] Rusticus was called in by the civic authorities, who were unable to persuade or force unnamed local people to disgorge their grain stocks. 'It is most unjust', he proclaimed, 'that the hunger (*fames*) of one's own fellow-citizens should be a source of profiteering for anyone.' This is not the kind of language that appears in the conventional honorific decrees that are the main epigraphical source for subsistence crises. It seems that we are up against a peculiarity either of the epigraphical sources (which systematically evade the subject of human suffering) or of the crises themselves (which never cause human suffering to a significant degree). In either case, the verdict already passed on the literary

---

[2] Cicero, *Dom.* 11; Polybius 1.19.7; Cassius Dio 55.27.1–3, 31.3–4; Appian, *Bell. civ.* 5.67.
[3] *AE* 1925, 162b.

sources is confirmed. Food crises cannot be characterised or contrasted merely on the basis of the language of the documents. It is necessary to look for enlightenment beyond word usage to the narratives and contexts.

'FAMINE NARRATIVES'

Drawing from Ps.-Joshua's full and detailed narrative, I find ten headings relevant to a qualitative analysis of food crisis. They divide into two unequal groups: the first four concern the setting of food crisis, and the following six the symptoms of food crisis and its impact on the consumer:

1 Immediate causes
2 Geographical range
3 Location
4 Duration
5 Price movements
6 Incidence of disease
7 Response of authorities
8 Behaviour of the people
9 Categories of victim
10 Mortality

1. Immediate causes

The famine at Edessa had natural causes, a plague of locusts combined with drought. The situation was then worsened by the outbreak of epidemic disease. Ps.-Joshua also gives an example of a famine that was entirely man-made, the siege of Amida in AD 504–5 by the Persians (Ch. 76).

The causes of food crises might be natural, man-made or a combination of the two. Natural causes include insufficient or excessive rainfall, unseasonable cold or heat, damage to or destruction of the crop by pests, disease that hits farmers, thus impeding production, and storms at sea that hinder the import of staple foods. Man-made causes include warfare, piracy, speculation and corrupt or inefficient administration.

Food crises might be unicausal. In particular, war by itself may produce food crisis. War can cancel out the benefits of a good harvest and an adequate supply system. Similarly, climatic irregularity might cause a food crisis, but its impact will be limited in scope unless there are additional aggravating factors. Those factors range all the way from a serious outbreak of epidemic disease to mild profiteering by landowners and traders. In the former case but not the latter, famine, as opposed to shortage, was a real possibility.

That causal analysis will be most informative which produces not a bare list of causes, but a qualitative assessment of each constitutive cause. War can be more, or less, destructive. In the worst cases, a city might come under siege. Some of the most vivid 'famine narratives' from antiquity relate to the sufferings of besieged urban populations. Similarly, there are many grades of harvest failure.

However, what counts is not the extent to which (for example) the harvest had slipped below a certain specified critical threshold, but the community's capacity to cope with the shortfall. At this point the historical background becomes relevant. It would be useful to know, first, whether the resources of the community had been recently depleted by food shortages or other critical events. To set off a food crisis, the level of crop shortfall or loss would not have to be as low following a crisis year as following a year of plenty. Secondly, the wider context has significance: in particular, the pressure of population (of special interest to historians under the influence of Malthus) and the state of class relations (the concern of Marxists). In a community where population growth had depressed living standards significantly, or where labour was heavily exploited, only a minor setback might be needed to trigger off a major subsistence crisis.

2. Geographical range

Siege-induced food crises apart, the more geographically circumscribed a shortage, the more speedily it could be relieved, and therefore the less serious its effects were likely to be.

According to Ps.-Joshua, the whole area from Antioch to Nisibis (about 600 km east) was afflicted with famine and disease. In AD 45–7 there were food crises in Egypt, Syria, Judaea and Greece. A wide area therefore was affected, even if the 'universal famine' of the author of Acts is an exaggeration. At some time in the late 330s or early 320s BC, perhaps in 328, Cyrene sent emergency supplies of grain to 41 Greek communities and two individuals in an area of Greece stretching from as far north as Epirus and Thessalian Larisa, through the northern Peloponnese, central Greece and Attica, to Crete, Rhodes and Cos in the south and south-east.

In contrast, a shortage might affect single communities, if induced for example by the destruction of harvests in war. Thus the Thebans were forced to send to Thessaly for emergency grain in 377/6 BC following crop damage inflicted in two years in succession by Spartan armies.[4] In addition, internal political factors, the breakdown of a food supply system or profiteering by the local rich might produce a very local subsistence crisis.

3. Location

Edessa lay more than 350 km from Antioch, its nearest port in northern Syria. Caesarea in Cappadocia was inland by about the same distance. A food crisis that hit Caesarea in the time of Basil, that is, in the second half of the fourth century AD, prompted Gregory of Nazianzus to make the following observation:

> There was a food crisis, the most terrible in the memory of man. The city languished but there was no help from any part, no remedy for the calamity. Cities on the sea coast easily endure a shortage of this kind, importing by sea the things of which they are short. But we who live far from the sea profit nothing from our surplus, nor can we produce what we are short of, since we are able neither to export what we have nor import what we lack.

What lies behind this comment is the backward state of communications and the expensiveness of freight, especially overland, which tended to isolate communities removed from the Mediterranean littoral, increased their vulnerability to food crisis and forced them to aspire to a high degree of self-reliance.

The case against land transport is sometimes overstated, as in the following comment: 'In the ancient world famine was never far away. Most districts aimed at self-sufficiency; they had no choice. The slowness and cost of transport made it impossible to bring essential supplies from a great distance, and a neighbouring region, subject to the same climatic conditions, was not likely to have an exportable surplus to meet a local dearth.'

Leaving aside the erroneous assumption of a homogeneous climate, why should it be conceded that cartage of essential supplies was out of the question? The cost of transport becomes less crucial to the price of wheat in periods of price-rise. If wheat doubled in price when hauled 200 miles, then cheap grain carried 200 miles would have competed with local grain that was fetching double its normal price on the market.

An incident in a food shortage at Antioch in AD 362–3 is sometimes discussed in this connection. The emperor Julian sent for large quantities of wheat from Chalcis and Hierapolis, 50 and 100 km away by land, respectively. Why hadn't the wheat been sent for earlier? To say

---

[4] Acts 11.27–30, with Gapp (1935); *SEG* ix 2+; Xenophon, *Hell.* 5.4.56.

that the operation was too expensive is misleading: many Thessalians had to haul their grain so far as a matter of course, and north Africans farther. To say, also, that only an emperor had the power to carry it out, is to give an incomplete answer. The brute fact is that men in authority in the city were themselves capable of relieving the crisis, by releasing their own grain or bringing it in from elsewhere, but were either cashing in on the high prices for food or unable or unwilling to prevent such profiteering.

The upshot is that if Gregory's words mean that grain was never carted overland in an emergency he was exaggerating. It was, however, an expensive operation, especially if carried out over a considerable distance, and would only be resorted to if the survival of a community was at stake. My guess is that there were usually sufficient local stocks to keep a community from going over the brink – the problem was how to extract them from profiteering landlords and merchants. In this case, as Gregory discloses, the speculators of Caesarea met their match in Basil. My inference is that Caesarea suffered a serious food shortage but not a famine. If the crisis was 'the most terrible in the history of man', then famine was indeed rare in Caesarea.[5]

4. Duration

A succession of bad or mediocre harvests had a more devastating effect than a single crop failure. Surplus stocks lasted only so long, and in the case of small farmers the limit was reached early. Even one year without a crop was sufficient to break the peasantry of Edessa, who swarmed into the city in search of food or moved off elsewhere. In Genesis, the seven lean years that followed the seven fat years did not trouble Joseph and his Pharaoh, because their arrival was predicted and prepared for; the people of Judaea did not share this intelligence and suffered in consequence. The seven-year drought on the island of Thera reported by Herodotus produced the forced emigration of a proportion of the population. For present purposes it is not vital to decide whether in either source a seven-year drought is credible.

At the other extreme, some shortages in the city of Rome in the late Republic and early Empire disappeared almost overnight, most notably on Pompey's appointments to suppress piracy in 67 BC and to

---

[5] Citations from Gregory Naz., *In laudem Basilii* 34–5 (Migne, *Patr. Gr.* 36,541–4, qu. Jones (1940), 350 n. 16), and from Brunt (1971),135. On land transport, see Duncan-Jones (1982), 366–9; Hopkins (1983a), 102–5. On Antioch, see Finley (1985), 33–4, 125–6 (stressing cost): cf. Hopkins (1983a), 105 (imperial power); Julian, *Misop.* 369c; Libanius, *Or.* 18.195 (speculation).

restore the grain supply in 57 BC, and on Augustus' taking personal charge of the grain supply in 22 BC. Those shortages could not have been as severe as the recurring though not continuous crises of 41–36 BC and AD 5–9 in the capital city.[6]

The Rabbinic literature is full of stories of sages who bring early-season droughts to an end by prayer and fasting, apparently before the prospect of a crop in the year concerned could be completely ruined. There is little sign of year-long droughts in these admittedly highly selective and idiosyncratic documents. As one commentator has remarked: 'Absence of rain at the beginning of the season was not infrequent in Palestine, and prayers for it do not prove that there was a drought during the whole season.' The prayers were usually answered, and in any case a year's drought did not necessarily result in a catastrophic food crisis.[7]

5. Price-movements

A rise in the market price of grain reduced its availability to those with limited purchasing power. Even in normal years prices fluctuated according to the season, rising significantly from a post-harvest low to a pre-harvest high.

In the Edessa famine, the main foods, wheat, barley and dry legumes (chickpeas, beans and lentils), in addition to wine, rose in price more or less simultaneously. The situation, in other words, was roughly comparable to that pertaining in France between 1590 and 1740, where all the staple foods became expensive and scarce together. In England in the same period lesser spring-grown grains (barley and oats) were substituted for failed winter-growing cereals (wheat and rye), and food crisis was avoided, or its effect reduced. The Edessans in the summer of the first famine year tried a 'catch-crop', three-month summer millet, but it failed.

In Edessa, moreover, the inflation in the prices of staples had a knock-on effect. Other foodstuffs (vegetables, meat, poultry and eggs) rose substantially in price, and non-edible commodities (clothes, household utensils, furniture) became cheaper. One indication that Athens in 329/8 BC experienced only a mild shortage is that prices for grain, clothing and basketware were all higher in that year than four years previously. Prices for grain were not so inflationary as to cause a

---

[6] Genesis 41, with Vergote (1959), 43–4; cf. Bonneau (1971), 132–4 (7 years of a low Nile 193–187 BC); Herodotus 4.151. For Pompey and Augustus, see Part IV, pp. 200–1, 220.
[7] See especially *Taanit*, Ch. 3. The citation is from Liebenam (1939–44), 435. See Patai (1939); Sperber (1974).

reduction in the demand for manufactured goods and a collapse of their price.[8]

The temple accounts of Delos in 282 and 281 BC show wheat and then barley becoming dear and scarce. The temple overseers purchased wheat for their slave-workers at prices fluctuating between 4 drachmas 3 obols per medimnos in the fourth month and 10 drachmas in the ninth. The series of prices for wheat dries up in the final months of the year, when the buyers switched to barley. In the following year, however (and in some other years), the masons were paid a food allowance of around 10 drachmas, suggesting that not only wheat but also barley was in short supply.[9]

Plutarch's 1,000 drachmas per medimnos as the price of wheat in Athens in 87/6 BC at the time of Sulla's siege of the city seems incredible: it amounts to twenty times the price-rise recorded for the siege of 295/4 BC. That is more credible; similar dramatic increases in the price of wheat (8–10 fold) are attested in Erythrae (Asia Minor) and Olbia (in the north of the Black Sea) in the third century BC, and, according to the Book of Revelation, in the late first century in Asia Minor. The pre-harvest price of wheat of 20 sesterces per modius in Sicily in 74 BC is very high in comparison with the standard (post-harvest?) price of 2–3 sesterces. Ps.-Joshua unfortunately never cites normal food prices, so the extent of deviations from the norm in the Edessa famine cannot be assessed.[10]

6. Epidemic disease

Among the most destructive crises were those in which shortage and disease combined. At Edessa the dead were so numerous that their disposal was a major problem. In the briefest of notices in a summary of Livy (supported by the late antique historian Orosius), 200,000 people are said to have died in the region around Utica and Carthage in 125/4 BC, following a plague of locusts.[11]

In the sources, famine and disease (*limos/loimos, fames/pestilentia*) make a pair. In Hesiod's *Works and Days* they are the punishment exacted by

---

[8] *IG* II² 1672; Clinton (1971), 111–12. See Appleby (1979) for the comparison of England and France.

[9] *IG* XI.2, 158 ll. 37–50; cf. 159, ll. 59–60; Clinton (1971), 110–11.

[10] Plutarch, *Dem.* 33; *Inschr. Erythrai-Klazomenai* 28; *Syll.*³ 495 = Austin 97; Plutarch, *Sulla* 13; Cicero, *2 Verr.* 2.3.214 cf. 2.3.84, 90, 173–5, 189, 194. See Duncan-Jones (1976a). By comparing Ps.-Joshua's figures one can see that in the first famine year wheat cost three times as much and barley almost four times as much as in the third year, which was one of partial recovery, while the cost of wine sank by more than 75% in one year. See also Patlagean (1977), 405–8.

[11] Livy, *Epit.* 60; cf. Orosius 5.11.1–7; etc.

Zeus from an impious city. In Thucydides' narrative of the 'plague' in Athens, we are reminded that the two were not in reality inseparable, although they were very closely associated in men's minds. *Loimos* struck the Athenians in 430 BC just after they had become embroiled in a war with the leading Dorian state, Sparta. An oracle about a Dorian war was recollected accordingly by ordinary Athenians. Thucydides comments ironically that the oracle would have been interpreted as referring to *limos*, if the Athenians had suffered famine and not epidemic disease.[12]

Shortage might be chronologically prior to disease, leading through the consumption of poor food-substitutes to sickness and death. The soldiers of Xerxes struggling homewards from Greece in 480 BC were reduced to eating grass, caught dysentery and fell by the wayside. Galen, the doctor from Pergamum, is a major source for starvation-induced disease. His treatise *On the Wholesome and Unwholesome Properties of Foodstuffs* begins with an extended account of the ill effects of consuming unhealthy foods, based on his own observation of country-folk in time of famine. In another place he offers an explanatory commentary to a passage of Hippocrates that records the bodily deterioration of the inhabitants of Aenus in Thrace, in consequence of their consumption of inferior cereals and vetch. But the shortage–sickness relationship can work the other way.[13] In the annals of early Rome it is sometimes recorded that disease killed off farmers (and their livestock), cultivation was interrupted and shortage followed.

7. Response of the authorities

Under this head I consider short-term measures designed to cope with a current crisis as a guide to its severity rather than long-term measures to ward off future crises or reduce their impact. The response of the authorities at Edessa, both ecclesiastical and secular, even if it was initially inadequate, confirms the gravity of the crisis. According to Ps.-Joshua, the ecclesiastical authorities took the lead in approaching the emperor, setting up infirmaries and interceding with the deity. While 'our father' Mar Peter was at Constantinople seeking remission of the capitation tax, the governor was extorting it from the landowners. The emperor for his part was at first willing to make only a partial remission. It was in the second year that 'famine relief' came to Edessans in the form of money, following a visit of the governor to the emperor at Constantinople. The governor's deputy, one Eusebius, had

[12] Hesiod, *Works and Days* 238–45; Thucydides 2.54.3.
[13] Herodotus 8.115; Galen IV 749ff. (Kühn); *CMG* V 126.4–6 L.

meanwhile distributed grain from the public granaries to anyone prepared to bake it. On his return from Constantinople, the governor gave out bread at the rate of one pound per day, established emergency accommodation and superintended the disposal of the dead.

The immediate reactions of the Roman authorities can be a useful indicator of the magnitude or otherwise of a crisis. In AD 19 the emperor Tiberius reacted to a rise in the price of wheat by fixing a maximum price and compensating traders. In AD 6, Augustus had expelled gladiators, slaves brought in for sale and foreigners, packed off senators and their entourages to their estates, rationed grain, cut back expensive celebrations and doubled the grain dole. In the historical record of Rome most of these measures are unique or nearly so.

It is difficult to make a fair comparison between the crisis of AD 19 and the other food crisis of Tiberius' reign, that of AD 32, when reports of popular protest at the price of wheat were brought to him in his retreat at Capri. His rule had seriously degenerated in the intervening period, and his reaction in AD 32 might have been quite irresponsible: he merely chided the senate and magistrates for not disciplining the populace. At any rate, it is evident from the response of Augustus in AD 6 (and from other indications) that this was by far the most serious crisis of the three.

Assessing religious response to food crisis (or the risk of food crisis) is a delicate operation. Consultation of oracles, seers and sacred books, religious innovation (including the introduction of new gods and cults), public ceremonies of purification or prayer, scapegoat rituals – these are signs that a community was experiencing something more serious than a mild shortage (although Jewish prayer and fasting requires separate evaluation). It is difficult to go beyond this, without forcing the evidence, making naïve assumptions about patterns of religious response in communities of similar religious culture, or indulging in shaky cross-cultural comparisons. For example, the slowing down of religious innovation in Rome after the early and middle Republic (always supposing the reality of such a development) may have little or nothing to do with the incidence of famine and other natural disasters. Again, scapegoat rituals occur in the Greek world as regular ceremonies with an apotropaic function; the expulsion ceremonies in Athens at the Thargelia and in Chaeronea in Boeotia are examples. They were available as purification rites in time of famine, but historical examples of their use are lacking. Does it follow that famines were rare? Not necessarily. The dilemma is similar in the case of consultations of the Delphic Oracle about natural disaster, which are common only in myth. Finally, differences between Jewish and Christian communities are highlighted by the speedy but routine recourse to public prayer and fasting in Rabbinic Palestine, and the (?surprisingly) late occurrence of public religious ceremony in Christian Edessa. But how reliable is the *Chronicle* on this point, and is it safe to generalise about Christian practice from this narrative?[14]

8. Behaviour of the people

At Edessa, the ordinary people sold their possessions, left their homes and were reduced to beggary in the city. For food they supplemented an inadequate grain ration with miserable scraps of vegetable matter, consecrated bread and human flesh. Children were abandoned by their mothers. Many died of starvation. In what follows I single out two items that occur in Ps.-Joshua's chronicle, consumption of alternative foods and emigration, and one item, popular protest, that does not.[15]

(i) *The consumption of unfamiliar foodstuffs.* At the risk of being over-schematic, I suggest five rough categories of foods, in descending order of desirability from the consumer's point of view: livestock not in ordinary circumstances destined for slaughter; 'inferior' cereals, either ranked low (for whatever reason) or damaged by pests or weather; regular animal food, such as vetch or acorns; 'last resort' natural products or non-foods such as roots, twigs, leaves, bark, leather; and finally, human flesh. The sequence in an incomplete version is on display in a pseudo-Quintilian oration: the inhabitants of a city under siege first consume animals, then herbs, trees, earth and the bodies of relatives. This is 'set piece' rhetoric. But cannibalism crops up also in historical documents, in particular, as might be expected, in the context of sieges, for example in Amida in AD 504–5, Potidaea in 430/29 BC and Athens in 87/6 BC in the account of Appian. He writes:

When Sulla discovered that the defenders of Athens were very severely pressed by hunger, that they had devoured all their cattle, boiled the hides and skins and licked what they could get therefrom, and that some had even partaken of human flesh, he directed his soldiers to encircle the city with a ditch so that the inhabitants might not escape secretly even one by one.

---

[14] For Augustus and Tiberius, see pp. 220–2. On expulsion, see Ammianus 14.6.19 cf. Ambrose, *Off.* 3.45–52. I know of no general treatment of the subject of religious response to natural disaster. Religious innovation at Rome has been treated by North (1976), and scapegoat rituals at Athens and elsewhere in Greece by, e.g., Bremmer (1983). See Harpocration, under 'pharmakos'; Helladios, in Photius, *Bibl.* 534a; cf. Scholiast on Aristophanes, *Knights* 1136 (Athens); Plutarch, *Mor.* 693E–694A (Chaeronea). On the Delphic Oracle, see Fontenrose (1978), Tables 5 and 10, pp. 41 and 54.

[15] For infanticide, sale of children and suicide, see e.g. Eyben (1980–1), 5–19; Oppenheim (1955); Livy 4.12.11.

A little later, in following the gory progress of Sulla's men through the captured city, Appian says that 'in many houses they found human flesh prepared for food'.[16]

The graver the shortage, the less desirable the substitute food, from a nutritional or moral stance. According to Hippocrates, the people of Aenus, a Greek city in Thrace, resorted to (only) unidentified inferior cereals and bitter vetch. The countryfolk of Asia Minor, as observed by Galen, were compelled to eat 'twigs and shoots of trees and bushes, and bulbs and roots of indigestible plants', in addition to wild herbs and grass. Their situation was comparable with that of the starving Finns of 1696–7, who turned for food to chaff, straw, roots, nettles and bark for making bread. Rabbi Johanan's reconstruction of the evolving diet of the Israelites during the seven-year famine of 2 Kings 8 owes a great deal to his own fertile imagination:

In the first year they ate what was in their houses; in the second that which was in the fields; in the third the flesh of clean beasts; in the fourth the flesh of unclean beasts; in the fifth the flesh of vermin; in the sixth the flesh of their sons and daughters; in the seventh the flesh of their own arms, to fulfil that which is stated 'And one snatcheth on the right hand and is hungry; and he eateth on the left hand and is not satisfied; they eat every man the flesh of his own arm.'

But besieged populations, as was seen, are not uncommonly said to have had to resort to human flesh.[17]

(ii) *Protest*. Three forms of food riot are distinguished in the historical scholarship of early modern Europe:[18]

1 Urban market riots, a reaction to shortage of grain for sale.
2 Rural riots, or 'entraves', the forcible prevention of the movement of grain from localities of production or distribution.
3 'Taxation populaire', or the popular requisition and sale of grain at a 'just price', a manifestation of what has been called 'the moral economy of the poor'.

Only the first category of food riot is directly attested in antiquity. 'Taxation populaire' is associated with the abandonment by national governments in France and Britain of traditional paternalistic

---

[16] Appian, *Bell. Mith.* 38; cf. Plutarch, *Sulla* 13 (no reference to cannibalism); Ps.-Quintilian, *Declam.* 12; Ps.-Joshua, *Chron.* Chs. 76–7; Thucydides, 2.70 cf. Ps.-Libanius, *Declam.* 13, with Russell (1983), 118 (Athenians accused of impiety over Potidaea). See also Diodorus 34/35.2.20 (Tauromenium, 132 BC: first children, then wives, then men); Caesar, *Bell. Gall.* 7.77 (Alesia: the elderly). It might be well to be suspicious of tales of cannibalism. As anthropologists have noted, it is always enemies or neighbours of a group who eat human flesh, and the stories can seldom be authenticated.

[17] For cannibalism in peacetime, see e.g. Vandier (1936), 8; Tucker (1981), 218–9 (Egypt); Galen, *Comm. in Hipp. Epid.* II = *CMG* v 126.4–6 L (Aenus); vi 749ff. (Asia Minor); Jutikkala (1955); *Bavli Taanit* 5a, transl. Epstein (1938), 16.

[18] Rudé (1964); Thompson (1971); Tilly (1971).

economic policies and the transition to *laissez-faire*. 'Entraves', in the sense of the prevention of export of essential foodstuffs, are less obviously tied to a specific historical context. They are not documented for antiquity, but are not inherently improbable; their absence in the documents can be attributed to the urban and upper-class bias of our sources and their general inadequacy.

A discussion of protest in an urban setting can usefully embrace non-violent demonstration as well as riot. The distinction is made explicitly by Tacitus.[19] In AD 32 when prices were high, the people raged for several days in the theatre against the emperor Tiberius 'with unusual insolence, almost crossing the border between demonstration and riot'. My impression is that peaceful protest was much more common than riot, and that only in the city of Rome itself in certain periods was the food riot a phenomenon of any significance.

In democratic Athens there were no food riots, because recognised channels of protest existed that were built into the constitutional framework and operated by the citizens themselves. Popular indignation against grain dealers whose conduct fell below expected levels received institutional expression in judicial sanctions, including the death penalty, imposed by the Council of Five Hundred on dealers and those who were supposed to supervise them (the several grain wardens). If Lysias is to be taken at his word, trials and executions of both categories of offenders were frequent.[20]

In states ruled by oligarchies, food riots were probably rather more common than appears at first glance. The literary sources which disclose their sporadic occurrence in the period of the Principate[21] are lacking for earlier periods, especially the Hellenistic age, where the evidence is predominantly epigraphic and weighted towards the successful resolution of food crises rather than their less cheerful aspects. Still, it is not unlikely that demonstration at festivals, shows and popular assemblies was usually sufficient to set in motion whatever coping mechanisms existed in the communities concerned. Euergetism, the public munificence of the rich, could usually be relied upon to ward off both starvation and unrest.

To turn to Rome: it might be imagined that popular complaint which did not degenerate into violence can be taken as a pointer to mild shortage, and violent protest to serious shortage. This suggestion appears to receive some support from Tiberius' refusal to take any emergency measures in AD 32, and from a passage of Dionysius under

[19] Tacitus, *Ann.* 6.13.
[20] Lysias 22.16, 18, 20.
[21] Dio Chrys. *Or.* 46; Philostratus, *Vita Ap.* 1.15.

493 BC where he puts rioting on a level with the consumption of strange foods. In fact, the correlations between demonstration and mild shortage and between riot and serious shortage do not apply.[22] First, in the unstable political conditions of late Republican Rome rioting was always in prospect in the event of a price-rise in essential commodities. Secondly, fear of famine rather than famine itself was enough to set people on the rampage, as in 57 BC or AD 51.[23] Thirdly, rioting became almost obsolete and demonstration the standard response, once power was concentrated in the hands of one man, whose rule rested to a significant degree on his ability to satisfy the economic needs of the urban plebs and who therefore made regular contact with the populace in the controlled environment of theatre and hippodrome.[24] The disturbance of 22 BC in the first decade of the Principate was the last of the 'old-fashioned' riots. Fourthly, rioting, whether in the Republican or Imperial context, is to be explained partly in political terms. The riot of 57 BC appears to have been at least in part a political event, in which Clodius, Pompey and Cicero played leading roles. The riot of 22 BC occurred because the people of Rome were unsure of Augustus' power and commitment to their cause after he renounced the consulship and refused a dictatorship.

(iii) *Emigration*. Poverty drove individual householders from their villages or towns at all periods in search of 'greener pastures'. For present purposes I am concerned with the movement of a sizeable section of a community, voluntarily or by political decision, in the context of what is invariably a serious subsistence crisis. The shortage-induced dispatch of a colony is a recurring motif in the historical tradition of early Greece. A seven-year drought forced the Therans, taking heed eventually of the instructions of the Delphic oracle, to 'send brother from brother, chosen by lot, and from all the seven districts, men', and to found a colony at Cyrene. Chalcidians from Euboea who participated in the foundation of Rhegium on the toe of Italy were men who according to an oracle were dedicated to Apollo – one man out of every ten – because of a failure of the crops. In Plutarch's anecdote, drought and plague in Corinth led to the foundation of Syracuse by Archias.[25]

Colonisation was not of this kind when undertaken by an imperial

---

22 Dionysius 7.18 cf. Williams (1976), at 74: 'There was no direct causal relationship between deprivation and protest' (in England in the 1760s).

23 Cicero, *Dom.* 11; Tacitus, *Ann.* 12.43; Suetonius, *Claud.* 18; Ammianus 19.10.

24 For the theatre and hippodrome as centres of popular demonstration see Nicolet (1976c), Ch. 9; Yavetz (1969); Kohns (1961), Ch. 3; Cameron (1974) and (1976).

25 Herodotus 4.151ff. Strabo 6.1.6. cf. Herakleides Lembos, *De Reb. Pub.* 25; Plutarch, *Mor.* 773A–B.

power, in particular Rome, but also fifth-century Athens. However, subsistence crisis in the city of Athens provides part of the background of the establishment of various cleruchies in the late 360s, the late 350s and the mid-320s.

9. Categories of victim

Food crisis confirms social inequalities in the ancient world. Ps.-Joshua's *Chronicle* provides a glimpse of inequality within the family as well as the more familiar inequality of wealth. Able-bodied men left the district altogether, abandoning farms and families: it was the sick, elderly, the women and the children who converged on the city of Edessa. Two years later in the Persian siege of Amida most of the available food and drink was given to the men in their role as soldiers, while the women supplemented their daily ration of a handful of barley with the flesh of the dead and with shoe-leather. The rich, who were typically large landowners, were able to ward off hunger by means of grain stored from good seasons, at Edessa and elsewhere. At Caesarea in Cappadocia in Basil's day, the rich still had food in their storehouses and were persuaded by Basil to part with some of it. The same function was performed, the story runs, by Apollonius of Tyana at the Pamphylian town of Aspendus in south-west Asia Minor during the reign of Tiberius. At Pisidian Antioch, in the reign of Domitian, the intervention of a Roman governor was required to achieve the same end. The rich and powerful suffered only when food crisis was combined with epidemic disease, as in Edessa, and in early Rome on several occasions. The implication of the sources is that it was disease rather than starvation which did the damage. As Ps.-Joshua wrote: 'Many of the rich died, but not of hunger.'[26]

In general, the ancient sources present a relatively undifferentiated view of society. In Livy, for example, we encounter essentially slaves, humble plebeians and nobility. The first two categories are said to have suffered first and most in a food crisis. In his narrative of the food crisis of 492–491 BC in Rome, Livy writes: 'It would have meant starvation for the slaves at least and for the plebeians, had not the consuls ... brought in grain.' The Roman authorities in 440–39, again according to Livy, among other actions ordered the reduction of rations for slaves and forced those holding grain stocks to declare and sell them. Despite this

---

[26] Cf. Eusebius, *Hist. Eccl.* 9.8.11: plague destroys those unaffected by famine 'because they were well provided with food' (Palestine, AD 312–13). On Apollonius' intervention, see Philostratus, *Vita Ap.* 1.15.

attempt to 'distribute the shortage', many plebeians committed suicide by throwing themselves into the Tiber.[27]

In order to deepen the analysis, it would be necessary to break down the monolithic blocks into which ancient society is divided by the literary sources. According to Amartya Sen, the vulnerability of particular social groups to famine will depend on their degree of access to and control over vital food resources, that is, on their 'entitlement'.[28] 'Entitlement' is defined as 'the set of alternative commodity bundles that a person can command in a society using the totality of rights and opportunities that he or she faces'. An individual's 'exchange entitlement' will vary in accordance with his or her occupation and place in the network of social, economic and legal relationships.

Sen's theory cannot be illustrated and tested with detailed case-studies from antiquity. It does however make possible a more intelligent use of such information as the sources provide, and permits the application of broader terms of analysis than those imposed by the sources. Thus, for example, the 'plebeians' or 'masses' (*plethos*), who in the annalistic tradition are usually presented as an undifferentiated group, can be broken down into sundry occupational groups (overlapping to a degree, to be sure), that are vulnerable to famine to a greater or lesser extent. In principle we would expect famine to make less impact on peasant-owners than on agricultural labourers or craftsmen. Peasant-owners have the capacity to produce food that is theirs and to build up reserves in the form of stored produce and livestock. In the case of agricultural labourers, however, access to food hinges on their capacity to sell their labour power, which is much reduced in time of famine. Craftsmen and traders are only marginally better off than agricultural labourers: they must buy food at high prices at a time when the demand for their own products and services has collapsed. As Ps.-Joshua wrote: 'Everything that was not edible was cheap.' In the *Chronicle* the attempt of urban householders to raise money for the purchase of food by selling off their possessions is a less clear index of the gravity of the crisis than the reduction of the peasantry to beggary within a year.[29]

We can complicate the picture, and draw closer to the perspectives of the sources, by taking into account not only occupational position, but also legal status and political, economic and social relationships. Thus slaves take their place as a social group lacking any effective legal

[27] Livy 2.34; 4.12.10.
[28] Sen (1981).
[29] See also Eusebius, *Hist. Eccl.* 9.8.6: precious possessions are exchanged for 'the scantiest supply of food'. Cf. Xenophon, *Mem.* 2.7: nobody will buy furniture immediately after the period of the Thirty (403 BC).

33

standing and completely dependent on their masters: slaves, presumably unsaleable in famine conditions, are among the last to starve; not the first, because their owners had an interest in keeping them alive which they lacked in the case of the free poor. (Livy, as we saw, puts the two classes side by side in his discussion of the crisis of 492–491, but we could hardly expect otherwise.) Again, the gap between peasants and the urban lower classes is seen to be less wide once we take into account the capacity of the city authorities to extract payments in kind or cash in the form of taxes and other imposts, and the easier access of city-dwellers to whatever redistributive mechanisms were in operation. Finally, the rich/poor, slaveowner/slave dichotomies were to some extent undermined by the existence of vertical relationships between the rich and powerful and select plebeians and slaves.

10. Mortality

According to Ps.-Joshua, somewhat over 15,000 dead were carried out of the lodging-house alone at Edessa in five months of one year. The main index of famine must be that it produces higher levels of mortality in the stricken community. It was found advisable in considering emigration to distinguish between the steady trickle of peasants abandoning their farms and a short-term upsurge of the same phenomenon, and to focus exclusively on the latter. In the same way my present interest is in the sudden effect on mortality rates of a collapse of the level of food consumption, rather than the continuous erosion of life due to chronic malnutrition.

The conventional sources, literary or inscriptional, are shy of mentioning death. There are surprisingly few texts comparable to Eusebius' description of hunger, plague and death in Palestine under Maximin in AD 312–13:

The customary rains, indeed, and showers of the then prevailing winter season were withholding their usual downpour upon the earth, and an unexpected food crisis broke out, and on top of this a plague and an outbreak of another kind of disease. This latter was an ulcer, which on account of its fiery character was called an anthrax. Spreading as it did over the entire body it used to endanger greatly its victims ... The tyrant had the further trouble of the war against the Armenians ... He himself was worn out along with his commanders in the Armenian war; while the rest of the inhabitants of the cities under his rule were so terribly wasted by both the food crisis and the pestilence, that 2,500 Attic drachmas were given for a single measure of wheat. Countless was the number of those who were dying in the cities, and still larger of those in the country parts and villages, with the result that the registers, which formerly contained the names of a numerous rural population, were now all but entirely wiped out; for one might almost say that the entire population perished all at once through lack of food and through plague. Some, indeed, did not hesitate to barter their dearest possessions for the scantiest supply of food with those better provided; others sold off their goods little by little and were driven to the last extremity of want; and others again injured their bodily health, and died from chewing small wisps of hay and recklessly eating certain pernicious herbs. And as for the women, some well-born ladies in cities were driven by their want to shameless necessity, and went forth to beg in the market-places, displaying a proof of their noble upbringing in their shamefacedness and the decency of their apparel. And some wasted away like ghosts of the departed, and at the last gasp, stumbled and tottered here and there from inability to stand, and fell down; then, stretched out prone in the midst of the streets they would beg for a small morsel of bread to be handed them, and with the last breath in their body cry out that they were hungry, finding strength for this most anguished of cries alone. Others, such as were regarded as belonging to the wealthier classes, amazed at the multitude of beggars, after giving countless doles, henceforth adopted a hard and pitiless frame of mind, since they expected that before very long they would be suffering the same misery as the beggars; so that in the midst of the market-places and alleys dead and naked bodies lay scattered here and there unburied for many days, presenting a most piteous spectacle to those who saw them. Some actually became food even for dogs; and chiefly for this reason those who were alive turned to killing dogs, for fear lest they might become mad and turn to devouring men. But worst of all, the pestilence also battened upon every house, especially those whom the famine could not completely destroy because they were well provided with food. Men, for example, in affluent circumstances, rulers and governors and numbers of officials, who had been left, as it were, of set purpose by the famine for the benefit of the plague, endured a sharp and very speedy death. So every place was full of lamentations; in every alley and market-place and street there was nothing to be seen but funeral dirges, together with the flutes and beating of breasts that accompany them. Thus waging war with the aforesaid two weapons, pestilence and famine, death devoured whole families in a short time, so that one might actually see the bodies of two or three dead persons carried out for burial in a single funeral train.[30]

In the historical record for Athens, Xenophon's three-times-repeated claim that Athenians were starving to death in 405–4 BC and Diodorus' dramatic confirmation ('the city was filled with corpses') are quite unique. Plutarch in his accounts of the sieges of Athens by Demetrius Poliorcetes and Sulla talks of acute *limos*, dearth of everything, consumption of strange foods, rocketing prices, but not death. Appian's evocation of the Sullan blockade omits any mention of death by starvation, unless it is implied in the references to cannibalism. The attention of both sources was drawn to the terrible massacre of

[30] Eusebius, *Hist. Eccl.* 9.8. Eusebius was a contemporary. His hatred of the persecutor Maximin explains his willingness to go into details, but does not impugn the essential veracity of the narrative.

Athenians by Sulla's men, but this cannot be a complete explanation of their silence. In the case of the Roman siege, archaeological evidence begins to fill the gap. A well in the agora, almost certainly closed up at the time of the Sullan siege, contained the remains of around 175 new-born infants and 100 dogs, presumably the first victims of chronic food shortage. Mortality rates certainly increased sharply under the impact of food shortage in 405–404, 295–294 and 87–86 BC.[31]

In the history of Rome the failure of a source to mention death by starvation or hunger-related disease cannot count as negative evidence. The crisis period 41–36 BC during which Rome under Octavian (the future Augustus) was intermittently blockaded by Sextus Pompeius gives a useful insight into the attitudes of the sources. The received record that was available to Appian and Cassius Dio writing, respectively, two and two and a half centuries after the event, evidently included some reference to starvation-induced deaths among the populace. But Dio's report of 'many deaths' is brief and almost casual,[32] while Appian in his longer narrative is silent on the subject.

Death crops up in the annals of early Rome less frequently than might have been expected, not for example in the context of siege. Livy is readier to record what might have happened had not the senate arranged for emergency supplies to be brought in, than what did happen when imports were held up. His notice under 440–439 BC to the effect that many plebeians escaped starvation only by drowning themselves in the Tiber is unique. In general, Livy and Dionysius report death only when it struck the nobility as well as the common people, that is, in the context of epidemics.[33]

Thus the reticence of the sources means that the incidence of death is not often a useful index for distinguishing severe from mild shortages. A sharp rise in the death rate is associated with the onset of epidemic disease, though epidemics could occur independently of shortage. At the other end of the spectrum, it is certain that even mild shortages increased the death rate among the poor and undernourished, although this has to be established with minimal assistance from the sources. Even Galen in his discussions of the deleterious effect on the body of a diet of substitute foods (or non-foods) focuses on disease, not mortality.

What this means is that spiralling mortality rates have to be inferred

---

[31] Xenophon, *Hell.* 2.2.11, 15, 21, with Diodorus 13.107 and Justin 5.8.1–3; Plutarch, *Dem.* 33; Sulla 13; Appian, *Bell. Mith.* 38; Angel (1945), inventory no. 116 on p. 311, Fig. 12 on p. 312.

[32] Cassius Dio 48.18.1.

[33] On holding up of imports, see e.g. Livy 2.34; 10.11.9. For upper-class deaths in epidemics, see Livy 3.32.2–4 cf. Dionysius 10.53–4; Livy 5.31.5–9 (but not Dionysius 13.4). For lower-class deaths, see Hopkins (1983), 208–11, referring to Lanciani (1888), 65–6.

from other details of the famine narratives. Plutarch in discussing the sieges of 295/4 and 87/6 says that the Athenians had to pay exorbitant prices for food, suffered acute hunger and ate 'alternative' foods. Given these conditions, the omission of reference to deaths would not be crucial, even if we lacked Appian and the grim remains in the agora well.

To sum up: on the basis of the ten indices introduced above, an attempt can be made to construct a profile of a particular food crisis and locate it roughly on the spectrum leading from mild shortage to disastrous famine. Siege-induced crises belong at the famine end of the spectrum. They are associated with the consumption of strange foods or non-foods, very high prices, and deaths by starvation and disease. The combination of shortage with epidemic disease provides another context in which a sharp rise in mortality can be inferred. At the other end of the spectrum can be placed the shortage which is short-lived, local, is manifested in higher-than-normal prices, and does not force the community to take drastic measures.

CONCLUSION

To return to the original question: how common was famine? In the Mediterranean region? In Athens and Rome? In the thousands of ordinary communities?

Athenians in the classical and Hellenistic periods suffered few famines. The three that are best attested, those of 405/4, 295/4 and 87/6 BC, were all siege-induced, and therefore relatively short-lived. In two cases they were associated with and overshadowed by greater disasters and humiliations, the abolition of independence and democracy by the Spartans (in 405/4) and the indiscriminate slaughter of civilians by the Romans (in 87–6). The list may not be complete, but I do not think many famines could have slipped through the record, incomplete though it is. In Roman history, sieges and shortages-cum-epidemics occurred with relative frequency in the early period, if the extant historical sources are to be trusted, but not thereafter. The populace of Rome may be supposed (the evidence is thin) to have suffered extreme hardship during the Hannibalic War and the civil wars of the 80s, 40s and 30s BC. Under the Empire the most serious crises appear to have occurred in the civil war of AD 68–9 and the last decade of Augustus' reign. However, in the latter instance the emperor was able to distribute double grain doles to 200,000 people on the distribution list throughout the most critical period (in AD 6).

For the mass of ordinary urban communities of the Mediterranean world we are thrown back onto the inscriptional evidence, supplemented by isolated anecdotes in the literary sources. It was earlier noted that words for hunger and starvation do not appear in the inscriptions. One explanation that suggests itself is that the crises of the inscriptions were invariably of minor significance: they were less than famines. This is less improbable than it sounds. The inscriptions in question are almost always honorific; they typically record an act or acts by which a crisis was alleviated or averted. Prices rose. Then a benefactor emerged in the shape of a local landowner or a trader offering cut-price grain or funds with which to buy grain. In the Roman period, external intervention was sometimes required to force the rich to disgorge. In both kinds of cases there was grain; it was simply being released too slowly and in too small quantities to satisfy the demand. So prices rose, people went hungry, some died – but there was no dramatic increase in the death rate. The crises were eased before they could evolve into catastrophe.

The Rabbinic literature is problematic in a similar way, in that it too is biased towards success, in this case the alleviation of drought, the first and primary cause of food shortage in rural Palestine. Here it is the duration of communal prayer and fasting which is the best indicator of a poor year to come. But the evidence does not entitle us to write off any year altogether. Even a fast which lasted for 6½ weeks and was then abandoned only takes us into the month of December; a late planting of the crop was still in principle feasible. In any case, unsuccessful fasts are rare in the sources.

There must have been genuine famines that do not figure in this literature, or (for a different reason) in the inscriptions. But in so far as one can reconstruct the norm on the basis of the Rabbinic literature, it is variable rather than poor harvests. Similarly, it is legitimate to conclude that the standard food crisis in the communities that produced the numerous inscriptions was of a kind described in those inscriptions, and it belongs at the shortage end of the spectrum of food crisis.

The first step in any historical study of famine or food crisis is the documentation of individual cases. This is in principle a straightforward, if laborious, task, and can be pursued by the traditional methods of the ancient historian: the combing of the primary sources, the assembling of references, the interpretation and authentication of texts. But documentation, however comprehensively and meticulously it is carried out, is not history. Historical analysis involves definition, classification, the integration of discrete but related phenomena into a pattern.

Weathermen call hurricanes 'Alice', 'Bertie', 'Charlie', or whatever, always using a different name, implicitly acknowledging that each hurricane has its own particular identity. Each food crisis, similarly, was an individual event. But if we are to offer a penetrating and analytical account of food crisis, then we must look for similarities and differences between particular occurrences, and make estimates of the frequency and magnitude of the general phenomenon. My answer to the questions 'How common?', 'How serious?', is that food crisis was common, but famine was rare. This conclusion is inevitably provisional, given the quality of the available data, and needs to be tested with all the methods at our disposal, including some that are not generally to be found in the armoury of ancient historians. Part of my aim in this section has been to show that to make progress in this area it is necessary to complement traditional with more novel methodologies. My general purpose has been to prove that a work of interpretation based on the qualitative analysis of the evidence is feasible, and that the history of food crisis need not be limited to the mere presentation of data.

PART II
SURVIVAL STRATEGIES

4

SUBSISTENCE AND SURVIVAL:
THE PEASANTRY

INTRODUCTION

The Graeco-Roman world was a relatively highly urbanised society sustained for the most part by the labour of small farmers, owners or tenants. The pattern and extent of urbanisation, the condition of particular cities and their relation to one another were constantly changing. Individual peasant households survived, were extinguished, migrated and were subjected to varying degrees of exploitation. But the essential structure of Mediterranean society and the character of its economic base remained relatively stable through the period of classical antiquity.

In this chapter and the next, I consider the problem of the food supply from the viewpoints of subsistence or near-subsistence producers and urban residents. The survival of the peasantry depended upon their success in following a low-risk production strategy, and in establishing and making the most of social and economic links with their equals and superiors in society.

As for cities, there was little regulation of the food supply by local governments. Fourth-century BC Athens and late Republican and Imperial Rome were exceptional in this respect. In most states the civic authorities intervened only in times of crisis, and their involvement lasted only as long as the emergency itself. Moreover, government or other public response to food crisis was rarely radical. Property redistribution was not entertained as a possibility, and such permanent institutions as were devised for dealing with food crisis were rudimentary. It was left very much to members of the elite acting in a private capacity to protect ordinary citizens against a breakdown of the food supply system.

Most farms in antiquity were small. Even where large tracts of land were in the ownership of one wealthy proprietor, it was common for the

43

land to be fragmented, in so far as it was arable rather than pasture or forest land. The estates of the rich were regularly not only fragmented, but scattered.[1]

How did large landowners farm their land? The ancient evidence, in particular the evidence for Italy, is skewed in favour of the 'slave estate', a property of a modest 25–60 hectares employing a permanent slave work-force under a slave overseer. The slave estate represents a style of farming which, even in late Republican and early Imperial Italy, the centre of agricultural slavery, can legitimately be called at most the 'dominant exception'. Moreover, in practice, few landowners dispensed with free peasant labour altogether. The economic viability of slave estates depended upon the availability of free labour at peak times in the agricultural year, especially during harvesting; it was also common in early Imperial Italy to employ peasants as tenants controlling a slave work-force. Finally, over the huge area covered by the Roman empire, the rural population, small proprietors, tenants and labourers (permanent or seasonal), was predominantly free. The ancient economy in all periods rested on the backs of peasants, not slaves.[2]

Peasants have been defined as 'small producers on land who, with the help of simple equipment, their own labour and that of their families, produce mainly for their own consumption and for meeting obligations to the holders of political and economic power, and reach nearly total self-sufficiency within the framework of a village community'.[3]

This definition marks off the peasant, smallholder or tenant (the categories are not mutually exclusive), from, on the one hand, the entrepreneurial farmer growing cash crops for the market, and on the other, the primitive cultivator or pastoralist isolated from the world outside his community. I am reluctant to admit political as well as economic dependence as a defining characteristic of a peasantry, because I wish to accommodate not only those peasant communities (no doubt the majority) that were locked into political relationships with cities or a central state, but also the pre-polis rural communities of early Greece such as the Boeotia of the poet Hesiod, where economic

[1] Garnsey and Saller (1987), 64–71.
[2] See Carandini (1981), 249–60 (slavery as 'the dominant exception'); Garnsey (1980), 41–3; Rathbone (1981) (interdependence of peasants and large landowners); Johne, Köhn and Weber (1983); De Neeve (1984) (tenants); Whittaker (1980) (free dependent labour).
[3] Shanin (1971), 39; cf. Scott (1976), 157. On modern peasants, see also e.g. Fei (1939); Redfield (1956); Wolf (1966); Popkin (1979); Forbes (1982). Useful historical studies include Montanari (1979) (1984); Le Roy Ladurie (1966) (the English translation of 1974 omits the important section on climate); Goubert (1986).

practices and moral values were recognisably 'peasant', and under-urbanised regions that were largely independent of or only loosely attached to urban centres. In Italy, for much of our period, the regions of Etruscan, Greek and Punic colonisation (and areas such as Latium and Umbria strongly influenced by the Etruscans), where cities and an urban pattern of culture were well established from pre-Roman times, can be clearly distinguished from much of the rest of the peninsula, characterised by isolated farmsteads and small population centres that were often little more than places of refuge or cult-centres with minor economic functions. In the north African and Danubian provinces of the Roman empire groups of veterans and their descendants made up communities of peasants on territory not originally dependent on a city.[4]

By adopting a broad definition of the peasantry I am making it more difficult to generalise about peasant responses to environmental con-straints and human demands. That was already an uphill task, and not only because of the lack of interest shown in small farmers in the sources, a product of the social and cultural elite. The behaviour of peasants has to be assessed in the light of a series of factors, above all system of tenure and size of farm, but also climate and soil fertility, nature of crop, technology and land use, material resources of cultiva-tors, family structure, demographic conditions, market-relationship and burdens imposed from outside. A brief comment on the first two of these variables will point to the disparities that existed and the implications for survival chances.

First, the means of subsistence were not equally accessible to smallholders, tenants and wage-labourers. The claim of wage-labourers to the product of the land was obviously weakest, and they were particularly vulnerable in times of food shortage when demand slumped and wages fell. In comparison with wage-labourers, tenant farmers had greater access to the resources of the landlord, who might feel obliged to guarantee their subsistence, at least until the crop was harvested. A lot hung on the terms of the lease and the landlord's attitude. The position of owner-occupiers was strongest, in that their control over the land and its products was superior in the sight of the law. In times of adversity, however, their independent position might actually work against them. Smallholders who were also a valued source of seasonal labour on a large estate were perhaps better

---

[4] Lehmann (1986) (agrarian capitalism); Millett (1984) (Hesiod); Frederiksen (1976); Gabba (1977) (Italy); D'Escurac (1967) (Africa etc.). On the peasantry in antiquity, see also Finley (1985), Ch. 4; Garnsey (1979) (1980); Foxhall (1986); Garnsey and Saller (1987), 75ff. On survival strategies see Halstead (1981) (1984) (1988).

45

cushioned against disaster, if they could accept their neighbour's aid without falling into debt and dependence.[5]

Secondly, as to farm-size: 'The optimum size of a peasant farm', writes Finley, 'is an obviously meaningless notion.' The concept of minimum size is equally meaningless. The size of farm that an ordinary Athenian (a thete) might have worked in the classical period has been estimated at around 2–4 hectares (20–40 *plethra*). The basic plebeian plot in Republican Italy was rather smaller, something in the range of 1.25–2.5 hectares (5–10 *iugera*). Many in each society would have worked larger or smaller plots than this. The essential point is that the 'basic' farm of Attica and Italy is universally considered too small to have supported by itself a peasant family, and the shortfall was significantly greater if animal labour was employed. It follows that access to other, typically uncultivated, land (and to other employment) was crucial, and that the fortunes of the peasantry fluctuated significantly with the availability of such land. Wherever there was pressure on the land, as a result of population growth or increased investment in rural property by the wealthy, the result would have been an expansion of the area under cultivation and under private ownership, and thus a contraction of the *incolto* and reduced access to such as remained.[6]

The range of diversity of peasant societies can of course be more fully appreciated through analyses of contemporary or near-contemporary rural communities than by means of the exiguous ancient sources. For example, a recent anthropological study of the Italian peasantry found that a deep divide exists between the peasantries of southern and central Italy. In the south, farms are typically small, irregular and scattered; they are worked by peasants who live some distance away; these peasants are isolated from owners and from each other; hired rather than exchange labour is the norm; property is continually circulating and the nuclear family is preferred. In central Italy, on the other hand, share contracts predominate; landlords and cultivators are

---

[5] Finley (1985), 105.

[6] See Burford Cooper (1977–8), on Athenian holdings; but note that thetes received plots of 4–6 hectares abroad. The Roman figures are drawn from semi-legendary anecdotes (Pliny, *Hist. nat.* 18.18, 20 cf. Columella 1 pref. 13) and more firmly based evidence for colonial allotments (e.g. Livy 8.21.11, 37.46.10–47.2, with Salmon (1969)). For the consensus on non-viability, cf. Brunt (1971), 194; (1972), 158; White (1970), 336 cf. 346; Jameson (1977–8), 131 (for family of) 5 read 4). The last two authors cite unpublished calculations of K. Hopkins. According to White (via Hopkins), 3.25 people need 1.75 – 2 ha (7–8 *iugera*) without, and 5 ha (20 *iugera*) with, a plough. Cf. Clark and Haswell (1970), 64–8 for the implications of employing animal labour. But access to other land is essential. All these views and calculations are based on the assumption that yields were low, but see Garnsey and Saller (1987), 77–82.

closely linked through patronage; cultivators live on or near the land; the preferred family type is the extended family; exchange labour is resorted to when necessary, and continuity in control of landholdings is normal.[7]

The ancient world no doubt witnessed contrasts equally sharp. However, it is likely that the emergence in the traditional societies of the Third World of powerful economic and political forces in the form of capitalism, colonialism and nationalism, and the unevenness of their impact on the countryside, has produced an exceptional degree of diversity in the peasant societies of the Third World, greater perhaps than in any historical epoch before the early modern period in European history. This does not give ancient historians licence to assume a high level of homogeneity, continuity and stability of values and systems in the rural societies of their period. Given the broad definition of the peasantry and the wide spatial and temporal range that I have adopted, it would be more reasonable to make an initial assumption of the particularity of any given rural society. Hesiod's Boeotians (eighth century BC), the countrymen of Attica who were full citizens and active members of the direct democracy (fifth and fourth centuries BC), the tenant farmers of early Imperial Italy bound only by a legal contract of lease (first and second centuries AD), and their successors in Italy and beyond, the *coloni* of the late Empire, bound to the soil (fourth and fifth centuries AD) belong to different worlds. The 'typical ancient peasant' is a chimera.

The high level of diversity among modern peasant societies has not of course discouraged generalisation. Judgements, often discordant, are made about representative peasant behaviour. Consider the following contrasting statements:[8]

Typically, the peasant cultivator seeks to avoid the failure that will ruin him rather than attempting a big, but risky, killing. In decision-making parlance his behavior is risk-averse; he minimises the subjective probability of the maximum loss.

Peasants are continuously striving not merely to protect but to raise their subsistence level through long- and short-term investments, both public and private. Their investment logic applies not only to market exchanges but to nonmarket exchanges as well.

For present purposes, the details of the debate matter less than the implicit and shared understanding that there is a central core of recognisably 'peasant' attitudes and practices that transcend cultures (and, I would add, epochs). This is an assumption that an ancient

---

[7] Silverman (1968), reacting to Banfield's study of 'family amoralism' in Lucania (1958).
[8] Scott (1976), 4; Popkin (1979), 4.

historian can accept. To give what might seem at first sight a trivial example, the following passages from the medical writer Galen[9] illustrate behaviour that is unlikely to have been peculiar to peasants from Asia Minor in the second century AD:

When our peasants are bringing wheat from the country in wagons, and wish to filch some away without being detected, they fill earthen jars with water and stand them among the wheat: the wheat then draws the moisture into itself through the jar and acquires additional bulk and weight, but the fact is never detected by onlookers unless someone who knew about the trick beforehand makes a more careful inspection.

In a bad year, there was a great deal of darnel in the wheat. The farmers failed to separate it out by the use of sieves that are handy for this purpose, for the total wheat crop was meagre; nor did the bakers bother, for the same reason.

In the attempt that follows to piece together a survival strategy of ordinary subsistence farmers, I focus on responses that spring from the essential nature of subsistence agriculture operating under ancient economic and environmental conditions, while making allowance for the divergencies that are (at least to some extent) a product of the interaction of the peasant economy with the wider political and economic environment.

Native cunning (as witnessed by Galen) and sheer physical and mental hardiness apart, the capacity of the ancient peasant to survive is best analysed under three headings: production strategies, social and economic relationships, demographic behaviour.

PRODUCTION

Subsistence farming is a minimum-risk enterprise. The farmer endeavours to reduce his vulnerability by dispersing his landholdings, diversifying his products and storing his surplus.

Dispersal of landholding

A typical farm in modern Lucania has been described in this way:

Such a farm is not likely to be all in one piece; it may be in three or four pieces scattered at various elevations on the mountain and even at opposite sides of it. Although it is a time-consuming and tiring task to walk from one field to another, most farmers prefer to have their land in at least two pieces as insurance against

---

[9] Galen, *Nat. fac.* 1.14.56; cf. VI 549ff. (Kuhn).

crop failure; the hailstorm that strikes one side of the mountain will leave the other side untouched.[10]

Fragmentation, the scattering of parcels of land, is an eternal feature of Mediterranean farming. Any existing pattern of land dispersal is the product of local inheritance and dowry rules and customs. But the practice of fragmentation is entirely natural; it fits the climate and the landscape. In this respect it corresponds to the Andean 'vertical archipelago' and the Alpine 'inclined peninsula' which span and incorporate a wide range of climates and microenvironments and provide a high level of security in the face of ecological constraints.[11] The opposite strategy, land concentration or unification, which land reformers have tended to regard as an absolute good, makes sense only in an ecologically homogeneous area. In the northern Mediterranean, in particular, large tracts of flat land are relatively rare. Thus, where crop failure consequent on irregularities in the climate is to be expected, spatial diversification is beneficial. It gives the farmer access to a variety of microclimates, only some of which will be adversely affected by unfavourable weather at the same time.

There is the further economic advantage to be gained from field scattering, in that even identical crops do not ripen simultaneously in different locales, and the energies of the labour force can therefore be spread over time. But the main advantage to the small farmer lies in the reduction of risk.

Diversification of product

The Mediterranean small farmer has traditionally practised mixed farming, the polycropping of arable and trees on the same land with the addition of a little livestock. The goal is self-sufficiency but also the minimisation of risk: since the growth requirements of the various products differ, the possibility that the farmer will be left with nothing is reduced. In what follows I make no attempt to give a comprehensive account of the peasant diet or to assess the relative importance of the elements that made it up. My aim is rather to demonstrate with reference to cereals, the leading member of the triad of staple foods (the others being olive oil and wine), how wide the range of crops was in

[10] Banfield (1958), 50. Popkin (1979), 49–50 says that plot-scattering is ubiquitous, provides a longer list of mini-disasters, and observes that land dispersal can be more extensive than is necessary, or simply inappropriate.

[11] Netting (1981), at 14–15. For reduction of risk in an Alpine setting see also Netting (1972); Rhoades and Thompson (1975); Orlove (1980). For the Andes, see e.g. Lehmann (1982); Guillet (1983), responding to classic studies by Murra (1975), etc.

antiquity and the extent to which this diversity was a response to uncertainty and hazard.

Mixed cereal and legume cultivation has been a common pattern in traditional Mediterranean agriculture. We think of wheat as the representative cereal. However, there were a number of varieties of wheat and their uses were in some cases complementary. In addition, many other seed crops were planted, as reliable performers in particular ecological zones and as substitute crops.[12]

Theophrastus (*c.* 370–285 BC) knew numerous kinds of wheat (distinguished in terms of colour, size, form, weight, growth cycle, food value and locality), barley (two-to-six-rowed) and lesser cereals (*tiphai, zeiai, olurai,* millets), and three sowing seasons (late autumn, early spring, summer). In the centuries separating Theophrastus, on the one hand, and Varro (116–27 BC), Columella (*floruit* mid-first century AD), Pliny the Elder (*c.* AD 23–79) and Galen (*c.* AD 129–99), on the other, the stock of available seeds and hence the farmer's crop mix had altered. Improvement in the quality of existing seed types through natural selection can be assumed rather than adequately documented. The progress made by naked wheats, bread wheat (*triticum aestivum*) in particular, at the expense of hulled varieties of wheat and barley, is rather more visible. The following comment of Galen is symptomatic: 'Among Romans, as among almost all their subjects, the purest bread is called *silignites*; the closest to it is *semidalites*. But the name *semidalis* is Greek and old, whereas *silignis* is not Greek at all. Yet it is the only name I can give it.'[13]

However, the hulled seed-crops were not displaced. In Varro's digression in praise of Italy, Campanian *far* (*semen adoreum* or emmer wheat) heads the list of products in which Italy led the world. A combination of archaeological finds (seed remains and mortars for de-husking grain) and literary sources show that the popularity of *far* had by no means vanished a hundred years after Varro. Columella began his discussion of kinds of seed by ranking *semen adoreum* with *triticum*, or naked wheat, as 'the two first and most serviceable grains for men'. He knew four kinds of *far*, one of them a three-month variety: in other words, it could be employed as a 'catch-crop' in the event of the failure of a main winter crop. In Columella's account, *far* and *triticum* were not mutually exclusive:

---

[12] The literary and other evidence is well surveyed by Spurr (1986), esp. Ch. 5. See, on north Italy in the early Middle Ages, Montanari (1979), 109–66.

[13] Galen VI 483. The shift in balance between the various cereals is a theme of Sallares (1986). His discussion supersedes those of Jasny (1941–2), (1944a).

For these kinds of seed, *triticum* and *adoreum*, should be kept by farmers for this reason, that seldom is any land so situated that we can content ourselves with one kind of seed, as some strip which is either swampy or dry cuts through it. Further, *triticum* grows better in a dry spot, while *adoreum* is less harmed by moisture.[14]

In addition, it is likely enough that ordinary farmers grew naked wheats for sale and less marketable cereals for their own consumption. Galen's Asian peasants followed this practice. The tenants on ecclesiastical estates in north Italy in the early medieval period grew wheat for their landlords and 'grani minuti', especially millet, for their own consumption.[15]

The extent of barley's popularity decline after the classical period is hard to gauge: the evidence comes in the main from outside Attica and the low-rainfall areas of south-east Greece, its preferred terrain. Barley was always a less significant crop in Italy than in Greece; but was grown still under the Empire, even if essentially for animals and for humans in time of emergency. Columella says that the variety called by the countrymen *hexastichum* or *catherinum* is recommended for this reason: 'It is better food than wheat for all the animals that belong on a farm, and is more wholesome for humans than is bad wheat; and in times of scarcity there is nothing better in guarding against want.'

Galen did not think highly of barley:

Among some peoples barley meal is used when bread is short. I myself have seen countryfolk eating barley-meal in Cyprus, even though they grow a lot of wheat. In the old days, people used to prepare barley-meal, but now its weakness in terms of food value is recognised. It gives little nourishment to the body. Ordinary people and those who do not take regular exercise find it quite sufficient, but for those who do take exercise in any way at all it is found wanting.

But barley, by Galen's own account, was more or less ubiquitous, and was to be classed with wheat as a superior cereal.[16]

As for the cereals outranked by wheat and barley, Galen's list does not diverge significantly from that of Theophrastus, but he is more informative about their role in production and consumption. On *zeia*, he writes:

---

[14] Varro 1.2.7; Columella 2.6.1–2. On plant remains, see e.g. Small (1981), 210: emmer, *triticum aestivum, triticum durum*, barley, oats; in addition, *vicia faba*, pea, lentil, vetch, alfalfa (at latest levels). On mortars, see Moritz (1958), Ch. 4.

[15] See e.g. Galen VI 513 (on *tiphe* and *olyra*, quoted below); Montanari (1979), 139.

[16] For barley in classical Greece, see Gallo (1983) and (1984); for the Roman period, see Columella 2.9.14; Galen VI 501ff., at 507; cf. Pliny, *Hist. nat.* 18.71–5: barley is preferred by 'the Greeks' for porridge (*polenta*), has declined in use (sc. in Italy), and is mostly animal food. See Sanders (1984), esp. 259 for (sound) conjectures on the importance of barley in the Cyclades in antiquity, based on later evidence.

Those who live in countries with a cold winter are compelled to feed on this and to sow it, because it is the grain which best resists the cold.

On *olura* and *tiphe*:

There is plenty of each of them in Asia, and especially in the region above Pergamum, as the peasants always use bread made from them because the wheat is carted off to the cities ... Hot breads from the best *tiphai* are much preferable to the *olura* breads ... when it is hot it is sought after even by city dwellers, being demanded with a particular kind of cheese.

On *bromos*:

This grain is very plentiful in Asia, and especially Mysia, which lies above Pergamum, where also *tiphai* and *olurai* are found in quantity. But it is food for pack-horses, not men. For men do not make bread from it unless smitten with severe hunger. In normal times however they eat it boiled in water with sweet wine or *hepsema* or honey-wine, like *tiphe*.[17]

Millet (Italian or common) is presented by Columella as an emergency resource for small farmers. 'In many regions,' he states, 'the peasants are kept going by food made from them.' Two generations earlier Strabo had written that millet was a sure defence against hunger for inhabitants of the Po valley when other crops failed. Ps.-Joshua gives an example of its use as a substitute-crop, which could be planted in the spring or summer because of its resistance to drought and short three-to-four-month growth cycle:

In the months of Khaziran [June] and Tammuz [July], the inhabitants of these districts were reduced to all sorts of shifts to live. They sowed millet for their own use, but it was not enough for them, because it did not thrive.[18]

The part played by dry legumes in the agricultural regime was not dissimilar. That is to say, they were grown as a matter of course or as catch-crops and famine foods. A convenient illustration of this last function is provided by Columella's discussion of lupine, which contains the following remark:

First consideration belongs to the lupine, as it requires the least labour, costs least, and of all crops that are sown is most beneficial to the land ... When softened by boiling it is good fodder for cattle during the winter; in the case of humans too it serves to ward off famine if years of crop failures come upon them.[19]

[17] Galen vi 513, 517, 522–3.
[18] Columella 2.9.17; Strabo 5.1.12; Ps.-Joshua, *Chron.* Ch. 38; Spurr (1986), Ch. 5.
[19] Columella 2.10.1ff. On turnips, see Columella 2.10.22ff. ('filling food for country people') and Pliny, *Hist. nat.* 18.127 ('a precaution against hunger').

Ancient writers in their discussion of seed-crops did not always distinguish firmly between cereals and legumes. The distinction between cultivated and wild plants is similarly imprecise. The 'kitchen garden' contained a wide variety of vegetables, some conventional, others less so. At one further remove from the farmhouse, a wide variety of greens growing in arable areas, particularly on fallow (without modern weed-killers to eradicate them), made a contribution to the peasant's diet.

Still further afield lay the resources of the *incolto*, uncultivated land. In his classic *L'Alimentation végétale*, Maurizio lists 621 'plantes de ramassage'. He does not treat the Graeco-Roman period specifically, but many of his edible plants are cited in ancient authors. Peasants have always been systematic foragers on uncultivated land, in woods, marshes and rivers. They gather both supplementary and alternative foods; or, in terms of a distinction made by Galen, foods that are eaten normally 'in the absence of famine' and others eaten only in famine conditions. The difficulty of sustaining this distinction is illustrated in the following text of Galen concerning the behaviour of Asian peasants. This alludes to the role played by domestic animals as a reserve of food, and may serve the further function of introducing the third arm of the peasant survival strategy, storage:

Countryfolk habitually eat the fruit of the cornel tree and blackberries and acorns and the fruit of the arbutus, and rather less those of the other trees and shrubs. But when famine grips our land, and there are plenty of acorns and medlars, they store them in pits and consume them instead of food from cereals throughout the winter and in early spring. Acorns were previously food for swine, then when the pigs could not be maintained in the winter in the usual way, first they slaughtered them and used them as food, then they opened up their storage pits and began to eat the acorns, preparing them as food in a variety of ways from place to place.[20]

Storage

Galen's peasants stockpiled famine foods as a matter of course. This is more striking than their use of domestic animals as a stored reserve, or the storage of foodstuffs that contributed to their usual diet – in particular, grain, but also dry legumes, dried fruits (figs, grapes), olive oil and wine.

Storage was an economic necessity for a peasant. For Hesiod there was an additional moral dimension. To live an honourable life one must

[20] Galen VI 620; Maurizio (1932); cf. Frayn (1979), 57–72; Evans (1980); Montanari (1979), 431–8 emphasises the crucial importance of the *incolto* in combating food shortage. On the kitchen garden, see App. Verg. *Moretum*, ed. E. J. Kenney.

work hard, fill one's barns and storage jars, and support oneself. His ideal is summed up in these words:

Thus the ears of your corn will bow down if Zeus himself finally gives you a good outcome, and you will sweep the cobwebs out of your jars; and I expect you will be happy when you take from the store you have gathered. You will have much until you come to bright springtime, and you will not look to others wistfully; but another man will need your help.[21]

Storage was designed to provide a level, uninterrupted flow of foodstuffs through the unproductive seasons of the year. This meant in normal years the winter and early spring, as the citation from Hesiod indicates. Similarly, Galen writes in connection with a legume he calls *dolichos*:

Anyone who wants to store them safely should dry them thoroughly first, as my father used to do. Thus through the whole winter they remain good and well preserved, offering the same service as peas do.[22]

Stored goods might, however, have to last through a barren summer. A prudent farmer alive to the risk of crop failure would aim to put aside a supply of food over and above the present year's requirements. To use a phrase coined by Allan in his study of East African peasants and applied by Halstead to neolithic Thessaly, the peasant's expectation is to produce a 'normal surplus':

Subsistence cultivators, dependent entirely or almost entirely on the produce of their gardens, tend to cultivate an area large enough to ensure the food supply in a season of poor yields. Otherwise the community would be exposed to frequent privation and grave risk of extermination or dispersal by famine, more especially in regions of uncertain and fluctuating rainfall. One would, therefore, expect the production of a 'normal surplus' of food in the average year.

Farmers in present-day Kosona, on the Methana peninsula in the Peloponnese, aim to set aside two years' supply of wheat and four years' supply of olive oil (since a reasonable olive crop could be anticipated only in every second year). They do not always succeed. Allan found that overproduction amongst the Tonga averaged 40% of subsistence needs.[23]

Small farmers did not hold onto grain for much more than two years. Their storage facilities were limited, and grain did deteriorate. Theophrastus' remarks on the durability of wheat carry a message that is pessimistic for growers (less so for consumers):

21 Hesiod, *Works and Days* 473–8.
22 Galen VI 546.
23 Allan (1965) 38, cited by Halstead (1988); cf. Forbes (1982).

For propagation and sowing generally, seeds one year old seem to be the best; those two or three years old are inferior, while those kept a still longer time are infertile, though they are still available as food.[24]

In practice, much depended on storage facilities. These ranged from the crude pits of the squirrel-like peasants of Asia Minor or Simulus' heap of grain in a dark corner (in the pseudo-Virgilian *Moretum*), to jars for relatively secure but still small-scale storage, to the sizeable structures for the bulk storage of grain described in the agricultural writers. Varro refers to units of 1,000 modii (over 3,300 kg).[25]

Seed could easily deteriorate through the action of rodents, fungus and above all insects, even supposing it could be protected successfully from the weather. All the agricultural writers have stories to tell about long-lived grain, but their continuing obsession with the problems of keeping out moisture and pests rings truer.

Wheat kept less well than some other grains and dry legumes, another reason for the use of the latter by ordinary farmers. Columella says that once dried in the sun millet kept longer than other grains. This follows the comment that in many regions peasants (*coloni*) are kept going by millet. Theophrastus thought the best grains for storage were the millets, sesame, lupine and chickpea. Galen makes continual reference to the preservation of foods by drying and pickling. We are even informed that soft thistles 'are thrown into brine or vinegar and kept to the next year'. In the case of fruit, his discussion is a useful reminder of the value placed in antiquity on figs and grapes in comparison with more perishable fruits. Galen held the latter in low regard: having long abstained from them under his wise father's supervision, at the age of eighteen and then again the following year he went on fruit-eating sprees in Pergamum with some friends, with the result that he was taken with an acute illness that had to be treated by venesection.[26]

SOCIAL AND ECONOMIC RELATIONSHIPS

Smallholders were shielded from economic adversity to a lesser or greater extent by relationships with members of their own or neighbouring communities and with men of superior wealth and influence.

---

[24] Theophrastus, *Hist. plant.* 8.11.

[25] *Moretum* 13–18; Varro 1.57 cf. Columella 1.6.9ff.; Pliny, *Hist. nat.* 18.301ff. For storage for sale, see Varro 1.16.2, 1.62 and 69; Columella 2.20.6.

[26] Galen VI 755–6; cf. Columella 2.9.18; Theophrastus, *Caus. plant.* 4.15.3.

Exchange

Exchange and storage are complementary. Goods that are surplus to requirements are exchanged for others in which there is deficiency. Some exchange of goods or services is unavoidable, for no household can be entirely self-sufficient. There need not, however, be a regular pattern of exchange, where food surpluses do not have to be rapidly eliminated, that is, where households can store surpluses in good years and fall back on stored staples in bad.

That form of exchange is most advantageous to the subsistence peasant which takes place outside the market context. Few producers could avoid contact with a market altogether. Simulus, the peasant of the *Moretum*, is as close to an ordinary subsistence peasant as the literature of antiquity can take us. The absence of meat from his diet is one of several indicators of his extreme poverty. Simulus grows, processes and consumes his own bread, having flavoured it with herbs, garlic and cheese. However, he needs to raise cash in order to pay for items in which he is deficient (such as salt) and perhaps also to meet demands for rent, tax or interest. To this end he grows vegetables in his 'kitchen garden' for market sale.[27]

It made a difference how much of a farmer's labour and resources went into the production of cash-crops. Too close a relationship with a market would undermine his subsistence base. In addition to the climatic uncertainties that were a 'given', a part of his permanent condition, he would be exposing himself to the vicissitudes of market exchange.

Reciprocal exchange was a more desirable alternative. Producers exchanged outside the market with others from the same community, typically kinsmen and neighbours, in order to acquire goods which were temporarily lacking following a bad or mediocre harvest. Such relationships might extend also to peasants in other communities no great distance away. It is worth recalling that both climate and yield vary strikingly both between and within regions in the Mediterranean, and that such variation was particularly marked in the broken landscapes of Greece and Italy.

Dio of Prusa, local politician and moral philosopher at the turn of the first century AD, provides a striking illustration of the role of reciprocity in a rural society. Dio enquired of his host, a peasant who farmed in the Euboean hills:

---

[27] *Moretum* 78–81. The editor suggests (p. 1, n. 60) that Simulus was a slave *colonus* saving up to purchase his freedom.

'Is she the one whose tunic you took off and gave to the shipwrecked man?' 'No,' he said with a smile. 'That daughter was married long ago and already has grown-up children. Her husband is a rich man living in a village.' 'And do they help you when you need anything?' I asked. 'We do not need anything', replied the wife, 'but they get game from us whenever we catch any, and fruit and vegetables, for they have no garden. Last year we borrowed some wheat just for seed, but we repaid them as soon as harvest time was come.'[28]

The twin notions of self-sufficiency and reciprocity are here on display. Subsequently we learn that the family's network of contacts reaches further than the extended family, to other local households. A young wild pig is exchanged for another, presumably domesticated, young pig, and wine is obtained for a special occasion.

Eight centuries previously, Hesiod had applauded competition between households on the grounds that it forced the peasant to work hard:

So, after all, there was not one kind of Strife alone, but all over the earth there are two. As for the one, a man would praise her when he came to understand her ... She stirs up even the shiftless to toil; for a man grows eager to work when he considers his neighbour, a rich man who hastens to plough and plant and put his household in good order; and neighbour vies with his neighbour as he hurries after wealth. This strife is wholesome for men. And potter is angry with potter, and craftsman with craftsman, and beggar is jealous of beggar, and minstrel of minstrel.

A comparison suggests itself between this pugnacious assertion of the self-sufficiency of the individual household and the 'amoral familism' ascribed to Lucanian peasants in a classic but controversial study. The ethic of the village community is captured in the following formulation:

Maximise the material short-run advantages of the nuclear family; assume that all others will do likewise.[29]

The comparison should not be pressed for several obvious reasons, not least the nature of the Hesiodic poem, 'a model of and a model for society' composed with the aim of influencing 'the reproduction of social values'.[30]

It is none the less undeniable, and uncontroversial, that individualism is a standard feature of peasant households. But individualism can be more, or less, pronounced, reflecting the degree of cohesiveness of the peasant community. In addition, even where it exists in an extreme, aggressive form (as in the south of Italy in modern times and in ancient Boeotia in the vision of Hesiod), it coexists with a recognition of the

[28] Dio Chrys. *Or.* 7. On the historicity of the speech, see Jones (1978), 61.
[29] Hesiod, *Works and Days* 20–6; Banfield (1958), 85.
[30] Quoted from Garnsey and Morris (1988). On Hesiod as peasant, see Millett (1984).

need for exchange and therefore of lateral links with other peasant households. Good relations between neighbours (and bad between kinsmen) characterised the Lucanian villagers, while Hesiod wrote:

It is good to take a measure from your neighbour, and good to pay him back the same, or better, if you can, so that if you are needy afterwards you will again find him sure.[31]

It remains to see what role was played by vertical relationships, in particular patronage, in protecting peasants against adversity.

Patronage

Patronage is a lasting relationship between individuals of unequal wealth or power involving the asymmetrical exchange of goods and services.[32] Patrons make available, as gifts or on loan, money, food, farming equipment or seed, and furnish legal assistance and protection. They receive in return labour, produce, political support and social prestige. A purely economic relationship between unequals is not patronage. Charity, a one-sided relationship between an active bene-factor and an essentially passive beneficiary, is not patronage. Can patronage and exploitation be distinguished? Not in the eyes of some. Rather than say that patronage is necessarily exploitative, I prefer to view patronage as a potentially unstable relationship which, because of the unequal bargaining position of the two parties, can easily slide into overt exploitation. What is involved in this transition is a change in the balance of services to the advantage of the stronger party, in the view of the weaker party. In a patronage relationship, a patron must meet the client's expectations of the treatment that is due to him if the relation-ship is to continue and not degenerate into something else.

The dilemma facing the would-be historian of patronage is clear-cut. We would expect patronage to have been a structural feature of rural society in antiquity, but we are hard put to show that it was. It is easy to demonstrate that communities and professional organisations, up-wardly mobile members of the Roman or provincial propertied classes and even respectable plebeians were caught up in patronal networks; in some cases they have received monographic treatment from modern historians. But rural patronage is largely invisible in the Mediter-ranean world before the late Roman Empire. If patronage was present in archaic Boeotia, Hesiod chooses to ignore the phenomenon: his was a

[31] Hesiod, *Works and Days* 339–41.
[32] On patronage, see Gellner and Waterbury (1977), especially articles by Gellner, Silver-man, Scott and Weingrod. Saller (1982) is best on private patronage in antiquity, but does not deal with agrarian class relations, on which see also Garnsey and Woolf (1989).

world of 'gift-devouring lords', serf-like labourers (*dmoes*), and stubbornly independent peasants. If Pliny, a substantial absentee landowner in Italy at the end of the first century AD, was a patron to his tenants in Tuscany and Cisalpine Gaul, he is silent on the subject.[33]

Gaul and Syria provide glimpses of vertical social relations in a rural setting involving for the most part the free poor. In Gaul, the basic social and administrative unit was traditionally the tribe, not the city. A succession of Roman or Graeco-Roman observers – Caesar, Varro, Tacitus, Strabo and Diodorus – reveal that in pre- and post-conquest Gaul *servi*, *clientes*, *ambacti* and *obaerati* were all in some way caught up in the magnetic field of chieftains. But information is lacking about their precise economic and occupational positions and the content of the relationship which bound them to their social superiors. Thus, in respect of *clientes*, we know only that they formed part of the regular escort and entourage of a chieftain in peace and in war. Five centuries after Caesar's conquest, Gaul was still relatively underurbanised, and Gallic nobles, as portrayed by and exemplified in Sidonius Apollinaris, Bishop and *grand seigneur* of Clermont Ferrand, were still recognisably Gallic chieftains, the centre of a network of asymmetrical relationships. But not all the vertical relationships of early or late Gallic society qualify as patronage. Slaves were not clients. Farm labourers and small tenants at the bottom of the social scale, whether or not they were debt bondsmen, must have been scarcely distinguishable from slaves, comparable perhaps to the *dmoes* of archaic Boeotia. Finally, Salvian, Bishop of Marseilles, wrote in a famous passage that because of heavy taxation and insecurity, the Gallic peasant had three choices: he could fly to the barbarians, join the Bagaudae, or seek the patronage of some neighbouring landed magnate, surrendering his land and freedom of movement in return for protection against barbarian raids and the demands of the central government. In effect, smallholders were being inadequately protected by traditional patrons and exploited by new ones. Salvian's apocalyptic vision of Gaul in turmoil serves as a foil to Sidonius' more optimistic picture of a relatively cohesive if fragmented society.[34]

The sources for late Imperial Syria introduce two kinds of vertical relationship, the one linking tenants with their urban-based absentee landlords, the other linking villagers with local men of power, whether

[33] Hesiod, *Works and Days* 38–9, 442 cf. 559–60; Pliny, *Ep.* 9.37.
[34] Diodorus 5.29.2; Varro 1.17.2; Caesar, *Bell. Gall.* 1.4; 6.15; etc.; Tacitus, *Ann.* 3.42; Sidonius, *Ep.* 4.18.2; 5.19; etc. with Wightman (1978); Salvian, *Gub. Dei* 5.8.38–40, no doubt exaggerated, cf. Jones (1964), 777. There are of course other spokesmen, ecclesiastical and secular, for late Roman Gaul, and Gallic social conditions were extremely diverse. For the Bagaudae, see Van Dam (1985).

military men, officials, ex-officials (*honorati*) or holy men.[35] In an
oration of Libanius they are both visible, and at odds. Libanius
complains that peasants were not following recognised procedures in
seeking help for themselves. He has in mind in particular some Jewish
tenants with whom he was himself in dispute. In the course of stating
his grievance, Libanius evokes a traditional pattern of patron-to-client
services which, it is implied, characterised his and his family's relations
with these tenants and their ancestors over four generations:

> They can even make their masters more kindly disposed towards them, so as either
> to allow a remission of debts, or even to offer a grant, and again, if they ever have
> need to have recourse to law between each other, they should approach the owner.

Contact had been broken in circumstances undisclosed, partly because
of patronal inadequacy, as Libanius tacitly admits. He goes on to say
that it was for the landlord to send the petitioners on to 'some more
powerful personage' if he could not himself carry out their requests.
Instead of approaching him, Libanius' tenants

> resorted to the usual trick and made for the general's quarters, their shield against
> the claims of justice. Then came the presents of barley and wheat, and ducks, and
> fodder for the horses. And the general ordained the release of those who had
> deserted their post, and the governor obeyed and promised to do so.

In the same oration Libanius tells how villages of peasant proprietors
raid other villages, having gained virtual immunity through the
protection of the local garrison-commander, whom they have won over
with gifts of wheat, barley and gold.

In a second oration, Libanius conjures up a patron called Mixide-
mus, who took over the patronage of some villagers from men on the
staff of the governor and proceeded to exact a payment in grain and
other produce from the peasants, using their wives as household
servants. His intention was to take over entire villages, not a forlorn
hope in view of the peasants' felt need for protection. This man, an
ex-official (*honoratus*), had in common with Salvian's Gallic magnates
an interest in expanding his landholdings at the expense of new
clients; the military men appear to have been content with payments of
one kind or another.

Patrocinium, here described by Libanius, emerged in the late Empire
essentially as a service for peasants oppressed by taxes and rents. It was
akin to patronage (food and services were given in exchange for
protection), but is better described as an illegitimate strain. It fell short

[35] Libanius, *Or.* 47 cf. 39; Brown (1971); Liebeschuetz (1972), 198–208, with bibl.; Patlagean
(1977), 287–95.

60

of patronage as it is normally understood in two ways: first, while it may be characteristic of a patronage system that it stands outside an officially proclaimed formal morality, *patrocinium* appears to go further in undercutting the existing moral codes and flouting the law: *patrocinium* is roundly condemned in a series of laws beginning in the 360s. Secondly, *patrocinium* was characteristically exploitative, resulting in the loss of the client's land and his general downgrading – though the laws indicate that some of these latter-day patrons also harboured men who had little or nothing to lose, runaway *coloni*, free tenants and labourers already subject to a generalised and authorised exploitation.[36]

Traditional patronage was in crisis in the late Empire. But how ubiquitous was patronage in earlier times and under what conditions did it flourish?

Patronage worked best when patrons were integrated into the rural community. It prospered (alongside other less balanced, more exploitative relationships) in Gaul, which, away from the 'Old Province' in the south, never became highly urbanised. Patronage was a force in the interior of Syria, where urban life was underdeveloped and villages many and independent. The problems arose where the natural patrons, large landowners, moved to the cities or were permanently resident there as a *rentier* class.

The city was the focus and symbol of Graeco-Roman civilisation. Its social, cultural and political life was attractive to the wealthy and ambitious. As cities grew in number, size and prosperity along the Mediterranean littoral, in the river valleys and in the immediate hinterland, the class of absentee landlords multiplied.

There are texts that present a stark picture of confrontation between urban and rural dwellers. The peasants in a passage of Galen quoted earlier were reduced to 'famine foods', having been forced to surrender their cereals and legumes to the urban populations. The blissful isolation of Dio's Euboean hillfolk was shattered when the authorities of the city discovered their existence and began to impose taxes, rents and compulsory burdens. Strabo, who lived under Augustus, wrote of the Gallic city of Nemausus (Nîmes): 'It has subject to its authority twenty-four villages that are exceptional in their supply of strong men, of stock like its own, and contribute towards its expenses.' Orcistus, a town situated on the borders of Galatia in central Asia Minor, sought from Constantine upgrading to city-status precisely because it was subject to a city, Nacola, and judged its rule oppressive. Finally, the

[36] *Cod. Theod.* 11.24 ('de patrociniis vicorum'). On the colonate, see Jones (1974a), cf. Finley (1976a).

arrival of peasants in the cities as seasonal or permanent emigrants in search of employment and subsistence is noted by a number of writers, including Libanius, who deplored their presence in Antioch, and Ambrose, who condemned the practice of expelling them from Rome when food was in short supply.[37]

The opposition of city and country can be too sharply drawn. Peasants did not lack access to the amenities of the city, especially if they were urban residents, as they sometimes were. Smaller cities were little more than overgrown villages, the centre of agricultural production for the area, and the seat of some or most of the farming population. In democracies peasants participated in the decision-making process and were protected from exploitation by legal and political institutions. Finally, the leadership of the (more typical) oligarchies neglected rather than tyrannised the peasantry. 'Libanius and his kind', writes Peter Brown, 'did not want duties that took them far into the countryside, away from the politics of the city and the delights of the great suburban villas at Daphne.'[38]

The evidence of Libanius that city-based landowners might act as patrons to their tenants should none the less be taken seriously. It is not out of the question that Pliny, though based in Rome, performed occasional patronal services for his tenants in Tuscany and Cisalpine Gaul, despite the impression conveyed in his letters that the relationships were purely economic. A landlord who was prepared, as Pliny was, to contemplate rent-remission and the conversion of fixed rentals into share-cropping arrangements can without difficulty be pictured intervening at law or arranging marriages for selected tenants. In general, the landlord–tenant relationship was potentially a fertile breeding ground for patronage, in so far as both parties had a stake in a common enterprise. In the same way, large and small landowners who recognised their economic interdependence might forge a relationship that extended well beyond the exchange of wages for labour. But many large landowners exploited their superior bargaining position to down-grade smallholders into tenants and drive free tenants into dependency; and if like Pliny they were inclined to paternalism, they were too remote to be active patrons.[39]

---

[37] Galen VI 749ff.; Dio Chrys. *Or.* 7.68–9; Strabo 186; *ILS* 6699; Libanius, *Or.* 41.11; Ambrose, *Off.* 3.45–52. See MacMullen (1974), 28–56.

[38] Brown (1971), 85. In addition, Libanius was kept busy by his urban clients, mainly his own pupils, see Liebeschuetz (1972), 192–8. See Garnsey (1979), on residence of peasants; De Ste Croix (1981), e.g. 96–7, on protection against exploitation under a democracy.

[39] Pliny, *Ep.* 9.37. On Pliny's finances, see Duncan-Jones (1982), 17–32.

To conclude: the peasant's first line of defence consisted of kinsmen, neighbours and friends in his own rural community. Patronage afforded supplementary insurance against disaster. For some it might even have functioned as an alternative to such a network of horizontal relationships, if the patron was active and accessible. Patronage often functions through a preferential distribution of resources and services to favoured clients, who are encouraged to put their own interests and those of their patron above all others. I suspect there was little peasant solidarity in Gallic society, where individual households were linked with chieftains or magnates in a variety of carefully graded vertical relationships of which patronage was one. In the Syrian context, in contrast, the strong patron did not play off villagers one against another, but promoted harmony and corporate action.

In traditional, mainstream Mediterranean society, the rural population needed both horizontal and vertical relationships of a patronal kind to meet the demands imposed on them by the city, and, where it existed, a central state. In so far as patrons were absentee urban-based landlords, a patronal relationship need not have seriously undermined the peasant's natural support system within his own community. By the same token, however, such patronage was often remote, unavailable and ineffective. When the burdens imposed from outside became sufficiently oppressive to jeopardise the material welfare of landowners as well as tenants, active exploitation was substituted for flagging patronal relationships, and former clients, already alive to the advantages of on-the-spot protection, looked for it with greater urgency and desperation.

DEMOGRAPHIC BEHAVIOUR

Malthus argued that in the long term population growth would outstrip the food resources of a nation, causing rising prices, falling earnings and a drop in the standard of living. The downward spiral might be arrested by the positive checks of famine and war, or alternatively and less tragically by the preventive check of 'the prudential restraint on marriage'. Malthus was confident that it was the preventive check which maintained the balance between population and food supply in the more advanced ('improved') societies of his time, and recent research has confirmed his judgement in the case of England. It has been shown with the aid of a set of parish registers covering the period between the sixteenth and nineteenth centuries that fluctuations in the food supply had a greater impact on nuptiality and fertility than on mortality patterns. These results and other comparative evidence should encourage the ancient historian to look for the operation of adaptive strategies in the Mediterranean world of antiquity.[40]

In ancient as in all pre-industrial societies, mortality rates were high and life-expectancy at birth low: between 20 and 30 years is a reasonable estimate.[41] The main determinant of the high level of mortality was disease. In addition, short-term fluctuations in the death rate occurred in consequence of war, epidemic and food shortage. The question at issue is whether voluntary family limitation – for example, through the adjustment of marriage age and the interval between births, the use of contraception, abortion and infant exposure – made a significant contribution to the determination of population trends in the long or short term.

Of the various modes of family limitation, exposure of the new-born child, who either died or was picked up and reared by another, typically as a slave, is the most visible in the sources. It was probably also the most commonly practised, especially among the poor. However, it is not easy to see how its significance could be demonstrated for any particular society or period, let alone for antiquity in general. The author of the most exhaustive survey of methods of population control in antiquity stops short of estimating the frequency of its use.[42]

The evidence is very varied and of unequal weight. One literary text with interesting demographic implications is Herodotus' well-known narrative of the colonisation of Cyrene from the island of Thera in the seventh century BC. If the interpretation offered below is broadly correct, then the story is an illustration of the interplay of positive and preventive checks in a community.[43]

The people of Thera, oppressed by a seven-year drought which had withered all but one tree on the island, passed a decree 'to send brother from brother, chosen by lot, and from all the seven districts, men', according to Herodotus. No women went on the expedition. In the so-called 'Founders' Stele', perhaps a later forgery, 'men, women, boys and girls' swore curses on those who disobeyed the decree, but only men were dispatched as colonists. The Ionians who left Athens to found cities on the Asia Minor coast had acted in similar fashion, as

---

[40] Malthus (1798; repr. 1970); Wrigley and Schofield (1981), 15–154; Schofield (1985); Hajnal (1965); Wrigley (1969), 108–43, esp. 116–27.

[41] Hopkins (1966) (25 years); Frier (1982) (21 years, early third century AD); cf. Frier (1983).

[42] Eyben (1980–1). Golden (1981) argues that Athenians practised female infanticide at the rate of 10% or more.

[43] Herodotus 4.150ff. cf. *SEG* IX 3; Herodotus 1.146 (Ionians). I have benefited from reading an unpublished paper of G. L. Cawkwell on the origins of Greek colonisation which contains a wide-ranging discussion of matters of demography.

Herodotus indicates: 'They set out from the city hall of the Athenians and counted themselves the noblest of Ionians. But they did not take women to the colony; rather, they got hold of Carian women, whose fathers they slew.'

One explanation of the absence of women colonists might be that women were in short supply at home as a result of the practice of infanticide. This is not the only possible interpretation: the Thera story shows, it might be said, that there was a superfluity of younger (adult) sons on a generally overpopulated island. But, in the first place, this image of seventh-century Thera is unrealistic: a community with an absolute surplus of manpower should have been able to spare more than the (at most) 200 men who could fill the pentekonters. Secondly, overpopulation was not the mainspring of the colonisation of Cyrene, but drought-induced famine. A community in which population and resources were already out of balance, thanks to an overenthusiastic application of the preventive check, was hit by a run of bad harvests, and only escaped the full impact of the positive check of famine by the drastic action of expelling a part of its population. Fortunately the Mediterranean world was not closed to emigration.

Other literary evidence is often impressionistic or tendentious. What is to be made of Plutarch's 'The poor do not bring up children'; or Posidippus' 'Everyone brings up a son, even if he happens to be a poor man; even a rich man always exposes a daughter'? Tacitus observed that exposure was unusually absent among the Germans and the Jews, and Strabo noted that the Egyptians zealously reared every child that was born. What, precisely, follows for Graeco-Roman society? That exposure was tolerated, familiar or endemic?[44] On the face of it, the 'law of Romulus' offers more enlightenment, at least in relation to early Roman society; it implies both that exposure of children of both sexes was frequent enough to be considered a threat to the community, and that girls remained at risk after the passage of the law, more so than boys. The law required Roman citizens to raise all boys (apart from any that were malformed) and the first-born girl. However, its authenticity must be doubtful. It is cited only by Dionysius of Halicarnassus in the course of his discussion of Rome's semi-legendary past, and is not picked up in any later legal document.[45]

[44] Plutarch, *Mor.* 497E; Posidippus, *Hermaphrodite*, fr. 11, Kock; Tacitus, *Germ.* 19, *Hist.* 5.5; Strabo 824 (cf. *P. Oxy.* 744: 'If it is a boy, rear it; if a girl, throw it out': a soldier to his wife).
[45] Dionysius 2.15 cf. 9.22.1 cf. Livy 1.9 (*penuria mulierum* and the Rape of the Sabine Women). The remarkable reticence of Republican Roman sources in general over infanticide has led some to doubt whether exposure was known in Rome until the Empire. See Bennett (1922–3); against, Eyben (1980–1), 14 n. 33. On the prevalence of exposure in antiquity in general, see Harris (1982), supporting Brunt (1971), 148–54, among others, against Engels

Pride of place among untrustworthy literary texts may go to Polybius' generalisation about the Greece of his day, the mid-second century BC:

In our own time the whole of Greece has been subject to childlessness and shortage of population, owing to which cities have become deserted and the land has ceased to yield fruit, though there have been neither continuous wars nor epidemics . . . For as men had fallen into such a state of pretentiousness, avarice and indolence that they did not wish to marry, or if they married, to rear the children born to them, or at most as a rule only one or two of them, so as to leave these in prosperity and bring them up to waste their substance, the evil rapidly and insensibly grew. For in cases where of one or two children the one was carried off by war and the other by sickness, it is evident that the houses must have been left unoccupied, and as in the case of swarms of bees, so by small degrees cities became resourceless and feeble.[46]

This moralistic diatribe has been treated with too much respect. Even to say that the passage documents voluntary decline in the birth rate among families of Polybius' own class and locality is to make an overambitious claim. It is unrealistic to attribute to Polybius or any other ancient observer such a high level of demographic consciousness.

Isolated literary texts have also been used to support the argument that the rural population of Republican Italy was not reproducing itself. Appian's narrative of the period of the Gracchi (composed about 250 years later) contains the following sentence: 'The land commissioners heard the lamentations of the poor, that they were being reduced from competence to extreme penury, and from that to childlessness, because they were unable to rear their offspring.' This text in combination with Cassius Dio's comment on the shortage of females among the Roman upper classes under the Augustan Principate does not justify the claim that 'The peasants of the Gracchan age, dispossessed of their lands, were unable to rear children.'[47]

A case can be made out for depopulation in Hellenistic Greece (and late Republican Italy), but it does not rest on evidence for the demographic behaviour of families, which does not exist. The Greek

---

(1980). Harris argues from early marriage for the structural importance of exposure, accepting Hopkins (1965): girls married at 12–15 and boys somewhat later. Hopkins' evidence is slanted toward the aristocracy. See Saller (1987), cf. Garnsey and Saller (1987), Ch. 7, for the argument on the basis of epigraphical evidence that men married in their late twenties and women in their late teens or early twenties, a pattern found in later Mediterranean societies. See Hajnal (1983). The implications for fertility of later age of marriage remain to be explored.
[46] Polybius 36.17; cf. Walbank, *Comm.* 680–1; Rostovtzeff (1941), 623, 1464 n. 23; Tarn and Griffith (1952), 100–1; Préaux (1978), 52; etc. On the matter of Hellenistic demography, I have profited from the shrewd insights of Sue Alcock.
[47] Appian, *Bell. civ.* 1.10; Cassius Dio 54.16.2; Brunt (1971), 152.

data are mainly archaeological. They show site abandonment, without, however, illuminating cause and context.[48]

Can epigraphy succeed where archaeology fails in throwing light on patterns of human behaviour and their motivation? Tarn, among others, was satisfied that inscriptions which appear to show a preponderance of boys within families establish the prevalence of infanticide in Greece in the late third and second centuries BC. But Tarn did not consider commemorative practice – in particular, the possibility that daughters existed who were not counted – nor did he enquire into either the origins or occupations of the families concerned. It makes a difference that the inscriptions from Miletus which produce the striking ratio of 118 boys to 28 girls concern a group of mercenaries from Crete. Female infanticide is likely to have played a part in producing the unnatural sex ratios, but the importance of its contribution is unknowable. Thus in this case epigraphy neither fills the gap in the evidence, nor combines with other data, also problematic, to produce a convincing reconstruction of demographic trends.[49]

An epigraphic document from Italy in the early second century AD is similarly suspect as demographic evidence. Trajan's alimentary scheme for the modest town of Veleia in the hills above modern Piacenza provided basic sustenance for 264 boys and 36 girls. If these figures were a true reflection of the boy : girl ratio in the community, then exposure of new-born girls had reached epidemic proportions and Veleia was in sharp decline. But it is obvious that those who devised the project had determined to give preference as dole recipients to boys and to select only a fraction of the available girls, perhaps those belonging to families that lacked non-adult sons.

If it can be assumed that Trajan's scheme was designed to give basic sustenance to children on or below the breadline, then it follows that a considerable number of girls were condemned to undernourishment, and presumably not just in Veleia, but in the 50 or so towns of Italy where alimentary schemes are attested. In other words, girls were systematically exposed, or neglected, or both.

The inscription therefore does have some demographic significance after all. It may be added to the very considerable body of evidence from antiquity that preference was given to males, whether as children or adults. A value system which permitted discrimination of the sort revealed at Veleia, which jeopardised the chances of producing a

---

[48] Bintliff and Snodgrass (1985); Van Andel *et al.* (1986); Runnels and Van Andel (1987).

[49] Tarn and Griffith (1952), 100–2. See the critique by Pomeroy (1983), who, however, seems to be suggesting that we can safely generalise from the behaviour of mercenaries because they were 'not atypical' of the age.

demographically stable community, could easily have accommodated exposure of new-born girls as a standard practice.[50]

To conclude: subsistence farmers throughout history have endeavoured to shape their families according to their material circumstances (static or changing), with results efficacious or otherwise for their own future and that of their community. In the words of A. V. Chayanov, drawing on Russian data from the bleak 1880s: 'It is evident that at a low level of material security, when there is the mere possibility of physical existence, material conditions influence family size with the force of a determinant.' Although the process cannot be documented for antiquity in the way that it can for early modern England or France, there is enough evidence to show that adaptive strategies were at work in the shaping of the family (and to show which strategies were favoured), as in the process of agricultural production and in social and economic relations. Hesiod's ideal of the only-born son was one that his brother Perses could actively pursue. Its realisation was not to be left entirely to nature.[51]

[50] *ILS* 6675, with Duncan-Jones (1964), 123; (1982), 294–300.
[51] Chayanov (1923); Hesiod, *Works and Days* 376. To be sure, Hesiod goes on to say that more than one son can be advantageous for production.

5

SUPPLY AND DISTRIBUTION:
URBAN COMMUNITIES

FIVE RESPONSES

States seeking to avoid food crisis or reduce its effects had in principle the following options:[1]

1 Extend domestic production: by increasing the proportion of home territory under cultivation, or by raising productivity on existing arable.
2 Extend the territory under control at the expense of other communities: imperialism.
3 Export a proportion of the population, so as to reduce the aggregate consumption requirements of the community: colonisation.
4 Import staple food items through trade and other methods of exchange.
5 Distribute available foodstuffs through the community to ensure the survival of the ordinary citizen consumer.

Of options 1 and 2, the more thorough exploitation of home territory and the exploitation of the territory of another state, the first is more or less an empty category. From time to time and in a variety of historical contexts (Attica and the Argolid in the fourth century BC are possible examples), land under cultivation was extended and higher productivity sought through intensification of farming practices. But this was done as a consequence of factors such as demographic pressure, not government direction. Civic governments did very little to regulate agriculture within their territories.

The second option, imperialism, was successfully exploited by relatively few states. Athens was one such, especially between 478/7 and 413/12, when her power at sea was unrivalled. During this period the Athenians were in a position to monitor and control the long-distance movement of grain, notably from the Black Sea, reduce enemies by blockade, feed a population far more numerous than their

---

[1] Cf. Garnsey and Morris (1989). The summary remarks on Athens and Rome that will be found in this chapter are expanded in Parts III and IV. The matter of religious responses to food crisis deserves separate treatment and will receive it on another occasion.

69

home territory could support, export citizens as settlers or garrisons on conquered land – and avoid food crises. The Romans, after an initial period of weakness marked by a chronically insecure food supply, from about the second quarter of the fourth century BC experienced significantly fewer food crises. The improvement in their situation coincided with the development of the empire in Italy and the Mediterranean. Food crises did become more frequent again in the century before the inauguration of the Principate in 27 BC. But the Romans brought these crises on themselves by incessant warfare, foreign and civil, and political strife.

However, with the exception of 'superpowers' like Rome, Macedon and Athens in her prime, imperialism was not in practice open to most cities on a long-term basis. The best they could hope for was to come out on the right side in a territorial dispute with a neighbour.

Options 3 and 4, colonisation and imports, were contrasting solutions to the same problem. The choice lay between exporting consumers and importing food. Colonisation was not a viable option for the great majority of cities. Colonisation shades into imperialism as soon as there is competition for land. In a relatively stable world, it can be indulged in with profit only by the powerful.

In practice, then, there were only two generally pursued lines of action, the import of essential foodstuffs and their distribution. How far did governments intervene in these areas?

IMPORTS

It is axiomatic that trade in antiquity was in private hands. Cities neither owned merchant ships nor employed those who sailed in them.[2] It does not follow that there was no contact between governments and the traders who brought in essential supplies.

Traders, when they come into the light of day in the classical period of Greek history, appear as a cosmopolitan group, not characteristically linked by ties of citizenship or even residence with any particular community that they habitually served. Nor were they mere clients of the aristocracy, as many of them appear to have been in archaic Greece.[3] The independent traders of the age of Demosthenes were more accessible to approach from city authorities than their counterparts in the archaic age had been.

Traders were usually 'small fry', with few resources of their own. They were therefore receptive to offers of loan capital from govern-

---

[2] For an introduction to the literature, see Cartledge (1983).
[3] Bravo (1977).

ments possessing the necessary revenues. In an inscription from the late
fourth century, the authorities of Teos and Lebedos, briefly united by
order of Antigonus Monophthalmus, the Macedonian king, are seen
negotiating with him aspects of the food supply. The representatives of
the cities wanted a sum of money to be provided from revenues which
could be loaned out to importers, who would repay the sum with
interest at the end of the year. The king was reluctant, but in the end
opted for the smaller amount recommended by Lebedos.[4] The source of
the money is not disclosed. Regular revenues were usually meagre in
Hellenistic states, but governments did succeed in raising funds from
private sources in emergencies (see below), or goods in lieu of funds, as
in the following passage from the Aristotelian corpus. This text shows
the city authorities of Clazomenae taking the initiative in obtaining
grain in co-operation with private shippers:

The people of Clazomenae, suffering from food crisis and scarcity of funds, passed a
resolution that any private citizens who had stores of oil should lend it to the state at
interest, this being a product which their land bears in abundance. The loan
arranged, they hired vessels and sent them to the marts whence they obtained their
grain, and bought a consignment on security of the value of the oil.[5]

In times of scarcity traders did not lack incentive to bring in cargoes
of wheat which could be sold at an inflationary price. But many
inscriptions show that for those traders who were prepared to moderate
their short-term profits, handsome rewards were available from grateful communities in the shape of sundry honours and material benefits.
An honorific decree from Hellenistic Oropus contains the following
resolution:

Be it resolved by the council and the people that Dionysius son of Ariston from Tyre
and Heliodorus son of Mousaeus from Sidon be *proxenoi* and benefactors of the city
of Oropus, and have the right to own property and housing and the rights of
equality in tax and asylum and safety by land and sea whether there is war or peace,
and that everything else be available to them that has been awarded to other
proxenoi and benefactors.[6]

Over time, cities developed contacts not only with traders, but also
with other communities, which could be activated in lean years. Some
were linked by kinship and common origin. Such a background lies
behind the assistance rendered Cos by the Thessalian cities, as attested
in fragmentary inscriptions from the Hellenistic period. One is a decree
of the *koinon* of Thessaly, another a decree of Cos in honour of the

---

[4] *Syll.*[3] 344 = Austin 40, para. 11.
[5] Ps.-Aristotle, *Oec.* 1348b17ff.
[6] *IG* VII 4262.

Thessalian cities. In a shortage, the Coans had secured from the *koinon* the right to import grain for which they had only partially paid.[7] The old thesis of a commercial motive for Greek colonisation in the archaic period is now largely discredited. Yet the colonial movement must have created networks of mutual assistance operating over long distances. The Greek settlers, those for example of the Black Sea colonies, mainly founded by Miletus, were not out of touch with the homeland and did import items from there. They may be supposed to have supplied in return basic foodstuffs, sent at times when supplies were short for reasons of weather or war, and offered at favourable rates.

The factor of distance coupled with poor communications ensured that contacts were most regular between cities in close proximity to each other. A decree of Chorsiae, a city of minor importance in Boeotia, granted the honorific status of *proxenos* (official local representative) to a magnate called Kapon from Thisbe close by for advancing grain and cash to the city in times of crisis. A roughly contemporary decree (of *c.* 200–180 BC) shows the city of Thisbe itself as a lenient creditor of its less prosperous neighbour. The recently published bronze tablets from Entella in Sicily of mid-third-century BC date include a decree honouring a number of Sicilian cities (and individuals) for contributing grain in an emergency. The cities in question had earlier participated in the resettlement of Entella, and their ties with the city were strengthened by the award of Isopoliteia (equal political rights) by the grateful Entellans.[8]

Neighbouring cities were not usually so closely linked, and some were from time to time on bad terms. Still, regular trading contacts operating in times of emergency between friendly neighbours must have been commonplace. A clause of the treaty between Athens and Clazomenae of 387 BC states that Clazomenae in the event of food crisis would continue to be able to seek help in the nearby city of Smyrna, and two other cities, which may have been Phocaea and Chios.[9] A second scrap of evidence from the same city, already quoted, shows the authorities obtaining grain from established (but unspecified) ports of call. The nature or even existence of an official relationship between Clazomenae and its neighbours is not explicitly indicated in these documents. It is not difficult to envisage a formal or informal agreement involving, for example, the exchange of oil from Clazomenae with grain from another nearby state.

[7] M. Segre, *Riv. Fil.* 12 (1934), 169ff.; cf. Sherwin-White (1978), 110, n. 141.

[8] Migeotte (1984), nos. 10–11, pp. 41–8; cf. Roesch, *Rev. Phil.* 39 (1965), 252–61; G. Nenci, *ASNP* 10 (1980), 1271–5; 11 (1981), 613.

[9] *Inschr. Erythrai-Klazomenai* 502. 17–19. Only]myrna can be read on the stone.

A reciprocal relationship of this kind between near neighbours can be teased out of two short Greek inscriptions from the Roman period.[10] The first is an altar inscription set up at Perinthus on the north shore of the Propontis by the Philapameis, Friends of Apamea – that is, the Bithynian city on the opposite side of the Propontis. The altar is dedicated to Homonoia, Concord. The territory of Perinthus and the Thracian hinterland as a whole is flat, grain and livestock country, whereas that of Apamea is cramped and hilly, rich only in the olive and other tree crops. Apamea could in principle lean for grain on its southern neighbour Prusa, but at least in the time of Dio of Prusa, the late first century AD, the two cities were at odds with each other. Two of Dio's surviving orations plead for Homonoia between the two cities on grounds of mutual interest.[11] The Perinthus inscription is a reminder that Apamea had other options.

Whereas the status of the Friends of Apamea in the eyes of the two city governments concerned is unclear, there is no ambiguity over the position of the donor of a second inscription at Perinthus. This was a grain official (*sitophulax*, Grain Warden) from Cyzicus, an important city on the south shore of the Propontis in the Roman province of Asia. His inscription honoured the governor of Thrace, whose base was Perinthus, for championing Homonoia between the two cities. Cyzicus was capable of producing a surplus of grain, but could also suffer shortfall. Even centres of grain production found it advantageous to cultivate relationships of reciprocity between each other.

The ordinary cities of the Mediterranean, then, were linked by informal or formal understandings and agreements that were brought into operation in times of need, with private traders functioning as middlemen. The task of activating these pre-existing relationships on any particular occasion was a public service (as opposed to a regular magistracy) undertaken by one or more officials with special responsibility for the grain supply. We have seen one of them at work for the city of Cyzicus in the Roman period, a Grain Warden (*sitophulax*). This and the very common post of Grain Commissioner, *sitones*, or an equivalent, circulated among the more wealthy and public-spirited members of each community.[12]

None of this evidence for institutional response to risk and scarcity makes much impression beside the machinery developed by Athens and Rome for bringing in the grain that they required. Their needs were greater than those of other states and the substantial urban

---

[10] Robert (1974).
[11] Dio Chrys. *Or.* 40–1, with Jones (1978), 91–4.
[12] On the *sitonia*, cf. p. 15, above.

73

elements of their citizenries were politically influential – in democratic Athens it was the ordinary consumers who decided policy.

In the case of Athens it is to the fourth rather than the fifth century BC that we must turn for evidence of state involvement in the grain supply. Athens, deprived of the bulk of its former empire, had to take special measures to secure the food supply. On the one hand, the Athenians gave traders additional incentive to serve them by securing most-favoured-customer status from a major supplier, the Bosporan kingdom, by instituting special courts to cope with commercial maritime cases and by rewarding generous service with public honour and concrete benefits. On the other hand, laws were enacted restricting the freedom of merchants based in Athens or making use of Athens-derived capital. The Romans secured vital grain by taxing their subjects in kind (unlike the Athenians), and, at least from the middle of the first century AD, made special efforts to encourage private shipowners to transport the grain to Rome by offering advantageous terms and facilities. The binding of shippers to the service of the *annona*, that is, the food supply of Rome, was a development of the late Empire. Under the Principate, however, bringing in the grain was a profit-making enterprise made more attractive by the favourable terms provided by the state.

DISTRIBUTION

Under this heading I consider standard measures, regular institutions or laws aimed at securing the situation of the more vulnerable citizen consumers through redistribution of available foodstuffs. There are two sub-headings: measures against speculation and mechanisms of distribution.

Anti-speculation measures

Domestic production was of vital importance to all states, even to regular bulk importers of food such as Athens. Governments to a large extent left the production and marketing of food in the hands of local landowners and traders. But they did from time to time intervene when the interests of large landowners, the socially and economically dominant class, came into conflict with those of ordinary citizens. The first such occasion in the historical record is associated with the career of Solon the Athenian in the early sixth century BC.

Solon in effect ruled that aristocratic control of production and distribution should issue in neither the enslavement nor the starvation of ordinary citizens. This is the implication of the laws declaring

74

debt-bondage illegal and forbidding the export of agricultural produce apart from olive oil.[13] This latter law is known only in broad outline from Plutarch, and its background and duration are mysterious. I believe that the law was an ad hoc measure issued in the context of a food crisis, and that the shortage had been aggravated by unscrupulous landowners who were sending their grain abroad in search of higher prices. Seen in such terms, Solon's law may be compared with a fourth-century BC regulation from Selybria near Byzantium, apparently enacted in a food crisis and specifically forbidding the export of grain. The source, the pseudo-Aristotelian *Oeconomica*, goes on to show that if the law banned exports altogether, it must have been only a temporary measure. The passage reads:

The people of Selybria had a law, passed in time of food crisis, which forbade the export of grain. Once, however, they were in need of funds; and as they had large stores of grain, they passed a resolution that citizens should deliver up their grain to the state at the regular fixed price, each keeping for himself a year's supply. They then granted right of export to any who wanted it, fixing what they thought was a reasonable price.[14]

On one dramatic occasion in the history of Hellenistic Boeotia, food was so short that 'all the cities' prohibited the export of wheat. This was the moment that Kapon of Thisbe chose to advance wheat to Chorsiae.

City authorities followed a flexible line on the movement of foodstuffs, oscillating between preventing and admitting exports as local supplies dwindled or were plenteous. A farmer such as Hesiod, had he lived under a polis government, would not have been discouraged from shipping his surplus to another community as long as food supplies were abundant. Exported goods earned useful tax-revenue. This was appreciated, for example, in Teos/Lebedos at the end of the fourth century BC and in Athens at the beginning of the second century AD. A clause in the Teos/Lebedos synoecism inscription of around 306–302 BC, already cited, states that grain brought into the city should in general be put on the market, but does not rule out re-export with the permission of the city authorities and on payment of a tax. The emperor Hadrian's law regulating olive oil export from Athens required exporters and shippers to clear their exports with the city authorities and pay a tax of one-third (or in some circumstances one-eighth). The back-

[13] Plutarch, *Sol.* 15; 24; Aristotle, *Ath. pol.* 2.2, 9.1.
[14] Ps.-Aristotle, *Oec.* 1348b33ff. See Chase (1983), on export (and maldistribution) of foodstuffs in time of food shortage in modern Poland, with which she explicitly compares eighteenth-century Poland: 'Poles know that Poland was the bread-basket of Europe in the eighteenth century but that the Poles consumed little of this plenty' (p. 79); cf. Braudel (1981), 125–6, quoting from a dictionary of 1797. For Chorsiae, see above, p. 72.

ground is one of deficiency in the midst of plenty. Landowners and merchants were putting personal profit before public interest and sending oil abroad for higher prices than they could secure at home. The inscription nicely complements, and may for all we know closely parallel, Solon's law allowing that only olive oil among agricultural products could be exported.[15]

The practice of stockpiling grain for export denied local consumers access to the staple food at any price. It was a particularly flagrant form of speculation, and provoked the most violent response. When the wonder-worker Apollonius of Tyana came to Aspendus in Pamphylia during the reign of Tiberius (AD 14–37),

he found vetches on sale in the market, and the citizens were feeding upon this and on anything else they could get; for the rich men had shut up all the grain and were holding it up for export from the country.

The *Life*, composed by Philostratus, continues:

Consequently an excited crowd of all ages had set upon the chief magistrate, and were lighting a fire to burn him alive, although he was clinging to the statues of the Emperor, which were more dreaded at that time and more inviolable than the Zeus in Olympia.[16]

Grain was of course also hoarded as a prelude to profitable sale in the home market. Such grain might be imported, in which case the culprits were likely to be traders, or home-grown, in which case landowners were the prime suspects. Hoarding is first attested in relation to imported grain. This practice, and the prevention of imports altogether, received hostile attention from the authorities in Teos in about 470 BC. An inscription lists curses to be repeated by the magistrates of the city three times each year, among them the following:

If anyone prevents grain from being imported into the land of Teos by any pretext or device, either by sea or from the mainland, or forces up the price of imported grain, that man shall die, both himself and his family.

The rich and powerful in Teos were physically preventing the entry of foreign grain or storing it away in order to aggravate the scarcity and eventually make a killing. To have provoked a reaction of this kind, such conduct must have been both common and judged deleterious to the interests of the community.[17]

[15] Hesiod, *Works and Days* 632 cf. 686; *Syll.*[3] 344 = Austin 40, para. 10; *SEG* xv 108 = Oliver (1953), 960–3.
[16] Philostratus, *Vit. Ap.* 1.15.
[17] Meiggs and Lewis 30, side A, ll. 6–11; Bravo (1983), 22–3, 28 n. 22. But I translate *anotheoie* (line 10) as 'force up [the price of]' (Buck) rather than 'repousser [hors du territoire de Teos]' (Bravo) or 're-export' (Meiggs and Lewis).

However, the hoarding of locally produced grain was undoubtedly the standard form of speculation. All landowners stored a proportion of the surplus; to do so was plain necessity. The difficulty lay in the absence of a clearly demarcated boundary between legitimate storage for domestic consumption and illegitimate stockpiling with a view to profiteering. In this matter the perspectives of the owner of the grain and the would-be consumer were likely to differ. Nor was there any one 'official view'. When civic authorities compelled those with stocks of grain to release it (see below), they might permit the retention in the household of as little as one month's rations (in Rome, in 440–39 BC) or as much as one year's rations, plus seed corn (in Pisidian Antioch in AD 92 or 93).[18]

Storage was routine. Thus in a food crisis the rich as a class could be assumed to be hoarding grain if they were not marketing it. When Dio of Prusa confronted a riotous crowd intent on raiding his barns and burning them down, he insisted that he had no grain. The crowd did not believe him.[19]

We can be sure that the rich were pressed to make grain available by both the civic authorities and the people at large, in public gatherings of one sort or another. If the response was inadequate, then governments, precisely to avoid the kind of trouble that erupted at Aspendus and Prusa, might issue a decree requiring the registration and compulsory sale of grain that was surplus to essential needs. Texts already cited give the impression that the rich at Clazomenae were routinely required to release surplus food stocks when the authorities needed to find grain or cash. Clazomenae may not have been typical.

As a last resort it was sometimes possible to solicit the intervention of someone from outside the community with special authority or char-isma. A Roman governor broke the deadlock at Pisidian Antioch. His measures were stern. All members of the community were given thirty days to declare the grain in their possession. They could keep grain for seed and a year's supply for the household, but the rest had to be sold to the Grain Commissioner of the city. All undeclared grain would be confiscated, and after the subtraction of one-eighth for informers, would be sold at one denarius per modius, such sales to cease on the first of August. The *deus ex machina* at Aspendus in the reign of Tiberius was, as we saw, Apollonius of Tyana. Apollonius persuaded the speculators to release their stock, thus saving the people from starvation and the chief magistrate from the flames – all this without saying one word. Procula of the town of Faviana in the Danubian province of Noricum Ripense

---

18 Livy 4.12; *AE* 1925, 126b.
19 Dio Chrys. *Or.* 46.

must have wished that St Severinus (d. AD 482) had likewise taken a vow of silence:

At that time a severe food-shortage had been oppressing a city called Faviana. The inhabitants believed that the only remedy for them would be to summon with devout prayers the man of God from the aforesaid town of Comagena. He had foreknowledge of their approach, and was instructed by the Lord to set out with them. On his arrival there he began to advise the citizens, saying, 'You can be set free from this great disaster of food-shortage by the fruits of repentance.' While they profited from such precepts, the most blessed Severinus learned from a divine revelation that a certain widow called Procula had hidden away a lot of crops. When she was brought out in public, he reproved her vigorously. 'Why,' he said, 'when your origins are of most noble birth, do you show and display yourself as the handmaid and slave of avarice, which the apostle teaches is the servitude of idols? See, although the Lord treats his servants with compassion, you will have no use for your ill-got supplies, unless perhaps you throw the wheat which you have cruelly withheld into the waters of the Danube, and exhibit to fish the humanity you have denied to men. For this reason bring aid to yourself rather than to the poor from what you are so far reckoning to hold back while Christ starves.' On hearing these words, the woman was terrified by a great fear, and willingly began distributing her supplies to the poor.[20]

Manipulation of the grain supply was a problem not infrequently faced by the municipal authorities; nevertheless a permanent institutional response was rare. The magistrates' curses at Teos are an exception to the rule. Fourth-century BC Athens developed an armoury of special officials to prevent speculation and regulate the profits of traders, millers and bakers. It is possible that some other states, in particular those with a democratic constitution, possessed similar if less elaborate machinery for protecting the ordinary consumer. We are ill-informed about the institutions of democracies apart from Athens. The indications are that temporary expedients were usually preferred.

Rome from the time of Julius Caesar or Augustus had an anti-speculation law, the *lex Iulia de annona*, that served as a model for similar regulations in cities founded or promoted by Rome in the western empire. A clause of a recently discovered Spanish municipal law from the Flavian age (second half of the first century AD), the *lex Irnitana*, reads as follows:

Rubric. That nothing may be bought up or hoarded.

No one in that *municipium* is to buy up or hoard anything or join with another or agree or enter into a partnership in order that something may be sold more dearly or not be sold or not enough be sold. Anyone who acts contrary to these rules is to be condemned to pay 10,000 sesterces to the *municipes* of the Municipium

---

[20] Eugippius, *Vit. Sev.* 3.1–2 = *CSEL* 9.2.

Flavium Irnitanum for each case and the right of action, suit and claim of that money and concerning that money is to belong to any *municeps* of that *municipium* who wishes and who is entitled under this statute.[21]

The existence of this clause of course carries no implications whatever for the mass of cities in the Greek world in the Roman period.

Distribution mechanisms

In the matter of the grain supply, as has been seen, city authorities did not leave the fate of citizen consumers entirely in the hands of large landowners and traders, and were capable of acting against private interests from time to time. The issue of government intervention may be taken further by asking what if any institutional apparatus evolved with the function of distributing available food throughout the community.

Crete, Samos and Rome distributed food to their citizens in various periods. The existence of these distribution systems does not imply a host of others like them. State governments did not commonly distribute cheap or free grain to the citizenry on a regular basis.

The Cretan common messes were famous and unique. They attracted the attention of Plato, who used them as the model for his supply and distribution system in the *Laws*, and of Aristotle, who compared them favourably to their Spartan counterpart:

Now the Cretan arrangements for the public mess-tables are better than the Spartan; for at Sparta each citizen pays a tax on produce, failing which he is excluded by law from active citizenship ...; but in Crete the system is more communal, for out of the crops and cattle produced from the public lands, and the tribute paid by the serfs, one part is assigned for the worship of the gods and the maintenance of the public services and the other for the public mess-tables. Thus all citizens are maintained from the common funds, women and children as well as men.[22]

The Cretan system was a relic of the past. It was a product of the idea, as old as the polis itself, that the polis was its citizens, and that whatever resources came its way in the form of booty, fines, dues or produce belonged to the citizens and should be shared out among them. In sixth-century Siphnos, the income from the gold and silver mines was distributed each year among the members of the community. For a brief period in the 480s after the discovery of a rich new seam of silver at Laurium, each Athenian received 10 drachmas annually as his share;

---

[21] Gonzales (1986), at 172,193 (Ch. 75).
[22] Plato, *Laws* 847; Aristotle, *Pol.* 1272a17. See Morrow (1960), 389–98; Huxley (1971).

Themistocles persuaded the Athenians to build 200 warships with the money.[23]

Thereafter, the distribution system in its simple, primitive form, fades from view, except in Crete. But the Cretan cities, as Aristotle indicates, had introduced significant modifications by the late fourth century: in particular, no longer was the whole income of the state divided among its members. In Hellenistic Crete, the food that was distributed came partly from public revenues and partly from tithes contributed by the recipients themselves. By the second century AD, distributions, which were now only biennial, were paid for by the wealthy.[24]

The idea that citizens had a stake in the revenues of the state outlived the archaic distribution system with which it was originally associated. It was alive in democratic and imperial Athens. Ordinary Athenians benefited from the revenues of the empire of the fifth century whose acquisition had been made possible by Themistocles. But Athenian democrats devised novel ways of looking after the poorer citizens. Regular distribution of food or money among all the citizenry was not one of them. Pay for office or jury service from the 450s BC was supplemented from 410/9 for five years by the *diobelia* (but in 405/4 grain was handed out instead of the two obols), in the fourth century by assembly pay, and from the 350s by the *theorikon*, ostensibly a grant to pay for festival tickets. Rowing in the fleet and work in the dockyards brought substantial cash benefits to thousands of Athenians, particularly in the fifth century, when the Athenians maintained a large fleet. Finally, mutual support between ordinary citizens linked by kinship, proximity of residence or friendship, and exemplified in the interest-free loan, was a defence against poverty, hardship and the personal patronage of the wealthy that was irreconcilable with democratic ideology.[25]

More surprisingly, there are echoes of the old ideology of distribution in the sources for 123 BC, when Rome's food distribution system was inaugurated on the initiative of the tribune Gaius Gracchus. 'What could be more just than that a people in need should be maintained from its own treasury?' These words of Florus were inspired by Gaius Gracchus, if they were not Gracchus' own. The Gracchan rhetoric was turned against him by his defeated opponent, L. Calpurnius

---

[23] Herodotus 3.57.2; 7.144.1 cf. Aristotle, *Ath. pol.* 22.7; Polyaenus 1.30.6; Latte (1948).

[24] Dosiadas in Athenaeus IV 143a; *Syll.*³ 527, ll. 123ff.; *Inscr. Cret.* I p. 84 no. 1; p. 190 no. 11.

[25] For *theorikon* and *diobelia*, see briefly Rhodes (1981), 355–7,514–17, with bibl.; for pay and its implications, see Finley (1983), 39–40, 58; Jordan (1972), 111–16; Markle (1985); and especially Millett (1989).

Piso Frugi, who joined the queue at the first monthly distribution in order to receive a share of 'my property'. Still, it had taken Roman politicians four centuries to embrace the argument that ordinary Romans had a claim to a share in the wealth of the state. Many remained unpersuaded, and the new system fell short of the ideal. The grain provided by the state was not available to all inhabitants of Rome of citizen status (except perhaps briefly from 58 BC), and for 65 years after the introduction of the distribution (123–58 BC) the grain was sold cheap rather than given away.[26]

It is tempting to argue that Gracchus found precedents for his distribution scheme in the cities of the Greek East. The difficulty is that only one continuous, annual distribution is firmly attested in the Greek world, at Samos from about the turn of the third century BC. More than 100 Samians contributed modest sums of money to a grain fund. The interest on the investment was put to the purchase of grain from the half-tithe on the temple estates of Hera on the mainland (Anaea) for distribution to all resident citizens of Samos at the rate of two measures per month until the grain ran out. It is not known how long the scheme lasted. In any case, its effectiveness is problematic. The amount of cash available was insufficient to purchase more than a small proportion of the grain requirement of the citizen population.[27]

No other city can be shown to have possessed comparable institutions. Grain reserves or grain funds existed at least in a few cities, but it is unclear that the ordinary citizen benefited greatly. An inscription from Thouria in Messenia of the second century BC shows the city authorities making arrangements for the disposal of a grain reserve in normal years with the financial interest of the city in mind: the grain was to be made available to individuals who needed it, presumably farmers, on condition that those who received it gave back at the end of the year more grain of quality as good. The accounts of the grain fund at Delos suggest that it was used primarily for profitable business. Doubtless in such cities grain purchased with special funds was made available to consumers in bad years, but there is no evidence that it was handed out gratis. At Delos and Thespiae the grain was certainly sold –

---

[26] Florus 2.1; Cicero, *Tusc. disp.* 3.20.48. For the background of the law, see Garnsey and Rathbone (1985); on Greek influences, see Nicolet (1965).

[27] *SEG* 1 366 = Austin 113. At Samos 98 people contributed on average *c.*165 drachmas each. If the 31 whose donations are unknown contributed at the same rate, the fund totalled 21,312 dr. At 10% interest, 2131 dr. p.a. were available for grain purchase. This would have purchased 400 medimnoi at most (at 5 dr. 2 obols, the stipulated minimum). At 5 med. per person/year, 80 people would have been fed for 12 months (or 320 for 3 months). The possibility that the list of subscribers at Samos was incomplete should be acknowledged. See Shipley (1987).

in Thespiae by three officials specifically designated Grain Sellers (*sitopolai*).[28]

State-funded distribution schemes were lacking because state funds were few. Wealth was essentially in private hands, and the city authorities, who were the wealthy of the community acting in an official capacity, were uninterested in building up the public treasury at their own expense by some kind of taxation system. What they, or some of them, were prepared to do, was undertake offices or public services for the community, and show generosity to the citizens in times of crisis.

By the second half of the fourth century BC or the first half of the third, city governments had to hand, as has been seen, an office or offices which could be called into service if prognostications for the harvest were poor.

These grain commissioners worked in concert with benefactors who put up either money for grain purchase or grain for sale at below market prices. Thus the public authorities were dependent upon the benefactions of private individuals, members of the local elite or, less often, outsiders. Euergetism, the public generosity of the rich, is the hallmark of the standard Mediterranean city throughout our period. After the virtual disappearance of democracy by the end of the fourth century BC, euergetism was the main safeguard of the common people of the towns against hunger and starvation in a subsistence crisis.[29]

The good works of these philanthropists of antiquity need to be assessed objectively in the light of the following considerations:

1 Euergetism was not motivated by altruism.
2 The class that produced euergetists also produced speculators.
3 Euergetism had definite limits.
4 Euergetism was essentially an ad hoc response, not a lasting solution.

1. Material rewards were available for benefactors, who gained enhanced status within the community through various public honours, as is illustrated in the inscription for Polycritus of Erythrae from the third century BC:

---

[28] Here I disagree with the standard view, expressed by e.g. Francotte (1905); Bolkestein (1939), 262–7; Tarn and Griffith (1952), 107–8; Hands (1968), 95–7; Rickman (1980), 156–7). The key documents include *IG* v 1 1379 (Thouria) with Robert, *BCH* 52 (1928), 426–32; Strabo 652–3 (Rhodes), with Wilcken, *RM* 90 (1941), 161–7; Fraser, *Samothrace*, no. 5 pp. 25ff.; Pouilloux, *Choix d'inscriptions* no. 34 pp. 126 (Thespiae), with Roesch (1965), 220–4; *Inscr. Delos* 442A 101; 399A 69–73, etc. (Delos), with Larsen (1938), 344–8, Vial (1984), 139–40, 237–9. None of these provide evidence for Samian-style regular distributions.

[29] See Veyne (1976); Gauthier (1985).

Wherefore, so that the people may be seen to be giving worthy rewards to good men, with the help of the gods, the council and people resolved: to praise Polycritus son of Iatrokleius, to honour him with a golden crown and a bronze statue because of his virtue and benevolence towards the people, to set it up in the market place by the stele on which the honours previously awarded him are inscribed; the games officials [should have] the honours given him [read out at the games] ...[30]

In a revealing passage, Aristotle points to the structural role of public spending as a safeguard for the perpetuation of oligarchic rule, and charges some members of oligarchies with having more in mind than mere honour:

And furthermore, the most supreme offices also which must be retained by those within the constitution must have expensive duties attached to them, in order that the common people may be willing to be excluded from them and may feel no resentment against the ruling class, because it pays a high price for office ... But at present the members of oligarchies do not adopt this course, but the opposite, for they seek gains of office just as much as the honour; hence these oligarchies are well described as miniature democracies.[31]

2. Public benefactors were not infrequently speculators. The inscription in honour of Polycritus suggests that he played such a dual role:

Later, when because of the grain shortage no one was bringing grain in to the market, he promised the people to advance money for a reserve fund to those about to be appointed grain commissioners, and to bring into the market for feeding the people the wheat he himself held. (ll. 25–9)

3. Euergetists rarely gave grain away. Moschion of Priene twice offered grain at reduced prices and once offered it gratis. More commonly, however, grain was sold and at a profit, even if at rates below the elevated market level. The inscription of Protogenes from Olbia in the Black Sea area states that he did not demand immediate payment, but was prepared to wait for a year. The implication is that it was normal for a benefactor at Olbia to require immediate payment for his cut-price grain, or demand repayment of capital plus interest. Other benefactors provided funds for the purchase of grain. But the money was loaned, rarely given, and often at interest (but Polycritus' loans were interest-free).[32]

4. Euergetism was typically a response to a specific crisis; it did not seek a lasting solution to the underlying problem. Euergetists emerged as individuals from the ranks of the rich as it were in rotation; they

---

[30] *Inschr. Erythrai-Klazomenai* 28 cf. *IG* vii 4262.
[31] Aristotle, *Pol.* 1321a, with De Ste Croix (1981), 76 on the anti-rich bias of democracies. See also Lysias 19.57.
[32] *Inschr. Priene* 108; cf., from the Roman period, *BCH* 40 (1920), p. 93, n. 28; *IGR* iii 493.

rarely combined their resources to strengthen the hand of the public authorities in dealing with food crisis in the long term. They apparently did not build public granaries, which are rarely attested. They did not combine to fund regular distribution schemes, also something of a rarity, as has been seen. There was never any prospect that such an institution, whether fed by donation or indiction, would displace ad hoc euergetism.

Rome, again, was different. Euergetism in the public sphere by private individuals was held to be incompatible with the collective rule of the oligarchy and subsequently with the one-man rule of an emperor, and played no part in the resolution of food crises. Rome, as we saw, did eventually develop a comprehensive distribution system.

Rome did not export either its distaste for euergetism or its reluctant approval of public distributions. The Mediterranean world under Roman rule witnessed no important changes in the character and centrality of euergetism, and, in general, in the mechanisms and practices designed to supply cities and ward off shortages. The stark contrast between public poverty and private affluence persisted. Public monies were no more available for the purchase of necessities than they ever had been, and the interventions of private benefactors still took the character of short-term responses. Thus permanent funds financing regular distributions were a rarity. In Egypt, there were distribution schemes in Hermopolis in AD 62 and in Oxyrhynchus, Alexandria and Hermopolis in the 260s and 270s AD. Only that at Oxyrhynchus is well-documented and demonstrably regular. A number of Lycian cities had lists of 'receivers of distributed grain', but the frequency of the implied distributions is unknown; in any case they appear to have been financed by private benefactors.[33]

So far little has been said about patronage. This is because ordinary citizens do not emerge in the sources as clients of the rich and powerful. In Rome the typical client was someone of moderate means or better, a Martial or a Juvenal. Despite Horace's charming story about a Roman senator, Philippus, who picked up a man of genuinely humble station called Mena, made him a regular guest at his table and gave him money and land, it would be absurd to suggest that the gap between rich and poor in Rome was regularly bridged in this way. Apart from Sparta, where patronage primarily served the function of recruiting the elite, as in Rome, the evidence for patronage from the Greek world is very thin.

[33] The inscriptions of the Principate produce a few examples of (i) provincial alimentary schemes, in which food or cash is distributed to children at private expense, as opposed to the central-government-funded Italian schemes; (ii) reluctant or absent benefactors. See Ch. 15.

For this the 'Athenocentricity' of the sources is partly responsible, though it was not to be expected that patronage between individuals, as a private matter, would receive much attention in the essentially 'public' sources of antiquity. Athenian democrats were hostile to patronage, no doubt aware that its function was to perpetuate rather than diminish social and economic inequality. In the sources for Athens, patronage surfaces in the oligarch Isocrates' vision of the 'Golden Age' before the democratic revolution of 462/1 BC, and in the behaviour of Cimon, the Athenian statesman who lost power to the radical democrats:

Cimon the Athenian stationed no guard over the produce of his fields or gardens, so that any citizen who wished might go in and harvest and help himself, if he needed anything on the estate. Furthermore, he threw his house open to all, so that he regularly supplied an inexpensive meal to many men, and the poor Athenians approached him and dined. And he tended to those also who day by day asked something of him. And they say that he always took around with him two or three youths who had some small change, and ordered them to make a contribution whenever someone approached and asked him. And they say that he helped out with burial expenses. Many times also, he did this: whenever he saw one of the citizens ill-clothed, he would order one of the youths who accompanied him to change clothes with him. From all these things, he won his reputation and was the first of the citizens.

Patronage on this scale is more aptly described as euergetism. It evokes the competitive largesse of the 'dynasts' of late Republican Rome, and at a more modest level, the generosity of numerous benefactors of the cities of the Graeco-Roman world, including Boulagoras of Samos, who numbered among his services, 'giving the best advice to the people publicly and privately to every citizen, reconciling those who have disputes and advancing loans from his own private means to many of the needy'.[34]

To sum up: the ordinary cities of the Mediterranean did not develop an extensive framework of institutions and laws capable of protecting the ordinary citizen consumer from hunger and starvation. The most thoroughgoing system of distribution was associated with the early polis, but after the archaic period it left few traces outside Crete. The old idea that citizens were entitled to a share in the whole resources of the state was out of place in the typical, oligarchic regimes of the Hellenistic and Roman periods. At most, there was a tacit assumption

[34] Mohler (1931); Gérard (1976); Horace, *Ep.* 1.7.46–76 (Rome); Cartledge (1987), Ch. 9 cf. Hodkinson (1983) (Sparta); Millett (1989); Theopompus in Athenaeus 12.532f–533c cf. Plutarch, *Cim.* 16.1–2 and Aristotle, *Ath. pol.* 27.3; Isocrates, *Areop.* 32–5 (Athens); *SEG* 1 366 = Austin 113, ll. 51ff. (Boulagoras).

that the civic authorities were obliged, when food prices were high, to take steps to secure emergency grain supplies and prevent the exacerbation of shortage by the hoarding or exporting of grain. Government action characteristically took the form of putting pressure on wealthy individuals to undertake services and make benefactions for the community.

So much for oligarchies; more might have been expected from democracies, and we know very little about the institutions of democratic states apart from Athens. In Athens a wide range of compulsory services or liturgies was expected of the wealthier citizens in the areas of finance, warfare, religion and culture.[35] But Athenian democracy developed in addition a variety of mechanisms and regulations to protect the ordinary citizens from poverty and hardship. The standard Greek democracy of the classical period, which lacked the financial strength of Athens, particularly fifth-century Athens, was correspondingly more dependent on the contributions of the more prosperous members of the community. In the oligarchic regimes which displaced democracy by the last quarter of the fourth century BC and remained entrenched thereafter, the crucial role was given to the elite whether as magistrates, liturgists or private benefactors.

CONCLUSION

The dependence of the cities on their most wealthy and influential citizens advertises the limitations of the public response to the inevitability of food shortage. It does not follow, however, that the existing system was not efficacious. One can imagine circumstances, such as prolonged siege or a series of harvest failures over a wide region, in which coping mechanisms proved ineffective and euergetism was stifled. Such occasions were relatively rare (though doubtless commoner than the sources suggest). Under normal conditions, traditional survival strategies operated reasonably effectively within their limits, and personal patronage and prudence blunted the sharp edges of confrontation between rich and poor, privileged and ordinary citizens.

[35] Davies (1971), Introduction.

PART III
FOOD SUPPLY AND FOOD CRISIS IN ATHENS
c. 600–322 BC

6

THE RESOURCES OF ATTICA

The food needs of the Athenians from the imperial period in the fifth century down to the Macedonian occupation of 322 BC could not be met from the resources of the territory of Attica alone. But the extent of Athens' dependence on external sources of supply remains problematic. There is a lack of precise and detailed information relating to land under cultivation, population level, food consumption rate, yield and sowing rate. Absence of data has not deterred scholars in the past from attempting to calculate the relative importance of home-grown and imported grain, and for better or worse their conjectures underpin current conceptions not only of the food supply policy of Athens but also of Athenian foreign policy in general over several centuries. Thus the conclusion that Attica could support only 60,000–75,000 people, 20–30% of the resident population as conventionally assessed (by my estimate about one-half of the figure actually supportable), underpins the doctrine that Athens' dependence on imports for 'by far the greater part of her corn supply … led almost inevitably to naval imperialism'; it also underpins the more radical thesis that Athens relied on foreign grain as early as the turn of the seventh century BC, well before the era of 'naval imperialism'. If, as I argue below, the productive capacity of Attica has been grossly underestimated, then a new interpretation of archaic Athenian history is demanded, one which is not shaped by conventional assumptions about Athens' early dependence on foreign grain.[1]

POPULATION

There are no reliable demographic data from ancient Athens. Recent estimates of the numbers of citizens of 18 years and over resident in Attica vary between 21,000 and 30,000 in the fourth century, and

[1] The quotation is from the brief discussion of De Ste Croix (1972), 45–9, at 46. Other treatments of the subject include the classic account of Gernet (1909), Jardé (1925), Gomme

between around 40,000 and 43,000 in the fifth century shortly before the Peloponnesian War. These figures imply, at an average of 2 children per household (but many would regard this as an underestimate), a total citizen family population of around 84,000 or 120,000 in the fourth century and of 160,000 or 172,000 in 431 BC.[2] Considerable short-term demographic fluctuations may be expected in response to Athens' changing fortunes in international affairs, warfare, migration and the incidence of famine and epidemic disease. Numbers of metics (resident aliens) and slaves must have varied enormously for similar reasons. My estimate is that the population of Attica proper, excluding the dependencies, rose from a low point of around 120,000–150,000 in 480 to a high point of around 250,000 just before the Peloponnesian War, and fluctuated between 120,000 and 150,000 (in 323/2) and 200,000 in the fourth century.

What population densities are entailed by these figures? Beloch calculated the surface area of Attica at 2,527 km², including Oropus and Eleutherae, two border areas Boeotian in origin and in Athenian possession from the late sixth to the late fifth century and for parts of the fourth.[3] Excluding them, we arrive at a base figure of around 2,400 km² for Attica.

Table 4. *Estimates of population density, persons per km², Greece*

Date	Area	Density (persons/km²)
Antiquity		
480 BC	Athens	50
431 BC	Athens	104
4th cent. (high)	Athens	83.33
4th cent. (low)	Athens	50–62.5
Modern period		
1838	Greece	15.8
1861	Greece	23.1
1889	Greece	34.1
1896	Greece	37.6
1896	Central Greece (less Greater Athens)	23
1896	Peloponnesus	42

(1933), 28ff., Isager and Hansen (1975), 1ff., 200ff., and Starr (1977), 152ff. The more radical thesis is found, e.g., in Grundy (1948), 67–9 cf. 64 and Rhodes (1981), 95–6, 577. Against, Noonan (1973); Bloedow (1975). For critical analysis of earlier discussions see Garnsey (1985), which should be read in conjunction with the present chapter.
[2] General discussions in Beloch (1886), Ch. 3; (1923), 386–418; Gomme (1933); Patterson (1981), Ch. 3; Hansen (1982) and (1986), with bibliography. On family size, see Raepsaet (1974).
[3] Beloch (1886), 56–7.

The population of Attica was high in the classical period (see Table 4). So was that of Boeotia – recently estimated at 85 persons/km². But at what point did population outrun resources? What was the carrying capacity of Attica?

Jardé, whose monograph on cereal cultivation is still the standard work on all these matters, estimated a population density threshold of 36 people/km² for Greece as a whole.[4] The corresponding figure for Attica is 33 people/km², if 10% of Attica's 2,400 km² were cultivated in any one year, as Jardé thought.[5] It would follow that the Athenian population outgrew its home territory when it reached the level of around 80,000, presumably at some stage in the archaic period.

There are grounds for questioning the values given by Jardé to each of the main variables – food needs, yield and extent of arable. Jardé worked from an average figure for wheat consumption of 3 hl per person/year, or around 230 kg.[6] I put the minimum requirement of cereals at around 150 kg and total minimum requirement in food at around 200 kg wheat equivalent, supposing that 75% of that requirement was furnished by grain. Secondly, his yield figure of 10 hl per hectare was for wheat, whereas the higher-yielding barley was the main cereal crop in Attica. (Nevertheless the wheat yield figure is not low; it is higher by 2 hl/ha than he conjectured elsewhere.) Finally, as will shortly appear, Jardé underestimated the amount of land under cultivation. In short, there is room for a less pessimistic assessment of the carrying capacity of Attica.

EXTENT OF ARABLE

Estimates of cultivable land range from 20% to 50% of Attica.[7] If the higher figure seems overoptimistic, the lower one is unduly pessimistic. We can test the plausibility of the latter by considering the implications

[4] Jardé (1925), 143.
[5] Jardé (1925), 142–3 with 52–3.
[6] See Foxhall and Forbes (1982); cf. Clark and Haswell (1970), 17. Jardé's estimate of 5.75 medimnoi per person/year is lower than other conventional estimates, which range from 6 medimnoi (3.1 hl at 51.7 l per med., or 240 kg at 0.772 kg/l or 2,095 kcals per day) to 7½ medimnoi. Even 5 medimnoi (2.625 hl, or 202.65 kg, or 2,021 kcals per day) is generous as an average basic allowance of wheat. Residents of Athens and Attica may be supposed to have taken as much as 25–30% of their food energy requirements from non-cereals. According to Braudel (1981), 130–2, the corresponding figure for Europe from the fifteenth to the eighteenth century was 25–50%, with the lower proportions generally coming from southern (i.e. Mediterranean) Europe and the countryside. It should be added that the widespread belief that women required less food than men (e.g. Xenophon, *Lac. pol.* 1.3; Aristotle, *Hist. anim.* 608b14–15) will affect any population calculations based on food consumption. I owe this point to Dr F. D. Harvey.
[7] Jardé (1925), 52–3; Osborne (1985a), 225, n. 82.

for landownership if only one-fifth of Attica were arable. Estimates of the number of Athenian hoplites (and knights) have varied from 18,000 to 25,000 in 431 and from 9,000 to 14,500 in 322.[8] Let us take the lowest and highest figures. If 9,000–25,000 hoplites owned all the land in Attica that was cultivable (which they did not),[9] and this land amounted to 20% of the surface area, then each hoplite had at his disposal an average of at best 5.3 hectares, at worst 1.9. We are asked to believe that the average hoplite (or knight) was operating below subsistence level (in 431 BC) or near subsistence level (in 322 BC), in terms of home-based arable land.[10]

It is worth pausing a moment to consider the implications of these calculations for Athens as an imperial power. In order to qualify for hoplite status, a significant number of hoplites would have had to declare land held abroad in cleruchies. Moreover, the value of cleruchic land to individual Athenians does not disappear if, say, one-half rather than one-fifth of Attica was cultivable, for even under those circumstances Athenian hoplites in 431 BC would have owned on average only 4.8–6.6 hectares of arable in Attica.

I adopt 35–40% as a reasonable estimate for the cultivable portion of Attica. The lower figure corresponds to recent cultivation levels in Attica, that is to say, in the modern eparchy of Attica, which has lost territory in the north-west that was once part of Attica but now belongs to the eparchy of Megara.[11] We have to reckon with the loss of agricultural land not only through administrative reorganisation, but also through the expansion of the built-up area (19% of Attica in 1961), which has encroached on good-quality agricultural land both outside and inside the city walls. In addition, the remains of ancient terracing imply that cultivation in some periods of antiquity was more extensive than it has been in modern times.[12] Finally, the First Fruits inscription from Eleusis as reinterpreted below shows that conventional estimates of cultivable and cultivated land are too low.

The amount of cultivable land actually put under cultivation in any one year would have varied from period to period in accordance with changes in population density and from year to year in line with the choices made by farmers. According to the conventional picture,

[8] Hansen (1981); Gomme (1933), 4ff.; Jones (1957), 161–81.
[9] For landholding by thetes, see Jones (1957), 79–80; for public lands, Lewis (1973), 198–9 (5% of agricultural land); cf. Andreyev (1974), 43 (*c.* 10%).
[10] Burford Cooper (1977–8) (endorsed by Jameson (1977–8), 125, n. 13) argued that a basic hoplite plot lay in the region 4–6 ha, and was doubtful about its viability (p. 171).
[11] Kayser and Thompson (1964), 301: 34.87% Attica except Greater Athens classed as arable.
[12] Bradford (1957), 29ff.; cf. Renfrew and Wagstaff (1982), 132: 14% cultivated now, 20% at some time in antiquity (Melos).

biennial fallow was more or less universal. Thus any estimate of arable in Attica must be halved to reach a figure for land actually worked. Jardé thought that 20% of Attica was arable and 10% was cultivated in any particular year. For reasons that are given below, I believe this judgement to be unduly pessimistic, whether or not we have in mind small farmers.

LAND USE

The reconstruction of ancient Greek agricultural practices takes place in the vacuum left by the disappearance of the numerous treatises on farming composed in classical and Hellenistic Greece, known only by their authors or titles. According to the conventional picture of farming in ancient Greece,[13] biennial fallow is demanded not only by the physical environment but also by the level of ancient technology (in particular, the absence of artificial fertilisers and irrigation), farm practices and crop choices. Attica is seen as a land sown for the most part with cereals, often intercultivated with the ubiquitous olive tree and the rather less frequent vine. Dry legumes were scarce and therefore cereal/legume rotation systems rare. Livestock except those used for traction or freight were little to be seen outside the winter months, when flocks of sheep and goats grazed the stubble and fallow and the lowland wastes. By the late spring they were on the move to the highlands to escape the heat of the summer. The pastoral and agricultural economies were separated for a half of the year, with the consequent loss of an invaluable natural fertiliser in this period.

A rival picture of ancient Greek farming is now gaining ground among historians and archaeologists, according to which small-scale, intensive, mixed farming was the norm in densely populated Attica in the classical period.[14]

This alternative model in the first place discards the assumption of universal biennial fallow. The advantages of fallow are clear: fallow rests the soil, enabling it to rebuild its stock of nutrients, especially if stock are turned onto it. Fallow also conserves water, a useful risk-reducing measure in a low-rainfall zone such as Attica was. Frequent tilling of the fallow breaks down and eventually pulverises the soil, thus reducing moisture-loss through evaporation by capillary action. Moreover, subjection of the land to regular tilling keeps down surface weeds, thus reducing transpiration from plant growth.

---

[13] Semple (1932), Jardé (1925), 81ff., etc.
[14] Halstead (1981), at 328; (1984), 315ff.; Jameson (1977–8); Gallant (1982). Against, Sallares (1991), Isager and Skydsgaard (1992).

93

Under a system of continuous cultivation the farmer runs the risk of exhausting the soil, his new crop is in greater danger from weeds and pests and less animal-given manure is available. But continuous cultivation does not necessarily mean that the same crop is sown on the same soil every year. Meanwhile, it is pertinent to ask, in respect of subsistence or near-subsistence farmers, whether they could afford to cultivate only one-half of their meagre plots each year.

The alternative model, secondly, accords greater significance to the growing of pulses as field crops for fodder and food and envisages the use of simple rotation systems, with an implied reduction of the role of fallow in the agricultural economy. Theophrastus discusses ten pulses including several variants, treats them along with cereals as field crops and can contemplate their cultivation on land which has just produced a cereal crop. Leases sometimes specify a rotation of cereals and pulses; a lease of sacred properties at Rhamnous includes an option to put half the fallow under pulses.[15]

Finally, the cultivation of pulses as a fodder crop implies livestock raising without or with minimal transhumance, and in symbiosis with rather than divorced from agriculture. The references in literature to small-scale maintenance of livestock in the lowlands, and to a connection between animal husbandry and cultivation, are scattered but cumulatively impressive. The evidence for a specialised, long-distance transhumant pastoralism in Greece as a whole is scanty. For Attica it is non-existent.[16]

The pattern of rural settlement is relevant to land use but thus far has proved difficult to recover. Farmers cannot be pinned down in the archaeological record to dispersed farmsteads. Recent archaeological surveys have uncovered evidence of scattered buildings, but their function is disputed.[17] They are unlikely to include many ordinary peasant farmhouses, which would not have survived the ravages of time. In any case, the argument for the prevalence of intensive farming does not depend on farmers residing on their properties rather than in nearby nucleated settlements.

---

[15] On the Rhamnous lease, see *IG* II^2 2493 (339/8 BC) with new fragment, discussed by Jameson (1982). Other leases include *IG* I^3 252, 12–13 (mid-5th century, according to David Lewis, pers. comm.); *IG* II^2 1243, 21–4; Theophrastus, *Hist. plant.* 8.5.1 cf. *Caus. plant.* 3.20.7. See Hodkinson (1986), Garnsey (1992).

[16] E.g. Thucydides 2.14, 7.25.5; Xenophon, *Oec.* 5.3; Aristotle, *Pol.* 1252b. See Hodkinson (1986), and articles by Cherry, Skydsgaard and Jameson in the same volume; also Garnsey (1986). For the traditional view (cf. Skydsgaard), see Georgoudi (1974).

[17] Pečirka (1973), 115ff.; Osborne (1985b); Bintliff and Snodgrass (1985), 139; Keller and Rupp (1983).

PRODUCTIVITY

No yield figures are available from ancient Greece. Barbagallo, writing at the beginning of the century, thought that wheat yields in Greece as a whole might have been 6.15 hectolitres per hectare (hl/ha), around 390 kilogrammes per hectare (kg/ha), a seed-yield : seed-sown ratio of 3 : 1, at a sowing rate of 130 kg/ha. By his estimate, barley yielded 10.5 hl/ha (around 670 kg/ha, 5 : 1), but in Attica with Oropus only 5 hl/ha (around 320 kg/ha, 2.5 : 1), and wheat 3 hl/ha (around 230 kg/ha, 1.75 : 1). Jardé estimated yield per hectare for Greece as a whole at 8–12 hl/ha for wheat, or around 600–900 kg/ha (a yield in the range of 4.5–7 : 1, at the same sowing rate of 130 kg/ha), and 16–20 hl/ha for barley (around 1,020–1,270 kg/ha, a yield of around 7.75–9.75 :1 at the same, standard, sowing rate). Jardé was apparently prepared to contemplate yield figures for Attica which are in line with his estimates of the minima for Greece as a whole.[18]

Barbagallo was misled by the false assumption that the harvest of 329/8, as calculated from the Eleusis First Fruits inscription, was a normal one in all the areas represented. Jardé shared this assumption, but it did not affect his calculations. He seems to have reached his figures simply by scaling down the national averages for the harvest of 1921 (13 hl/ha for wheat, 19–24 hl/ha for barley). This harvest appears to have weighed more with him than three other factors: the harvest of 329/8 BC, the intuition that average yields were probably lower in Attica than elsewhere in Greece because more marginal land was cultivated, and finally his low opinion of the fertility of Attica.[19]

The poor agricultural potential of Attica is a commonplace. The account of Cary in his standard work of historical geography is fairly typical.[20] After discussing the 'ill favoured' climate and especially the low rainfall, which 'barely suffices for the cultivation of wheat', Cary continued:

The two central plains of the Attic Cephissus (in which Athens lies) and of the Mesogaea (between Hymettus and Pentelicus) and the coastal lowlands of Thria (near Eleusis) and of Marathon, contain small areas of richer soil, but Attica as a whole is, in the words of Plato (Critias 111bc), a discarnate skeleton, whose bones show through in large slabs of bare rock. Only one-quarter of Attica is estimated as cultivable, and part of this is ill-suited for anything save the drought-resisting

[18] Barbagallo (1904); Jardé (1925), Ch. 3, esp. 53, 60n. Jameson (1977/8), 131 adopts 400 kg/ha (= 5.25 hl/ha), close to Barbagallo's estimate for Greece as a whole. Bintliff (1977), 634 opts for a higher figure.
[19] The harvest of 1921 yielded in Athens and Boeotia 697 kg/ha (= 9 hl/ha) and 789 kg/ha (= 12 hl/ha) for wheat and barley, respectively. See Hopkins (1983a), 91: an average of 620 kg/ha (= 8 hl/ha) in Greece between 1922 and 1938.
[20] Cary (1949), 75–6.

olive-tree. In the fourth century only one-third to one-quarter of the Athenian requirements in cereals was home-grown (mostly barley), and from the time of Solon the importation of foreign grain into Attica was a matter of such importance as to require state regulation.

Other ancient sources, including Thucydides, Strabo and Plutarch, made disparaging remarks about the soil of Attica.[21] But as Cary himself concedes, not all of the soil of Attica is light or thin (*leptos*). Moreover, barley yields well in light soils in dry climates. Theophrastus, who did know his crops and soils, writes: 'At Athens the barley produces more meal than anywhere else, since it is an excellent land for that crop.' The suitability of the soil and climate of Attica for olives and vines, then as now, needs no special stress.

Philippson, in his standard work on the geography of Greece, gets it right:

> But it is no way true that Attica is to be classed as infertile, as is too often stated with assurance. This judgement is based on the appearance of the landscape in summer and autumn, and is coloured by the assumption of a Northerner that fertility is bound up with lush green growth. The light soil of the Athens and Eleusis plains and slopes brings very good returns of grain, oil and wine, and the plains of Marathon and especially that of Mesogeia actually have relatively rich soil with a relatively deep plough-zone.[22]

Just as travellers have been led astray by the appearance of Attica at the height of the summer drought, so scholars have misconstrued such ancient evidence as impinges on agricultural productivity. 'In the fourth century', writes Cary, 'only one-third to one-quarter of the Athenian requirements in cereals was home-grown (mostly barley), and from the time of Solon the importation of foreign grain into Attica was a matter of such importance as to require state regulation.' The two pieces of evidence from the fourth century which underlie the first part of this statement are a passage of Demosthenes (*Against Leptines*, 20.31–3), and an inscription recording the First Fruits offered to Demeter at Eleusis in 329/8 BC (*IG* II² 1672).

DEMOSTHENES ON IMPORTS

In his speech *Against Leptines*, Demosthenes attacked the law proposed and carried by one Leptines that cancelled all immunities from public

---

[21] Thucydides 1.2; Strabo 9.1.8; Plutarch, *Sol.* 22; cf. Menander, *Dysc.* 3 (Phyle); Lucian, *Tim.* 31; contra, Theophrastus, *Hist. plant.* 8.8.2.
[22] Philippson (1952), 783.

services (liturgies), except those enjoyed by descendants of the tyranni-
cides Harmodius and Aristogiton, and made it illegal to grant such
honours in the future. Those affected, and slighted, by the action of
Leptines, included, says Demosthenes, that 'perpetual benefactor' of
the Athenian people, Leucon, king of the Bosporus, and his children.
Demosthenes went on to remind his audience that Athenians consumed
more imported grain than any other people, and to assert that as much
grain came from the Pontus as from other foreign suppliers put
together. A little later he added that Leucon sent about 400,000
medimnoi, as any one could see if he checked the records of the
sitophulakes, the officials concerned with the grain market.

Demosthenes was claiming documentary support only for the latter of
these two statements, that concerning the 400,000 medimnoi. The
former, to the effect that half Athens' imports came from the Pontus, is
less secure. It would be unwise to take it literally, and even more so to
treat the two statements as of equal value and capable of yielding a figure
for annual imports. Some have opted for 800,000 medimnoi, others for
some larger amount, in the belief that Demosthenes had deliberately
underestimated the volume of non-Pontic imports. One commentator
wrote with brutal frankness, that as Demosthenes 'was a politician and
so was probably not speaking the truth', an estimate for imports of
around 1,200,000 medimnoi was a reasonable one.[23] The truth is that no
figure for non-Pontic imports can be safely derived from the speech.
Even the 400,000 medimnoi has dubious value. It cannot be safely
assumed that this figure represents a regular, annual import from the
Pontic region, rather than merely the amount imported in one year,
which might have been the recent bad year to which Demosthenes refers
in the same passage. In that case it would support the limited point that
Athens might have had to import in any particular year as much as
400,000 medimnoi from one source (enough to provide adequate sustenance for 80,000 people or to keep alive more than 100,000).

A second stray figure for Pontic imports deserves brief consideration.
According to Strabo, who lived under Augustus and came from the
Greek city of Amaseia not far from the south shore of the Black Sea,
Leucon sent 2,100,000 medimnoi from Theodosia in the Bosporus to
Athens. This volume of grain would represent about 84 million kg,
enough to feed around half a million people. But was the grain sent in
one year (and if so in a normal or an abnormal year?), or in the course of
the four decades in which Leucon was king of the Bosporus? Or was it

---

[23] Gomme (1933), 32–3 (quoted); Isager and Hansen (1975), 18–19; Jones (1957), 77–8.

Table 5. *The harvest of 329/8 BC (accounts of the epistatai of Eleusis, IG II² 1672)*

	Barley			Wheat		
	First fruits	Total medimnoi[a] (×600)	Total kg	First fruits	Total medimnoi (×1,200)	Total kg
1. Erechtheis	33 m	19,800	661,320	0 m 2 h 2 ch	250	10,000
2. Aigeis	84 m	50,400	1,683,360	2 m — 7 ch	2,575	103,000
3. Pandionis	51 m 7 h 3 ch	30,987.5	1,035,000	1.5 m — 2 ch	1,850	74,000
4. Leontis	86 m 11 h —	52,150	1,741,800	3 m — 10 ch	3,850	154,000
5. Akamantis	68 m 5 h —	41,050	1,371,060	3 m — 2 ch	3,650	146,000
6. Oineis	47 m 1 h 3 ch	28,287.5	994,820	2 m 11 ch 2 ch	3,550	142,000
7. Kekropis	38 m 3 h —	22,950	766,560	1 m — —	1,200	48,000
8. Hippothontis	56 m — 6 ch	33,675	1,124,760	4.5 m — 3 ch	5,475	219,000
9. Aiantis	43 m 4 h —	26,000	868,380	2 m 1 h —	2,500	100,000
10. Antiochis	57 m 8 h 2 ch	34,625	1,156,500	1 m 9 h 2.5 ch	2,162.5	86,500
Attica total	566 m 7 h 2 ch	339,925	11,353,560	22 m 6 h 2 ch	27,062.5	1,082,500
11. Drymus	1 m — 2 ch	625	20,880	2 m 5 h 1 ch	2,925	117,000
12. Oropus	20 m — —	12,000	400,800	5 m 9 h —	6,900	276,000
13. Salamis	40 m 10 h 2 ch	24,525	819,120	— — —	—	—
14. Skyros	48 m — —	28,800	961,920	8 m — —	9,600	384,000
15. Myrina[b]	162 m — —	97,200	3,246,480	23 m 5 h —	28,100	1,124,000
16. Hephaestia[b]	252 m 2 h 2 ch	151,325	5,054,280	23 m 10 h 2 ch	28,650	1,146,000
17. Imbros	43 m 4 h —	26,000	868,380	36 m 10 h —	44,200	1,768,000
Total (11–17)	567 m 5 h 2 ch	340,475	11,371,860	100 m 3 h 2 ch	120,375	4,815,000
Total (1–17)	1,134 m	680,400	22,725,420	122 m 10 h 1.5 ch	147,437.5	5,897,500

[a] 1 medimnos = 12 hemihekteis = 48 choinikes; 1 medimnos of wheat = 40 kg; 1 medimnos of barley = 33.4 kg.   [b] On Lemnos.

sent from Theodosia as distinct from Panticapaeum, or from both ports? The discussion must be inconclusive.[24]

The inscription for 329/8 gives total production figures for barley and wheat in Attica and in dependent territories for the year concerned, on the assumption that the contribution amounted to not less than 1/600 in the case of barley and 1/1200 in the case of wheat – the proportions operative in the late fifth century.[25] The sums, for Attica, are 339,925 medimnoi of barley and 27,062.5 medimnoi of wheat (see Table 5). The net combined cereal crop could have fed around 53,000 people at 175 kg p.a. or around 58,000, if farmers underestimated their harvests by, say, 10%.

It is abundantly clear that the harvest of 329/8 BC was inadequate to feed the population of citizens, metics and slaves in this or any other year between 480 and 322. The difficulty is that there is no other harvest to provide a comparison. On the face of it, we cannot know whether the harvest in question was normal or abnormal. In this situation, the correct response might seem to be not to use the inscription at all. Instead, most commentators have assumed that the harvest was normal and have accepted the pessimistic view of Attic agriculture which this implies.[26]

The picture is even bleaker if we believe that for the Athenians barley was regarded as exclusively food for animals, slaves and the poor. Jardé has even suggested that the barley crop of 329/8 was only sufficient to feed the animal population of Attica. Yet wheat made up only 8% of the crop of 329/8, measuring by volume, or 9.5%, measuring by weight. It looks as if conventional estimates of grain imports are too low.[27]

A comparison of the performances in 329/8 of Attica and the two communities on the island of Lemnos, Myrina and Hephaestia, puts a quite different perspective on the matter. Jardé pointed the way forward in a footnote, but did not rewrite his text in the light of his

---

[24] Strabo 7.4.6; Hopper (1979), 90–2: 52,500 med. p.a. from only Theodosia over a 40-year period. His third chapter, on imports, is unreliable.

[25] *IG* I³ 78 (425–2 or *c.* 422–1 or 416–15). See now Garnsey (1992).

[26] But see Gernet (1909), 296; Isager and Hansen (1975), 202; Jones (1957), 77–8. There are no other data relevant to the food supply of 329/8. Food shortages are firmly attested in 330/29 and 328/7 (*IG* II² 360; Demosthenes 34.38; etc.).

[27] See Jardé (1925), 125–7, and, for an extreme version, Jones (1957), 77. Like Isager and Hansen (1975), 17–18, and Gallo (1983) (1985), I believe in the widespread consumption of barley in Athens and Attica. The implications of the Scholiast on Aristophanes, *Ach.* 548 is that in some years, at least, a lot of barley was *imported*: the Great Stoa at Piraeus was also called 'The Barley Hall'.

discovery.[28] He saw that 329/8 could not have been a normal year if his own conjectured normal returns for wheat and barley are acceptable. By applying to the product of 329/8 his lowest yield figures, 8 hl/ha for wheat and 16 hl/ha for barley, he reaches the conclusion that grain land as a proportion of the surface area of Attica was a mere 5.65%, an embarrassingly low figure. He writes: 'The percentage figure seems too low and therefore the yield figures too high. This is a confirmation of the hypothesis often floated and considered by us undemonstrated, according to which the agricultural year 329/8 was bad.'

Earlier in the same chapter, Jardé had made the sound observation that his 10% figure for land under cultivation as a proportion of surface area is inappropriate for Lemnos, because it produces an unacceptably high yield figure of 33 hl/la for wheat and barley combined for the year 329/8.

On the other hand, Jardé was prepared to let the figure for Attica of 8 hl/ha stand: 'These two figures are so far apart, the second more than four times higher than the first, that even after conceding that the land of Lemnos was exceptionally fertile, we have to admit that 10%, if it is correct for Attica, is too low for Lemnos.'

Curiously, the sentence that follows suggests that Jardé was on the point of reversing this implied judgement on Attica, and revising his figure for arable upwards and his yield figure downwards: 'To be sure, because of its needs, Attica despite the extension of its vineyards and olive groves had to give over as much land as possible to wheat and sow cereals even in regions where the results were mediocre, and that accounts for a reduction in the average return for the country.'

The Attica/Lemnos comparison may now be reintroduced, but with the application of a uniform figure for yield (Jardé's minimum 8 and 16 hl/ha) rather than for arable (see Table 6).

There is no escape from the conclusion that Lemnos had an average or good year, and Attica a bad one. To test this we could lower the yield to, for example, 4.5 hl/la for wheat and 9 hl/la for barley. This gives the result that 44.27% of Lemnos was under cereals (6,621 + 14,497 = 21,118 hectares). Even taking into consideration the fertility of Lemnos, this is clearly too high a figure for land under cultivation (as opposed to cultivable land). The same yield figures, when applied to Attica's harvest, give 9.6% as the area under cereals (3,157 + 19,829 = 22,985), which is marginally below Jardé's figure. It is only by lowering the yield estimate radically that more reasonable figures for land under cereals in Attica are arrived at. Thus, for example, a yield of 2.25 hl/ha for wheat and 6 hl/ha for barley gives a

[28] Jardé (1925), 52–3, 6on.

Table 6. *Attica and Lemnos: product and estimated area under grain in 329/8 BC (from IG II² 1672)*

	Attica	Lemnos
Wheat (medimnoi)	27,062	56,750
Wheat (volume, hl)	14,208	29,794
Wheat (yield, hl/ha)	8	8
Wheat (sown area, ha)	1,776	3,724
Barley (medimnoi)	339,925	248,525
Barley (volume, hl)	178,461	130,476
Barley (yield, hl/ha)	16	16
Barley (sown area, ha)	11,154	8,155
Total area under grain (ha)	12,930	11,879
Total area (ha)	240,000	47,700
% of total area under grain	5.4	24.9

total for land under both crops of 36,058 hectares, or 15% of Attica, while yields of 2.25 hl/ha (wheat) and 4.25 hl/ha (barley) give a total of 48,305 hectares, or approximately 20% of Attica. It is only by lowering yields to, for example, 1.5 hl/ha and 3.6 hl/ha for wheat and barley respectively, that one can produce a percentage figure for land under cultivation which is almost equivalent to that arrived at for Lemnos by applying the much higher yields of 8 and 16, respectively: 24.6% of Attica, 24.9% of Lemnos.

HOME PRODUCTION AND THE CONSUMER

The conventional picture – little land under cultivation, low total product, few consumers fed, very high level of imports – is based on the erroneous belief that 329/8 was a normal year in Attica. The capacity of Attica to feed its resident population needs to be reassessed. The calculations in Table 7 and Figure 1 (overleaf) are offered as an indication of the range of the possible. The notes that follow comment on the key variables.

Production in Attica

I have not taken into consideration the contribution from dependencies, in particular those mentioned in the First Fruits inscription – the Boeotian border lands of Drymus and Oropus, the islands of Salamis, Lemnos, Imbros and Skyros. In 329/8 these areas between them produced a little more barley and just under five times more wheat than

Table 7. *Consumers supportable by domestic grain production in Attica*

	Minimum	Likely	Maximum
Area under grain as % of Attica	10	17.5	30
	(31)[a]	(55)	(94)
% grain land under barley	67	80	90
	(52)	(55)	(56)
Output wheat (hl/ha)	4	8	12
	(50)	(55)	(59)
Losses wheat (seed, etc.)	1/6	1/3	1/2
	(57)	(55)	(52)
Output barley (hl/ha)	8	12	20
	(39)	(55)	(85)
Losses barley (seed, etc.)	1/6	1/4	1/2
	(60)	(55)	(39)
Consumption (kg person/year)	150	175	230
	(64)	(55)	(42)

Modal answer: 55 consumers per km², or 132,000.

[a] Figures in parentheses represent number of consumers per km² if all other inputs remain at their most likely value.

the ten tribes of Attica put together. It can be assumed that Athenians were able to tap a considerable proportion of the surplus of these territories as landowners and residents within them and as consumers in Attica itself. The wheat surplus would have been especially welcome, in view of the uncertainties and small scale of wheat-production in Attica. Lemnos was an obvious target for a special tax in a crisis.[29]

Area under grain

This is a crucial variable, in that the value it is assigned will materially affect the result. If anything, my 'likely' figure is on the low side, if my earlier estimate of cultivable land at 35–40% and my arguments against universal biennial fallow are accepted.

Wheat : barley ratio

Attic farmers can be expected to have shown a marked preference for barley as a low-risk, high-yield crop. My 'likely' figure gives wheat a greater significance as a crop than has conventionally been thought. It

[29] A new law of 374/3 BC 'concerning the 8⅓% tax on the grain of the islands' shows Lemnos, Imbros and Skyros contributing to the food-supply of Athens, presumably in an emergency. A full publication is awaited. See Shear (1987).

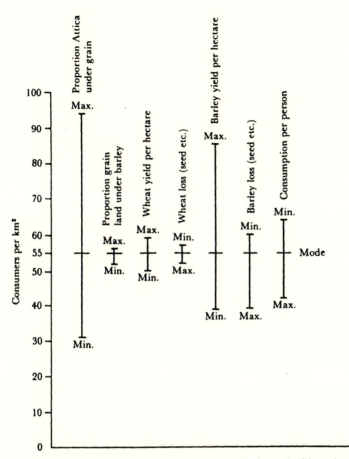

Figure 1. Graphical representation of Table 7. Each vertical bar shows the effect on consumers per km² of changing that input from its minimum, through its most likely, to its maximum value, with all other inputs remaining at their most likely value.

is usually assumed on the basis of the First Fruits inscription that the Athenians customarily put ten times as much land under barley as wheat. But if 329/8 was a bad year, then barley is likely to have done better than wheat, which needs more rain in the growing season.[30] That is to say, barley's share of the crop would therefore have been substantially larger than its share of the seed sown and of land cultivated. In fact, this variable produces a narrow range of values. The effect

[30] Arnon (1972), II, 4 (300 mm for wheat), 74 (200–250 mm for barley).

on the number of consumers of substituting a different value is minimal.

Output of wheat and barley

In the case of wheat, the range of values is narrow. Substitution of the minimum value would still produce a carrying capacity of 50 persons/ km² or 120,000 in total. In contrast, varying the barley yield would produce widely different estimates of carrying capacity (39–85 persons/ km²). My 'likely' figure of 12 hl/ha for barley is more conservative than Jardé's of 16 hl/ha, and is considerably closer to the estimated minimum than to the maximum.

Losses of wheat and barley

The losses represent deductions for seed, wastage and animal feed. The lower figure in the case of barley reflects the higher return on seed. Again, it is the result for barley which makes a significant difference to the equation.

Consumption rate of grain

The 'likely' figure for consumption is quite generous; it implies total food consumption of over 230 kg/person/year, if grain provided 75% of food energy requirements. Consumption of grain at an average rate of 230 kg/person/year reduces the number of supportable consumers to 42 per km², or a little over 100,000 people.

To sum up: by my estimate (and I do not insist on the figures on which it is based), Attica was capable of feeding in the region of 120,000–150,000 people, and this without the aid of other territories, under normal conditions.

'Attica was capable ...' Attica's potential might not have been realised. Choice of crop, extent of land to cultivate and production targets lay with individual farmers and landowners. The decisions they made were dependent upon, among other things, their assessment of market demand. The preference of some for imported bread wheat, it might be argued, would have reduced the demand for home-grown cereals (among which barley was predominant), and created an artificial demand for imports. The issue is difficult to resolve. In my view, population levels in the middle decades of the fifth century were sufficiently high to absorb all that Attica could produce, as well as a generous supply of imports. In the fourth century the demographic burden was not so heavy, but imports flowed less freely, and demand for the local product is unlikely to have slackened. Finally, some, perhaps the majority, of Athenians may have preferred wheat, but most of them put up with barley. There was not always any choice.

'Under normal conditions'. The agricultural performance of Attica varied with political, social and economic conditions, and also the behaviour of the climate. Attica is one of the driest parts of Greece. Variability of rainfall in the growing season is very high. The risk of crop-failure is pronounced, especially in the case of legumes and wheat (almost 3 bad years in 4, more than 1 bad year in 4, respectively, on the basis of modern rainfall statistics). In bad years, therefore, and particularly when the barley crop failed (about 1 year in 20), Athens' order for foreign grain must have been enormous.[31]

How much grain did Athens regularly import? As we have seen, no firm figure can be derived from the passage in Demosthenes' Speech *Against Leptines*. In the fourth century, Athenians had a group of regular suppliers in the form of Athenian citizens or, more usually, metics based in Attica or supported by Athenian capital. These men were prohibited by law from taking their grain anywhere else than to the Piraeus.[32] But the amount they brought in must have varied according to supply and demand as well as political and climatic conditions. As for importers not subject to Athenian law, they would only have unloaded their grain at Athens if they thought the price attractive or if there were other benefits involved.

CONCLUSION

Athens was a regular importer of foreign grain, and these imports had to be substantial if the Athenians were to maintain the level of population and the standard of living appropriate for a great power. This is not at issue. However, my calculations suggest that Athens never in a normal year had to find grain from outside Attica, narrowly defined, for more than one-half of its resident population. Athens was less dependent on foreign grain, and in particular on distant sources of grain, than is generally assumed.

A second conclusion follows, if the general tenor of my argument is accepted: that Athens became dependent on grain from foreign sources later than is generally assumed. A serious disequilibrium between Athens' food needs and its capacity to meet them from Attica and nearby dependencies did not develop until well into the post-Persian-

[31] Cf. p. 10.
[32] Demosthenes 34.37; 35.50; 56.6 and 11; Lycurgus, *Leocr.* 26.7.

War period in consequence of population growth. Even in this period food crises were rare thanks to Athens' control of the sea, particularly the grain route from the north, and her attractiveness to suppliers, because of both the size and stability of her market and the certainty of a return cargo in the form of silver.[33]

[33] A theme of Xenophon, *Poroi*.

7

THE BEGINNINGS OF DEPENDENCE

INTRODUCTION

When did Athens become dependent on foreign grain? At what stage did imports become inevitable, no matter how good the harvest was? As with most aspects of early Greek history, the data that throw light on this issue are scanty. They consist of brief notices, often in late literary works, of various foreign adventures undertaken by Athenians and of shadowy regulations issued by Solon; of coin and pottery finds in Egypt and the Black Sea respectively, difficult to date and interpret; and of some funerary evidence from Attica which might or might not have significance for demographic trends.

On the basis of such unpromising material, the doctrine has evolved that the population of Attica had outrun its resources and was dependent on imports by the late archaic age. A prohibition on the export of agricultural products apart from olive oil, attributed to Solon by Plutarch, has been taken to imply an absolute shortage of cereals. Athenian activity abroad has been interpreted as similar in origin and purpose to the earlier colonisations in which Athens did not participate, that is, as essentially designed to reduce the number of domestic consumers and facilitate the import of grain. Recently this general argument from the nature of the colonisation movement has been complemented by the claim that the pattern of burials indicates very fast population growth in eighth-century Attica.

Recent reference works and textbooks reflect the impressive consensus that has grown up around this issue.[1] Rhodes states in his substantial commentary on Aristotle's *Constitution of the Athenians* that Athens already relied on imported corn to supplement the local crop by the end of the seventh century and the beginning of the sixth. The same

---

[1] See, in order of citation, Rhodes (1981), 95–6, 577; Bury and Meiggs (1975), 122; Boardman (1980), 264, quoting Starr (1977), 176; Austin and Vidal-Naquet (1977), 69. See also, e.g., Jardé (1925), 144, 198–9; Grundy (1948), 67–9; French (1956), 11; (1964), 59 cf. 46–9; Salmon (1965), 37ff.; Hammond (1967), 180–1, 191–3; Hart (1982), 18.

view is propounded, if with rather less conviction, in Bury and Meiggs' standard history of Greece:

Another problem may have been affecting the city rather than the countryside. By the fifth century Athens was heavily dependent on imported corn; we have no firm evidence when that dependence started, but there may be hints that the position was already becoming precarious. Toward the end of the seventh century Athens planted a small settlement at Sigeum near the entrance to the Hellespont: it may have been intended to stake a claim on the corn route from the north coast of the Euxine which was later to be the main source of Athens' supplies.

Boardman, in his important work on Greek colonisation and trade, notable for its full exploitation of archaeological evidence, draws a contrast between an earlier period, when Athens failed to participate in overseas foundations and trade, and the turn of the seventh century, when 'Athens made a deliberate bid to secure a footing on, and indeed control of, the Hellespont, "surely to secure strongpoints on an artery of growing commercial importance to her".'

Finally, Austin and Vidal-Naquet, who are usually alive to the dangers of modernistic 'economic' explanations in Greek history, agree substantially with this position, while emphasising that Athenian imports in the fifth century were of quite a different order:

During the sixth century Athens began to show interest in the problem of the import of foodstuffs. Solon placed a ban on the export of all Athenian agricultural produce from Attica with the exception of olive oil. Though there may not be any proof of Athenian activity in Egypt at this period, the Athenians sought on the other hand to secure the control of the straits leading to the Black Sea, perhaps already in Solon's time, and in any case certainly under the tyranny of Peisistratus (cf. the Athenian settlements at Sigeum and in the Thracian Chersonese). One is still a long way from the policy of large-scale food imports known in the classical period, but this is at least the prelude to it.

Noonan has been one of the few to challenge the orthodox position. On the basis of literary and archaeological evidence (pottery finds), he reached a negative conclusion on the extent of the trade links between the northern Black Sea and Greece before the turn of the sixth century:

An examination of the written and archaeological evidence strongly suggests that the export of grain from the northern Black Sea to Greece could not have begun until the late sixth or early fifth century BC at the earliest. It is only at this time that the Greek colonies developed a trade of sufficient volume with the natives to permit the export of grain abroad. Consequently we should not be surprised that the earliest possible written reference to grain exports from the northern Black Sea dates to about 480 BC. Only in the fifth century BC, when written sources confirm the existence of grain exports to Greece, do significant amounts of Greek imports appear in native settlements. Thus, the written and archaeological evidence are in basic agreement both during the sixth century BC and later.[2]

This deviation from the traditional doctrine has not gone completely unnoticed. It is enshrined in the revised *Cambridge Ancient History* that grain imports into Greece 'were minor until almost 500 BC'. The position of Athens however is left obscure. In an earlier monograph on the society and economy of archaic Greece the same writer, Starr, in a brief and ambiguous statement on Athens, had suggested obliquely that Athens and other unnamed cities had become interested in the Pontic trade somewhat earlier than some other cities: 'Assumptions that this trade ran far back into earlier centuries are too easily made, and Athens and other importing cities were exceptions in Greece.' This suggestion is neither confirmed nor denied in the *Cambridge Ancient History*. Other contributors to that work also avoid confronting the problem directly but appear to be operating within the framework of the traditional theory.[3]

There must be serious doubt as to whether grain was imported in bulk into Greece in the early sixth century not only from the Black Sea region but also from Egypt. The Athenian owl coins found in hoards on Egyptian sites, and usually taken as evidence of corn exports to Athens, are dated no earlier than the end of the tyranny of Peisistratus or the beginning of that of his son Hippias, that is, in the last quarter of the sixth century.[4]

The arguments from pottery and coin finds also tell against the hypothesis that the tyranny of Peisistratus in the mid-sixth century was the watershed in the history of the Athenian food supply. Thus far a bold champion for this view is lacking, perhaps because the weakness of the orthodox view has not been appreciated. Athenian foreign ventures under the tyranny, whether inspired by the tyrant or the result of individual initiative, do not provide secure grounds for a counter-argument, because their background and motivation are obscure. It is by no means clear that the grain supply was a major consideration in these proto-imperialistic activities.[5]

One could make out a better case for the late sixth century or early fifth as the turning-point. Attica was by now, in my view, approaching

[2] Noonan (1973), e.g. 241; cf. the intuition of Gernet (1909), 317.
[3] Starr in *CAH* III².3, 427 cf. 430; in the same volume, Andrewes p. 405 and Graham p. 121. See Starr (1977), 68, 164–5. Otherwise, Noonan's article has hardly been noticed in the literature. See Legon (1981), 87 n. 2.
[4] Kraay (1964) (date); Crawford (1982), 19ff. (date and corn/coin exchange).
[5] Cf. Bloedow (1975), urging against De Ste Croix (1972) that the search for grain does not explain Athenian imperialism in the pre-Persian War period. A more careful statement of the position is required.

the danger zone, where a better and better harvest was required if the need to import grain on a regular basis was to be avoided. But the whole argument needs reconsideration at a number of different levels.

GRAIN IMPORTS

There is no direct evidence of grain imports into Athens in the archaic period. Scholars have had to argue for their existence in a roundabout way from the evidence for the export of artefacts, agricultural products (primarily olive oil) and silver, and from a problematic text of Plutarch.

Archaic Athens as an industrial centre, capable of paying for the staple foods that it needed by the sale of manufactured goods, is an anachronism.[6] For present purposes, the point to be stressed is the implausibility of the suggestion that fine pottery was an exchange item for grain. The bulk of it went to the West, particularly to Etruria, through the agency of non-Athenian traders. Grain from this region is not attested in Athens before the second half of the fourth century.[7]

It is unsafe to infer the existence of a substantial export trade in wine and oil from the wide diffusion of decorated vases. The counter-arguments remain powerful.[8] In any case, an expansion of oleoculture and viticulture in Attica from the time of Solon and through his initiative is quite conjectural. Solon's prohibition of the export of agricultural produce apart from olive oil implies, if anything, that olive cultivation was already well developed. Plutarch does not say that Solon was encouraging the extension of the olive. This is a modern interpretation of his actions, based on the prior assumption that Athens was already dependent on grain imports and needed to build up an export crop to pay for them.[9] An alternative interpretation of Solon's prohibition is available (see below).

The argument for an Athenian coin / Egyptian grain exchange has been purged of its earlier excesses but still retains some implausible

---

[6] Starr (1977) exaggerates the scale of Athenian 'industry'. See Cook (1972), 270–4; Morris (1991).

[7] See p. 151, below. In Herodotus 7.158.4, Gelon of Syracuse offers equipment, men and supplies to the Greeks – not specifically to the Athenians – in 480 BC. This suggests at least that in *c.* 450 Sicily was known to be a grain exporter on a considerable scale. However, surplus Sicilian grain could go not only to Greece, but to Carthage, other western Phoenician cities and central Italy – and within Greece, it would go less naturally to Athens than to the Isthmus, the Peloponnese and the Dorian Aegean. On the diffusion of decorated pottery, see Johnston (1979); Perreault (1986).

[8] Vallet (1962), 1556–7; cf. Johnston (1979), 50.

[9] E.g. Murray (1980), 46. It is a gratuitous inference that a consequence of the expansion of oleoculture was a decline of cereal production; cf. Green (1970), 17: 'But to export oil meant planting new olive groves, which in turn reduced the acreage available for cereals.'

elements.[10] Nobody believes that the widely dispersed Thracian and Macedonian silver coinage was intended specifically for the purchase of grain in Egypt. Why then should it be assumed that the Athenian coins that replaced it were minted with such an exchange as the prime aim? The coinage was issued in the first instance for a variety of immediate uses, including no doubt diplomatic gift-giving, payments to mercenaries and construction workers and the receiving of dues and fines. In so far as Athenian coin was left in Egypt (and it also went to the Levant and south Italy and Sicily), it was taken and paid over in the last of a succession of – to us – invisible transactions by mainly foreign traders in exchange for grain, among other things, which found its way to Athens, among other places. The coin hoards prove Egypt's need for silver much more firmly than Athens' need for grain. They establish the case for a regular, annual import of grain, into Athens neither at the turn of the seventh century (when Athens had no coinage) nor at the turn of the sixth.

Solon's law prohibiting the export of agricultural produce apart from olive oil should be taken at its face value, as an attempt to check the free movement out of the country of the crucial staple, grain.[11] I imagine that grain shortage following harvest failure forms the background and precipitating cause of Solon's action. Large landowners could apparently get higher prices for their product and acquire more (or more interesting) things in exchange in towns like Aegina and Megara than at home in Attica, even or especially in years of mediocre or bad harvest. In sending grain abroad, they were putting their own interests and the benefit of other peoples, including rivals and enemies, before the welfare of Athenian consumers. The law, thus interpreted, may be taken as indirect evidence of the coexistence of surplus and want in Athens, but hardly of an absolute shortage and still less of a permanent deficiency of grain in Athens. It takes its place alongside Solon's abolition of debt-slavery in Attica, Peisistratus' loans to the poor to permit them to farm and his tax on produce of 10% (or 5%), as measures designed to mitigate distress and raise the legal and material position of the poor. There is no need to invoke excessive population as an explanation.

The distinction between permanent and temporary deficiencies is a crucial one, and it permits us to differentiate between two kinds of grain-importing states. Most Greek states belonged to the latter

[10] See Crawford (1982), 19ff. I share the scepticism of Finley (1965) and Austin (1970), 37–40, 72–4, with bibliography, attacking, e.g., Sutherland (1943).

[11] Garnsey and Morris (1988). Bravo (1983), 21, is too optimistic when he says that the grain only went abroad in good seasons. See pp. 74–6 above for other laws prohibiting grain export.

category. That is, they did not invariably produce enough grain for the needs of their population. This was the situation of archaic Athens.

It is impossible to say how often Athens had to import grain to counter shortage. Food shortages are difficult to identify in the meagre sources. As suggested above, Solon may have been reacting to a temporary grain shortage created or (more likely) aggravated by the behaviour of the rich; alternatively, the use of grain export as a weapon of the rich against the poor was fresh in his memory. Camp has argued that a number of innovations in cult and ritual cluster around the later eighth century, when in his view Athens was suffering from a prolonged drought.[12] He has in mind a sanctuary of Zeus the Rain-Bearer (Ombrios) on Mt Hymettus, a cult of Artemis at Brauron to counter *limos* (or perhaps *loimos*), the introduction of Dionysus and of the Great Mother Cybele into Athens, the sacrifice of the daughters of Leos, the institution of the Diipoleia and of agricultural sacrifices, the inauguration of Demeter's cult at Eleusis and the foundation of a Field of Limos in Athens. Much of the cult evidence can probably be accounted for with reference to the normal risks and uncertainties of cultivation rather than major shortages and crises. Moreover, since virtually no cults of any kind are known from the Dark Age, the identification of cults concerned with agriculture in the archaic period need not point to anything distinctive about the condition of archaic-age agriculture.

Thereafter, the Solonian law apart, there is nothing further in the sources which might relate to food crisis until right at the end of the archaic age. Ostraka (potsherds) from the large Kerameikos dump in Athens, datable to the years after 487 BC (the date of the first ostracism), call for the ostracism of one Limos Eupatrides, Hunger for which the Eupatrids, the aristocracy, are to blame.[13]

There is nothing improbable in the notion that the Athenians did suffer periodic food crises in the archaic age and that importing grain was one response. But such grain need not have come any distance: Euboea, Boeotia and Thessaly were ports of call within the region. Unless some more convincing arguments surface in the next section, it

[12] Camp (1979), 402.
[13] Thomsen (1972), p. 104, n. 342. There is nothing of relevance to this period to be gleaned from the Scholia to Aristophanes, *Plutus* 178: 'In the days when Amasis was king of Egypt, the Athenians sent to him in time of scarcity and asked him for corn. He sent them a plentiful supply. On this account the Athenians sent the Egyptians a body of troops to help them in the war with Persia, and the two peoples combined to be allies and friends' (Rutherford's translation). Amasis was king in the mid-sixth century. See Lewis (1977), 147 n. 73 on the 'wild guessing of the scholia', of whom even the best confused Amasis with Akoris (king *c.* 393/2–381/0).

must be concluded that a regular grain trade with the northern Black Sea or with Egypt in the archaic period is a figment of the imagination.

OVERPOPULATION

The traditional theory revolves around the supposition that Athens was overpopulated by the end of the seventh century or a little later. Until that time Attica was able to absorb rising population levels without resorting to colonisation, the drastic remedy for overpopulation. Athens therefore missed out on the movement of colonisation in which many Greek city states were involved over a period of about 150 years from the eighth century.

The significance of the new argument of Snodgrass from Athenian burial patterns is that it both confirms the suspicion that Attica was half empty at a time when other states were feeling the strain, and predicts a later crisis period induced by population pressure and characterised by a wave of colonisation. The period beginning in the second half of the seventh century offers itself as such a time. Snodgrass writes:

I have tried elsewhere to calculate the rate of growth in one area, Attica, at this time, using the evidence of the datable burials from this region. My conclusion was that in the space of two thirty-year generations, between about 780 and 720 BC, the population may have multiplied itself by a factor of approximately seven, and I tried to show grounds for finding this credible.

The Argolid apparently experienced a similar growth rate.

Camp turned Snodgrass' argument on its head by asserting that the increase in burials attests population decline, not increase. But the rival interpretations have similar implications, for Camp believes that colonisation was 'an important feature of Athenian foreign policy' from the early sixth century. The difference is that in his theory colonisation was a consequence of a serious and very sustained drought from the middle of the eighth to the first quarter of the seventh century.[14]

These reconstructions can be questioned at two points. First, is a unitary explanation of colonisation in terms of overpopulation satisfactory? Secondly, was Athens in fact overpopulated?

The first question merits a negative answer along the following lines. First, population growth is not a 'prime mover'; it is itself part of the phenomenon that requires elucidation. Secondly, overpopulation as

[14] Snodgrass (1977) and (1980), e.g. 23, supported by Murray (1980), 65,107; Camp (1979), e.g. 405. Snodgrass (1980), 93 did acknowledge 'that the rise in population had stopped, rather abruptly, after 700'. Camp showed this to be an understatement. See Morris (1987), Fig. 54.

ordinarily understood is the product of a long-term development in the course of which population and resources gradually move into disequilibrium. As such it seems an inadequate explanation for those occasions where colonisation was a response to a short-term crisis in the internal development of a state. One might try to reformulate the theory in terms of 'relative overpopulation', as in the following statement:

We may take it as axiomatic that no one leaves home and embarks on colonisation for fun. This means that by definition there was overpopulation in the colonising states, since overpopulation is a relative concept and there were certainly large numbers of people for whom conditions at home were so unsatisfactory that they preferred to join colonising expeditions. On this argument, even if all participants went voluntarily, there was overpopulation, but in fact we know that sometimes colonists were conscripted, because the community decided that it could not support the existing population. This is most clearly attested in Thera's colonisation of Cyrene ...[15]

However, the concept of 'relative overpopulation' has little explanatory power in itself and may actually be a hindrance to understanding. At best it merely points one back to the substantive cause or causes of particular instances of colonisation such as political faction-fighting, famine, or exploitation of the poor by the rich.

As for Athenian overpopulation: advocates of the thesis of overpopulation will not find supporting evidence in the archaeological data, whether for settlement, wells or burials.

To judge from the site-maps (published in 1973), the fifth century was the period of rapid and substantial growth. There was population increase at an impressive level in the eighth century, but the process of infilling a relatively empty landscape was far from regular (there is a sudden fall of the number of settlements known for the seventh century) and remained incomplete; large tracts of Attica, especially the north and north-west border areas and the south, remained underpopulated at the end of the archaic period.[16]

Developments in the water supply of Athens have provided ammunition for those arguing for overpopulation. In particular, an alleged trebling of the wells in the Agora has been held to indicate a substantial expansion of population in the eighth century. It may be noted as a preliminary point that there was no unilinear progress: if the number of wells in the Agora trebled in the eighth century, they were almost halved in the half-century following. Next, the assumption that the ratio of users to wells remained constant is distinctly dubious, and the failure to consider other factors, notably the changing role of the Agora,

[15] Graham, *CAH* III².3, 157.
[16] Travlos and Tsimbides-Pendazos (1973).

weakens the argument. More fundamentally, wells are distinctly problematic as indices of population growth. We only have the dump fills that closed the wells; at best we know when they were abandoned. Many appear to have been cleared out for reuse from time to time. This means that there is no way of establishing that the eighth-century wells were not in use in previous centuries.[17]

Burial patterns have traditionally been used as an index of demographic change in Attica. The new arguments have their implausibilities: a 4% p.a. rise in the birth rate is exceptional by any historical standards and is virtually impossible for ancient Athens, while a drought lasting most of a century is problematic conceptually and empirically. More seriously, the assumption of a direct link between numbers of graves and ancient population levels has been exploded by the demonstration that the significance of the burial pattern is primarily political and social, not demographic. The increase in burials around 750 BC represents an expansion of the category of those entitled to be formally buried to include those of low rank and children; it coincides with the emergence of the polis and the enhanced status of the ordinary citizen within the polis structure.[18]

A similar argument accounts for a second sudden increase in burials at the end of the sixth century. The mid-eighth century development was reversed within a half century, and it seems that for the next two centuries the old restrictions on access to formal burial were reimposed. 'Suddenly, just about 500 BC, the proportion of the Athenian population represented in formal, archaeologically recoverable burials expands to include not only a fuller age structure but also a much larger proportion of the adult population.'[19] Again the explanation is to be found in the political context. These changes were part of the reassertion of the polis ideology and the enhanced role attributed to the ordinary citizen in the reforms of Cleisthenes.

Though the burial evidence does not indicate dramatic population increase in the Cleisthenic period (any more than it does in the mid-eighth century), it is likely that the population grew steadily in late archaic-age Attica. But by how much?

Athenian demography is a leap in the dark. The population resources of Athens in 480 BC have been the object of some debate, but there is very little in fact to go on, and it is all in Herodotus, whose numerical data are often unreliable. Herodotus thought there were

[17] Coldstream (1968), 360; Camp (1979). Critiques in Morris (1987), 237–8; Snodgrass (1983), now challenged by Dontas (1983); cf. Robertson (1986).
[18] Morris (1987), Chs. 4–10.
[19] Morris (1987), 101.

8,000 Athenian hoplites at the battle of Plataea. He is also responsible for the suggestion that the Athenians could only man 180 ships at the battle of Salamis. At 200 men per ship this points to an adult male citizen population of 36,000.[20] Gomme settled for 35,000 and a total citizen family population of 140,000. One factor that would force a revision of the figure downwards is the presence of non-citizens among the rowers and supernumeraries, a regular policy in later periods, and not unattested for 480: Pausanias tells of slaves fighting on the Athenian side at Marathon. Beloch had earlier opted for the figure 30,000, which points to a citizen population of more than 120,000, though 30,000 is a commonly recurring conventional figure; Patterson suggests 25,000–30,000. Gomme did not try to assess metic or slave numbers, though he suggested there may have been 'very few metics indeed, only some hundreds', and the account of the building of the walls at Athens inclined him to believe that the slave population was 'not large'. Patterson mentions, though only incidentally, figures of 1,000 and 2,000 for metics and slaves respectively. The latter figure at least is most improbable, especially in view of the development of the silver mines, which was under way from the late sixth century and acceler-ated after the large strike of 483 BC. There were surely several thousand slave miners in Laurium by 480 BC, before agricultural and domestic slaves in Attica at large are counted in. I suggest a total population figure, citizens and non-citizens, in the range of 120,000–150,000 by 480 BC.[21]

This discussion has shown how flimsy our data base is for the period in question, and how risky it is to give weight to the occasional literary passages bearing on population. The case for an overpopulated Athens, to be persuasive, must rest on firmer foundations.

At first sight the overpopulation thesis might be rescued by an indirect argument from the demographic requirements of the Cleisthe-nic constitution introduced in 508–7 BC. Hansen has calculated that the Athenian *boule*, as manned by the Athenians in the fourth century, required 'a minimum population [sc. of adult male citizens] well above 21,000, perhaps 25,000, perhaps even 30,000'.[22] The higher figure is the same as Beloch's for 480 BC and implies a total citizen population of more than 120,000.

Hansen's argument cannot simply be transferred from the fourth century to the last decades of the archaic age, unless there are good

---

[20] Herodotus 8.17; 8.44; 9.28.
[21] Beloch (1886), 60; Gomme (1933); Patterson (1981), 51–6; Hansen (1986), 26; Lauffer (1956), II 904–16 (mines); Pausanias 1.32.3 (slaves at Marathon).
[22] Hansen (1986), 64.

grounds for thinking that the membership restrictions applying in the fourth century (both *de iure* and *de facto*) were in operation from the time the Council was first constituted, in about 501/0 BC. It would have to be believed not only that the Council was from the first a body with an annually rotating membership made up of citizens of thirty years of age who had already served no more than once, but also that the other regulation with demographic significance was already in place, that a councillor could serve as chairman of a prytany only once in a lifetime. It would further have to be accepted that the behaviour of Athenians was similar in the late archaic and in the late classical ages: for example, that they characteristically served as councillors at 40 rather than 30 years of age.

I have a less static view of the development of democracy in Athens; I am inclined to give Ephialtes and Pericles rather more to do in designing Athenian institutions; I see no reason for believing that attitudes to Council membership remained frozen over almost two centuries; and I find it implausible that the citizen population was no lower in 500 BC than the highest point it reached in the fourth century.

COLONISATION AND IMPERIALISM

It remains to consider the evidence for Athenian colonisation in the late archaic age. According to the traditional view, imperialistic activity leading to colonisation is to be seen as one solution to population pressure on domestic resources.

A cautionary note should be sounded at the outset. It would be unwise to assume that a domestic food supply problem is the only conceivable or the most likely stimulus for Athenian imperialism in any age, or that every outpost of empire was automatically and immediately a supplier for the imperial capital.

The sketchy sources for archaic Athens refer to a number of foreign ventures.[23] Some were close to home: war with Aegina in the eighth or seventh century, war with Megara over Salamis at the time of Solon and again before the tyranny of Peisistratus, perhaps the installation of a cleruchy in Salamis in the last decade of the sixth century, war with Chalcis leading to the seizure of the lands of the aristocratic Hippobotae in around 506 BC and the settlement of 4,000 or 2,000 Athenians (if the event is not to be dated 60 years later), and the seizure of the border

[23] Herodotus 5.82–9 (Aegina); Plutarch, *Sol.* 8–10 cf. Aristotle, *Ath. pol.* 14.1; *IG* I³ 1, but cf. Graham (1964), 168 n. 6 (Salamis); Herodotus 5.94–5; Strabo 599–600; Alcaeus frag. H 28; X (7) 15–20; Z 105 (b) Lobel and Page (Sigeum, Thracian Chersonese); Herodotus 5.77.2 cf. 6.100.2 (Chalcis); *RE* s.v. 'Oropus' 1153; Herodotus 6.137–40 cf. *IG* I² 948 (Lemnos; ?Imbros); Berve (1937), 33–4 (Phrynon); Frost (1984), 288.

territory of Boeotian Oropus and Eleutherae at about this time, if not earlier in the time of the tyrant Peisistratus.

Other events took place further afield. Sigeum on the south side of the entry to the Hellespont received Athenian settlers at the turn of the seventh century under Phrynon, and was subsequently lost and retaken by Peisistratus more than half a century later. An Athenian presence was established on the other side of the Hellespont in the Thracian Chersonese by the elder Miltiades in the mid-sixth century. The island of Lemnos, first port of call south of the Hellespont, was taken at the expense of the Pelasgians, perhaps at the beginning of the fifth century under the younger Miltiades, the future victor at Marathon. Imbros perhaps fell to Athens in the same period.

Some of this activity, notably the wars with Aegina and Megara, is reducible to the tug-of-war between neighbouring city states that was a regular feature of international relations in Greece. The activities in the north smack of adventurism, and official involvement or even interest cannot always be assumed. Phrynon is a shadowy figure. Peisistratus is said to have established his own son Hegesistratus as tyrant at Sigeum, but his motives and those of Phrynon are obscure. It is an unlikely construction that they were influenced by the 'pressure of population'. Similarly, there is no need to speak of an official effort 'to favour Athenian trade' or of 'Athens' interest in imported corn'. No source links Sigeum with Athenian interests in the Black Sea, and the town was in any case poorly placed to forward such interests. The Athenians who established themselves in the Chersonese under Miltiades, also under the tyranny of Peisistratus, were no better placed to control Hellespontine commerce, though sporadic piratical raids on shipping can be envisaged. In the account of Herodotus, Miltiades was not the founder of an official Athenian colony in the Chersonese. Rather, he was the choice of the local Thracian tribe, the Dolonci, as their leader against the neighbouring Apsinthii. Miltiades was a rival of Peisistratus and the latter was glad to be rid of him.[24]

The acquisition of Lemnos by the younger Miltiades was brought up by his friends as a point in his favour during his trial in Athens in 489 BC. His abortive attack on Paros, not, incidentally, a station on the so-called 'northern trade route', is characterised frankly by Herodotus as opportunistic fortune-seeking. The Lemnos expedition might also have been private enterprise. This explanation is not incompatible with Herodotus' story, which reads like *ex post facto* official apologia, that

[24] For Miltiades as independent, see Berve (1937); Graham (1964), 32ff. Allowance might have to be made for Herodotus' use of sources biased towards Miltiades and his family, the Philaids. See Hart (1982), 16–24.

Lemnos was captured as an act of vengeance on the Pelasgians for crimes committed earlier against the Athenians. Despite Herodotus' silence on the matter, Miltiades was doubtless aware that Lemnos was strategically important, relatively fertile and had good port facilities. But we should be wary of attributing to him or to Athenians in general motives and intuitions which they may well have possessed two decades later.

The punishment of Euboean Chalcis around 506 BC was severe by the usual standards of neighbourly warfare, but the Athenians had recently defended themselves against an unusual coalition of enemies. This was an act of revenge on Chalcis for its part in the invasion of Attica by Cleomenes I of Sparta and his Boeotian, Megarian and Euboean allies. It is unnecessary to claim that the purpose of the move was the siphoning off of excess population from Athens and Attica. Some settlement of conquered land, short-lived in this case, was inevitable. It shows that Athens had reserves of manpower, not that she was overpopulated. The further suggestion that the Athenians already had in mind the strategic position of Chalcis on the 'route to the north' is quite gratuitous.

CONCLUSION

Fifth-century Greeks knew the Athenians as singularly energetic, adventurous and interfering. It is not difficult to detect the emergence of these qualities in the late archaic period. The tempo quickens from the last years of the sixth century, a key event being the traumatic experience of the Spartan-led invasion of Attica. Victory in this year, coinciding with the political reforms and the organisation of a citizen army associated with the name of Cleisthenes, gave Athenians an injection of aggressive self-confidence. This manifested itself in the occupation of part of the territory of Chalcis, the seizure of Boeotian Oropus, and the swashbuckling adventurism of men like Miltiades that secured Lemnos and Imbros for Athens. These actions do suggest greater land greed on the part of the Athenians, but not necessarily domestic overpopulation. Between this period of transition and the foundation of the 'Delian League' under Athenian control stood the morale-boosting repulse of two Persian invasions and the tenfold expansion of the navy. The springtime of Athenian imperialism had arrived. But the first direct literary evidence for regular Athenian grain imports comes considerably later. So does the explosion of population which made this necessary. Athenian imperialism became a response to food supply problems only in the mid-fifth century.

8

RULERS OF THE SEA

CONTROL AND INTERFERENCE

As head of the 'Delian League' from its foundation in 478/7 BC, Athens
was in a position to monitor and control the long-distance movement of
grain. The destruction of the Persian fleet at the battle of Eurymedon
(?469 BC) left the Athenians without a serious rival in the Aegean sea,
and their supremacy was thereafter not in doubt until the Sicilian
débâcle of 413 BC. The career of the Athenian navy was not un-
chequered. In particular, something in the region of 200–250 ships were
lost in Egypt in 454 BC. But no state or combination of states took the
opportunity to mount a serious challenge to the Athenians. Again, the
Athenians were never in a position to control all the major sea-routes.
However, for geographical reasons it was relatively easy to monitor the
route from the Black Sea, most of the grain imported into Old Greece
came this way, and Athenian authority remained more or less unchallenged in this area throughout the period.

It does not follow from the apparent fact that the Athenians
controlled this or that grain-route that they actually exploited their
position of power at the expense of other states. It is appropriate to
begin by addressing this concrete issue in relation to the Hellespont.
Did the Athenians detain at Byzantium ships heading for the ports of
other states, and did they actively steer grain ships toward the Piraeus?

The 'Old Oligarch', an anonymous critic of Athenian democracy of
the third quarter of the fifth century, expresses a view only on the issue
of Athenian interventionism at the expense of other states.[1] His
message appears to be that the Athenians were actively interventionist,
to the extent that only cities subject to Athens were allowed freedom to
trade:

Of the Athenians' subject cities on the mainland, some which are large are ruled
because of fear, and some which are small are ruled because of actual need. For

---

[1] Ps.-Xenophon (Old Oligarch), *Ath. pol.* 2.2–3.

there is no city which does not have to import or export, and these activities will be impossible for a city unless it is subject to the rulers of the sea.

If this should turn out to be an exaggeration, it would not be the only one of which this eccentric pamphleteer is guilty. On the other hand, the passage which it follows, on the ineffectiveness of rebellion among island polities, is unimpeachable, as the fates of Samos and Lesbos in 440/39 and 428/7 testify:

Subject peoples on land can combine small cities and fight collectively, but subject peoples at sea, by virtue of being islands, cannot join their cities together into the same unit. For the sea is in the way, and those now in power are thalassocrats. If it is possible for islanders to combine unnoticed on a single island, they will die of starvation.

The Athenians could reduce rebels by blockade. It can also be accepted (though doubt has been expressed) that the sanctions imposed on Megara by the so-called Megarian decree banning Megarians from the Athenian Agora and from the harbours of the empire really did bite, despite the difficulties of enforcement.[2] What is not known is how regularly the Athenians put into operation the much simpler procedure of holding up at Byzantium grain destined for particular cities. The Mytilenaeans were anxious about just such a cargo in 428 BC, and against their will and better judgement initiated their revolt before its arrival. As Thucydides reports:

Straight after the invasion of the Peloponnesians, all Lesbos except Methymna revolted from Athens. The Lesbians wished to do this even before the war, but the Lacedaemonians had not taken them into their alliance, and even now they were forced to revolt sooner than they had intended. For they were waiting until the work should be finished of blocking their harbours, building walls and constructing ships, and until the arrival of what they needed from the Pontus – archers and grain and whatever else they were sending for.[3]

The war with the Spartans and their allies was in full swing. But the blocking of the Hellespont was surely a regular part of Athenian procedure in dealing with a rebellious ally. However, an inscription dating from 426/5 BC might contain a reference to special wartime procedures at the Hellespont:

Resolved by the Boule and the Ekklesia, Hippothontis held the prytany, Megakleides was Secretary, Niko— presided, Kleonumos made the motion. The Methonaeans shall be permitted to import from Byzantium up to the amount of ...

[2] Legon (1981), 213–17, against De Ste Croix (1972).
[3] Thucydides 3.2.

thousand medimnoi each year. The Wardens of the Hellespont shall not themselves prevent them from exporting it or allow anyone else to prevent them, and
if they do, they are to be liable to a fine of 10,000 drachmas each. After giving
notice to the Wardens of the Hellespont, they shall export up to the permitted
amount. There shall also be exemption from payment for the ship carrying
it.[4]

A parallel concession was given to Aphytis, a city situated just south of
Potidaea on the western-most finger of Chalcidice, and at about the same
period. Aphytis was permitted to import up to 10,000 medimnoi of grain
from Byzantium at a price equal to that paid by the people of Methone.[5]

Methone on the western coast of the Thermaic gulf was a relatively
new ally or subject of Athens, having joined the League perhaps as
recently as 432/1. It was a particularly valuable catch. Athens now had
an enclave in Macedonian territory. Athenian relations with the
Macedonian king Perdiccas were never stable, and the alliance with
Methone was an additional unsettling factor.

Methone was valuable, but also needed protection. In 430 BC Athens
had sent envoys to inform the king,

that justice required him to allow the people of Methone free use of the sea and that
he should not restrict them, but allow them to carry on their normal trade with the
interior. He should neither harm them nor be harmed by them and he should not
lead a military force through their territory against their will.

At about the same time the Athenians passed a decree exempting
Methone from tribute payments except for the quota to Athena.[6]

In granting similar privileges to Aphytis, the Athenians were recognising the strategic and administrative importance of this city. But
in addition the Athenians betray concern over the loyalty of the city in
exacting an oath to Athens and to her colonists in Potidaea, settled in
about 429 after a long and expensive revolt. The Athenian purpose may
have been to reconcile Aphytis to the establishment of a new colony
that perhaps ate into her territory.

These inscriptions show much more thoroughgoing interference with
the grain traffic than is implied by the passage of Thucydides on
Mytilene. It was one thing to cut off the flow of grain to hostile states,
and quite another to set limits on the grain imports of a privileged ally.
Unfortunately we do not know for how long Wardens of the Hellespont
(*Hellespontophulakes*) had been installed or the nature of their peacetime

---

[4] *IG* i³ 61, 32–41.
[5] *IG* i³ 62. See Meritt, *Hesperia* 13 (1944), 211–29, citing Thucydides 1.64.2 (432 BC) for the role of Aphytis.
[6] *IG* i³ 61, 5–7, 16–23.

duties. It is perfectly possible that their regular activity consisted of the exaction of customs dues on grain (dues from which Methone was specifically exempted) and on everything else that flowed through the Hellespont in either direction.[7] There may not have been any necessity to interfere with grain shipments, beyond detaining those heading for rebel cities. It is compatible with this interpretation that there was no wholesale intervention before the outbreak of the Peloponnesian War, and before the Spartan pre-harvest invasions of Attica raised new anxieties about the food supply of Athens itself.

GRAIN FOR ATHENS

How many consumers were there in fifth-century Attica?[8] For my purpose very rough orders of magnitude are sufficient. A population which by the middle decades of the century had passed the 200,000 mark (citizens and their families, metics and slaves), and may have topped 250,000 by the outbreak of the Peloponnesian War, had far outrun the resources of Attica and its dependencies. Regular bulk imports of grain were needed.

The first explicit reference in the sources to regular grain imports belongs to the period of the Peloponnesian War. In Thucydides' *History*, Nicias is made to say the following, in a speech assigned to 415 opposing the Sicilian expedition:

They have wealth too partly in private possession and partly in the temples of Selinus; and to the Syracusans tribute has come in from time immemorial from certain barbarians also; their chief advantage over us, however, is in the fact that they have many horses and use grain that is home-grown and not imported.[9]

Fourth-century sources are not short of such references. The absence of comparable texts datable to or even referring to the period between the Persian and Peloponnesian Wars is striking, though not altogether surprising, given that oratorical evidence comparable to that available for the fourth century is lacking. The 'Old Oligarch', whose treatise may date to the 420s (or belong at earliest to the late 440s), excludes himself by failing to mention anywhere the food needs of Athens itself. Xerxes, according to Herodotus, saw Pontic grain ships when he arrived at the Hellespont in 481 BC, but they were heading for Aegina and the Peloponnese. In the same year, if we can believe Herodotus, the

[7] Cf. Meiggs and Lewis 58 = Fornara 119.
[8] The main discussions are by Beloch (1886), (1923), Gomme (1933) and Patterson (1981). Also Hansen (1986) and (1982 publ. 1985). Travlos (1960) estimates the population of the city at 36,000, but the proportion of city to country dwellers is unknown.
[9] Thucydides 6.20.4.

Syracusan tyrant Gelon made an offer 'to provide grain for the whole Greek army till we have made an end of the war', but the passage makes no specific mention of Attica. Thucydides has nothing about grain imports to Athens in a pre-Peloponnesian War context. The most that can be said is that dependence on imports is implied in Pericles' advice to the Athenians that they should become as it were islanders: 'We must abandon the land and our houses.'[10]

The most promising literary text for our purposes comes from a speech of Isocrates of about 393 BC, and refers to Athens' special relationship with a king of the Bosporus, Satyrus, who reigned from 433/2 (or a little later) to 393/2 (or again a little later).

It is right also that you keep in mind both Satyrus and my father, who have always esteemed you above all the other Greeks, and frequently in the past, when there was a scarcity of grain and they were sending away empty the ships of other merchants, granted you the right of export.[11]

An Athenian decree of 346 BC in honour of later Bosporan rulers refers to the favoured treatment accorded Athens by the same Satyrus:

The People of Athens praises Spartacus and Pairisades because they are good men and promise the People of Athens to see to the export of wheat as their father did, and say that they are ready to furnish the People with whatever they need. The envoys are to be asked to report to them that in these conditions they will suffer no disappointment from the Athenians; and since they award the Athenians the privileges that Satyrus and Leucon had accorded them, the People is to grant Spartacus and Pairisades the privileges which it granted to Satyrus and Leucon and to crown each of them at the Great Panathenaia with a crown of gold worth 1,000 drachmas.[12]

At most these texts push back the establishment of favoured status for Athens, and an implied regular import of grain from the Bosporan kingdom, to the beginning of the Peloponnesian War or just before. There is, on the other hand, no sign of fifth-century precursors of the grain laws and officials that are familiar from the fourth-century evidence. There is not even any guarantee that the food supply was debated in the Athenian assembly every prytany in the fifth century as it was in the 330s.[13]

Foreign grain might have come into Attica irregularly, in the context of food shortage. The evidence for food shortage is thin and problematic. Prior to the Peloponnesian War there are only two allusions that

---

[10] Thucydides 1.143.5; Herodotus 7.147, 158.
[11] Isocrates 17.57. On the Bosporan kingdom, see Gajdukevic (1971).
[12] *Syll.*[3] 206 = Harding 82.
[13] Aristotle, *Ath. pol.* 43.4.

might be relevant. One is fragmentary and conveys little information. It consists of a few words from a decree of perhaps 450/49 referring to a grain shortage.[14] The other reference, to an event of 445/4, is distinctly problematic. Psammetichus, who is called either 'king of the Egyptians' or 'king of Libya', gave 30,000 medimnoi of grain to the Athenians. So says Philochorus, an Atthidographer who flourished in the early third century BC and a reliable source, cited three times by a scholiast on Aristophanes' *Wasps*; Plutarch in his *Life of Pericles* gives the higher figure of 40,000 medimnoi.[15] In *Wasps*, Bdelycleon attacks the untrustworthiness of the political leadership with reference to recent trouble in Euboea and a handout of grain (apparently in 424/3 BC):

But when they have something to be afraid of, they offer you Euboea and undertake to provide wheat at fifty medimnoi a head. They have never yet given you the fifty, only five, and made even that hard to get by accusing you of being a foreigner and handing it out a choinix at a time – and then it turned out to be barley.

The best of the Scholia is the Venetus, which has the following three paragraphs:

This is because at the grain distributions a severe examination was carried out to establish who were the genuine citizens, with the result that people were brought to court on charges of making illegitimate claims to citizenship. So Philochorus says that 4,760 were discovered to have been improperly entered on the registers ... just as has been shown in the text. The reference to Euboea agrees with the Didascaliai [on the date of the play], for the previous year in the archonship of Isarchus they sent an expedition against the island, according to Philochorus. Perhaps he is referring to the gift from Egypt, which Philochorus says Psammetichus sent to the people in the archonship of Lysimachides, 30,000 medimnoi – though the numbers do not agree – and five medimnoi for each citizen. For he says that those who received the grain numbered 14,240.

When there was a shortage of grain in Attica, Psammetichus, king of Libya, sent grain to the Athenians at their request. When the distribution of grain occurred, the Athenians got rid of foreigners, and in separating out the genuine citizens they discovered that foreigners had been put onto the registers. So he says that in the enquiry (Philocleon) himself, because he was accused of being a foreigner, got his

[14] *IG* I³ 30.
[15] Plutarch, *Per.* 37; Aristophanes, *Wasps* 718, ed. Koster and Helwerda, *Scholia in Aristophanes, ad loc.* = Philochorus, *FGrH* 328 no. 90. I am grateful to Dr S. Halliwell and Professor E. Handley for their advice in interpreting the Scholia. On the episode, see Gernet (1909), 16–17; Gomme (1933), 16–17; Labarbe (1961). On the expedition to Euboea, Mattingly (1961); Nenci (1964).

five medimnoi with difficulty, and these not all at one go, but one choinix at a time. He says 'of barley', because there is no difference between grain and barley.

The point is that there was a food shortage, and foreigners were separated off (that is, officially examined) to see whether they were citizens or not.

Plutarch has a briefer version:

And so, when the king of Egypt sent a present to the people of 40,000 medimnoi of wheat, and this had to be divided up among the citizens, there was a great crop of prosecutions against citizens of illegal birth by the law of Pericles, who had up to that time escaped notice and been overlooked, and many of them also suffered at the hands of the informers. As a result, a little less than 5,000 were convicted and sold into slavery, and those who retained their citizenship and were adjudged to be Athenians were found as a result of this scrutiny to be 14,040 in number.

The precise details of the episode are irretrievably lost. It is not even certain that there was a grain crisis. There is no notice to this effect in Plutarch or in the first and best note in Venetus (which leans on Philochorus). The much inferior and briefer second note begins 'A food shortage having arisen in Athens', and this is picked up by the composer of the third note, who begins his miserable one-line summary with 'A famine having arisen'. Can we be sure that the inventiveness of a historicising scholiast does not lie at the bottom of this?

This is not the end of the matter. Some would say, invention or no, there must have been a food crisis.[16] I prefer to say there could have been a food crisis.

Meiggs in his basic work on the Athenian Empire presents (but does not juxtapose) two versions of the episode, without making it clear whether he thinks they are genuine alternatives or merely represent different points of view, Athenian and Egyptian.[17] It matters little: what Meiggs gives us is the raw material for two different scenarios. According to the first, there was a grain crisis to which Psammetichus responded: the 'large gift of corn', says Meiggs, 'seems to have been badly needed'. According to the second, compatible with but by no means entailing the first, the donor is identified as a son and brother of anti-Persian rebel leaders, who, says Meiggs, 'may have thought of reviving his father's cause', and acted in the traditional way by approaching the greatest naval power in the Aegean. A note in Plutarch implies that not long before the Peloponnesian War there were some Athenians who wanted to make another attempt on Egypt.

[16] Labarbe (1961), 203.
[17] Meiggs (1972), 95, 268.

If there was a food crisis, we have to believe it was not serious, or, against the silence of the sources, that the gift from Egypt only went part of the way toward resolving it. Thirty thousand medimnoi of wheat would not in itself have alleviated a grave shortage. More than a century later, in perhaps 328 BC, Athens received five times as much wheat from Cyrene, and for a considerably smaller citizen population. Psammetichus' gift would have fed around 24,000 people, perhaps 10% of the population, for three months (at 5 medimnoi per head). There remains however the third possibility, that there was no crisis to which Psammetichus was responding.

Two general points are clear. First, in and by themselves references to food shortage do not establish Athens as a regular importer of grain. Psammetichus' convoy of grain, whatever the context, has the hall-marks of a one-off gift. Secondly, food shortages very rarely show up in the record of the inter-war period.

Does it follow that Athens was more or less immune from food crisis? There are many gaps in the sources. There is no explicit reference to regular Athenian grain imports, no sign of laws or institu-tions to control the grain trade, no evidence for interference with Black Sea shipping, and finally, little sign of food shortage or of measures to secure emergency grain stocks. Of these four lacunae, only the last is not puzzling. It is quite certain that Athens in the fifth century was a regular importer of grain on a large scale. It is almost as obvious that Athens did not tolerate a free market in grain in all circumstances, and from time to time took steps to divert grain ships away from hostile ports and toward the Piraeus. Again, officials with special responsi-bility for the grain trade must have existed in the fifth century, even if in smaller numbers than in Aristotle's day. On the other hand, it would be surprising if the dominant sea power in the Aegean had been unable to enjoy more or less uninterrupted abundance of food supplies.

There is however another kind of evidence still to be considered which might put a different complexion on things: Athenian imperial-istic activity in the inter-war period. It might be proposed that overpopulation and a search for essential food supplies lie behind the expedition to Egypt in the 450s, the alliances made with three Greek cities in the West (Egesta, Rhegium and Leontini) from 457 to the late 430s, and the colonies and cleruchies which can be dated for the most part in this period. All this frenetic activity, it might be suggested, shows that Athens' food supply remained problematic even when the Empire was in its prime.

OVERPOPULATION, COLONISATION AND THE QUEST FOR GRAIN

I begin with the account of Meiggs. First, on Egypt:

Thucydides once again gives us a bare record of events and does not explain the reasons for the intervention in Egypt. No other reason may be needed than the hope of further crippling Persia, but it is probable that economic factors also appealed to Athens and her allies. By the time of the Peloponnesian War Athens seems to have depended on the Euxine for her corn supplies, but it is doubtful whether the Euxine alone could have provided adequate supplies for Athens before Pericles' expedition in the thirties. It is perhaps significant that when in 445-4 Psammetichus, an Egyptian 'King', sent a large gift of corn from Egypt to Athens, it seems to have been badly needed. The prospect of Egyptian corn may have influenced policy; more generally, an independent Egypt from which Phoenician trade could be virtually excluded would be a richer market for the Aegean Greeks than a Persian province. The Ionians will have remembered the wealth that they drew from Egypt in the sixth century; the Egyptian enterprise was probably popular with the League so long as it seemed likely to succeed.

This passage runs against the tenor of Meiggs' narrative. A little earlier we were told that, as one can read in Thucydides, the League force of 200 ships was sent to Cyprus and not to Egypt (probably in 460 or 459), and that the expedition was diverted to Egypt in response to an appeal from the initially victorious rebel king Inarus; and, furthermore, that the 'vigorous offensive' in the eastern Mediterranean 'need be no more than a logical sequel, delayed by the revolt of Thasos, to the victory of the Eurymedon'.[18]

In fact, the Athenians and their allies were indulging in 'profitable aggression' at the expense of the Persians.[19] This was a policy which could not hope to achieve permanent results, as was confirmed by the later expedition to Cyprus of 450 from which a detachment was sent to Egypt. The economic value of Egypt was certainly appreciated by all Greeks, but it is gratuitous to reduce this to Athens' grain needs and to promote it as a major motive of the whole expedition. In taking up this stance, Meiggs was influenced by the conviction that the northern sources of supply were regularly inadequate until Pericles sailed into the Euxine some time in the 430s. Pericles' expedition does catch the eye, as the only known occasion when Athens took a fleet beyond Byzantium. But it is implausible to suggest that the grain flowed freely only after this event. The grain gift of Psammetichus certainly does not justify this inference.

It would be equally implausible to suggest that Sicily was looked to

---

[18] Meiggs (1972), 93–5.
[19] De Ste Croix (1972), 312; cf. Salmon (1965), 129–33, with bibliographical survey.

as a major supplier of Athens either in the 450s prior to the Egyptian disaster of 454 (apparently the date of the alliance with Egesta), or in the decades that follow. Meiggs is rightly cautious, influenced by a clear statement of Thucydides under 427 BC. Athens in that year sent an expedition to Sicily consisting of 20 ships and two years later a reinforcement of 40 ships. Thucydides states the aims as twofold: to stop grain coming from those parts to the Peloponnese, and to explore the chances of bringing Sicily under Athenian control. Athens did not need Sicilian grain as long as existing sources of supply were maintained.[20]

The settling of citizens abroad in colonies and cleruchies was a characteristic feature of Athenian imperialism in the 440s and 430s above all. Is this to be seen as a solution to overpopulation at home and the inability of the Athenians to provide basic supplies for the residents of the city and of Attica? Meiggs thought that supplies from the Black Sea were inadequate until Pericles' expedition of perhaps the mid-430s, one aspect of which was the establishment of Athenian settlers in several Greek cities on the southern Black Sea coast. But this seems to be merely an inference from Athenian interest in Egypt and the evidence (which was seen to be scanty) for food shortages in Athens. If Meiggs is right, then we have to accept that earlier settlements abroad either were not intended to meet the domestic food supply problem or had failed in this purpose. In fact, the drift of Meiggs' discussion of the settlements of the 440s is that their end was primarily strategic. They were intended to restore Athenian authority in areas where it had been challenged during the movement of revolt which in his view swept the empire after the Peace of Callias (450/49). There is a later parallel in the garrisoning of Potidaea and Lesbos through cleruchs in 429 and 427 after heavy losses from plague and warfare.[21]

In the case of the major Athenian-sponsored settlements at Thurii in Italy in 443 and Amphipolis in the north Aegean in 437, there is

[20] Thucydides 3.86.4, 115.3–5. See Meiggs (1972), 101 cf. De Ste Croix (1972), 220–4, 379; Westlake (1969), Ch. 6. Contrast Green (1970), Ch. 2. See Sophocles in Pliny, *Hist. nat.* 18.65, for the first reference to Italian grain (but no import trade is implied). The Hermippus fragment 63 of *c.* 427 BC is about imports into Athens, but 'Italian' (referring to *chondros*) is an error for 'Thessalian'.

[21] M. H. Hansen, in an unpublished paper 'Athenian losses 431–403', which he kindly made available to me, calculates that plague in 430/29 and 429/8 (also 427/6) caused the death of some 14,000 adult male Athenians. A further 430 fell at Spartolos in 429/8 and an unknown number at Potidaea in 432–429. For cleruchies and colonies, see Meiggs (1972), 121–3 cf. 157–60; 178–81, 185, 195ff., 197–8. Also Brunt (1966a), cf. Jones (1957), 167–77 (cleruchs stayed at home); contrast Gauthier (1966) and (1973). The motive for the Brea colony, notable for the amendment stipulating that the colonists should come from the two lowest census groups, is usually regarded as strategic. See *IG* I³ 46 = Fornara 100 (450–430, perhaps 446/5).

additional reason for concluding that an explanation in terms of response to overpopulation is irrelevant. Athenians constituted a small minority of those who went out. Meiggs finds it doubtful 'whether Pericles was thinking primarily in economic terms', and conjectures in relation to the colony at Thurii that the 'main concern' was 'to raise the prestige and general influence of Athens in the West'.

It was noted by Brunt that Athenians were sent to places lying 'on the vital corn-route from the Crimea', but this does not account for all the colonising activity of the 440s, and is in any case reconcilable with Meiggs' picture of an Athenian effort to reassert their authority throughout their sphere of influence.

The finding that Athenians were always alive to their strategic interests is not very remarkable, and is quite different (as Brunt acknowledges) from the claim that the Athenians were interested in running down their domestic population because of a chronic deficiency of essential foodstuffs and a permanent incapacity to make up the deficiency with imports. Gauthier's demonstration that many of the settlements abroad had the character of garrisons, most obviously the cleruchies established after the expulsion of entire populations or population segments, reinforces the case against the primacy of demographic or economic considerations. In passing, it should be noted that the view that cleruchs characteristically stayed at home instead of residing on the properties assigned to them is hard to reconcile with the overpopulation thesis.

An explanation of Athenian settlements abroad in terms of overpopulation and a more or less permanent crisis in the domestic food supply is far too simple. Most obviously, it fails to explain the limited participation of Athenians in the colonial enterprises at Thurii and Amphipolis when manpower was in theory abundant, and conversely their whole-hearted commitment to the garrisoning of Lesbos when their numbers were depleted. More generally, it misses the point that the settlement of territory was a regular tactic of imperial states. It was employed even by Sparta, notably at Heraclea Trachinia in 426 BC. The Spartans, notoriously, were short of manpower (and took *perioikoi*, non-citizens, as colonists on this occasion), not arable land.[22]

Athens, as an imperial power in its prime, was well able to plant a proportion of its citizen body in alien territory. This would not have been possible had not Athens built up substantial resources of manpower. Athenian manpower, however, is not to be regarded as a burden on the state, as constituting a mass of consumers who had somehow to be fed. It was an asset to be deployed, militarily in regular and

[22] Thucydides 3.92–3; Diodorus 12.59.3–5; Andrewes (1978).

sometimes multiple wars against enemies or rebels, as in the 450s, and strategically as settlers or garrisons on conquered land or land whose location or natural resources attracted the interests of a power with vital needs in food, timber and metals.

There are two further considerations, the absence of either taxes in kind or regular food distributions.

First, Athens, unlike Rome, did not impose a regular grain tax on allies. At most the Athenians may have allowed or required some states to pay a part or the whole of their annual tribute in some years in the form of supplies for the Athenian navy. The contribution of First Fruits for the Goddesses of Eleusis by the various regions of Attica, Athens' dependants and allies, was not a substitute for a grain tax. It amounted to a mere 1/600 of the barley crop and 1/1200 of the wheat crop, and may have been instituted no earlier than the 430s.[23]

Secondly, as far as we know, grain was handed out to Athenian citizens only in 445/4 (the gift of Psammetichus), 424/3 (a wartime crisis), and in 405/4 (the final crisis of the war). The Athenian practice was to give to ordinary citizens not grain, but money to buy grain, whether in the form of payment for office, jury service, attendance at the assembly, service in the fleet, the *diobelia* (two-obol payment), or the *theorikon* (festival ticket money). The handout of 405/4 broke a sequence of *diobelia* payments. Even as the war drew toward its close, money was still available to be distributed – and grain to be bought.[24]

The implication is that fifth-century Athens experienced no standing food supply problem. The Athenians could cope on the basis of their own territorial resources and those of their closest dependants, the appeal to traders of their market and their silver, and, in the last resort, their ability to commandeer supplies and steer them toward the Piraeus.

CONCLUSION

Domestic production remained vital in the interwar period, supplemented by contributions from the permanent dependencies. But existing grain resources had increasingly to be supplemented by new channels of supply. The capture of Sestos from the Persians and the expulsion of the Spartan admiral Pausanias gave the Athenians control over the route from the north. This became an important source of grain, especially as Athenians grew to appreciate the soft bread wheat,

---

[25] *IG* i³ 78 = Fornara 140. For an irregular grain-tax in 374/3 BC, see Shear (1987).
[24] See pp. 80, 125 above, for references.

triticum aestivum or *vulgare*, grown in south Russia.[25] However, a considerable amount of grain could have come from the Aegean islands and mainland. In 329/8 Lemnos, another producer of bread wheat, and Imbros between them appear to have produced almost four times as much wheat as the whole of Attica, that is, over 100,000 medimnoi, or more than four million kg of wheat. Athens was the obvious place to dispose of surplus grain.[26]

As mentioned above, changing tastes may have played some part in encouraging imports, as wealthy Athenians and urban residents as a whole developed a preference for wheaten bread. Attica was unable to produce sufficient wheat to feed more than a fraction of the resident population. But population growth provided the main incentive for the import of grain.

To some extent the Athenians spread the burden of feeding their population by securing supplies for the military and naval forces from allied or friendly states in the theatre of operations, and by sending citizens to reside abroad where they could live off local resources. Such strategies eased the pressure at home, but are not to be accounted for only or primarily with reference to economic motives. Similarly, Athenian imperialism as a general phenomenon is not reducible to the provision of Athenians with necessities.[27]

Under normal conditions, the Athenians are unlikely to have had to go in search of grain. There was no need to intercept shipments of grain intended for other states, nor to force subjects to pay tribute in the form of foodstuffs. The people received their share of the revenues of empire in the form of cash, not grain. Athens was attractive to traders: it could offer a huge and relatively stable market, a valuable return cargo of silver and a secure passage. Food supply was occasionally but never regularly a problem.

The outbreak of the Peloponnesian War was a crucial turning-point. Thereafter the Athenians were not in total control of their own territory.[28] They became more heavily dependent on imports, and also had to take active steps to secure them, probably for the first time. In the years following 431, the Athenians tightened their hold on the Hellespont. They actively intervened to deny grain from this route to

---

[25] For 'Russian' bread wheat, see Janushevich and Nikolaenko (1979), 115–34; Janushevich (1981), 87–96; Van Zeist and Casparie (1984), 267–76, 277–83.

[26] *IG* ii/iii² 1672, 253ff. For wheat from Lemnos cf. Theophrastus; *Hist. plant.* 8.4.4–5; *Caus. plant.* 4.9.6. For the extraordinary grain-tax of 374/3 BC, see Shear (1987).

[27] Nesselhauf (1933), 63 against primacy of economic motives; also Romilly (1963), 71–4, and much earlier, Gernet (1909), e.g. 382.

[28] Note the projected raid on Piraeus in 429 BC, in Thucydides 2.93–4. Hanson (1983) plays down the extent of the dislocation of Attic agriculture.

enemies and to secure it for friends, and presumably for themselves. No document earlier than the first decade of the war refers to the Wardens of the Hellespont. The Athenians also put increased pressure on their subjects in this period. It is not impossible (evidence is lacking) that they now began encouraging allied states to sell grain to Athens over and above their First Fruits contributions. In particular, the Athenians leaned on Euboea, treating the island as virtually an extension of Attica and the first place from which to exact supplies when food was short (as apparently it was in 424/3).[29] When Euboea rebelled and left the alliance in 411, Athens was thrust back increasingly onto long-distance suppliers. Once Lysander had seized the Hellespont in the late summer of 405, Athens was doomed.

[29] Westlake (1948), referring to Thucydides 7.28, 7.98, 95.2, 96.2; and see above, p. 125, in connection with Psammetichus.

9

VULNERABILITY AND VIGILANCE

Democracy was unexpectedly restored in Athens in 403/2 by the Spartans and more predictably abolished by the Macedonians 81 years later. After a period of subservience to Sparta, Athens staged a revival dating from the battle of Cnidos in 394, which was followed up by the recovery of the islands of Lemnos, Imbros and Skyros in 392, and the capture of Byzantium and imposition of a 10% toll on all transit goods in 390. The revival had run its course by 388/7 (though the three islands remained Athenian possessions). The Spartans had retained their footholds in the Hellespont at Abydos and Sestos. Now they reasserted their authority by closing the Hellespont (while 'pirates' raided the Piraeus) and imposing peace on the Greek world with the aid of the Persian King (387/6). A second and more lasting Athenian resurgence was soon in progress. Profiting from the unpopularity of Sparta, the Athenians were already by the late 380s beginning to strike alliances with important states (Chios was an ally by 384), and in the summer of 378 formed the Second Athenian League. By 373 there were about 60 member states.[1] Athens was arguably once again the strongest naval power.

The League had ceased to function as an instrument of power-politics by the mid-350s, when Athens was defeated by her allies in the Social War (357–355 BC). However 338, the date of the Macedonian victory at Chaeronea, was an even more crucial turning-point in the history of Athens. Before Chaeronea the Athenians were competing with other mainland states and latterly the emerging power of Macedon for influence and prestige in the Greek world. After Chaeronea empire-building by Athenians and other Greeks was at an end. This chapter assesses the efficiency of the Athenian food supply system down to Chaeronea against the background of the changing fortunes of Athens in the international arena.

[1] Tod II 123, to be read in Cargill (1981), 14–47.

THE NECESSITY OF GRAIN IMPORTS

The fourth-century sources, unlike those for the fifth, are full of explicit references to the importance of grain imports to Athens.[2] Demosthenes twice claims that the Athenians were the major grain-importing Greek state, once in the speech *Against Leptines* composed in 355 and once in 330 in the speech *On the Crown*, where the following is stated:

When Philip was driven out of Euboea by your arms and also ... by my policy and my decrees, he cast about for a second plan of attack against Athens; and observing that we consume more imported grain than any other nation, he proposed to get control of the carrying trade in grain. He advanced toward Thrace and the first thing he did was to claim the help of the Byzantines as his allies in the war against you.

The words attributed by Xenophon to Jason of Pherae and allegedly delivered by his fellow Thessalian Polydamas to the Spartans were written in the mid-fourth century, though their dramatic date is 375:

And who are likely to be better able to maintain the sailors, we who on account of our abundance even have grain to export to other lands, or the Athenians, who have not even enough for themselves unless they buy it?

To these texts may be added three more that are equally familiar. Xenophon stipulates that a political orator must base his speeches on the knowledge of, among other things:

how long the grain grown in the country will maintain the population, and how much is needed annually, so that you may not be caught napping should the city at any time be short, and may come to the rescue and relieve the city by giving expert advice about food.

In a parallel passage from the *Rhetorica* attributed to Aristotle, the key subjects on which orators were expected to speak persuasively are listed as ways and means, war and peace, the defence of the country, imports and exports and legislation. A little later the same author shows that imports and exports are reducible to food, on which subject an orator must base his speeches on knowledge of the following:

what amount of expenditure is sufficient to support the state; what kind of food is produced at home or can be imported; and what exports and imports are necessary in order that contracts and agreements may be made with those who can furnish them.

---

[2] Demosthenes 20.31–2; cf. 18.87; Xenophon, *Hell.* 6.1.11; *Mem.* 3.6.13 cf. Ps.-Aristotle, *Rhet.* 1.4.7,11.

The message of the sources is that the Athenians were permanently in need of imported grain. It remains to investigate with the aid of demographic evidence whether it is possible to stipulate more precisely the requirements of the Athenians.

Calculating the population of Attica is just as hazardous a business for the fourth as for the fifth century. It is worth stressing that the only direct evidence for the numbers of citizens, metics and slaves (21,000, 10,000, 400,000 respectively) is provided by a census taken by Demetrius of Phaleron at some time between 317 and 307. It was taken therefore after the Lamian war, the occupation of Athens, the suppression of the democracy, the voluntary and enforced migration of citizens and, on the other hand, the return to Athens of the cleruchs on Samos, and the fluctuations in the numbers of metics and slaves that certainly occurred in consequence of these events. The source is a fragment of a historical work by Ctesicles (about whom almost nothing is known) preserved in the *Dinner Table Conversations* of Athenaeus, a writer of the early third century AD. The figure for slaves is generally considered worthless, and that for metics, the most mobile element of the resident population, tells us nothing about their numbers at other times. In any case, we do not know whether the census included women, foreigners of free birth exempt from the tax on metics, and metics considered ineligible or unfit for military service. It is disputed whether the 21,000 citizens of the census represent all adult males of 18 or above, or only those fit for military service, in which case a total adult citizen population of around 29,000 is suggested.[3]

The next most promising piece of evidence, often linked with the text of Athenaeus, is marred by a conflict between the sources. When Antipater imposed oligarchy on Athens in 322/1 he restricted citizen rights to the owners of property worth 2,000 drachmas, who numbered 9,000 (Diodorus), and expelled the remaining 22,000 (Diodorus) or 12,000 (Plutarch).[4]

The rest of the evidence (from army and navy levies, the population base required to run the Council of 500, ephebic lists, Public Arbitrator lists) is indirect and indecisive, though recently Hansen by ingenious and sustained argument has tilted the balance toward the higher figure of 31,000 suggested by the passage of Diodorus.

Athenaeus apart, there are no 'figures' available for metics or slaves. It is therefore obvious that any estimates of the total residential

---

[3] Athenaeus 272c. See Hansen (1986), 30ff. on slave numbers (cf. Hyperides frag. 29 for another implausible figure), and in general for bibliography and argument. See also Sallares (1986).

[4] Diodorus 18.18.5; Plutarch, *Phoc.* 28.7.

population would be mere guesses, even if accurate figures for citizen numbers were available.

I settle for 20,000–30,000 adult male citizens, implying a total citizen population of rather more than 80,000–120,000, and guess that the total resident population was in the range 150,000–200,000. I make a virtue out of the impossibility of providing any more precise figure. Any estimate, to be realistic, should reflect the demographic fluctuations which occurred in consequence of war, food shortage, disease, emigration and immigration. By Hansen's own account, the resident population of adult citizens fell from around 40,000 in 431/0 to 20,000 in 405/4, rose in the following years to 25,000–30,000, sank again just as quickly to 25,000, rose to 30,000 by the mid-360s, fell to 25,000 by 350/49, reached 28,000 by 325/4, 30,000 by 322/1 and 29,000 by 317/16–307/6.[5] These figures, as their author is aware, are not much more than plausible guesses. Some are less plausible than others: in particular, the last figures take too little account of the food crises, emigration and military and political disasters of the 320s. But the point is made: an average population figure for Attica in the fourth century is a meaningless concept.

We cannot hope to quantify Athens' grain imports by means of demographic data which are conjectural and controversial. Nor do my estimates of Attica's productive capacity furnish more than a rough guide to the scale of the demand for foreign grain. It can be agreed that Attica always produced less grain than was required to feed its residents, even when there were as few residents as 150,000, in my view at the beginning and end of the fourth century. This conclusion is compatible with both population estimates and my conjecture that Attica was capable by itself of feeding 120,000–150,000 people under normal conditions. A background of defeat in war, political collapse and food crisis do not constitute normal conditions.

BRINGING IN THE GRAIN

The Athenian strategy for topping up their domestic grain supplies with foreign imports may be summed up in four words: diplomacy, incentive, regulation and force.

Diplomacy

A superficial reading of the sources might incline one to believe that Athenian diplomatic efforts were directed exclusively toward the

[5] Hansen (1986), 68.

Bosporan kingdom. The Bosporan kings had access to a large wheat surplus, they appear to have controlled the grain export trade directly, and the Athenians worked hard to establish and maintain the status of most favoured customer. But the trade networks of Athens as of other Greek states encompassed less distant (and less visible) suppliers as well, and these long-established links were underwritten by formal and informal understandings made with public authorities and private traders. Just as the Athenians appear to have reformulated their relationship with traders in the fourth century (see below), so the terms secured from the Bosporan kings need not have been standard and traditional.

In the speech *Against Leptines* Demosthenes justified honours for Leucon the Bosporan king with the following argument:

Leucon, who controls the trade, has granted exemption from dues to merchants conveying corn to Athens, and he proclaims that those bound for your port shall have priority of lading.[6]

To be sure, Demosthenes' political enemies attributed to him disreputable motives:

Do you think he got nothing for proposing free meals and a statue for Diphilus, conferring citizenship on ..., putting up in the market bronze statues of Berisades, Satyrus and Gorgippus the tyrants from the Pontus, from which he receives 1,000 medimnoi of wheat a year?[7]

Personal contacts did underlie the promotion and continuation of the special relationship between Athens and the Bosporan kingdom, but that relationship predated the career of Demosthenes. Both these points emerge from a passage of the *Trapeziticus* of Isocrates of about 393, which looks back to the reign of Satyrus (*c.* 433/2 – *c.* 393/2). The Athens-based son of a grain merchant who was a courtier of King Satyrus addresses the Athenians in this way:

It is right also that you keep in mind both Satyrus and my father, who have always esteemed you above all the other Greeks, and frequently in the past, when there was a scarcity of grain and they were sending away empty the ships of other merchants, granted you the right of export.[8]

The Bosporan kings remained solidly on Athens' side in the generation after Leucon, as the honorific decree for his sons Spartacus and Pairisades dated to 346 BC indicates. Thereafter the relationship between the two states is not easy to trace in detail. It is difficult to

---

[6] Demosthenes 20.31.
[7] Dinarchus 1.43; cf. Gernet (1909), 321.
[8] Isocrates 17.57.

believe that the Macedonians did not periodically disrupt the flow of commodities through the Hellespont after it fell under their control. Nevertheless the special friendship of Athens and Bosporus can be shown to have survived into the third century BC.[9]

It is not hard to see why the Athenians made diplomatic approaches to the Bosporan kings and gave them public honours in return for their favours. Their need was greater than that of any other state. Conversely, it suited the Bosporan kings to make concessions to the greatest consumer of imported grain.

Incentive and regulation

Given that trade in antiquity was in private hands, the concessions given by one state to another took the form of privileged treatment to those traders who served the latter. This had the consequence of confirming any predisposition that traders had to serve the state in question.

Athens was already attractive to traders. It offered the largest and most stable market in the Aegean, good port facilities and financial backing, and a valued return cargo. In addition, at some point in the mid-fourth century the Athenians introduced special courts (*dikai emporikai*), to cope with commercial maritime cases involving a written contract providing for trade to or from the port of Athens. These courts appealed to traders because they offered quick settlements in the winter months when sailing was inadvisable, and were accessible to Athenians and non-Athenians, metics or non-metics.[10] Finally, after Chaeronea if not before, the Athenians began bestowing public honours, including citizenship and the right to own property in Athenian territory, on traders who had given them generous service in situations of crisis.

However, fourth-century Athenians exploited these advantages by passing laws which restricted the freedom of merchants based in Athens or making use of Athens-derived capital.

The laws laid down two main rules:[11]

1 Any voyage made by a transport vessel that was financed by a maritime loan negotiated by an Athenian, resident alien or one in his power (typically

---

9 *Syll.*[3] 206 = Harding 82 (346 BC); *IG* II² 1485.21–4, with Burstein (1978a), but the date of the dedication of the crown is 306 or 305 (D. M. Lewis, pers. comm.); *IG* II² 653 of 285/4, with Burstein (1978b).

10 Cohen (1973); Rhodes (1981), 582–3 (on *Ath. pol.* 52.2), 664–6 (on 59.5), following Gernet (1938), 1–2, in suggesting that these courts were introduced between *c.* 355 and 343/2. See also Isager and Hansen (1975), 84–7 (after 355 and before 347).

11 Demosthenes 34.37, 35.50, 56.6 and 11; Lycurgus, *Leocr.* 26–7.

a slave) had to issue in the import of necessities, particularly grain, to Athens.

2 No one who lived in Athenian territory could transport grain to any other port than the Piraeus.

The penalty for breach of these laws was death.

The laws were not necessarily totally effective. The Dionysodorus case shows how slippery traders could be. It concerns a trader who allegedly took out a maritime loan at Athens for the round trip Athens–Egypt–Athens, went to Egypt, picked up grain – and unloaded it at Rhodes.[12]

Another law required traders to transport two-thirds of the grain they were importing up to the city of Athens. It was the responsibility of the port superintendents (*epimeletai* of the *emporia*), numbering 10 according to Aristotle, to enforce this and other rules, as part of their function of supervising the docks and the transactions that took place at or near them.[13] The point of the regulation was probably to ensure that city residents were not disadvantaged as against port residents at times when grain was relatively short.

What happened to the remaining one-third of a shipment of grain? Was it re-exported (the normal view), or are we to suppose (as has recently been suggested) that this practice was outlawed and the grain was sold in the market of the Piraeus?[14] Unloaded grain would not have lacked customers at the Piraeus, nor would the numerous watch-dog grain officials have permitted grain brought in under contract to be taken out again. But importers who were neither Athenians nor metics nor non-metic borrowers of local capital, and who had sailed into the port of Athens to see if grain was selling at an attractive price, were in a different position. It was not in the interests of the Athenians to discourage such merchants from bringing in their cargoes when prices at Athens were not the highest in the region. The case for legislation forbidding re-export is therefore not attractive. The only sanction available to the Athenians against a non-metic trader reluctant to unload his grain was probably the seizure of his boat and its cargo (*katagein*). There is a presumption that the state would pay something for the grain it commandeered.

In sum, the regulations imposed on the maritime grain trade did not discourage merchants from serving Athens. The residents of Athens and Attica made up the largest concentration of population in the

[12] Ps.-Demosthenes 56.

[13] Aristotle, *Ath. pol.* 51.4 cf. Ps.-Demosthenes 35.51; 58.8–9. See also *SEG* xxvi 72, ll. 18–21 (375/4). See Stroud (1974), and the criticisms of Buttrey (1979) and (1981).

[14] Gauthier (1981). My interpretation is influenced by Michael Jameson (pers. comm.).

Aegean and offered the certainty of regular custom to suppliers of grain and other commodities. The 'law of the two-thirds' caused only minor inconvenience to traders, who presumably passed on to the customer the expense of transporting the grain from port to city. Nor did the more central regulations and the dire penalty provided for therein frighten them away. As long as Athens had the ability to protect merchant shipping, there was never likely to be a shortage of suppliers willing to serve her.

To complete the survey of the regulation of the grain trade it is necessary to consider the retail side: laws first, then officials. There was a law restricting the amount of grain that dealers (*sitopolai*) could buy. Lysias' speech *Against the Grain-dealers* indicates that they were permitted to purchase no more than 50 baskets (*phormoi*), presumably in one day. The capacity of a basket is unknown; it may or may not be equal to a medimnos. In any case, the purpose of the law is clear. It was designed to prevent stockpiling and speculative profits. A second law, briefly alluded to in the same speech of Lysias, restricted profits: 'for they were bound in selling to add no more than one obol to the price'. In both cases offenders were liable to the death penalty.[15]

The *sitophulakes*, Grain Wardens, supervised grain market operations within the city and Piraeus. The first indication of the numbers of such officials is given in the Aristotelian *Constitution of the Athenians*, which states that there used to be 5 for the port and 5 for the city, but that now (that is, in the 320s) the numbers are, respectively, 15 and 20. Their duties were to see that unground grain was put on sale in the market at a fair price, that millers sold barley meal at a price corresponding to that which they paid for raw barley, and that bakers sold loaves at a price corresponding to that which they paid for the wheat. They also fixed the weights. In 375/4 their competence was extended to cover breaches of a new law regulating coinage, in so far as the offence was committed in the grain market of the city or of the Piraeus.[16]

None of these laws and institutions can be closely dated. Lysias' speech, of about 386, shows that the two laws governing the retail trade and an unknown number of Grain Wardens were in place by this date. The expansion in the numbers of these officials was a product of the food crises of the 330s and 320s. The laws regulating the wholesale side of the trade are not referred to before this period, but the Port Superintendents who enforced them existed as early as 375/4, when they were empowered to try offences under the coinage law of that year unless such offences were committed in the grain markets. There is no

[15] Lysias 22.5, 8. It mattered that the dealers were mainly metics.
[16] Aristotle, *Ath. pol.* 51.3; *SEG* xxvi 72, ll. 18ff. (for bibl. see n. 13, above).

sign, and in my view no likelihood, that the bulk of the laws and institutions in question predate the fourth century. Some elements may go back into the Peloponnesian War period. That is to say, they may have been war measures which were kept on, or revived under the restored democracy.

Force

In August 362, a meeting of the Athenian assembly received bad news from the Hellespont, among other places, and voted that the trierarchs launch their ships forthwith. One of the trierarchs, who subsequently sued the man appointed to relieve him, reports the requests of several states in the region for aid, and adds:

When further the merchants and shipowners were about to sail out of the Pontus, and the Byzantines and Chalcedonians and Cyzicenes were forcing their ships to put in to their own ports because of the scarcity of grain in their own countries; seeing also that the price of grain was advancing in the Piraeus, and that there was not very much to be bought, you voted that the trierarchs should launch their ships and bring them up to the pier, and that the members of the council and the demarchs should make out lists of the demesmen and reports of available seamen, and that the armament should be despatched at once, and aid sent to the various regions.[17]

On this occasion the Athenian fleet arrived in time. It was equally successful in the following year, when it was recalled to escort the merchant ships from the Cimmerian Bosporus out of the Black Sea, in the face of renewed attempts by Byzantium and Chalcedon to seize the ships and their cargo.

The conduct of the fleet after it had fulfilled its mission is interesting. It was turned to the profitable task of hiring out its services to other states seeking safe passage for their grain, specifically Maroneia and Thasos. Entrepreneurial activity of this kind shades into piracy in the hands of an unscrupulous admiral such as Diopeithes, whose operations of about twenty years later are described defensively by Demosthenes in his speech of 342 BC *On the Chersonese*. In one passage it is revealed that Diopeithes has been detaining merchantmen. A little later Demosthenes generalises about the activity of Athenian admirals in the north:

Athenian generals raise money from Chians, Erythraeans, from whatever people they can, I mean the Greeks of Asia Minor. Those who pay, purchase for the merchants sailing from their own harbours immunity from injury or robbery, or a

---

[17] Ps.-Demosthenes 50.6.

safe conduct for their own ship, or something of that sort. They say they are granting benevolences.[18]

According to Demosthenes, this activity was absolutely necessary. Without it Athens could not run a fleet, could not pay and feed her rowers.

Katagein, the seizing of ships, bringing them to port and compelling the unloading of their cargoes, has been described as 'a tacitly recognised right' of any city suffering a grain shortage, rather than an act of war.[19] The only remedy was to send warships to escort the grain convoy. It is precisely in the matter of securing safe passage for the grain ships that the comparative weakness of fourth-century Athens shows up. *Katagein* by other states and freebooting pirates was a much greater menace in the fourth century than in the fifth. In the heyday of Empire, Athens had garrisons and officials in key points such as Byzantium (the Wardens of the Hellespont) and, according to Plutarch, a fleet of around 60 ships in permanent patrol of the Aegean.[20] It had been Athens' self-imposed obligation and right to keep the peace of the seas.

The first danger point was the Hellespontine region. In 387 the Spartans repeated the tactic of closing the Hellespont which had brought the Athenians to their knees in 405. Xenophon reports: 'Antalcidas, who had more than 80 ships, was master of the sea; he could thus stop ships from the Pontus sailing towards Athens and force them to Sparta's allies.'[21]

The Spartan seizure of the Hellespont was a prelude to a diplomatic offensive culminating in the King's Peace, which did much to restore the influence of the Spartans in old Greece at the expense of, among others, Athens and Thebes.

In due course Philip of Macedon surfaced as a more permanent threat. He could in the first place obstruct Athenian counter-measures against interference by other states, in particular Byzantium. In 362, as we saw, Athens was able to stand up against three local states acting in concert. But in 346 Demosthenes complained that the peace with Philip in effect left the Byzantines free to grab the ships. This was nothing compared with Philip's own seizure of 230 (or 180) merchantmen in the autumn of 340 and of the force of 20 ships sent by the Athenians to

---

[18] Demosthenes 8.24–8.
[19] De Ste Croix (1972), 47 and App. 8.
[20] Plutarch, *Per.* 11.4 cf. Meiggs (1972), 427; Cartledge (1979), 235.
[21] Xenophon, *Hell.* 5.1.28.

protect them.[22] After Chaeronea the blocking of the Hellespont was a sanction that the Macedonians could always impose on the Greeks if they proved too independent.

If the grain fleet was most vulnerable at the Hellespont, it could also be attacked at other points closer to its destination. In 376 the grain fleet met serious trouble at Cape Geraestus at the south-east corner of Euboea, in the form of a Spartan fleet under Pollis. It was saved by a hurriedly assembled fleet under Chabrias which drew the enemy south by attacking Naxos and won the subsequent battle. A year later the Athenians sought to make peace with the Spartans, worn out by, among other things, piratical raids from Aegina. The line between piracy and official or semi-official acts of warfare was a fuzzy one. Alexander of Pherae in Thessaly who descended on the Piraeus in 361 and kidnapped some merchants is branded by Xenophon a 'villainous pirate'. But freebooting pirates were a constant menace; their operations embarrassed Macedonians as well as Greeks.[23]

FOOD CRISIS

The network of suppliers and transporters, laws and officials described above no doubt reduced the risk of food crisis, but did not eliminate it altogether. The Athenians were prepared for trouble. They kept the state of the food supply under constant review. It can bear repeating that the standing agenda of the main assembly meeting of each prytany included discussion of the food supply, by the late 330s anyway, when the Aristotelian *Constitution of Athens* was composed.[24] The Athenians were geared to a quick response if a deficit on the 'grain account' looked likely: the second passage from the *Rhetoric* quoted earlier hints at the existence of a standard procedure for contracting with traders for emergency supplies. This task was already in the hands of a special Grain Commissioner, *sitones*, in the latter part of our period. Alternatively, if warships were required to rescue a fleet of merchant ships destined for Athens, trierarchs were alerted, crews prepared, and the expedition sent off with despatch.

How prone were fourth-century Athenians to food crisis? We should

---

[22] Demosthenes 5.25 (346 BC). On the incident in 340/39, see Philochorus, *FGH* 328 F 161–2 (230 ships) cf. Theopompus, *FGH* 115 F 292 (180 ships); cf. Demosthenes, 18.73ff. (20 ships).

[23] Xenophon, *Hell.* 5.4.6off., Diodorus 15.34.3 (Chabrias); Xenophon, *Hell.* 6.2.1 (Aegina raid); Polyaenus, *Strat.* 6.2.2 cf. Xenophon, *Hell.* 6.4.35 (Alexander); Xenophon, *Hell.* 6.2.19; Demosthenes 19.315; cf. Ormerod (1924); Ziebarth (1929); McKechnie (1985), Ch. 5 (piracy).

[24] Aristotle, *Ath. pol.* 43.4.

first be on our guard against the suggestion that Athens was in extended or continuous crisis. The idea of a prolonged drought lasting from the 360s to the 320s is a priori implausible, and is not entailed by the evidence, which points to a number of individual crises.[25] In any case, harvest failure did not necessarily issue in food shortage. The second theory is more familiar and deeply entrenched in the scholarly literature: Athens was perpetually in crisis because of overpopulation. This is considered proven by the despatch of cleruchies and the emigration of individuals, to reside elsewhere or to contribute to the mercenary armies that were a feature of the age.[26]

Mercenaries were not a new phenomenon in Greece as a whole or in Athens; they both were a product of and fed on endemic warfare, political instability and the inability of the public authorities in the Greek states to redistribute the wealth of the community. The scale of private emigration cannot be quantified; it may have reached new heights in fourth-century Athens, but we do not know. There is, similarly, no way of showing that emigration at a significant level was continuous rather than sporadic, the product of wars or food crises. The second alternative has greater plausibility. Finally, much emigration was temporary; it involved circulation rather than absolute loss of manpower.

Athenians were sent as cleruchs to an unknown destination in 370/69, to Samos in 365/4, 361/0 and 352/1 (to the number of 2,000), to Potidaea possibly in 364/3 and (?again) in 362/1, to the Thracian Chersonese in 353/2 and 344/3. Cleruchies were a weapon of empire unpopular with the Greeks and renounced by Athens in the charter of the new League in 378/7. Their reappearance (at the expense of non-league states) following the extensive conquests of Timotheus are clear evidence that Athenian imperialism was entering a second, harsher phase. The Athenians were returning to old tricks – and old haunts. To be sure, there was poverty in Athens, and the worse-off thetes benefited from occupying the land of others. But cleruchs in this as in other periods are not to be seen merely as 'surplus mouths'.

This said, the domestic situation helps explain the cleruchies of 361/0 and the late 350s. The Athenians had suffered food crisis in 362/1. In 353/2 Athens was in a state of exhaustion after the disastrous war which severely weakened her league (357–355). By 353, according to Demo-

[25] Camp (1982).
[26] On mercenaries, see Parke (1933); Griffith (1935); Pritchett (1974), Ch. 3; McKechnie (1985), Ch. 4. For the overpopulation thesis, see e.g. Ehrenberg (1960), 149: 'The whole development of the Hellenistic age cannot be understood unless we recognize the fact, beyond doubt for the fourth and third centuries BC, that Greece was seriously over-populated.' Cf. Hornblower (1983), 170ff.

sthenes, the treasury did not contain a single day's supplies.[27] The actions of 353/2 betray desperation. The Chersonese was settled after Chares' capture of Sestos, the Samians were disgracefully expelled from their island and Chares was ordered to maintain the siege of Chios lest his large army come back to Athens. A generation later, the food crises of the late 330s and early 320s provide part of the background for the despatch of colonists to the Adriatic in 325/4.[28]

In short, grand theories of secular crisis are both implausible and lacking in explanatory value. They are no substitute for the analysis of particular crises, to which I now turn.

The merchant fleet was held up at the Hellespont in 387/6 by the Spartans, at a time when unnamed 'pirates' operating from Aegina were blockading the Piraeus, in 362/1 and again in the following year by states from the Hellespontine region, and in 340/39 by the Macedonians. On all but the last of these occasions there are allusions in the sources to food shortage in Athens.

The unhappy situation of consumers in Athens in the winter of 387/6 is touched on in the speech of Lysias *Against the Grain-dealers*. A defendant admits to having bought up grain in excess of the legal limit of 50 measures, but claims that he was ordered to do so by officials. Two denied any knowledge of the matter; the testimony of the third, as summarised in Lysias, was as follows:

Anytus stated that in the previous winter, as the grain was dear, and these men were outbidding each other and fighting amongst themselves, he had advised them to cease their competition, judging it beneficial to you, their customers, that they should purchase at as reasonable a price as possible: for they were bound, in selling, to add no more than an obol to the price. Now, that he did not order them to buy up the grain for holding in store, but only advised them not to buy against each other, I will produce Anytus himself as witness.

The incidents of 362/1 and 361/0 coincide with, and must have aggravated, a food shortage in Athens. Byzantium, Chalcedon and Cyzicus had seized the grain fleet in the late summer of 362/1 because they were themselves short of grain. The year was perhaps a bad one in Attica as well; at any rate, already in August, not long after the harvest, grain was rising in price and was in short supply in the market of the Piraeus. In the year that followed, Attica experienced a severe drought: the speaker of Oration 50 in the Demosthenic corpus, Apollodorus, son of Pasion, reports that while he was away in the north on the second of his two missions as trierarch, the land had produced no crop, the water

[27] Demosthenes 23.209.
[28] On cleruchies, see Griffith (1978), 137ff.; Hansen (forthcoming); more briefly, Hansen (1986).

had dried up in the wells, and there were not even any vegetables in the garden. This statement refers to the harvest of 361/0, not that of 362/1, when Apollodorus was still in Athens. There were two difficult years in succession.[29]

Speeches of 355 BC refer twice briefly to food shortage. In *Against Androtion*, Demosthenes says the following: 'In the last war with the Lacedaemonians, when it seemed unlikely that you could despatch a fleet, you know that vetch was sold for food. But when you did despatch it, you won peace on your own terms.'[30]

The reference may be to the year 376/5, when the naval victory of Chabrias at Naxos enabled the grain ships to leave Euboea for the Piraeus. According to Xenophon, Sparta's allies put pressure on Sparta to prosecute the war more actively, arguing that they were in a position to starve Athens into surrender. Xenophon's own comment was that with the Spartan fleet deployed near Aegina, Ceos and Andros, 'the Athenians were as good as besieged'. Or Demosthenes had in mind 374/3. An inscription of this year records the imposition of a tax of 8⅓% 'on the grain of the islands' (Lemnos, Imbros and Skyros). The Athenians, says Xenophon, were 'worn out' by war taxes and piratical raids from Aegina.[31]

In *Against Leptines* there is, again, a brief reference to a 'universal grain shortage', securely dated to 357 BC.[32] It coincided with the beginning of the war with the allies, the so-called Social War. As in 362/1, other states besides Athens suffered distress. Harvest failure was aggravated by action taken against the grain fleet by Hellespontine states, especially Byzantium, one of the rebellious allies of Athens.

This list of shortages is not complete. Lysias' speech *Against the Grain-dealers* of around 386 BC states that the Athenians were used to receiving 'bad news' about the loss or capture of 'their' grain ships, that retailers were frequently charged with speculating in grain, and that Athenian officials were regularly punished for permitting these practices. There is some confirmation, from both Xenophon and Isocrates, of supply problems in the 390s, when the Spartans were still a force to be reckoned with at sea.[33] In addition, dissatisfaction at the vulnerability of Athens' food supply in the present (and not merely nostalgia for the great days of empire) is expressed in the slogan 'walls cannot

---

[29] Ps.-Demosthenes 50, esp. 4–6 and 61.
[30] Demosthenes 22.15.
[31] Xenophon, *Hell.* 5.4.60; 6.2.1; Shear (1987).
[32] Demosthenes 20.33.
[33] Lysias 22.8, 13–14, 16, 18, 20; Xenophon, *Hell.* 4.8.20; Isocrates 17.35–6; cf. *Hell. Oxy.* 7.1.

feed us', which circulated among the pro-war party at Athens, that is, among the opponents of the conservative politician, Andocides, in 392/1, the date of his speech *On the Peace with Sparta*.[34]

One point that Andocides does not make in his speech is that war had an adverse effect on grain imports. This was apparently understood by one Xenocleides, who opposed the motion to help the Spartans against Thebes in 369/8. The reason given by the speaker of the *Against Neaera* is that Xenocleides 'had purchased the right to collect the 2% tax on grain during the peace'. Andocides had himself held the contract about three decades earlier. It was precisely in time of war or other such emergencies that the retailers of grain in Athens were most active in subverting the laws, according to Lysias:

For their interests are the opposite of other men's: they make most profit when, on some bad news reaching the city, they sell their grain at a high price. And they are so delighted to see your disasters that they either get news of them in advance of anyone else, or fabricate the rumour themselves; now it is the loss of your ships in the Black Sea, now the capture of vessels on their outward voyage by the Lacedaemonians, now the blockade of your trading ports, or the impending rupture of the truce; and they have carried their enmity to such lengths that they choose the same critical moments as your foes to overreach you.[35]

Again, 357 was not the only year of shortage in the 350s. Isocrates in 355 in *On the Peace* refers in general terms to the disruption of agriculture and trade in the three years of the war with the allies, and adds that the city was now not only short of money, but had also been abandoned by 'traders, foreigners and metics'.[36] The desperation measures taken in 353–351 in the aftermath of Athens' defeat have already been mentioned.

Athens' food supply system was chronically insecure in the period down to 338. It was insecure at the beginning of the fourth century when the Spartans were masters of the sea, because the flow of grain was dependent on Spartan good will and interest in policing the main trade routes. Both were limited. It was insecure when the Athenians had thrown off the Spartan yoke and were pursuing imperialistic ambitions, because they lacked the necessary financial resources and naval power to eradicate piracy and interference by rival states. For all that, food crises do not appear to have hit Athens with any frequency until the last decade and a half of Athenian democratic government, after Philip had tamed the Greeks at Chaeronea and taken firm control

[34] Andocides 3.36. See on this speech Missiou-Ladi (1986).
[35] Ps.-Demosthenes 59.27; Andocides 1.133; cf. Lycurgus, *Leocr.* 19; Lysias 22.14–15.
[36] Cf. Isocrates 7, Demosthenes 22 and 14, Xenophon, *Poroi*, all dating from this dark period in Athenian history.

of the Hellespont. Down to the 330s, Athens was comparatively successful in securing the grain that was needed from external sources. This was a considerable achievement for a state which was no longer a great power, even if it continued to behave as if it was one.

10

FROM UNCERTAINTY TO CRISIS

After the battle of Chaeronea in 338, the external food supply of the Athenians was as much in the hands of others as it had been at the beginning of the century. It is difficult to believe that grain flowed as freely from the north, given the demonstrably increased vulnerability of the Athenians to food crisis in this period. It is noteworthy that imports from the west and south-east come into prominence in the sources only after Chaeronea.

The Athenians did little to endear themselves to the rulers of Macedonia. Philip's seizure of the grain ships in 340 was repeated at some point in the following decade. The speaker of *On the Treaty with Alexander*, delivered in 331, complains:

For they have grown so arrogant that they forced all the ships coming from the Black Sea to put in at Tenedos ... and refused to release them until you passed a decree to man and launch 100 triremes instantly.[1]

The grain fleets were most vulnerable when war was being waged between Macedon and Greek states, especially in 338/7 and 323/2 (the Lamian war), but also in 335/4 (the Theban war) and 331/0 (the revolt of Agis of Sparta, a limited enterprise). The Persian fleet was a force in the Aegean from 334/3 to the early summer of 332. Other states, for example, Byzantium, periodically obstructed the passage of the grain ships. Finally, piracy flourished during the period of Macedonian ascendancy.[2]

---

[1] Ps.-Demosthenes 17.19. On the date of the speech, see Cawkwell (1961). I do not find plausible the suggestion that this was not a genuine *katagein*.

[2] Ps.-Aristotle, *Oec.* 1346b30ff.; *IG* ii² 360 ll. 29ff.; Lycurgus, *Leocr.* 18 (*katagein*); *IG* ii² 1623.285 (two ships sent in 335/4) (piracy). See Potter (1984) for the argument that *IG* ii² 399 refers to war captives. In Philip's lifetime, at any rate, Macedon also suffered from piracy, according to Demosthenes 18.145; cf. 19.315.

GRAIN IMPORTS

Grain was still routinely sought in the Black Sea in the late 330s and 320s by traders serving Athens. Many of these traders would have come from the Pontus; in particular, the Heracleotes formed a substantial community in Athens, on the evidence of gravestones. The speaker of the *Against Phormio* (Oration 34 of 327/6) had a partner based in the Bosporus and a slave wintering there, and had lent money to the defendant for the 'double voyage' to the Bosporus and back.

The Athenians had not lost their special relationship with the Bosporan kingdom. Reference is made in *Against Phormio* to the most recent republication by the Bosporan king Pairisades of the traditional decree 'that whoever wished to transport grain to Athens for the Athenian market might export it free of duty'. Lampis, a rogue associate of Phormio, was on hand to take advantage of this decree. He flouted the law by unloading at Acanthus in Chalcidice rather than at Athens.[3]

Quite apart from difficulties caused by slippery traders and the seizure of cargoes (and rigging) by other states, political and economic conditions in the north did not always favour trade. Phormio arrived in the Bosporus to find Pairisades embroiled in a war with the Scythians, and was unable to sell his goods or take on a return cargo.[4]

The next piece of evidence relating to contact with the Bosporus belongs to 323/2. In a fragmentary inscription of this year some persons were honoured in connection with a mission to the Bosporus. This was also the year of the Greek rebellion against the Macedonians known as the Lamian War. This war, which included a sea-battle in the Hellespont fought under the command of the nauarch Euetion, must have disrupted trade with the north and caused hardship in Athens.[5]

Also in 323/2, according to the *Oration Against Dionysodorus* (Oration 56 in the Demosthenic corpus), Sicilian grain arrived in Athens and Egyptian grain was expected. Grain was actively sought from both these areas in the 330s and 320s. An inscription of the late 340s or early 330s honours a Salaminian who brought in grain from Egypt and sent home some Athenian captives from Sicily after paying their ransom. It was presumably the grain trade between Sicily and Athens which led him as shipowner and trader to Sicily.[6]

[3] Ps.-Demosthenes 34.36.
[4] Ps.-Demosthenes 34.8; *IG* ii² 360 = *Syll.*³ 304, ll. 29ff. (rigging seized).
[5] *IG* ii² 369+ = Schweigert, *Hesperia* 9 (1940), 395ff. no. 42 = Osborne (1981–2), D 25; *IG* ii² 398a, linked with 438 in Walbank (1987).
[6] *IG* ii² 283. It is unclear whether these Athenians were mercenaries (which might point to a date in the late 340s) or captives of pirates.

The contribution of Egypt to the feeding of Athens is impossible to measure. The evidence only hints at the regular export of grain from Egypt, while giving the firm impression that Egypt was a less desirable supplier than might have been expected, thanks to the profiteering of Cleomenes, Alexander's financial official and then governor in Egypt (331–323). A work in the Aristotelian corpus preserves two anecdotes about Cleomenes' entrepreneurial activities:

While Cleomenes of Alexandria was governor of Egypt, at a time when there was some scarcity in the land but elsewhere grievous hunger, he forbade the export of grain. On the local governors' representing that if there were no export of grain they would be unable to pay in their taxes, he allowed the export, but laid a heavy duty on the grain. By this means he obtained a large amount of duty from a small amount of export, and at the same time deprived the officials of their excuse.

At a time when the price of grain in Egypt was 10 drachmas, Cleomenes sent for the growers and asked them at what price they would contract to supply him with their produce. On their quoting a price lower than what they were charging the merchants, he offered them the full price they were accustomed to receive from others; and taking over the entire supply he sold it at a fixed rate of 32 drachmas.[7]

Egyptian grain and Cleomenes are brought into relation with Athens in the speech *Against Dionysodorus*, which refers back to events of 323/2. Certain traders are accused of unloading in Rhodes a cargo of grain which they had contracted to bring to Athens. The speaker goes on to level the charge that his opponents were a gang of crooks whose dirty work was masterminded by Cleomenes, governor of Egypt:

In accordance with this agreement, men of the jury, Dionysodorus here and his partner Parmeniscus, when they had got the money from us, despatched their ship from Athens to Egypt. Parmeniscus sailed in charge of the ship; Dionysodorus remained in Athens. All these men, I would have you know, men of the jury, were underlings and confederates of Cleomenes, the former ruler of Egypt, who from the time he received the government did no small harm to your state, or rather to the rest of the Greeks as well, by buying up grain for resale and fixing its price, and in this he had these men as his confederates. Some of them would despatch the stuff from Egypt, others would sail in charge of the shipments, while still others would remain here in Athens and dispose of the consignments. Then those who remained here would send letters to those abroad advising them of the prevailing price, so that if grain were dear in your market, they might bring it.[8]

It would be dangerous to base any statement on the significance of Egyptian grain for Athens on this tendentious source. The importance of the trade route from the west is more firmly established. The earliest

---

[7] Ps.-Aristotle, *Oec.* 1352a17ff.; 1352b14ff.

[8] Ps.-Demosthenes 56.7–8. On this speech, see Isager and Hansen (1975), 200ff., and Carey and Reid (1985).

references appear to belong to the 330s, although dates are disputed. The honorific inscription for the Salaminian, who, among other things, ransomed some Athenians in Sicily, suggests that Sicilian grain was reaching Athens by the 330s (or possibly the late 340s). Hieron, a native of Tyre, and his son Apses are thought to have brought grain to Athens not only from Sicily but also from Italy and Carthage not much before 332 BC; another inscription shows Carthaginian ambassadors in Athens at about the same time. In the speech of about 330 BC *Against Zenothemis*, composed by Demosthenes for Demon, it is alleged that certain rascally traders had been foiled in their plans to scuttle their ship laden with an Athens-bound cargo of Sicilian grain. Finally, in 323/2, Dionysodorus and his men were persuaded to break contract and take their grain elsewhere by the effect on the grain market of the arrival of 'the ships from Sicily'. The wording suggests that this was a regular event, while the fall in prices points to a substantial cargo.[9]

As with the northern so with the western route, security of passage was far from guaranteed. The inscription for the man from Salamis is one of several indications that piracy was a persistent threat on the route from the west. Some references to piratical activity are unspecific as to the sphere of their operations. An example is the navy list of 334/3 which records Diotimos' expedition 'to ward off pirates' in the previous year. On the other hand, 'Etruscan' pirates, whose main sphere of operations was presumably the west, are singled out on more than one occasion, most notably in the naval accounts which reveal the despatch of a colony in 324 with the following end in view,

to secure for the people for all time its own ports and passage of grain, and by the establishment of a naval base of its own, to guard against the attacks of Etruscan pirates.[10]

Grain arrived from time to time from other sources, certainly Cyrene and Cyprus, perhaps Asia Minor and Syria. In general, traders looked for grain where they had connections and where they knew a surplus for export was commonly to be found. There was nothing new about this. The major development was the emergence of western states, particularly in Sicily, as regular suppliers of Athens, if the sources are to be trusted. We may speculate that substantial colonisation of Sicily under Timoleon from 342 to 336 stimulated pro-

[9] *IG* II² 283; *IG* II² 342 + *SEG* 24 104, cf. *IG* II² 418, with Walbank (1985); Demosthenes 32 and 56. See also *Hesperia* 43 (1974), 322–4 no. 3 (a man from Akragas).
[10] See nn. 2, 19.

duction, in the first instance for the home market, at a time when imports from the Black Sea were problematic as never before.[11]

Athens' loss at Chaeronea of 3,000 men, 1,000 of them dead, the rest taken captive, was compounded by the disruption of the food supply. The appointment of Demosthenes as Grain Commissioner (*sitones*) and his gift of one talent, presumably to the grain-purchase fund, belong to the period immediately after the war. In Lycurgus' speech *Against Leocrates* it is said that when the rumour that the Piraeus was blockaded reached Rhodes, the Rhodians sent triremes to seize the merchant ships en route to Athens and secure their grain and other cargo for themselves. This detail, though not necessarily Leocrates' personal responsibility for the events, may be accepted as authentic. The Athenians suffered more than a collapse of morale and a manpower crisis immediately after Chaeronea.[12]

In 335 Alexander wiped out Thebes, and Athens suffered the first of three crises in which Chrysippus, the speaker of the *Against Phormio*, claims to have performed signal services to the people of Athens. I consider it likely that the Athenians suffered food shortages in all three instances, and not simply in the last two, where the text is explicit on the point. On this assumption, the gift of one talent contributed by Chrysippus and his brother in 335 was paid over to a grain commissioner appointed to raise money and buy grain.[13]

The second food crisis is to be assigned to 330/29. Chrysippus says that he and his brother brought in more than 10,000 medimnoi and charged 5 drachmas per medimnos at a time when the market price had reached 16 drachmas. The event is not precisely dated in the speech, but the inscription honouring Heracleides of Salamis in Cyprus indicates that 330/29 was a year of grain shortage (*spanositia*), and only one such year is needed between the first and third crises, which fell in 335/4 and 328/7. The Heracleides inscription consisting of five decrees is dated to 325/4 but refers back to the archon year 330/29, in the course of which Heracleides, like Chrysippus and his brother, sold grain at 5 drachmas per medimnos. Heracleides brought in 3,000 medimnoi, rather less than Chrysippus and his brother. He still saved the consumer 33,000 drachmas or 5½ talents, at 11 drachmas per medim-

---

[11] Talbert (1974), 165–6. For other sources of grain, see *IG* II² 401 (Asia restored; cf. 416); 407; Tod II 196; cf. 343 (a Sidonian, who might be a metic).

[12] Demosthenes 18.248; Lycurgus, *Leocr.* 18; Plutarch, *Mor.* 851A.

[13] Ps.-Demosthenes 34.38–9. The anti-pirate expedition of 335/4 (*IG* II² 1623.285) suggests an interruption of the flow of grain in that year.

nos. Moreover, Heracleides had the distinction of having been 'the first of the traders who came into Athens during the shortage to charge 5 drachmas'. His reward was to be praised, awarded a gold crown, made a *proxenos* and benefactor and given (in 325/4) the right to own property in Athenian territory (*enktesis*). Another sign that his services were valued by the Athenians is the sending of a special envoy to demand of Dionysius, tyrant of Heracleia Pontica, that he return the sails of Heracleides' ships and refrain from molesting traders who served Athens.[14]

The third crisis of *Against Phormio* fell in 328/7. In this year Chrysippus and his brother gave one talent towards the purchase of grain (*sitonia*). Heracleides in the same year gave 3,000 drachmas, or half as much as Chrysippus. He was joined by others. The inscription runs: 'and again, when the contributions (*epidoseis*) were made, he gave 3,000 drachmas towards the grain supply' (ll. 10ff.). Demosthenes may have given a second gift of a talent towards grain purchase in this year, according to one reading of a text of Plutarch. The names of a number of other donors are tucked away in the naval accounts of 326/5, the authority for their inclusion having been given by a decree of Demades of that year. It appears that trierarchs had had difficulty meeting the cost of fitting out ships launched somewhat earlier, and faced a fine of double the original cost. Demades promulgated a decree to the effect that, if a trierarch or a friend of a trierarch contributed to the grain fund, his fine should be reduced by that amount. As a result of this 'fiddle', the list of donors to the grain fund can be lengthened, and some non-donors identified, with the aid of the naval records. The records in question are dated to 326/5 and give a *terminus ante quem* for the contributions to which they refer. The probability is (there is no proof) that they cluster in the year 328/7. Assuming this to be the case, the total of known contributions comes to 7 talents, 2,500 drachmas (see Table 8).[15]

A public subscription is in any case securely dated to 328/7 by the Heracleides inscription. This is the first known subscription of its kind in Athenian history, the only instance where money was contributed for the purchase of food rather than, for example, to finance a public building project. The implication is that the third of the three crises was especially severe. The nature of the responses of Heracleides, Chrysippus and his brother points in the same direction: they contributed not

[14] *IG* ii² 360 = *Syll.*³ 304, ll. 29ff. (rigging seized). On privileges, see Pečirka (1966).
[15] I agree with D. M. Lewis (pers. comm.), following Kuenzi (1923), and against Migeotte (1983), at 146ff., that there was one subscription. The reconstruction of donors in Table 8 is that of D. M. Lewis. In the case of Demosthenes' gift (Plutarch, *Mor.* 851B) there may be a doublet; cf. Davies (1971), 137 (κ cf. ο).

Table 8. Sitonia *contributions, ?328/7* BC

		IG II²	1628	1629	
3,000 dr	Herakleides of Salamis				
1 T	Chrysippos and brother				
1 T	Demosthenes				
1,000 dr ?+	Konon Timotheou Anaphlystios	358–63	880–84		
3,000 dr ?+	Panther Demonikou Lakiades	363–66	884–86		
1,000 dr ?+	Meidon (Samian resident in Piraeus)	366–68	886–88		
2,500 dr ?+	Neoptolemos Antikleous Meliteus	384–86	904–06		
2,500 dr ?+	Philippides Philomelou Paianieus	393–95	911–14	cf. 1631.8–10	
2,300 dr ?+	Arrheneides and Charikles Paianieis	410–11	930–31	(2,200 dr)	
1,000 dr ?+	Menelaos Menelochou Myrrhinousios	412–13	932–34		
950 dr ?+	Xenokles Xeinidos Sphettios	414–16	934–36		
250 dr ?+	Hieron Chariou Palleneus	416–17	936–38		
500 dr ?+	Neoptolemos Meliteus	418	938–39		
2,000 dr ?+	Python Pythokleous Sounieus	431–32	953–54		
3,500 dr ?+	Xenokles Xeinidos Sphettios	434–35	955–56		
3,000 dr ?+	Pheidippos Xypetaion	444–50	[971–75]		
2,000 dr ?+	Archestratos Euthykrates Amphitropeus	450–51			

(*Authority for inclusion of these contributions in the naval lists given by decree of Demades of 326/5 – IG II²
1628.334ff., 1629.859ff. The figures should be treated as minima.*)

Therefore

1 T	Chrysippos and brother
	Demosthenes
4,450 dr	Xenokles
3,000 dr	Herakleides of Salamis
3,000 dr	Panther
	Pheidippos
	Neoptolemos
2,500 dr	Philippides
2,300 dr	Arrheneides and Charikles
2,000 dr	Python
	Archestratos
1,000 dr	Konon
1,000 dr	Meidon
	Menelaus
250 dr	Hieron

7 T 2,500 dr ?+

grain but money. In the previous crisis they were able to furnish cut-price grain. The inference is that there was less grain available in 328/7 than in 330/29. None of our three generous traders appears to have had any. Alternatively and less probably, they had previously brought in grain and it was not enough. There was still a grave deficiency.

Next, there is a reference in a fragmentary inscription to a grain shortage in Athens contemporaneous with, and no doubt aggravated by, a naval battle in the Hellespontine region. The Greek rebellion against the Macedonians (the Lamian War) of 323/2 supplies an appropriate context.[16] The speech *Against Dionysodorus* referring back to the same year provides some confirmation, but without much enlightenment: we learn merely that prices were high, and therefore, by implication, that food was short. Traders took out a maritime loan at Athens for the round trip Athens–Egypt–Athens. The contract stipulated, as such contracts customarily did, that the grain was to be conveyed to Athens and to no other port. According to the speaker, Darius, the traders were prepared to accept this clause because 'when they despatched their ship from Athens they left the price of grain here pretty high'. Darius goes on:

Afterwards, however, men of the jury, when the ships from Sicily had arrived, and the prices of grain here were falling, and their ship had reached Egypt, the defendant straightaway sent a man to Rhodes to inform his partner Parmeniscus of the state of things here, well knowing that his ship would be forced to touch at Rhodes. The outcome was that Parmeniscus, the defendant's partner, when he had received the letter sent by him and had learned the price of grain prevailing here, discharged his cargo of grain at Rhodes and sold it there in defiance of the agreement, men of the jury, and of the penalties to which they had of their own will bound themselves.[17]

The prosecutor would have us believe that Cleomenes and his men were chiefly responsible for any discomfort suffered by Athenian and other Greek consumers. But he had an axe to grind: he wanted to brand his opponent as a creature of Cleomenes. In both the anecdotes of Ps.-Aristotle, Egypt was suffering shortage and therefore had little grain to sell, and none of it cheap. The responsibility for bad harvests can hardly be laid at the door of Cleomenes. That said, it can be accepted that the activities of this 'mafia' network, always assuming it was not a figment of the orator's imagination (which seems improbable), did have an impact on the grain market in Athens, by forcing up the price when grain was short, and by impeding the storage of grain by the responsible officials when supplies were adequate.

So far, five food crises: 338/7, 335/4, 330/29, 328/7, 323/2. Can the list be lengthened? There may have been shortages at Athens in 332/1, 329/8 and 325/4. The case for 332/1 as a crisis year is not very strong. The Persian naval offensive in the Aegean had now petered out,

---

[16] *IG* II² 398. See Walbank (1987), who identifies *IG* II² 438 as a fragment of the same stone.
[17] Ps.-Demosthenes 56.9–10. The contract was apparently made in Metageitnion (or July) 323, too late for it to be interpreted as a response to a 'normal' (typically, pre-harvest) price-rise.

without, incidentally, having affected prices in Athens in 333/2. The Macedonian seizure of grain ships near Tenedos, to which allusion is made in a speech of 331, presumably took place earlier in 332/1, but the implication of the source is that the Athenians coped with the crisis by launching 100 triremes instantly. The suggestion that it was in this very year that Cyrene sent a large quantity of grain to Athens (and lesser amounts to many other Greek communities) is unconvincing. There is no indication that food shortage was widespread in this year, and in any case it is an integral (and plausible) part of the argument that the initiative and money of the Macedonians lay behind this extraordinary event.[18]

For 329/8 the main evidence is furnished by the First Fruits inscription. I have argued that the performance of the leading producer of 'Greater Attica', Lemnos (and no doubt those of Imbros and Skyros), was closer to the norm than that of Attica itself, and that harvest returns in Attica were lower than usual, indicating a bad year. The argument is relevant only to the level of local production. A shortage would have been averted if stocks were reasonably high after the search for emergency grain of the previous year, and if the grain convoy encountered no difficulties. There is a suggestion in the First Fruits inscription of price-fixing by the assembly. At one point it is stated that the popular assembly had laid down the prices of 3 drachmas for barley and 6 drachmas for wheat. These are artificially low prices, below the current rates.[19] In another inscription from the same year, prices for food and other consumer items are shown to have been noticeably higher than four years previously, but to have risen together. In a serious food crisis, the demand for non-food items (here, baskets, hats, shoes) might be expected to collapse. Finally, anything more serious than a mild shortage accompanied by modest price-rises in 329/8 seems to be ruled out by the silence of the prosecutor of Phormio, who knew only three food crises – unless he is to be charged with having deliberately passed over a shortage which he did not help to alleviate.

The naval accounts reveal the despatch in 325/4 of a colony (*apoikia*) 'to the Adriatic'. The destination (perhaps Spina or Adria) is not certainly known.[20] The details must have been contained in the original decree of the people, which does not survive. What we have is the follow-up decree of Cephisophon, 'in accordance with which Miltiades took over the triremes and quadriremes and the triaconters and their

---

[18] Ps.-Demosthenes 17.19 with Cawkwell (1961); Clinton (1971), 111–12 (prices in 333/2); *SEG* 9.2 = Tod II 196 = Harding 116 (Cyrene edict), assigned to 332/1 by Kingsley (1986). The theory of Macedonian involvement goes back to Oliverio (1933).

[19] *IG* II² 1672.283–7, with Isager and Hansen (1975), 202; Clinton (1971), 111–12.

[20] *IG* II² 1629; Isager and Hansen (1975), 26–7.

tackle' (ll. 163ff.). The decree directs that in order to execute the decree of the people 'concerning the colony to the Adriatic' (ll. 171–6), the curators of the dockyards shall hand over to the trierarchs the ships and their tackle (ll. 177–83), and the appointed trierarchs shall bring them alongside the jetty before Munichion 10 (4 May 324), fully prepared to sail (ll. 183–90). The first, second and third to present themselves shall be rewarded. The aims of the colony are stated as 'to secure for the people for all time its own ports (*emporia*) and passage of grain (*sitopompia*), and by the establishment of a naval base of its own to guard against the attacks of the Etruscan pirates' (ll. 215ff.)

For those who think that colonies and cleruchies from the eighth to the fourth century were invariably designed to ship off surplus mouths, no special explanation need be sought for the dispatch of this colony. In my view the immediate background is always crucial to the interpretation of any particular case. Here the inscription itself provides few clues, and there is no evidence from oratory. The loss of two speeches on piracy, one by Dinarchus, the other by Hyperides, is particularly regrettable. By one reconstruction, the Athenians had had a difficult winter, thanks to attacks on the western grain fleet in the late summer and early autumn. As soon as the seas were open to shipping again they sent off what was in effect a garrison to combat these problems at source. The alternative explanation, that the colony was a delayed reaction to the problems of the first half of the decade, is less plausible.

Other references to grain crisis are not precisely dated. On the occasion of a food shortage (*sitodeia*) in Greece, already alluded to, Cyrene provided grain for no fewer than 41 states and for the mother and sister of Alexander, Olympias in Macedonia and Cleopatra in Epirus. The amount of grain sent was 805,000 medimnoi by the Aeginetan standard, which comes to 1,207,500 by the more familiar Attic standard (see Figure 2). Athens received 100,000 Aeginetan or 150,000 Attic medimnoi, one-eighth of the total, weighing about 6 million kg and sufficient to feed around 30,000 people for one year (or 60,000 for 6 months, or 120,000 for three months). The inscription, which is undated, is normally placed in the period 330–323 (although 332/1 has recently been suggested by an ingenious argument). My inclination is to place it in 328/7 because of other indications that the crisis in this year was particularly grave. On this interpretation, the event falls within a period when the Greek states were not actively resisting control by the Macedonians. The idea that Macedonian inspiration, organisation and finance lie behind the event is attractive, though nothing of this surfaces in the inscription.

The composition of the list remains a mystery. It is too simple to say

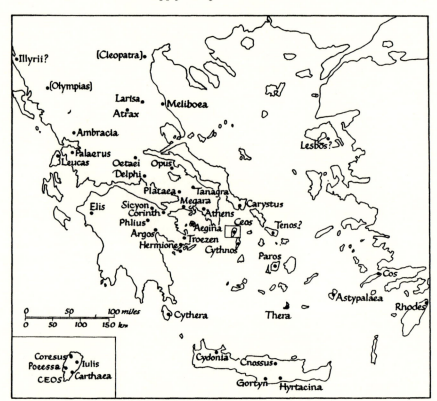

Figure 2. Communities receiving grain from Cyrene (as listed in *SEG* IX 2 = Tod II196)

Line nos.		Aeginetan medimnoi	Line nos.		Aeginetan medimnoi
46, 50	Aegina	10,000	58	Icetyrii?	1,000
19, 56	Ambracia	16,500	54	Illyrii?	3,000
7	Argos	50,000	45	Iulis (Ceos)	5,000
47	Astypalaea	5,000	8	Larisa	50,000
5	Athens	100,000	16	Lesbos?	15,000
24	Atrax (Thessaly)	10,000	20	Leucas	15,000
51	Carthaea (Ceos)	4,000	14, 36	Megara	30,000
21	Carystus	15,000	13, 37	Meliboea	28,500
53	Ceos	3,000	18, 41	Oetaei	21,400
10	Cleopatra	50,000	6, 22	Olympias	72,600
31, 59	Cnosus	10,900	26	Opus	10,000
55	Coresus (Ceos)	3,000	35	Palaerus (Acarnania)	10,000
9	Corinth	50,000	29	Paros	10,000
28	Cos	10,000	39	Phlius	8,000
27	Cydonia	10,000	44	Plataea	6,000
48, 52	Cythera	8,100	11	Rhodes	30,000
25	Cythnus	10,000	12	Sicyon	30,000
30	Delphi	10,000	32	Tanagra (Boeotia)	10,000
34	Elis	10,000	15	Tenos?	20,000
33	Gortyn	10,000	17	Thera	15,000
40	Hermione	8,000	43	Troezen	6,000
49	Hyrtacina	5,000			
				Total	805,000

Note: 1 Aeginetan medimnos = 1.5 Attic medimnoi.

that states were included and excluded primarily out of political considerations; that, for example, Macedon was on good terms with, or anxious to impress, among the western islands, Leucas but not Corcyra, Cephallenia and Zacynthus, and in Euboea only the city of Carystus. The drought, which was presumably the primary cause of the shortage, cutting a swathe across the Greek world from the north-west to the south-east, would have had an uneven impact on the states that fell in its path. Local climates were diverse, and civic governments were more or less equipped to cope with harvest shortfall. A sizeable number of communities may be assumed to have had no pressing need for the grain.[21]

Two passages in the Demosthenic corpus refer directly or indirectly to food crisis, but without indication of date.[22] In *Against Phaenippus*, the defendant is accused of, among other things, enriching himself by selling food and drink at the 'famine' prices of 18 drachmas per medimnos for barley and 12 drachmas per measure for wine. In *Against Phormio*, Lampis is accused of unloading Bosporan grain at Acanthus in Chalcidice. This was done

at a critical time, when those of you who dwelt in the city were having their barley-meal measured out to them in the Odeum, and those who dwelt in Piraeus were receiving their loaves at an obol each in the dockyard and in the long-porch, having their meal measured out to them in half-sixths of a medimnos, and being nearly trampled to death.

Rather than multiply food crises, we should assign these texts to those crises already identified. The crises of 330/29 and 328/7 appear to be the best candidates.

The prosecution speech against Dionysodorus contains the charge that the sharp practices of Cleomenes and his cronies were injurious to Athens and other Greeks 'from the time he received the government'.[23] If the year 323/2 is excepted, the allegation is quite general: the speaker does not identify any other specific food crisis that Cleomenes and his men might have aggravated. Ps.-Aristotle does appear to be supplying a historical context rather than dealing in blanket generalisations when he refers to the prohibition of the export of grain from Egypt 'at a time when there was some scarcity in the land, but elsewhere grievous hunger (*limos*)'. But without more detail it is impossible to pinpoint the

---

[21] See n. 18, above. The political situation in Cyrene may be relevant. See Coster (1951), at 10; cf. Applebaum (1979). Reynolds (1978), 113 and 117 suggests that it is this event that is recalled centuries later in a Hadrianic inscription.

[22] Ps.-Demosthenes 42.20; 34.37.

[23] Ps.-Demosthenes 56.7.

crisis in question. Did Cleomenes' meanness coincide with the arrival of grain from Cyrene?

Finally, a number of inscriptions of uncertain date honour benefactors for bringing in or presenting grain.[24]

CONCLUSION

This was a bleak period for the Athenians, who suffered at least five food crises between 338/7 and 323/2. Other states also had difficulties securing the grain they required, which made things harder for Athens. Even Egypt, one of the three main surplus-producing areas in the Mediterranean, appears to have had two bad years between 331 and 322. Thessaly, another state capable of producing large surpluses, experienced deficit in the Larisa area and also in Magnesia in perhaps 328/7. Three Thessalian cities between them received gifts from Cyrene totalling 88,500 Aeginetan medimnoi, or 132,750 Attic medimnoi. The supposition must be that the other Thessalian cities could not make up the deficiencies of these three, even if they had enough grain in reserve for themselves.

Athens was involved in the campaigns against the Macedonians at Chaeronea (338/7) and Thebes (335/4), and then in the Lamian War (323/2). On each occasion the Athenians were on the losing side, and suffered, among other things, some disruption of their food supply.

Cargo seizure by other states or by pirates was an ever-present threat. Expeditions undertaken specifically to combat piracy begin to surface in the sources in the post-Chaeronea period, and culminate in the sending out of a colony to ease the passage of grain ships in an area which the Athenians were finding hard to police.

The insecurity of the northern route means that the dominance of the Bosporan kingdom among Athens' suppliers becomes questionable in this period. Grain from the west was now vital to Athens, and recourse was had also to Egypt, at least in emergencies.

Pressure was applied to traders serving Athens to be generous and not to charge the market rate for grain where the price was inflated. The honorific decree to the trader-benefactor was born, at least as regards Athens, in the post-Chaeronea period, though Xenophon had earlier pointed out the advisability of making a display of gratitude.[25]

Pressure was put also on wealthy men, Athenians or metics, to contribute cash for the purchase of grain. A number of testimonia relate

[24] *IG* II² 342 (+ *SEG* XXIV 104); 363, 407, 408, 409, 416, 423; *Hesperia* 9 (1940), 332–3, no. 39; 43 (1974), 322–4, no. 3; 49 (1980), 251–5, no. 1.
[25] Xenophon, *Poroi* 3.3–4.

to the contributions of private individuals in 328/7. This special subscription (*epidosis*) has no known parallel in Athenian history. In addition, prominent Athenians were given more opportunities than ever before to provide personal, and no doubt also financial, service in offices relating to the grain supply. Grain commissioners (*sitonai*), unattested before Chaeronea, were appointed whenever food was short, and the board of Grain Wardens (*sitophulakes*) was expanded dramatically from 10 (5 for the city, 5 for the port) to 35 (20 for the city, 15 for the port), probably in the 320s.

Finally, if the behaviour attributed to the 'Boastful Man' in Theophrastus' *Characters* is anything to go by, patronage by the rich, ideologically incompatible with the radical democracy and practically invisible in the sources since the heyday of Cimon, was making a reappearance towards the end of the fourth century:

> In the food shortage, he gave handouts of more than five talents to needy citizens – he doesn't know how to refuse. He then tells the men sitting next to him, who are strangers, to set out some counters; and by reckoning in sums of a thousand drachmas and in round minas, and by plausibly attributing a name to each of them, he makes it ten talents. He says that these are the monies he has contributed in *eranos* loans.

The Boaster, significantly, has intruded into the world of interest-free (*eranos*) loans, an institution of mutual support among ordinary citizens which under the democracy had served as a defence mechanism against patronage.[26]

In sum, Athens after Chaeronea was in effect already showing some of the essential features of the typical Greek city of the Hellenistic period, above all, a chronic tendency to food crises, and a dependence for their resolution on wealthy and generous individuals, whether residents or outsiders. The transition was completed with the destruction of the navy, the occupation of the city and the suppression of democratic institutions, including those like the theoric fund that had served the material interests of ordinary Athenians. Athens returned to democracy, a moderate, not radical democracy, in 228, but independence was lost for ever. Hellenistic Athens was a prey to foreign powers and chronically vulnerable to food crisis. As illustration, I cite part of a decree of 270/69 in honour of an Athenian, Callias, for his role in the fruitless revolt against Macedon in 286, and a passage of Pausanias showing the weakness of Athens and its helplessness in the face of Roman power in the mid-second century BC. A central part of the inscription for Callias, after the prolegomenon and before the award of

[26] Theophrastus, *Characters* 23; with Millett (forthcoming).

honours (a golden crown, a bronze statue and a front seat at all games) reads as follows:

Whereas Callias – when the revolution of the People took place against those who were occupying the city, and they expelled the mercenary soldiers from the city, but the fort on the Mouseion was still occupied, and the countryside was in a state of war at the hands of the troops from the Piraeus, and while Demetrius with his army was approaching from the Peloponnese to attack the city – Callias learned the impending danger to the state, and choosing a thousand of the mercenary troops stationed with him on Andros, paying their wages and providing rations of grain, he came at once to the city to help the People, acting in accordance with the good will of King Ptolemy toward the People; and he marched his troops into the countryside and made every effort to protect the harvest of the grain so that as much grain as possible could be brought into the city.

And whereas, when Demetrius had arrived and encamped to besiege the city, Callias fought on the side of the People, and attacking with his troops, although a wounded man, he did not shrink from any danger, not at any moment, for the sake of the deliverance of the People ...

And whereas, upon the succession to the monarchy of the younger King Ptolemy, Callias was staying in the city and when the generals called upon him, explained the situation in which the city found itself, and begged him for the sake of the city to hasten to King Ptolemy in order that aid in the form of grain and money might be forthcoming as quickly as possible for the city, Callias himself sailing at his own expense to Cyprus and there conversing earnestly with the king on behalf of the city brought back 50 talents of silver for the People and a gift of 20,000 medimnoi of wheat, which were measured out from Delos to the agents sent by the People ...

Pausanias tells of an appeal lodged with Rome by the state of Oropus, victim of an Athenian atrocity, and of disciplinary action taken against the Athenians by the Romans, the imposition of a fine. The Athenian action and its motivation are here the main interest:

The Athenian people sacked Oropus, a state subject to them. The act was one of necessity rather than of free will, as the Athenians at the time suffered the direst poverty, because the Macedonian war had crushed them more than any other Greeks.[27]

[27] Shear (1978); Pausanias 7.11.4.

PART IV
FOOD SUPPLY AND FOOD CRISIS IN ROME
c. 509 BC – AD 250

11

THE BEGINNINGS OF EMPIRE

INTRODUCTION

Early Rome is notoriously hard to approach. The main access-route is through the annalistic tradition, which is full of fiction. The food crises of the regal period, specifically of the reigns of Romulus and Tarquin the Proud, cannot be given credence, plausible though they may appear to be. I take those recorded for the early period of the Republic rather more seriously. In this I am influenced by a passage from the *Origines* of the elder Cato, indicating that there was a tradition of systematically recording food shortages or their symptoms (among other things) in the *annales maximi*:

I am not satisfied merely to report what is in the table that is with the Pontifex Maximus, how often food is expensive, how often mist or something else cuts off the light of the moon or sun.[1]

A critic might argue that Cato's statement is evidence only for the early second century BC, that later writers did not consult any original *tabulae* or an edition of them, and in general that there is nothing in the accounts of the early shortages which could not have been invented by a Roman (or Greek) writer of the second or first century BC. My position, to which I cannot hope to convert a determined sceptic, is that the basic fact of food crisis where it is mentioned in the annalistic record can be accepted as authentic, and that the historian in confronting the 'famine narratives' can legitimately concern himself with the problem of identifying contamination by later writers and separating it off from the 'naked' annalistic accounts.[2] In this I am following the lead of Momigliano, who in an exploratory paper of 1936, which is still very

---

[1] Cato, frag. 77 P. = Gellius, 2.28.6.
[2] I follow Ogilvie (1965), on 2.9.6. My view is that there is an authentic core in the record of food crisis, which justifies an analysis such as I have attempted. However, to treat the evidence for early Rome and for later periods together, as Virlouvet (1985) does, is open to serious and obvious criticism.

influential, gave good grounds for believing that some at least of the details in the narratives can be salvaged, for example, the tradition that grain was sought in emergency in Campania and Sicily.[3] But in addition, something of use can be derived from patterns in the tradition: for example, the concentration of food crises in the first century and a quarter of the Republic (508–383), and their virtual absence thereafter until the invasion of Hannibal. The literary sources for much of the third century (291–220) are thin, as only the *Summaries* of Livy survive. But there is still the contrast between Livy's first and second five books to be explained. It is perfectly credible that the Romans should have been much more vulnerable to food crisis in the first period, when they were weak, than when they were continuously expanding their territory and resources at the expense of other Italians.

In this chapter I examine the food crises of early Rome chronologically (in bare outline) and then thematically (taking in more detail), with a view to separating what is credible in the annalistic record from what reflects later historical events and the attitudes of Roman writers and their sources.

FOOD CRISES

1. In 508 (according to the tradition), Lars Porsenna of Clusium in Etruria invaded Roman territory. Livy says that the senate sent for grain to the Volsci and to Cumae, 'nationalised' the trade in salt, and withdrew taxes on the plebs – all this for a political motive, if it can be believed (it cannot), to head off defections to the enemy when the inevitable siege and shortage ensued. Dionysius has the Romans seeking grain in Cumae and in the cities of the Pomptine plain (Volscian territory) while the siege and shortage were actually in progress, and gaining some temporary respite thereby. Whether an extended blockade actually occurred is unclear. Rome surrendered to the enemy. Patriotic pride required that the minds of Romans should be distracted from this unpalatable fact by stories of protracted siege and heroic exploits on the Roman side (Horatius, Mucius, Cloelia). The occurrence of food shortage following perhaps a short siege need not be doubted.[4]

2. Under 496 Dionysius records a scarcity of provisions following the absence of a crop and the obstruction of imports by war. A temple of Ceres, Liber and Libera was vowed and three years later dedicated. Livy allotted only half a chapter to the years from 498 to 496. He says

---

[3] See Momigliano (1936); Frederiksen (1984), 164–6.
[4] Livy 2.9–14; Dionysius 5.21–7, 32, 65.

nothing of Ceres. He does however note the senate's direction to the people that the consul whom they chose to dedicate the temple of Mercury should also, among other things, preside over the grain supply. The implication is that grain was short in the late spring. The date of the dedication is given as May 15, 495.

Ceres (Demeter) was a Greek deity as indeed was Hermes (Mercury). The cult was probably introduced from Campania; her temple was embellished with paintings and statues by two Greek artists, Damophilus and Gorgasus. The establishment of this cult implies the existence of relations with the Greek world of Italy and Sicily in the sphere of not only culture but also commerce, and these are confirmed by the archaeological evidence.[5]

3. Under 492 it is recorded that a rise in the price of grain was followed by a severe food crisis 'such as hits a city under siege'. The root cause is given as the secession of the plebs, which left the fields uncultivated. Grain was sought from Etruria, the Volsci, Cumae and Sicily, but of these possible sources only that from Etruria came through with dispatch. The arrival of this grain and the sending out of colonists to 'top up' an existing colonial settlement at Velitrae and to found Norba eased the situation. The ships sent to Sicily spent the winter there and arrived back in Rome the following year with a substantial cargo of grain. This was eventually made available to purchasers at a below-market price.

The embassy to Sicily and the food crisis which necessitated it receive some confirmation from a passage in Dionysius. In the process of criticising a number of Roman historians for mistaking the Sicilian tyrant who received the embassy, Dionysius reveals the existence of independent, presumably Greek, sources, who knew of the embassy and assigned it an Olympian date:

For the embassy appointed to go to Sicily set sail in the second year of the seventy-second Olympiad, when Hybrilides was archon at Athens, seventeen years after the expulsion of the kings, as these and almost all the other historians agree.[6]

4. War with the city of Veii in southern Etruria placed by the sources in 477 brought food crisis (*annona premente*), which would have been more serious had the Veientes been permitted to blockade the city. Thus Livy. According to Dionysius, enemy raids had prevented the

---

[5] Dionysius 6.17, 94; Tacitus, *Ann.* 2.49; Pliny, *Hist. nat.* 35.154; Cicero, *Balb.* 55; Valerius Maximus 1.1; Livy 2.21.7 cf. 2.26.5. See Le Bonniec (1958); on commercial links, see Frederiksen (1984), 158–73, with bibliography.

[6] Livy 2.34–5; Dionysius 7.1–2, 12–15; etc.; Plutarch, *Cor.* 16; Cassius Dio 5.18.4; cf. Livy 2.41.8–9, Dionysius 8.70.5. See Diodorus 11.37.7 for Spurius Cassius' later attempt (in 486) to have the purchase money returned to buyers. And see n. 3.

land being sown and kept merchants away. The situation was eased (*laxior annona*) by the arrival of grain from Campania, the release of hoarded grain, and above all the cessation of the war.[7]

5. Livy, under 456: 'Affairs were quiet both at home and abroad. There was a shortage of grain owing to excessive rains. A law was passed opening up the Aventine to settlement.' This reads like an unembellished annalistic entry.[8]

6. In 453, according to Livy, 'two terrible misfortunes came at the same time, food crisis and epidemic disease' (*fames pestilentiaque*). The corresponding passage in Dionysius mentions first only disease at Rome; but a later reference to the double affliction (*limos* plus *loimos*) of Rome's neighbours, to whom the disease spread, might have been intended to cover Rome as well. In any case, Dionysius goes on to indicate that while the disease finally ceased in the following year (452), food shortage due to the impact of disease on the rural population was only eased in the beginning of spring with the arrival of foreign grain.[9]

7. 440–439. 'The troubles began with a harsh food crisis', probably following harvest failure. L. Minucius was given responsibility for the grain supply (in Livy his title is *praefectus annonae*) and sent for grain by land and sea, but with little success. His next moves were not much more successful: he attacked the grain-dealers, reduced the rations of slaves and forced those with stocks to disgorge them. Many plebeians committed suicide by jumping into the Tiber. In contrast with the meagre success of Minucius, a private citizen Spurius Maelius secured ample quantities of grain from Etruria and Campania and sold it for 2 instead of 12 denarii. He was assassinated by Servilius Ahala, who either bore the official title of Master of the Horse or acted as a private citizen on behalf of the senate. Minucius distributed the grain assembled by Maelius at 1 as per modius, and the shortage came to an end in the second year.

This story has rightly been found incredible in the form it has come down to us. We are faced with several options, if we wish to reduce the problematic element. One is to remove one of the two leading characters, Minucius and Maelius.[10] But which one? The Minucii were associated with the grain supply in later ages: a portico named after them was located in a grain market and was used for the grain distributions from the time of the emperor Claudius. It is true that the

---

[7] Livy 2.50–52.1; Dionysius 9.25–6.
[8] Livy 3.31.1. See 3.32.7 cf. Dionysius 10.31–2 for the antiquarian tradition that a tribune Icilius promoted the law.
[9] Livy 3.32.2; Dionysius 10.53–4; Orosius 2.13.1; Augustine, *Civ. Dei* 3.17.
[10] Momigliano (1936) favours Minucius, but Ogilvie (1965), 550–1 Maelius. See also Gagé (1966); Lintott (1970), 13–18; Crawford (1974), 273–5, no. 242; Pollera (1979).

portico could not have been erected earlier than the third century BC. On the other hand, no good reason has yet been suggested for impugning the historicity of a fifth-century Minucius. The central part of the Maelius/Servilius strand of the story also has claims to authenticity; the Fasti support Servilius, and Maelius too, if the tribune Spurius Maelius of 436 is a double. Again, there seems no good reason for suppressing one of the sub-plots rather than the other. Neither is in itself improbable: the appointment of a special official in a serious shortage; and the eruption of a serious political crisis in the context of such a shortage. The authentic core of this multi-layered fabrication defies identification.[11]

8. An outbreak of epidemic disease is recorded for 433. A temple was vowed to Apollo. The magistrates predicted food crisis because of the ravages of the disease among farmers, and were able to avoid it by sending for grain to Etruria, the Pomptine district, Cumae and Sicily.[12]

9. In a digression concerning A. Cornelius Cossus, Livy says that his consulship, which he places in 428, 'fell within a period of about three years when there were no wars owing to a pestilence and a dearth of crops (*inopia frugum*)'. Livy and Dionysius both report under 428 a drought and disease but not specifically a food shortage.[13]

10. An epidemic broke out at the beginning of 412. This was followed in the consular year 411 by a food shortage (*inopia frugum*) due to neglect of cultivation. The efforts made to remedy the situation read suspiciously like those of 492, and Livy wrongly reports tyrants in Sicily in 411. There is however one new detail, that the Samnites had conquered Capua and Cumae and prevented the import of grain from Campania.[14]

11. In 399 there was a severe winter followed by a summer of epidemic. But shortage was avoided (there was no rise in price) because adequate supplies had been imported earlier.[15]

12. In 392 drought and heat brought food crisis and disease.[16]

13. In 390, according to the tradition, the Gauls occupied Rome after winning the battle of the Allia. The troops in the citadel are said to have been starved into surrender. This is suspect, along with the whole story of the siege. Roman propagandists produced their own versions of this traumatic episode in Roman history. Rome was taken, but the Romans may simply have evacuated the city in advance of the Gauls'

---

[11] Livy 4.12–16; Dionysius 12.1–4; Pliny, *Hist. nat.* 18.15; Orosius 2.13.1.
[12] Livy 4.25.3–6, 26.5.
[13] Livy 4.20.9, 30.7.11; cf. Ogilvie (1965) 563–4; Dionysius 12.6; Orosius 2.13.9.
[14] Livy 4.52.
[15] Livy 5.13.4 cf. 14.3; Augustine, *Civ. Dei* 3.17.   [16] Livy 5.31.5; Dionysius 13.4.

arrival. That the war interfered with the food supply of Rome and brought hardship to its inhabitants need not be doubted.[17]

14. Under 384 the death of Manlius is recorded, followed by an epidemic, and subsequently a food shortage (*inopia frugum*).[18]

15. In 299 the Romans were engaged in war with the Etruscans and Samnites and experienced a rise in food prices. The aediles prevented a disaster by energetically acquiring and distributing grain.[19]

16. In 296 in the course of the Samnite war the Etruscan seer Manius prophesied victory, epidemic and a food crisis so serious that the people would be forced to look for alternative foods. The prophecy is said to have been fulfilled in all respects, though there are no details of any food crisis in the historical sources.[20]

Did shortages consequent on epidemics occur also in 472, 463 and 436? All serious epidemics had a detrimental effect on the food supply, in so far as local production was halted or greatly reduced. Thus under 412 Livy talks of neglect of cultivation as usual in such times. But in 433 and 399, according to Livy, shortage was avoided after an epidemic by precautionary action taken by the magistrates.[21]

ANALYSIS

At the outset I adopted the position that there was a kernel of truth in the historical record of food crises (to which may be added epidemics). In cataloguing recorded crises I made a start in separating out the more obvious fictional detail in the narratives. In the schematic presentation of the main features of the food crises that follows, the same purpose is pursued but on a broader front.

Causes

War is the most commonly attested cause of food crisis. The adverse effect of war on food supplies needs no special demonstration. War and subsistence crisis (*bellum/fames*) are stock conjunctions, as are siege and subsistence crisis (*obsidio/fames*). Siege-induced crises were the worst. Livy admits this in an indirect way, when he says that the serious peacetime crisis of 493 was 'such as comes to besieged cities'.[22]

[17] Livy 5.39–48; Plutarch, *Cam.* 23.1; Appian, *Hist.* 4.6; Orosius 2.19.8.
[18] Livy 6.20.15, 21.1–6.
[19] Livy 10.11.9 cf. 10.9.10–14.   [20] Zonaras 8.1.3 cf. Cassius Dio frag. 36.28.
[21] Dionysius 9.40 (472); Livy 3.6–8 cf. Dionysius 9.67–8 (463); Livy 4.21.3, 5–6 (436); Livy 4.52.4 (412); 4.25.3–6 (433); 5.13.1 (399).
[22] Livy 2.34.2.

If the sources are to be believed, and there is good reason for scepticism on this point, there were two classic sieges of Rome, one Etruscan (508) and one Gallic (390), and one 'near-miss' (Etruscan, 477). There is doubt over whether the Romans on the occasions in question held out for long enough to provoke a siege, rather than surrendering or abandoning their city.

In any case, Rome was constantly involved in wars, and these were not wars of expansion. Rome in the fifth century was forced onto the defensive, its territory was regularly attacked by one of the many rival cities or tribal groups in the neighbourhood, its economic life was disrupted, the flow of food from the countryside cut off, and the city population swelled somewhat by the influx of people from the country (though early Rome, essentially an agricultural community, knew no sharp urban/rural divide). It is significant that food crises are frequent in this period rather than the fourth and third centuries when Rome was in the ascendant, no longer exposed to continual attack, and able to obtain food supplies at the expense of other states.

After war, epidemic disease is the next most common explanation given for food crisis. In 453 and 413 (and probably in 384), disease hit the farming population and disrupted production. No conjunction between disease and shortage is recorded under 472 and 453, while timely imports warded off shortage in 433 and 399. In 428 and 392 disease was a secondary phenomenon, following drought or a harsh winter.

Climatic irregularities are cited as a cause of food crisis in 428 and 392 (drought) and 456 (excessive rainfall). In addition, the crisis of 440 was probably caused by a bad harvest, if we accept the 'plebeian' version, and reject the 'patrician' charge that politics and 'bright lights' had lured farmers away from the fields. It is extremely significant that such notices are rare, and entirely absent from the record after the Gallic invasion. The agricultural performance of Rome's home territory was less relevant to the situation of Roman consumers as Rome's capacity to acquire supplies of food from other states, by force if necessary, increased.

Finally, the food crisis of 492 was brought on by civil dissension, culminating in the plebeian secession. Livy writes:

This year there was no war to occasion trouble from without and the breach at home had been healed. But another and a much more serious misfortune befell the nation. First the price of grain went up, from men's failure to cultivate the fields during the withdrawal of the plebs. This was followed by food crisis, such as comes to besieged cities.[23]

[23] Livy 2.34.1–2.

173

Dionysius offers chronological precision:

Rome suffered from a great scarcity of grain, which had its origin in the secession. For the populace seceded from the patricians after the autumnal equinox, just about the beginning of seedtime ... and from that time the two classes remained aloof from each other until the state was composed and reunited, the reconciliation being effected not long before the winter solstice. During that interval, which is the season in which all planting of grain is best done, the land was destitute of people to cultivate it, and remained so for a long time.[24]

The struggle between the patrician and plebeian orders had reached a critical phase. Out of this crisis would emerge the office of tribune of the plebs, distrusted by Livy, a good conservative Italian/Roman of the first century BC. At one point he comments that the senate could always have neutralised the tribunes by ensuring that the people received an ample flow of inexpensive grain.[25] The lesson for Rome of the last century of the Republic is clear.

The Struggle of the Orders was not identical with the conflict between rich and poor: the former was between two status-groups, the latter between two classes. In Dionysius' account of the secession, the 'more prosperous' joined the patricians, while the 'thetic' element went over to the secessionists. But well-heeled plebeians were skilful at manipulating the class strife over debt, in particular, in order to obtain the political ends they were seeking.

Behaviour of the people

The material assembled under this heading is overtly political in content and strongly reflects the struggle of the last century of the Republic between 'conservative' and 'radical' politicians in Rome.

Dionysius, as a foreigner, presents himself as impressed by the absence of violence in early Roman politics, by the way in which the Romans settled their differences by persuasion and reason.[26] The only clear reference to violent action taken by the poor in a food crisis comes under 477, during the Etruscan invasion. A serious food shortage was aggravated by the influx of countryfolk. The enlarged urban population was volatile:

This multitude was not easy to placate. They were exasperated at their misfortune, and gathering together in the Forum, clamoured against the magistrates. They rushed in a body to the houses of the rich and endeavoured to seize without payment the provisions that were stored up by them.[27]

---

[24] Dionysius 7.1.1–2.   [25] Livy 2.34.7.
[26] Dionysius 7.66.5.   [27] Dionysius 9.25.

In contrast, Dionysius can write under 492, the first year of the food crisis induced by the plebeian secession, when upper-class/lower-class relations were at their nadir:

However, their hatred did not lead to any irreparable mischief as often happens in like disorders. For on the one hand the poor did not attack the houses of the rich, where they suspected they should find stores of provisions laid up, nor attempt to raid the public markets.[28]

What is to be made of this? The annalists are least reliable when they are reconstructing the political struggles of the early Republic. Dionysius and his sources may well have deliberately played down the incidence and seriousness of popular disorder, lest the impression be given that the senate was not in control of the situation. Predictably, Dionysius follows up the second remark quoted above with the assertion that the rich, for their part, did not oppress the poor by violence. He knew, and says so in this passage, that political violence was endemic in Italy in the first century BC. His purpose was to condemn the recent past by contrasting it with a remote, idealised epoch, the true character of which was irretrievably lost.

This same passage of Dionysius contains a classic text for the consumption of strange foods by the hungry. He says that they did not riot, 'but consented to buy small quantities of food for a high price, and when they lacked money they sustained life by using roots and grass for food'.[29] This cannot be accepted as an authentic notice. On the other hand, the reference to emigration to neighbouring cities has been thought to relate to the so-called 'right to migrate' (to Rome), and if so may be historical at base.[30]

There is an unusual element in Livy's description of the behaviour of the hungry poor in 440–439: 'Many of the plebeians lost hope, and sooner than suffer torment by prolonging their existence, covered up their heads and threw themselves into the Tiber'.[31] Livy has uncharacteristically lifted the lid off something here. Ogilvie comments: 'An unexpected glimpse, probably a literary adaptation of an old ceremony, employed in time of famine, of throwing pensioners into the Tiber as a sacrifice (Festus 450L *sexagenarios de ponte* ...). The employment of such a ceremony would surely have figured in the Annals.' But Livy, or his sources, has not faithfully reported this antique ritual, but rather transformed it into an act of voluntary suicide, while maintaining its religious character.

---

[28] Dionysius 7.18.3.   [29] Cf. Dionysius 13.4.
[30] Humbert (1978), 86ff., 91ff.   [31] Livy 4.12.11.

175

Behaviour of the rich

Speculation and 'euergetism', or the public display of generosity, are two possible responses of rich Romans, to judge from evidence from other communities of antiquity. Do they surface in the sources for early Rome?

The line between the legitimate storage of necessities and the stockpiling for the purpose of profiteering is an imprecise one, and the ancient sources are for the most part equivocal or uninformative. Those with stockpiled grain were commonly forced by civic authorities to empty their storehouses faster and more completely than they might have done otherwise, but the charge of speculation is very rarely levelled overtly, and the context sometimes suggests that such an accusation would be inappropriate. An example is the crisis of 440–439, where in Livy's version Minucius, the 'prefect of the grain supply', among other things compelled men to declare their stock of grain and sell the surplus above the requirements of one month. It is clear that Livy wants us to remark upon the harshness of Minucius' measure rather than any illegal or immoral behaviour on the part of those forced to disgorge. Moreover, Livy goes on to say that grain-traders (*frumentarii*), who were presumably not identical with the grain-hoarders just referred to, were attacked; their alleged offence could only have been profiteering.

Livy in his narrative of the food crisis of 476 does suggest that certain individuals at least failed to co-operate with the state authorities: we hear that 'men brought out the stores which they had concealed', apparently after the crisis had subsided. The version of Dionysius merely has the consuls ordering those with 'more than a moderate amount of grain for their own subsistence' to bring it forward.

Under 508, Livy says that marketing of salt was taken over by the state because private individuals were charging a high price. The notice is unique in its overt reference to speculation and its specification of salt as a commodity in demand. Whether it deserves more credence for these reasons than the other texts just discussed is a moot point.[32]

Euergetism is also (almost) absent from the documents. Here the case is different. It is a legitimate suspicion that hoarding and speculation in necessities by wealthy landowners and traders were standard occurrences that were soft-pedalled by the upper-class sources, and rarely formed the subject of an annalistic notice. The public display of generosity, however, was not compatible with Roman political practice.

[32] Livy 2.9.6, 52.2; 4.12.10.

Spurius Maelius is the only private benefactor to figure in the narratives of food crisis in early Rome. According to the tradition an equestrian and therefore not a member of the 'political class', he was spectacularly successful in bringing in grain from all sides. He did this, moreover, at a time when the official in charge of the grain supply could only produce a trickle of grain from Etruria – not the only implausibility in this fantastic story. Maelius proceeded to sell his grain cheap or (according to Dionysius) to give it away to the very poor. He was put to death on the grounds that he was aiming at tyranny.

Why were private benefactions of this type the object of official displeasure? Why could it be so readily assumed that Maelius was aiming at unconventional office or power? Maelius acted purely on his own initiative, came – though wealthy – from the wrong social background, and spread his bounty indiscriminately.

In Rome, the job of securing and distributing emergency grain rested on the shoulders of elected magistrates. If there was gratitude to be earned for feeding the hungry, this was the preserve of senior senators. This largely accounts for the resentment fastened on tribunes (the 'double' of Maelius in Livy was a tribune)[33] when they emerged in the late Republic as sponsors of grain laws and in general as favourites of the populace. Private individuals were not called upon to show generosity in the public arena in the manner that was standard among Greek cities of the Hellenistic and Roman periods, and anyone who acted in this way without invitation could expect to be viewed with hostility and suspicion, especially if he was not a practising politician. Finally, Maelius did not behave as a typical patron giving sustenance to his clients. His distributions or cheap sales were for the benefit of 'the poor', not merely his own dependants.

Private patronage is also rarely on display in the documents. But patronage, unlike euergetism, can be assumed to have existed. Rich men supported their poor retainers. The practice does not feature in the annalistic record because it was regarded as essentially a private matter.

Something akin to patronage surfaces once, though not in a 'famine narrative', and in a form 'larger than life'. Manlius, when pleading for his life in 383, 'brought forward nearly 400 men to whom he had lent money without interest, thus saving their goods from being sold and their persons from enslavement'. Manlius' patronage is better described as euergetism. His generosity was not confined to his own clients, but embraced all those in need. In the view of Livy, he was the original 'popularis' patrician, the first to take up the cause of the

[33] Livy 4.21.3.

177

plebeians.[34] Hence he was dangerous in the eyes of conservative senators.

Government response

1. *Imports.* Grain was sought in emergencies from the Pomptine plains in Latium, that is, from the communities of the Volsci, from Campania (specifically Cumae), Sicily and Etruria. The historicity of these missions can be accepted.

Such notices apparently did not specify the quantity of grain brought in. Dionysius' note under 492 is an exception:

Then too Geganius and Valerius, who had been sent earlier as envoys to Sicily, arrived with many merchantmen in which they brought 50,000 medimnoi of wheat, one half of it purchased at a very low price and the rest sent by the tyrant as a free gift to the Romans and conveyed at his own expense.[35]

This looks ahead to Livy's notices concerning the generosity of Hiero of Syracuse in the late third century, but is not necessarily to be impugned on that score. However, it is most likely that the annals merely stated that grain in quantity had arrived from Sicily – on the model of the later notices under the years 203, 202 and 200 BC.[36] Who was sent in search of grain, or who was responsible for its acquisition? Here the message of the sources rings true. Details are furnished under 508, 492, 440, 412 and 298. Acquisition of emergency or supplementary grain supplies was an obligation of the consuls in office, until the aediles emerged in the early third century as the responsible officials. Thus, for example, in 492 and 412 the consuls sent for grain, and in time to head off a food crisis. There was a tradition that once, in 440, an extraordinary appointment of a grain commissioner was made by the senate, whom Livy calls *praefectus annonae*, recalling the permanent official with that title instituted in the last years of the emperor Augustus and after the composition of Livy's *History*. There are many problematic elements in the story of Minucius and Maelius, as has been seen, but some such appointment is not to be rejected simply because of its rarity.

Anyway, there is no doubt in the minds of the sources that the senate collectively, and its leading magistrates in particular, bore responsibility for the grain supply, and that this was a service rendered the mass of the people. The preoccupation of later annalists with this last theme and its implications is the origin of various elaborations and embellishments in the narrative. Under 508 Livy represents the dispatch of

[34] Livy 6.11.7, 20.6.   [35] Dionysius 7.20.   [36] See below, p. 193.

envoys to buy grain as one of the 'many concessions' offered by the senate to the plebs at this time. It was a favour they could ill afford to neglect if they wanted civil peace. Dionysius says the consuls of 492 were sensitive to this:

The consuls ... took great care to supply the city plentifully with both grain and all other provisions, believing that the harmony of the masses depended on their well-being in this respect.[37]

The plebeians are often represented as having accused the patricians of negligence and dishonesty in the management of the grain-supply.[38] The lengthy debate in Dionysius over the price at which the Sicilian grain should be sold is in fact concerned with the broader issue of senatorial responsibility. The debate is sheer invention. It would not have been difficult for historians to conjure up a full-scale political confrontation between hard-liners and liberals on the basis of reports of later debates of this kind. There were in all ages senators who argued against cheap grain for the poor and were in general opposed to making concessions to the lower classes. Livy took sides in this debate. It was his opinion that the creation of the tribunate could have been blocked, and that even afterwards tribune-inspired civil strife (*seditio*) was avoidable, if the senate had behaved responsibly.[39]

2. *Warfare and colonisation.* Under 476 Dionysius writes:

Servius Servilius and A. Verginius succeeded to the consulship, both being men of experience in warfare. To them the Tyrrhenian war, though great and difficult, seemed pure gold in comparison with the conflict within the city walls.[40]

In 492, according to Livy, the senate's response to the popular outcry over debt was to distract the people with more warfare, this time against the Volsci. In the course of the war Suessa Pompetia was sacked, the territory of Velitrae seized and the city colonised. No motive is offered in Livy, but Dionysius comments:

After this, he, Valerius, sent out colonists to occupy the land they had taken from the Volscians, choosing them from among the poor; these would not only guard the conquered country, but would also leave the seditious element in the city diminished in number.[41]

Moreover, Dionysius offers a fuller explanation, and this time introduces food shortage as a factor, at a later stage in his narrative.[42] Plague had wiped out most of the population of Velitrae. The survivors

---

[37] Dionysius 7.20.　　[38] Livy 3.12.7 cf. Dionysius 7.73.3.　　[39] Livy 2.34.7.
[40] Dionysius 9.25.1.　　[41] Dionysius 6.43 cf. Livy 2.25.5, 17.6.　　[42] Dionysius 7.12–13.

sent envoys, surrendered the city and asked for additional colonists. The Romans resolved to send a large colony there,

in consideration of the many advantages that would result to them from that measure. For the place itself, if occupied by an adequate garrison, seemed capable of proving a serious check and hindrance to the designs of any who might be disposed to bring a rebellion or create any disturbance; and it was expected that the shortage of foodstuffs under which the city then laboured would be far less serious if a considerable part of the citizens moved elsewhere. But above all other considerations, the sedition which was now flaring up again, before the former one was as yet satisfactorily appeased, induced them to vote to send out the colony.

The motives attributed to the Romans for going to war are a fabrication of the annalistic historians. They are none the less plausible up to a point. In the first place, it is a fair inference from the decisions and actions of the leaders of the Roman state, that warfare was the preferred alternative to civil justice at home and a fair distribution of Rome's economic resources among her citizens. It was precisely because Rome was an inegalitarian society, in which the means of production were dominated by the few, that the lower classes were so vulnerable to debt and food crisis. Secondly, warfare undoubtedly provided short-term gratification for the destitute in the form of booty.

Whether the Romans were seeking long-term advantages in this period, however, is another matter. The reality of a causal chain leading from domestic disturbance (food crisis, debt crisis) through warfare to the colonisation of alien territory is dubious. The dispatch of colonists is recorded on several occasions in the troubled 490s – to Signia in 495, to Velitrae in 494 and 492 and to Norba in 492. Rome organised these colonies, but they were of Latin not Roman status, some of the colonists came from elsewhere, and they did not technically constitute an expansion of Roman territory.[43]

A brief notice in Livy does point to Roman gains, although he makes nothing of it. Sandwiched between the resettlement of Signia and the (dated) consecration of the temple of Mercury, we read, under 495: 'At Rome 21 tribes were formed.'[44] The required sense is given by the epitome of Livy: 'The number of tribes was increased to 21.' The Romans had exploited their victory over the Latins at Lake Regillus in 496 to take land from neighbouring states and establish on it eleven new rural tribes. Thereafter, however, there was virtually no Roman expansion and no augmentation of rural tribes for approximately one hundred years, that is to say, until the defeat of Veii and the division of its territory between Romans and Etruscans in the period between 393

[43] Livy 2.21.7; 2.31.4; 2.34.6; Dionysius 7.12–13. Salmon (1969), 42ff.   [44] Livy 2.21.7.

and 387. The fifth century, unlike the fourth, was a period of alliance with the Latins against mutual enemies (the Etruscans, Volsci, Aequi and Sabini), not of aggrandisement at their expense.[45]

CONCLUSION

The fifth century has claims to uniqueness in Roman history, as the only period in which the Roman state lacked the capacity to alleviate the distress of poor Romans by the fruits of conquest. The relative weakness of the Romans is reflected in the susceptibility of the community to food crisis arising from warfare and civil dislocation. A turning-point was the defeat of their powerful northern neighbour Veii and the digestion of its territory, a process slowed up temporarily by the Gallic invasion. Thereafter, the vulnerability of the Roman consumer was substantially reduced, as Roman armies steadily expanded the sphere of influence of the Roman state. At first, the activity was concentrated close to home. The Romans fed their hungry on the crops of their neighbours and planted them on land ceded by defeated enemies. The conquered were required also to furnish supplies (and manpower) for the next stage of conquest. In time, the Romans would be raiding and exploiting systematically the resources of regions across the seas. It was on the surplus extracted from subject states that Rome's soldiers and non-producing civilians would be fed.

---

[45] Humbert (1978), 58–64. New tribes (4) were added in 387, and also (2 each) in 458, 332, 318, 299 and 241. See Taylor (1960).

12

RULERS OF THE MEDITERRANEAN

In 123 BC Gaius Gracchus as tribune of the plebs carried a measure providing for the monthly sale of grain to citizens of Rome at the fixed, low price of 6⅓ asses per modius, and for the construction of state granaries. Regular distributions of grain were a novelty in Rome and, on the scale envisaged in the Gracchan law, quite unparalleled in the earlier history of the Mediterranean world. Their institution presupposes an extraordinary expansion of Rome's power and resources, the development of a comprehensive network of supply, and a dramatic growth of the population of the city of Rome to the point where the vulnerability of its poorer inhabitants to hunger and starvation could become a political issue. This chapter sets out the main developments in the matter of supply and distribution, and assesses the ability of the Roman state to feed a fast-rising city population, in the century that separated the beginning of the Hannibalic War from the tribunate of Gaius Gracchus.

SUPPLY

Overseas suppliers

Cicero in a speech of 66 BC tells how Pompey as Grain Commissioner 'visited Sicily, explored Africa and sailed to Sardinia ... and secured those three sources of our country's food supplies'. In the age of Cicero, Sicily, Africa and Sardinia were all provinces which paid taxes to Rome in kind in the form of grain. The tithe of Sicily brought in around 3 million modii of grain each year, but the Roman government sometimes drew as much again, or more, from the province. Africa might have been sending around 8 million modii of grain to Rome as tax in the same period.[1]

---

[1] Cicero, *Imp. Pomp.* 34; *2 Verr.* 3.136 (Sicily). The only figures relevant to Africa are in Plutarch, *Caes.* 55 (for Africa Nova) and Livy 43.6.13 cf. 11 (for Cirta and Carthage).

This trio of provinces was not complete until 146, when the north African province was carved out of the old Carthaginian empire, and production presumably took some time to reach the late Republican levels. Part of Sicily and Sardinia were made provinces as early as 241 and 238 respectively, but a tax in grain was not instituted immediately, and the amount of grain coming to the city of Rome from these sources was insubstantial until the last years of the third century. The Romans did not control the kingdom of Syracuse, which contained some of the most productive areas of Sicily, until 211. Furthermore, the two fledgeling provinces had to be garrisoned, certainly from 218, and the resident army fed on provisions raised locally or sent from Rome. Livy attributes the following judgement to Roman senators in 215: 'Sicily and Sardinia, which before the war had paid taxes in kind, were hardly feeding the armies that garrisoned them.'[2]

In this transitional period (down to 210), more grain came from Sicily than through tax. Similarly, African grain reached Rome or Rome's armies before the inauguration of the province in 146. Such grain came from 'friends and allies' of the Romans, most conspicuously, Hiero II of Syracuse (down to 215) and Massinissa of Numidia (between 200 and 170), but also from Rome's defeated enemies, the Carthaginians (also 200–170).[3] How frequent and how substantial were these offerings, and on what basis were they made?

Hiero II of Syracuse provided grain for Roman soldiers or civilians on a number of occasions between 263, when he abandoned the Carthaginian alliance and negotiated a peace treaty (renewed in 248), and 215, the year of his death. Polybius reports that the Romans accepted his offer of friendship in the first instance in the expectation that he would furnish them with supplies.[4] In fact, the Romans appear to have received grain from him in the course of the First Punic War only in emergencies, during the sieges of Agrigentum in 262 and Lilybaeum in 250.[5] Polybius' narrative for 251–248 suggests that the responsibility for supplying their armies in Sicily ordinarily lay with the authorities in Rome, and that their efforts were supplemented by allies who paid taxes. Roman armies also foraged when opportunity offered. In emergencies, they leant on allies for further contributions, and

---

[2] Livy 23.48.7.

[3] Livy's narrative is lost after 167 BC. One-off gifts of grain came in addition from Sicily and Spain. See Livy 33.42.8; 30.26.5–6.

[4] Polybius 1.16.6–10 cf. Diodorus 23.4.1; Zonaras 8.9. I follow Eckstein (1980), in holding that this was a treaty of peace and not a formal alliance; cf. Gruen (1984), 67–8.

[5] But the only source for the gift of 250 is Diodorus 24.1.4, an exact doublet of 23.8.1. See also Polybius 1.18.11.

approached friends.[6] Hiero, as a friend, was not bound by the terms of his treaty to aid the Romans, nor was he turned to regularly for grain or equipment.

Hiero gave grain to the Romans at least twice in the inter-war period (240–219). In 237 he appeared in person in Rome with 200,000 modii of wheat as a gift to the Roman people. This dramatic gesture is to be understood in the light of two recent occurrences, the Mercenary War in which Hiero sent aid to Carthage, and the Roman seizure of Sardinia from the Carthaginians. His provision of grain to the Roman armies in the Celtic War of the 220s was of a different character; he was paid for it after the war ended.[7]

Hiero's most handsome services to Rome date to the first years of the Second Punic War. As in the first war, it was almost invariably Hiero who took the initiative. In 218 he met the consular army in the straits of Messina, and promised the consul 'that with the same spirit with which in his youth he had helped the Roman People in the former war he would help them now as an old man, and would furnish grain and clothing gratis to the legions of the consul and the naval allies'. Hiero was only once asked to fulfil his promise, in 216, and then as a last resort, after the praetor in Sicily had been told by the senate that there were no supplies or money in Rome. 'Titus Otacilius sent legates to Hiero, the mainstay of the Roman people, and received what money was needed for pay, and grain for six months.'[8]

Earlier in the same year Hiero had sent, as a gesture of sympathy to the Romans after the disastrous defeat at Lake Trasimene, a golden Victory weighing 220 pounds, 300,000 modii of wheat and 200,000 modii of barley (with more available on request), and 1,000 archers and slingers, with the earnest request that these gifts be accepted. In 215 he sent 200,000 modii of wheat and 100,000 modii of barley to support a Roman force guarding the Adriatic against possible aggressive movements by the Macedonian king, Philip V. In 210 Roman senators would refer to Hiero as 'that most loyal servant of the Roman empire' who had made his kingdom in south-eastern Sicily 'the granary and treasury' of the Roman people.[9]

By 210, however, Hiero had been dead for five years, and his teenaged grandson and successor Hieronymus had changed sides and had eventually lost his kingdom to the newly enlarged Sicilian

[6] Polybius 1.39.8, 1.52.5 (supplies from Rome); 1.18.4 cf. 1.52.8 (contributions from allies regular or extra); 1.17.9 (foraging).

[7] Diodorus 25.14; Eutropius 3.1.3 cf. 2.1 (237).

[8] Livy 21.50.9–10 (218); 23.21.5 (216); cf. 23.21.6 for contributions from Sardinian allies.

[9] Livy 22.37; 23.38.13; 24.21.9; 26.23.2.

province. The wisdom of Hiero's 'corn diplomacy' was dramatically vindicated. Thereafter, grain from south-eastern Sicily would come to Rome not sporadically as gifts but annually as tribute.[10]

After the Hannibalic War, a deutero-Hiero emerged in the form of a king of Numidia, Massinissa. In 200 Massinissa sent 200,000 modii of wheat and 200,000 modii of barley to Macedonia where the Roman army was operating. In 198 he sent 200,000 modii of (indeterminate) grain to the army in Greece. In 191 he promised 500,000 modii of wheat and 300,000 modii of barley for the army in Greece, and 300,000 modii of wheat and 250,000 modii of barley for the city of Rome. On this occasion the answer was given 'that the Roman people would use the grain if payment was accepted for it'. In 170 he promised 1,000,000 modii of wheat and 500,000 modii of barley to wherever the senate and Roman people wanted it delivered.[11]

Massinissa's motives are transparent. In 200 and 170 he was matching a Carthaginian offer to the Romans. In 191 the Carthaginians had offered perhaps 500,000 modii of wheat and the same of barley; Massinissa promised more.[12] In 198 Massinissa was on his own. Clearly he was hoping and expecting to make territorial gains at the expense of his humbled neighbour and rival.

Thus the offerings of Hiero, Massinissa and independent Carthage were sporadic and often unsolicited. They were also not very substantial, considering the resources of the territories concerned and the needs of Rome. Hiero was at his most generous by far in 216. Between the battles of Trasimene and Cannae, he gave 300,000 modii of wheat, by Polybius' figures for rations and size of legions enough to feed around 2.5 Roman legions for 6 months, while after Cannae he fed the whole army in Sicily for 6 months (the 2 legions of citizen foot-soldiers alone required around 200,000–240,000 modii of wheat). There were, however, 13–14 legions in service in 216, the lowest number of citizens under arms until 201 (and for 12 months in the year). Carthage's contributions, which average out at only one per decade, range from 200,000 to 1,000,000 modii of wheat (plus barley). The latter quantity, sent to the consul in Macedonia in 170 for the war against Perseus, was

---

[10] Hiero's offerings were, from his point of view, gifts (cf. Polybius 7.5.7; Livy 22.37), for which he expected in return only protection and the maintenance of his kingdom (cf. Polybius 1.16.10). The Romans from time to time insisted on paying for his help (cf. Livy 23.38.12). This was a way of indicating that their relationship with benefactor states was not between equals: Rome did not need gifts. But in the critical years of the Hannibalic war this was patently not the case.

[11] Livy 31.19.4; 32.27.2; 36.4.8; 43.6.11.

[12] Livy 36.4.8. The amount of the Carthaginian wheat offering is lost in a corrupt text.

enough to feed more than three legions and accompanying allied troops for 6 months.[13]

In sum, the grain contributions of the old Syracusan kingdom and the old Carthaginian empire (not to mention the Numidian kingdom) became regular and substantial only on their incorporation into the Roman provincial system. Until that time the contributions were not part of an organised system for supplying Rome and the armies. At best they can be described as a way of coping with war-related fluctuations in demand.

In Sicily a new era began in 210 for both the original province and the former kingdom of Syracuse. Some passages of Livy bear striking witness to the activity of Roman officials in the enlarged Sicilian province. First, the consul Laevinus

compelled the Sicilians to lay down their arms at last and turn their attention to tilling the soil, so that the island might not only produce food enough for the inhabitants, but might relieve the grain market of the city of Rome and of Italy, as it had done on many occasions ...

Next, the consul M. Valerius is reported to have informed the Roman senate

that there was not a Carthaginian in Sicily, that not a Sicilian was absent; that those who had been absent, banished by their fears, had all been brought back to their cities, to their lands, and were ploughing and sowing, a deserted land was again under cultivation, productive at last for the farmers themselves and for the Roman people in peace and in war a most dependable source of grain.

In the following year, Valerius is said by Livy to have

roamed around his province in order to visit the farms and to distinguish between cultivated and uncultivated lands, and to praise or upbraid the owners accordingly. So, owing to such diligence, such a crop of grain was produced that he sent grain to Rome and also transported it to Catania, whence it could be supplied to the army which was to have its summer camp near Tarentum.

By 191, if not earlier, both Sicily and Sardinia were capable of furnishing double tithes to the Romans. If we had Livy's narrative of the 140s, we might see Roman officials operating in a similar way in the new province of Africa with the aim of promoting agricultural production and raising Rome's total tax revenues.[14]

Finally, the Romans on at least two occasions looked to states in the eastern Mediterranean for emergency supplies of grain. Polybius says

[13] Livy 43.6.13–14 (170); Polybius 6.39.13 (rations, with Duncan-Jones (1976b), 46–7 n. 16); 6.20.8 (size of legion).
[14] Livy 26.40.13–16; 27.5.1–5; 27.8.18 cf. 29.1.14; 36.2.12.

that Rome sent to Ptolemy for grain at a time of a very serious shortage. The year was probably 210.[15]

A decree of the Thessalian *koinon* concerns the dispatch to Rome of 430,000 baskets (*kophinoi*) of wheat after a visit by the Roman aedile Q. Caecilius Metellus while a certain Petraeus was chief magistrate (*strategos*) of Thessaly. The most likely date is 129. There is no sign that the Romans made a habit of going to Thessaly for grain for their capital city, although Roman armies operating in Greece and Macedonia in the middle or late Republic made more or less free use of the food resources of these areas.[16] This was an emergency: Rome was suffering from food shortage.

Why did the Thessalians contribute grain? It might be said that they had no choice in the matter. But there is more to it than that. Thessaly, like Numidia under Massinissa, was free and independent. Both states had benefited greatly from the defeat by the Romans of a powerful neighbour. In 186 Philip V had been forced to withdraw to the ancient boundaries of Macedonia, which meant that the Thessalians recovered their traditional boundaries. In 167 Perseus and in 148 the false Philip Andriscus were defeated by Rome and the new-found integrity of Thessaly preserved. Thessaly was apparently untouched in the reorganisation of Greece which followed the defeat of the forces of the Achaean League and the sack of Corinth in 146. There was much to be grateful for. In case the Thessalians did show reluctance in providing the grain that was needed, the Romans sent a member of the family which had had as much to do as any other in carrying out the pro-Thessalian policy. Q. Caecilius Metellus the consul of 206 had led the three-man embassy of 186 which forced Philip out of Thessaly. A Q. Metellus had been sent with two other young men to convey news of the defeat of Perseus at the battle of Pydna in 168; this was probably the Metellus who later routed Andriscus and earned the title Macedonicus. His uncle had earlier been sent with two other senators to the Roman commander Flamininus in Greece in 197, and was later honoured by the Thessalian *koinon*. If it was his great-nephew who went cap in hand to Thessaly in about 129, then he had special qualifications for the job.

This was a singular event. The Romans did not regularly seek grain for the city of Rome in Thessaly, any more than Ptolemaic Egypt was a

---

[15] Polybius 9.11a.3. Livy 36.4.2 under 191 refers to the refusal of an Egyptian offer of gold and silver, not grain, for the war against Antiochus.

[16] See e.g. Livy 42.64–70 cf. Appian, *Bell. Mac.* frag. 18.3; Livy 43.4.9, 6.3; Appian, *Bell. Mith.* 30; Caesar, *Bell. civ.* 3.5, 34. On the Thessalian decree see Garnsey *et al.* (1984); revised date in Garnsey and Rathbone (1985), Appendix.

normal port of call for this purpose. The suppliers of Rome were located in the west, and not only in the provinces.

Italy

Livy writes, under 203:

The year was marked by a great conflagration in which the Clivus Publicius was burned to the ground, and by floods, but also by the low price of grain, because not only was all Italy open by reason of peace, but also a great quantity of grain had been sent from Spain. M. Valerius Falto and M. Fabius Buteo the curule aediles distributed this to the population by precincts, at 4 asses [sc. per modius].[17]

Italy had always been the major supplier of grain to the city of Rome, and still held that position at the end of the third century. The Hannibalic war severely disrupted the production and distribution of grain and other agricultural products. Hannibal helped himself to such crops as he could secure. The Roman armies did more or less the same. In addition, the government in Rome ordered peasants to destroy and abandon their farms and sent them to war in large numbers.

These farmers-turned-soldiers (a small number of 'urban' legions were also raised) consumed in aggregate vast quantities of grain. Around 50,000–80,000 Roman citizens were under arms (11–18 legions) in 217–205 while Hannibal was in Italy, and a larger number of allied troops, perhaps twice as many, plus cavalry. By Polybius' figures for rations, which are perhaps too high to apply to these critical years, the citizen foot-soldiers alone would have consumed 200,000–320,000 modii of grain per month, or 2,400,000–3,840,000 modii per year.[18]

Italy supplied the bulk of the food and equipment required by the legions and allied contingents deployed in the peninsula and in Sicily, and was also turned to for substantial contributions to campaigns further afield. In 215 the Scipios reported from Spain that despite their successful operations

money for pay, also clothing and grain, were lacking for the army, and for the crews, everything. So far as pay was concerned, if the treasury was empty, they would find some way of getting it out of the Spaniards. Everything else, they said, must in any case be sent from Rome, and in no other way could either the army or the province be kept.

The implication is that in normal circumstances the Roman authorities were responsible for maintaining the flow of cash and all manner of supplies to the Spanish armies. It was only extensive commitments

[17] Livy 30.26.5–6.   [18] Brunt (1971), 416–34, for legionary numbers.

elsewhere, above all in Italy itself, which had prevented the senate sending a routine shipment of supplies to supplement that sent in the winter of 217–216.[19]

Etruria maintained its position as a surplus-producer well placed to send grain to Rome by river and sea right through the period of the Republic. It was the area where fifth-century Romans sought grain in emergencies, where Varro in the mid-first century BC knew of returns from cereals of 10-fold (and then again 15-fold), and where Scipio turned for provisions and equipment for his volunteer army of 205, the army he would take to north Africa:

First the Etruscan communities promised that they would aid the consul, each according to its own resources. The men of Caere promised grain for the crews and supplies of every kind, the men of Populonia iron, Tarquinii linen for sails, Volaterrae the interior fittings of ships, also grain. Arretium promised 3,000 shields, an equal number of helmets; and they would furnish a total of 50,000 javelins, short spears and lances with an equal proportion of each type; also axes, shovels, sickles, baskets and hand-mills, as many as were needed for 40 warships; 120,000 modii of wheat also; and that they would contribute allowances for petty officers and oarsmen. Perusia, Clusium and Rusellae promised fir for shipbuilding and a great quantity of grain.[20]

In the annalistic tradition for early Rome, grain was also imported from Campania, when political conditions were favourable. In 343 the Romans accepted the decision of the Campanians to go over to Rome by a formal act of submission, *deditio*. They did so on the expectation that the easily accessible agricultural wealth of this potential 'granary of the Roman people' would level out 'the fluctuations in their grain supply' (*varietates annonae*), although they knew that in doing so they were breaking a treaty with the Samnites and provoking them to war. In the Samnite and First Punic Wars Campania served as a base and supply depot as well as a recruitment ground for the allied troops who accompanied the Roman legionary and naval forces. Hannibal, lured into Campania by his need for food and his determination to break up the Roman alliance, secured the defection of Capua in 216. For five vital years the flow of grain from the heart of Campania to Rome was cut off.[21]

Rome's terrible revenge on Capua as on Syracuse included the confiscation of the agricultural resources of the community. The

---

[19] Livy 23.48.4–5 cf. 40.35.4 (180); Polybius 3.106.7 (217–16); Richardson (1986), 35–42.
[20] Livy 28.45.15ff.; cf. Livy 2.34.5 (492) etc.; Varro 1.44.
[21] Livy 7.31.1 (343); cf. Cicero, *Leg. agr.* 2.80 ('horreum legionum, solacium annonae'). For a contribution of grain from Nola and Naples in 215, see Livy 23.46.9. In general, see Frederiksen (1981), and (1984), *passim*.

Campanians remained on their lands, but they now belonged to the Roman people, and the Romans had a new interest in systematically exploiting them. Campanians, like the Sicilians, were put to work for the benefit of the Roman state and individual Romans. Together with the Sardinians, they brought in a regular flow of rent- and tax-grain.

Apulia was a major grain producer, as Hannibal appreciated, but too far from Rome to have been a regular supplier of the city.[22] Latium is usually thought not to have maintained a role as a grain supplier of Rome because of its very proximity.

The issue of grain production in Latium is one aspect of the wider question of the fate of cereal cultivation in Italy in general in the middle and late Republic. It has long been a conviction of scholars that Italian grain production slumped dramatically after the Hannibalic war, never to recover. The wide range of supporting arguments utilised have included the increased employment in agriculture of slaves, a form of labour particularly unsuitable for cereal cultivation (or so it has been alleged); the high cost of transport, which meant that only the most profitable cash crops, that is, olive oil and wine, could be economically hauled overland; soil exhaustion; and grain importation from abroad. Recent commentators have set limits to the contraction of cereal production in Italy by stressing the inaccessibility to provincial grain of most Italian consumers outside Rome. It has also been pointed out that 'plantation agriculture' characterised by the production of 'cash crops' by slave labour was concentrated in a restricted zone in central and southern Italy. But the thesis of the collapse of cereal cultivation in Latium in consequence of the influx of foreign grain and the expansion of specialised production for the Roman market, and the idea that Italy as a whole played 'a small part' in supplying Rome's food, have only recently begun to be challenged.[23]

The problem is complex. None of the key variables is known, and in any case they did not remain static over two centuries. They include the needs of Rome and of the army, the amount of surplus Italian and

---

[22] See Varro 1.2.6 on the quality of Apulian grain. Medieval Naples leant on Apulia and Sicily for grain, and Florence and Venice competed for access to it. See Abulafia (1981), at 381–2.

[23] For the traditional view, see Staerman and Trofima (1975), 31ff.; Yeo (1952); Toynbee (1965), ii 298–9 (on slavery); Yeo (1946); Martin (1971), 278–86 (on transport); Mommsen (1854–6), viii Ch. 12, iv Ch. 11; Gummerus (1906); etc. (on grain imports). For a welcome corrective, see Spurr (1986). There are modifications of the traditional line in Brunt (1971), Ch. 20; Rickman (1980), 101–19; cf. Veyne (1976), 522 n. 319. However, Rickman implicitly accepts the displacement of grain production in Latium (p. 103) and writes of 'the small part played by Italy in supplying the Roman market from the third century BC' (p. 104). Brunt limits the decline in cereal cultivation in Latium to 'Old Latium' and some coastal areas (pp. 126–30, 345–50).

provincial grain, and the way available grain was distributed between civilian and military consumers. I make the following suggestions, with the aim of provoking further discussion.

1. The contribution of Italy became proportionately less important as grain-exporting provinces increased in number and produced a larger surplus.

2. This development is not to be confused with a decline either in overall grain production in Italy or in the amount of Italian grain available for Roman civilians and soldiers.

3. The proportionate reduction in Italy's contribution did not occur overnight. In particular, Rome was without a province of Africa until 146.

4. In some years at least, provincial tax-grain was sent to the army overseas, and Italy's contribution to the feeding of the capital city was correspondingly more significant (see below).

5. Competition with other crops was a negligible factor in any decline of cereal production. It does not follow from the fact that wine production and consumption increased that cereal production (or consumption) went down. The products of Ceres/Liber, *pain/vin*, are inseparable; they were, in combination, the essential foodstuffs of Italians.[24]

6. On the other hand, harvest levels were adversely affected by war, insecurity and the displacement of peasants in Italy. The implication is that, other things being equal, total production and the amount of surplus grain were lower on average in the first century than in the more tranquil second.

7. Widespread urban expansion in Italy[25] is incompatible with a slump in Italian grain production.

8. Demand remained high for Italian grain in the rapidly expanding capital city. Rome's inhabitants could use all the grain they could get.

THE CONSUMER IN ROME

The population of Rome may have risen from around 180,000 in 270 to 375,000 in 130 and to 1,000,000 under Augustus. On these figures, the wheat requirements of the city of Rome rose from between 4 and 5½ million modii in the early third century to between 8½ and 11¼ million modii in the Gracchan period.[26] How did Rome's inhabitants fare in

---

[24] Tchernia (1986), 10–11.
[25] See Gabba (1972); Brunt (1971), 294ff. (first-century urbanisation).
[26] The first two population figures are from Brunt (1971), 69, and are accepted here merely as working estimates. The third figure is 25% higher than Brunt's. I employ 22.5 modii per

the period in question, and what steps if any did Roman governments take to protect them from hunger and starvation?

The Hannibalic War

The presence of Hannibal cut deep into the food resources of the residents of Rome and central and southern Italy. Appian says that the senate was influenced among other things by food crisis, when it instructed the consuls for 216 to finish the war as quickly as possible. In fact they led the army to disastrous defeat at Cannae. The defection of Capua followed quickly. Syracuse abandoned the Roman cause in 215. A Sardinian rebellion erupted and was quelled in the same year. Against this background the consternation felt in Rome in the late summer of 215 at the request of the Scipios for money, grain and clothing can be readily understood.

In these years, everything went into the military effort and the civilian population inevitably suffered. Livy is silent on their condition; he is totally preoccupied with the war. Appian records a food crisis in Rome in 211 which led Hannibal to march on the city. A fragment of Polybius refers to a 'serious shortage', not precisely dated, but belonging to the same time. He writes:

The Romans sent envoys to Ptolemy wishing to procure a supply of grain because of the serious shortage they were suffering. All the crops of Italy up to the gates of Rome had been destroyed by the armies, and help from abroad had not been forthcoming, since all over the world except in Egypt there were wars in progress and hostile forces in the field.[27]

Polybius adds the detail that in this shortage grain rose to 15 drachmas per Sicilian medimnos, or 90 denarii per modius, an extraordinarily high price.

That production did not pick up significantly in Italy in the five years that followed, in effect, until Hannibal had been driven out of Italy, is suggested by the elder Pliny's comment that the arrival of the cult of Magna Mater in Rome (in 205) coincided with a harvest larger than any other over the preceding decade.[28]

Epidemic disease in city and countryside (therefore damaging to food production) is recorded for 208. Another outbreak in 205 affected

person p.a. as the minimum grain requirement and 30 modii for the average rate of consumption. See Garnsey (1983), 118.
[27] Polybius 9.11a; Appian, *Bell. Hann.* 17 (216); Livy 23.34.10–17; 23.40–1 (Sardinia); Livy 23.48.4–12 (Scipionic letter).
[28] Pliny, *Hist. nat.* 18.16.

both armies and led to the consultation of the Sibylline books and the summoning of Magna Mater.[29]

Post-Hannibalic War

In the second century, epidemic disease is recorded under 187 and from 182 to 180, and in the second of these years a drought lasting 6 months and a food shortage. A serious food crisis and epidemic occurred in 165 and again in 142.[30]

Problems with the food supply are not mentioned again until the Gracchan period. However, no continuous narrative of Livy is available after 167.

Livy has some enlightening entries on the feeding of Rome, in particular for the years between 203 and 189. On the basis of his narrative it is possible to detect three different types of situation between which the Romans fluctuated. It is impossible to say which of the three was the more typical; it is something to know that each was possible in the period between the Hannibalic War and the Gracchi.

1. In the years 203, 201–200 and 196 grain was sold cheaply by the curule aediles to the people, as one text says, by districts or precincts (*vici*). The notice under 201 is typical:

Dramatic performances at the Roman games in that year were given with splendour and magnificence by the curule aediles L. Valerius Flaccus and L. Quinctius Flamininus. The performance of two days was renewed. They distributed to the people a vast quantity of grain which P. Scipio had sent from Africa, at 4 asses (*sc.* per modius), earning the greatest credit and favour thereby.[31]

These were years of plenty. Italy was back into production, as announced in the entry for 203. Also grain arrived unexpectedly each year from foreign parts. It seems clear that without such a windfall there would have been no distribution.[32]

Further, the Roman military commitment was tapering off very strikingly in this period. The legions in service for 206–200 numbered: 20, 18, 19, 20, 15, 14, 8.[33] Some provisioning of legions was done from Italy, Sicily and Sardinia; legions were operating in northern Italy against Gauls and Ligurians, and the two provinces were garrisoned.

---

[29] Livy 27.23.6 cf. 9.3; 28.46.15 cf. 29.10.1.
[30] Livy 38.44.7 (187); 40.29.2; 40.36.14 (3 years); cf. Obsequens 6 (181), 10 (175).
[31] Livy 31.4.5 (201); cf. 30.26.5–6 (203); 31.49.8–50.1 (200); 33.42.8 (196).
[32] In 202 grain was abundant and the price fell. The quantity that came in from Sicily and Sardinia, presumably by regular channels, was unexpectedly large. See Livy 30.38.5.
[33] For legionary tallies, see Brunt (1971), 418, 424, 432–3.

But the total burden was significantly reduced. More grain was available for civilian purposes.

2. The record for 199–197 and 195–192 is empty. It can perhaps be surmised (since Livy is interested in the grain supply at this stage of his history) that the provincial tithe was coming in, and dearth was avoided in the city.

There was no great military commitment in these years. Between 199 and 192 the legions numbered 6, 8, 6, 10, 10, 8, 10.

In short, conditions were normal and stable. There was no special military effort, and the provincial tithes could proceed to Rome.

3. During 191–189, and then again in 170, Rome's grain supply was in jeopardy.

In 191 two tithes were sent from Sicily east to the army.

In 190 two Sicilian tithes and one tithe (Livy says 'a part') from Sardinia went east. The other tithe went to Rome. In this year alone grain from north Africa (perhaps 550,000 modii all told) was sent to Rome rather than to the armies.

In 189, and again in 170, both double tithes went east to the armies, and nothing came to Rome. There is an indirect indication of food shortage in Livy under 189:

Also twelve gilded shields were set up by the curule aediles, P. Claudius Pulcher and Servius Sulpicius Galba, out of the money that they had condemned the grain traders to pay for hoarding grain.[34]

Thus for three years in succession, and again in 170, Sicilian tax-grain was completely lost to Rome. Moreover, all or most of the additional surplus grain from Sicily went elsewhere. The smaller contribution of Sardinia was diverted completely in 2 years out of 4; in the remaining years Rome received 1 or 2 Sardinian tithes.

This came about largely because of the wars with Antiochus and his Aetolian allies, and then with Perseus. The major military effort is reflected in the legionary totals. For 191–188 they were 12, 13, 12, 12, the highest until the middle of the century. In 171 there was a sudden rise from 6 to 10 legions.

In sum, the food supply of Rome in the 40 years following the departure of Hannibal from Italy has an air of instability and unreliability. This situation was likely to prevail as long as the Romans remained heavily committed to warfare and imperialistic intervention abroad.

If the sources were available, we would probably find that provincial tithes were doubled and sent to the army at the expense of the consumer in Rome in the context of other major military crises in the second

[34] Livy 38.35.5; cf. 37.50.9 (189). See 36.2.12–13 (191); 37.2.12 (190); 42.32.8 (170).

century. The years immediately preceding the grain law of Gaius Gracchus were one such period.

The background to Gracchus' law

The Gracchan period saw considerable disruption of production in Sicily, Sardinia and Africa, sharp fluctuations in the distribution of grain as between military and civilian consumers, and food shortages in Rome, actual or feared. It did not see, as has been supposed, a dramatic rise in the prices of grain in the Mediterranean region as a whole, or a downturn in public building and therefore a slump in employment opportunities in the city of Rome.[35]

In 142 Rome was hit by food crisis and epidemic disease. In 138 rising prices led a tribune C. Curiatius to try to stimulate the senate into seeking supplementary grain. The consul Scipio Nasica refused to move, rather as the elder Cato had done in similar circumstances earlier in the century. Probably in 129 the aedile Q. Caecilius Metellus arranged for grain to be shipped from Thessaly to Rome, in the words of the Thessalian decree, 'because the situation in his country at the present time is one of dearth'.[36]

The food supply of Rome in this period was affected by slave revolts, first in Campania in 143 and 141, and then rather more seriously in Sicily. The Sicilian rebellion began in 139 (or 135) and occupied one or two legions continuously until 131. For the duration of the rebellion Sicily was in no position to send its normal tithe to Rome. The Illyrian campaign of 129 required two new legions, the feeding of which placed an extra burden on Italy. No wonder the Romans took the unusual step of seeking grain in the east in this year.[37]

The legionary count from 125 signals the beginning of another period of strain. The number of legions, having sunk to five in 128, rose in 125 to 7 and in 124 to 9. The new legions were engaged in Gallia Narbonensis and Sardinia; that is, they were near, and presumably

[35] Garnsey and Rathbone (1985), 21, on Heichelheim (1930), e.g. 51–2, 67–8, 72–7, 118–22; Coarelli (1977) on Boren (1957–8).

[36] Obsequens 22 (142); Valerius Maximus 3.7.3 cf. Plutarch, *Cato Maior* 8.1; Garnsey *et al.* (1984), 36 ll.7–8. Coins of 135 and 134 BC, issued by moneyers (two Minucii and one Marcius) recalling semi-legendary grain distributions by earlier members of their houses, hint at distributions by the responsible officials (aediles) in these years. See Crawford (1974), 242–3, 245.

[37] For the slave wars, see Frederiksen (1981), 277; (Orosius 5.9.4; Minturnae and Sinuessa in Campania, 450 and 4,000 executed, respectively); Finley (1979), 137–47 (Sicily; the sources suggest 130,000–200,000 slaves involved, but they may not all have been active participants). For the legionary count in these years, see Brunt (1971), 433.

provisioned by, Italy. Supplies were diverted from Rome, and Sardinia fed, if anyone, Roman and allied soldiers.

Even the occupying force was short of food in Sardinia at some stage between 126 and 124. Gaius Gracchus happened to be there as quaestor during these three years. He exploited his family connections to obtain supplies from Sardinians and Numidians (in the person of Micipsa, son and successor of Massinissa), from the former clothing and other equipment during a harsh winter, from the latter grain. In 125–124 the province of Africa suffered a ruinous plague of locusts that was immensely destructive of plant, animal and human life. In 124, Gaius Gracchus left Sardinia for Rome to stand for the tribunate.[38]

CONCLUSION

Some observations are prompted on the position of civilians and the attitude of governments in the second century BC.

The imposition of a provincial grain tax ensured that under normal conditions some grain would be available in the market. It must have been written into contracts made with the private individuals and companies who collected the grain that they should transport it to Rome. However, the amount of grain that came to Rome in this way varied with the size of the harvest. The price of grain fluctuated accordingly.

Sharp price-rises and food shortages occurred in Rome in consequence of harvest failure in Italy or a grain-exporting province, the outbreak of epidemic disease which disrupted production, or military campaigns; whether fought on the territory of a grain-exporting province or elsewhere, wars reduced the amount of grain available to civilian consumers. There are many gaps in the historical record, especially after 167, but the vulnerability of the populace is visible in the first decades of the century and again in the quarter-century preceding the passage of the Gracchan grain law.

To cope with food crises, the Roman authorities fell back on traditional, ad hoc remedies. The responsible magistrates, that is to say, the aediles, sent for emergency grain supplies. They presumably made the grain available at below current (high) prices, though this is not specifically attested, unlike the sale of cheap grain when supplies were abundant, as occurred on several occasions at the turn of the third century. There was credit to be gained with the populace by an aedile or general who secured grain or distributed it cheap. But these bonanzas were unpredictable, sporadic occurrences, and they were less

[38] Plutarch, *G. Gracch.* 6; Livy, *Per.* 60; Obsequens 30; Orosius 5.11.1–3.

advantageous to ordinary citizens than regular, monthly distributions. Gaius Gracchus in person denounced a promagistrate who sent a cargo of grain to Rome from Spain, and compelled the senate to send payment to the communities that had supplied it.[39] This was a symbolic act marking the end of an era. The grain law was introduced shortly afterwards.

The Roman state was capable of taking measures of more long-term significance with implications for the quantity of tax-grain and rent-grain. Grain production was stepped up in Campania and Sicily after 211, and several attempts were made to stop the encroachment of private individuals on public land in Campania in the first decades of the second century.[40] Finally – an event provoked, to be sure, by considerations other than the food needs of Rome – Africa was transformed from a cash-indemnity-paying ally into a grain-tax-paying province in 146.

Such adjustments, at least in the short term, did not compensate for the increase in the food requirements of the city population, which grew dramatically in the course of the century.

To sum up: the inexorable pressure of a rapidly rising population exposed the inadequacy of the traditional ad hoc response to the problems of food supply and food crisis in Rome.

The regular distribution of grain at a fixed, modest, price had clear advantages from the consumer's point of view over the traditional strategy of dealing with each emergency as it approached or occurred. In particular, it offered protection against fluctuations in the supply and price of grain.

However, many noble Romans were opposed to the institution of cheap food for the plebs. They preferred a system which gave individual politicians a chance to win popular favour and gave aristocratic houses a monopoly over the dispensing of patronage or charity. Some opposed making concessions to the mass of the people on principle. For these reasons, and others connected with the personalities and careers of the brothers Gracchi, the Gracchan reform amounted to a revolution.

---

[39] Plutarch, *G. Gracch.* 6. Gaius' own behaviour in Sardinia was comparable.
[40] Livy 28.46.4–6; 38.28.4, 36.5–6; 42.1.6, 19.2; Cicero, *Leg. agr.* 2.82 cf. Granius Licin. 28.29–37 (ed. Criniti). See Frederiksen (1981), 275–7.

13

FOOD AND POLITICS

Monthly sales of cut-price grain were introduced into Rome by the state authorities in 123 BC following the passage of the grain law of Gaius Gracchus. They were abolished in 81, remained in abeyance until 73, and sporadically ceased to function in times of civil strife. Otherwise the system operated more or less continuously. However, Rome in the late Republic was by no means free from food crisis. The explanation lies both in the disturbed political climate of the time and in the inadequacy of the distribution system.

FOOD CRISES

1. In 104, when Saturninus was quaestor, grain rose in price. The senate deprived him of his responsibility for supplies and transferred it to M. Scaurus, the leading senator (*princeps senatus*). Stung by this insult, Saturninus became a demagogue, according to Cicero.[1]

2. In 100 the senate authorised the purchase of supplementary stocks of grain. A denarius of this year shows on the obverse the head of Saturn and a serrated sickle, and on the reverse the two quaestors Caepio and Piso seated on a bench, at each end of which there is an ear of corn. The reverse bears the inscription: 'Ad Fru[mentum] Em[undum] Ex S[enatus] C[onsulto]' ('For the purchase of grain following a senatorial resolution').[2]

This special grain purchase undertaken with senatorial authority may perhaps be seen as the conservative counter to Saturninus' more radical proposal, also of 100 (but some favour 103), to reduce the price of distributed grain from $6\frac{1}{3}$ asses to $\frac{5}{6}$ as per modius. The proposal was successfully blocked by the violent action of the quaestor Caepio.[3]

---

[1] Cicero, *Har. resp.* 43 cf. *Sest.* 39. Diodorus 36.12 says Saturninus' job was to see to the transport of grain from Ostia. Only the first passage refers to difficulties with the food supply (*caritas annonae*).

[2] Crawford (1974), 73, 616.

[3] I follow Rickman (1980), 162–4 rather than Brunt (1971), 377–8 and Crawford (1974), 73.

If this reconstruction is along the right lines, then 100 provides a foretaste of the political manoeuvring that took place when a shortage of food in the market exposed the shortcomings of the food supply system.

3. Obsequens writes under 99 BC: 'A roar that seemed to rise from the depths of the earth to the sky foretold scarcity and hunger.' There is a presumption (not proof) that Rome suffered food crisis in this year.[4]

4. In 91–89 Italy was the setting for a destructive war between the Romans and their Italian allies. A rhetorical passage of the historian Diodorus under the year 90 has Romans and Italians doing battle over the current harvest:

Since the ripe ears were there before them ready to be reaped, they settled with their blood the question who was to have the essential food. No one waited on the urging of his commander. Nature itself, confronting them with the cold logic of deprivation, spurred them on to bravery. Each man stoutly faced the prospect of dying by the sword because he feared death from privation.

The fifth-century historian Orosius, drawing from the lost books of Livy, records the disappointment of the senate at the lack of worthwhile booty accruing from the capture of the town of Asculum in 89. He adds that the treasury was so short of funds by the end of the war that there was no money even to pay for soldiers' grain rations.[5] It can be inferred from the shortage of military rations and cash that civilians were in dire straits at this time.

5. In 87 Cinna was declared a public enemy, and in collaboration with Carbo, Marius and Sertorius besieged the city with three armies. Marius prevented food getting through from Ostia or by way of the upper Tiber; he also seized grain 'stored for the Romans' in neighbouring towns. The senate was worried lest the scarcity of grain (*sitodeia*) be protracted, and sought peace. Meanwhile 'fear of famine' (*limos*), coupled with a desire to be on the winning side, induced many citizens to desert to Cinna. The senate capitulated and the subsistence crisis, not however the political crisis, was at an end.[6]

6. Coinage issued by the aediles of 86 indicates that there were supplementary distributions of grain in their year of office. The inference is that there was a shortage of grain in the market.[7]

7. In 82 Rome's inhabitants were already suffering from hunger (*limos*) when Sulla's army approached the city, and a blockade was unnecessary. Sulla's enemies in Rome had taken desperate measures to

---

[4] Obsequens 46; cf. 69.   [5] Orosius 5.18.26–30; Diodorus 37.24.
[6] Appian, *Bell. civ.* 1. 67–70; Plutarch, *Mar.* 42.
[7] Crawford (1974), 367, no. 351.

collect soldiers, provisions and money against him in 83 (but their preparations had in fact begun in 85). When they finally abandoned the city, they will have drained it of its last stocks of grain.[8]

8. 75–73 BC. In 75 Cicero was quaestor of Sicily. In a later speech he boasted that his quaestorship 'was the sole topic of conversation at Rome'. He continued:

I had sent off a vast amount of grain at a time when prices were extremely high (*in summa caritate*). The universal opinion was that I was civil to the financiers, fair to the traders, generous to the Sicilian cities, kind to the allies.

A fragment of Sallust records riots in Rome in 75 arising from an extreme grain shortage (*annonae intolerabilis saevitia*). Octavius and Cotta, the two consuls, and Metellus, the praetorian candidate they were escorting, were chased along the Sacred Way and took refuge in Octavius' house. At some point in the same year when grain was expensive (*caritas annonae*), the aedile Hortensius distributed grain at the rate of 1½ modii per man.[9]

The evidence for shortage in 74 is less conclusive. In that year M. Antonius was given wide-ranging powers (*imperium infinitum*) to combat piracy throughout the Mediterranean. He held this office continuously until he was utterly defeated by the Cretan pirates in 71. The fact that his sphere of operations for the first year of his command was the west suggests that supplies for Rome were seriously disrupted by piratical activity in this or the previous year. In 74 M. Seius the aedile won singular public honour by distributing grain at 1 as per modius.[10]

The passage of the Lex Terentia Cassia with the authority of the senate suggests ongoing difficulties with the grain supply. The law restored regular grain distributions after an 8-year hiatus. No details are known apart from the size of the ration, which was 5 modii per person per month. In addition, Verres as governor of Sicily was told to purchase a second tithe of 3 million modii at 3 sesterces per modius, and an additional 800,000 modii at 3½ sesterces. He did so for each of his three years in office. The information comes from a casual reference in the *Verrine Orations* of Cicero; it is not to be excluded that other governors were given similar instructions.[11]

9. In 67 the grain convoys were intercepted by pirates, now oper-

[8] Appian, *Bell. civ.* 1. 76, 79, 81, 88.
[9] Cicero, *Planc.* 64; Sallust, *Hist.* 2. 45; Cicero, *2 Verr.* 3.215.
[10] Cicero, *Off.* 2.58; Pliny, *Hist. nat.* 18.16. For M. Antonius (Creticus), see Broughton (1952), under 74–71 BC.
[11] Cicero, *2 Verr.* 3.163; 5.52 cf. Sallust, *Hist.* 3.48. Despite Rickman (1980), 45 cf. 166, Cicero does not say that the supplementary purchases became a permanent arrangement. Note Cicero's charge that Verres' rapacity drove farmers off the land in Sicily: *2 Verr.* 3.48, 119.

ating unchecked in the waters of Italy. Ostia was raided and ships were burned. Cassius Dio says the import of grain was completely cut off, and blames the senate for negligence over a long period of time. Appian observes that the inhabitants of Rome were suffering terribly because of their numbers. Extraordinary powers were proposed for Pompey to combat piracy, and carried by violence over the protests of the senate. Cicero, writing over a decade later, recalls the sequel:

On the very day Pompey was appointed, the price of grain, which had been very dear and in short supply, suddenly plummeted, because of the hope that everyone had in one man and because of his reputation.

Plutarch says that Pompey found the markets of Rome full of provisions when he visited the city only 40 days after the beginning of his campaign.[12]

10. In 58–56 Rome experienced grain shortages characterised by wild price fluctuations.[13]

(i) The grain price was high and grain scarce when Cicero departed into exile in early April 58.
(ii) The price was high again on the eve of his restoration on 8 August 57.
(iii) It fell unexpectedly on that day, 8 August.
(iv) It was high less than a month later, on Cicero's arrival in the city on 4 September 57. Crowds instigated, it was claimed, by Clodius, besieged the senators on the Palatine, threatening to burn them alive.
(v) On 7 September 57, Cicero proposed that Pompey be put in charge of the grain supply. The price of grain fell, probably immediately, certainly by the end of the month when the speech *De domo* was delivered.
(vi) In February 56, Clodius tried to provoke a fresh riot over food supplies.
(vii) On 5 April 56, the senate awarded Pompey 40 million sesterces for his grain commission. There was little grain in the market.

11. In 54 a freak flood ruined a large quantity of grain. Pompey left the city in search of emergency supplies.[14]

12. The civil war that broke out in 49 between Caesar and Pompey put the inhabitants of Rome at risk. Blockade of the city was more or less inevitable, as Cicero had hinted in a letter of December 50. In March 49 Cicero reported to Atticus Pompey's 'first plan': it was 'to throttle Rome and Italy and starve them, then to lay waste and burn the country, and not to keep hands off the riches of the wealthy'. A few

[12] Cicero, *Imp. Pomp.* 44 cf. Plutarch, *Pomp.* 26.2; 27.2; Cassius Dio 36.22–4; Appian, *Bell. Mith.* 14.93–6.
[13] Cicero, *Dom.* 10–12, 14–18; *Att.* 4.1; Cassius Dio 39.9.3, 24.1; Cicero, *Q. fr.* 2.5; *Har. resp.* 31; Plutarch, *Pomp.* 49.4–50.2; etc.
[14] Cassius Dio 39.63.3 cf. 61.

days later Cicero was gloomily predicting a terrible war, 'ushered in by famine'. He was aware that a large fleet was being prepared 'to cut off the supplies of Italy and blockade the grain-producing provinces'. In June he advised Terentia and Julia to head for the family estate at Arpinum if grain became more expensive. When Caesar arrived back in the city from Spain, he found the people 'starving'. He had grain brought in from the islands and distributed.[15]

13. On 9 April 44, within a month of Caesar's assassination, Cicero reported in a letter that builders at his villa in Tusculum had gone to Rome for grain and come back empty-handed, bearing the strong rumour that Antony was stockpiling the grain at his house, presumably in preparation for civil war. Either the distributions had lapsed, or there was no grain in the market, or both. The praetors (and assassins) Brutus and Cassius were sent to purchase grain in Asia and Sicily respectively, primarily to allow them to leave the city with dignity. They may never have carried out the commission.[16]

14. In 43 the senate, acting out of political considerations, ruled that no one man should be made superintendent of the food supply. Behind this notice may lie a food shortage and attempts to alleviate it. An outbreak of epidemic disease over virtually the whole of Italy is recorded for this year.[17]

15. From late in 43 to 36 Sextus Pompeius was entrenched in Sicily (and his lieutenants in Sardinia and Africa), and able to exploit his naval superiority to cut off shipments of grain to Rome. By 42 many were dying in the city. In 41 the reservation of available grain for soldiers provoked food riots. Meanwhile cultivation was disrupted in Italy. In 40 the crisis deepened as Antony moved against Italy. Octavian negotiated a new agreement with Antony, but Pompeius' blockade and the food shortage went on. More riots ensued, in the course of which the triumvirs were stoned. The mobs were savagely disciplined by the troops, but their demand for peace was temporarily heeded. Octavian reluctantly concluded a treaty with Pompeius at Misenum which regularised his position in Sicily and Sardinia. The agreement proved fragile, war and food crisis resumed, only to cease when Octavian and Antony in combination defeated the forces of Pompeius in 36.[18]

[15] Cicero, *Att.* 7.9.2, 4; 9.9.4; *Fam.* 14.7.3; Appian, *Bell. civ.* 2.48; Cassius Dio 41.16.1.
[16] Cicero, *Att.* 14.3.1; Cassius Dio 44.53.3; *Att.* 15.9–12; Appian, *Bell. civ.* 3.6.35; 4.57 cf. Cassius Dio 44.51.4.
[17] Cassius Dio 45.17.8ff.; Obsequens 69: an oracular pronouncement.
[18] See esp. Cassius Dio 48.18.1; 48.31; Appian, *Bell. civ.* 5.67–8.

CONTEXTS OF CRISIS

Food crises in Rome were not usually unicausal. Even contemporary observers would have found it difficult at times to disentangle the various causal strands and judge their relative significance, especially when the shortages were somewhat mild and characterised by price fluctuations. In the case of the crisis of 57, it is possible to find support in the sources for the following contributory factors: harvest failure, speculation, Clodius' grain law of the previous year (which abolished the charge for state grain and lengthened the list of recipients), and Cicero's return from exile (which temporarily swelled the city population). Some of the more obvious causes are isolated below, without any implication that they operated independently or with equal force.

Warfare

Production in Italy and consumption in Rome were frequently disrupted by wars and civil strife in this period, more particularly between 91 and 81, in 78–77, 73–70 and 63–62 (the rebellions of Lepidus, Spartacus and Catiline), in 49–46 and 44–36. The city was fought over and besieged on several occasions. Rival generals drained its stores of grain to feed their soldiers.

Campaigns overseas had the effect of diverting grain from civilian to military consumers. The classic text is a speech given by Sallust to Cotta, the consul of 75, explaining the crisis to the people in terms of Rome's heavy commitments abroad:

You have elected us to the consulship, Romans, at a time when our country is in dire straits at home and abroad. Our generals are calling for money, men, arms and supplies, and they are forced to do so by circumstances, since the defection of our allies and the retreat of Sertorius over the mountains prevent them from either contending in battle or providing for their necessities. Armies are maintained in Asia and in Cilicia because of the excessive power of Mithridates, Macedonia is full of enemies, as is also the sea-coast of Italy and of the provinces. In the meantime our revenues, made scanty and uncertain by war, barely suffice for a part of our expenditures; hence the fleet which we keep upon the sea is much smaller than the one which formerly safeguarded our supplies.[19]

Rome was supporting 24 or 25 legions in 75 BC, 5 more than in the previous year. Another 5 were added in 74, and yet another 4 in 73, a grand total of 33 or 34, not counting Perperna's 5 rebel legions fighting with Sertorius against Pompey in Spain. Pompey happens to have been one of those commanders who wrote letters to the senate as Cotta

[19] Sallust, *Hist.* 3.48.

reported. His complaint was of inability to secure sufficient supplies in Spain or in Gaul (where harvests were bad), and grain had to be sent out to him as to the army in Spain in 215. There were 11–12 legions in Spain in 75 and 13–14 from 74 to 71. The war against Mithridates required 8 legions from 74 to 68. In Italy itself armies were assembled, initially of 4 legions, later of 10, to counter the Spartacus rebellion from 73 BC.[20]

Foreign wars form part of the background of the shortages of 104 and 100. Fighting against the Cimbri and Teutones had begun in Transalpine Gaul in 109, requiring two legions. By 105, however, there were 6 legions in the north, 4 confronting the enemy in Provence and 2 in Cisalpine Gaul standing guard over Italy. The sharp rise in the number of legions from 7 to 11 in this year increased the demand for surplus grain from Italy and the western provinces. The commitment in the north stayed at the same high level for 5 years.

In the last years of the second century, increased demand for military supplies was compounded by the disruption of production in a vital grain-exporting province. Sicilian slaves were on the rampage from 103, requiring first 1 legion (in 103 and 102) and then 2 (in 101 and 100). Sicilian agriculture had not yet recovered in 100, in which year the legionary total dropped dramatically from 11 to 5 following the cessation of hostilities in the north. When M'. Aquilius was in command in Sicily in 101–100, the Sicilian cities themselves had to be given grain on loan by the Roman commander.[21]

Piracy

In the second year of the slave war in Sicily, M. Antonius as praetor for 102 was entrusted with a special command against the pirates. He was still in Cilicia, his sphere of operations, until late in 100, and was instrumental in establishing the province of Cilicia. A comprehensive law concerning pirates was issued in 100, the year of Saturninus' second tribunate.[22] The problems posed by piracy for the Roman grain supply at this stage are debatable. In 74–71, when the younger M. Antonius held a command against the pirates, he was operating in the region of Liguria, Spain and Sicily. A few years later, the harassing of shipping

---

[20] Brunt (1971), 449; Sallust, *Hist.* 2.98 cf. Plutarch, *Pomp.* 20. Note that after the Italian allies secured the franchise following the Social War they fought in the legions as citizens. One second-century legion plus allied support equals 2–3 legions of the 70s and later.

[21] Cicero, *Leg. agr.* 2.83.

[22] Livy, *Ep.* 68; Obsequens 44; Cicero, *De orat.* 1.18.82; *ILLRP* 1 342; Cicero, *Rab. perd.* 26, with Broughton (1946), 35–40; Hassall, Crawford and Reynolds (1974).

by pirates along the west Italian seaboard caused food crisis in Rome – and Pompey's career received a significant uplift.

Natural causes

Flood, pestilence and harvest failure play minor roles in the 'famine narratives' of late Republican Rome. Part of the background to the food crisis of 75 is formed by fluctuating harvests in the western provinces. Harvest failure in Gaul aggravated Pompey's army supply problems in Spain. Sicily's record was patchy in these years. The good harvest of 76 was followed by a very bad one in 75.

If Cicero in his explanation of the crisis of 57 was not merely guessing, then harvest failure in the grain-producing provinces was partly responsible.[23]

Speculation

Cicero offers a tripartite explanation, as follows: 'the grain-growing provinces did not have grain'; 'they had sent it abroad to other lands through what can only be described as the avarice of the dealers'; 'they had stored it in custody, so that its arrival in the midst of hunger might be the more gratifying: they could produce it as an unexpected surprise'.

The three items, harvest failure and two kinds of manipulation of the grain supply, do not together make a convincing package. Cicero's reconstruction of the motives of the hoarders is disingenuous, and his location of this activity in the provinces suspicious. The fluctuations in the supply of grain implied in the pattern of price movements on the Roman market could only have been produced by hoarders based in Rome. That they included friends of Pompey working in his interest, as Clodius charged, is a possibility – but proof is out of the question. Pompey's attested contacts with traders date from the period of his commission, not before. The return of food shortage in 56 so soon after his appointment shows that the speculators were not all or not always on the side of Pompey.[24]

Also in 67, Pompey was a beneficiary of the strategies or impulses of those with grain stocks in or around Rome. But the events of that year, in so far as they can be reconstructed, do not undermine the hypothesis

[23] Cicero, *Dom.* 11; *2 Verr.* 3.214–15 (Sicily).
[24] Elsewhere Cicero blamed Clodius' law, see *Red sen.* 34; *Dom.* 25. For the charge against Pompey, and the consul Spinther, see Plutarch, *Pomp.* 49.5. The speculators remain shadowy figures. P. Sittius is thought by J. Heurgon (1950) to have been one, on the basis of Cicero, *Fam.* 5.17.2. A Pompeian trading contact: Cicero, *Fam.* 13. 75. 1–2 (cf. n. 50).

that speculation, even in the highly charged political atmosphere of late Republican Rome, was primarily an economic phenomenon.

POPULAR REACTION

The standard reaction of the people of late Republican Rome to food shortage was hostile demonstration, for which the typical setting was the public meeting (*contio*) or the show. Such protest sometimes turned into riot. At the games in honour of Apollo in July 57, P. Clodius 'collected a crowd of commoners and, having excited their anger at the price of grain, made them drive all the spectators out of the theatre'.[25] Two months later, violence was turned directly against the political authorities. A mob allegedly instigated by Clodius rushed to the Palatine where the senate was in session and threatened to burn the senators alive.

The citation (from Asconius) might give the impression that Clodius' organisation of violence was casual and ad hoc. A quite different account of his activities can be derived from the pages of his personal enemy Cicero. Having secured in 58 the legalisation of clubs and associations (*collegia*) banned by the senate in 64, Clodius proceeded to mobilise their membership as paramilitary gangs for his own political purposes.[26]

Clodius was not the only politician of the 50s who organised support in this way among the lower classes, but his radical corn law did give him a special appeal among the people of Rome. The grain recipients (*plebs frumentaria*) as much as the plebeian associations (*collegia*), whose membership will in any case have overlapped, formed a basic source of recruits for his gangs.[27]

Hunger or fear of hunger had driven the plebs to protest long before the era of organised violence or orchestrated demonstration had arrived. Their behaviour was no less spontaneous for the fact that it customarily won support from sympathetic politicians, usually from the ranks of the tribunate, a plebeian magistracy. As early as 138, a tribune, C. Curiatius, had acted as spokesman for the people in demanding that emergency grain stocks be sought. Such champions of the people were often conspicuously alive to their own or another's advantage. Moreover, when it came to a trial of strength with the senate, the 'progressives' could sometimes draft in outside forces to tilt

---

[25] Asconius p. 48c. On popular riots see now Virlouvet (1985).
[26] Lintott (1968), 77–83.
[27] On Clodius and his law, Asconius p. 8; Schol. Bobb. p. 132; Cicero, *Sest.* 55 (alleged cost); Nicolet (1976a); Flambard (1977).

the balance in their favour. Thus, for example, Gabinius with the support of the populace, no doubt reinforced by Pompey's veterans (who were not yet settled on land allotments), won Pompey his 5-year command against the pirates. It makes no difference: genuine popular discontent remains the mainspring of the action.

Confrontation between the plebs and the political authorities in the context of food shortage could take various forms. In the incident of 138, known unfortunately only through an anecdote, no force was used on either side. A vocal but not violent crowd was subdued by a consular rebuke. No continuous narrative is available for the events of 75. The people rioted, and the consul Cotta, though he had been personally endangered, used persuasion to restore order – but the evidence is fragmentary. In 67 violence was used on both sides. The supporters of Pompey's pirate command had to counter the determined and violent resistance of conservative senators. As Cassius Dio reports:

They adopted his motion and immediately all except the senate turned to Pompey. But that body preferred to suffer anything whatever at the hands of the freebooters than put so great command into Pompey's hands. In fact they came near slaying Gabinius in the very senate-house, but he eluded them somehow. When the people learned the feeling of the senators, they raised an uproar, even going so far as to rush upon them as they sat assembled; and if the senators had not got out of the way, they would certainly have killed them.[28]

There can be little doubt that of the three possible scenarios, violence by neither side, by one side, and by both sides, it is the last which best fits the climate of Rome in the post-Gracchan period.

In the riots of the early 30s, the authorities (the triumvirs) used repression to quell mob violence. These riots were more serious and prolonged, and the situation of the populace more desperate, than in any earlier food crisis. There is another important difference: upper-class leadership for hungry Romans was conspicuously absent. The political context had changed dramatically with the collapse of the Republic. There were no politicians and no political institutions to mediate between the consumers of Rome and the triumvir, Octavian, who posed as their leader, but who pursued policies flagrantly at odds with their material welfare. The face-to-face confrontation that took place is described graphically by Appian:

Now Rome succumbed to food crisis, since the traders of the east could not put to sea for fear of Pompeius, who controlled Sicily, and those of the west were deterred by Sardinia and Corsica, which the lieutenants of Pompeius held, while those of Africa opposite were prevented by the same hostile fleets, which infested both

[28] Cassius Dio 36.34.

shores. Thus there was a great rise in the cost of provisions, and the people considered the cause of it to be the strife between the leaders, and cried out against them and urged them to make peace with Pompeius. As Octavian would by no means yield, Antony advised him to hasten the war on account of the scarcity. As there was no money for this purpose, an edict was published that the owners of slaves should pay a tax for each one, equal to one-half of the 25 drachmas that had been ordained for the war against Brutus and Cassius, and that those who acquired property by legacies should contribute a share thereof. The people tore down the edict in fury. They were exasperated that, after exhausting the public treasury, stripping the provinces, burdening Italy itself with contributions, taxes, and confiscations, not for foreign war, not for extending the empire, but for private enmities and to add to their own power (for which reason the proscriptions and murders and this terrible famine had come about), the triumvirs should deprive them of the remainder of their property.

They banded together with loud cries and stoned those who did not join them, and threatened to plunder and burn their houses, until the whole populace was aroused, and Octavian with his friends and a few attendants came into the forum intending to intercede with the people and to show the unreasonableness of their complaints. As soon as he made his appearance, they stoned him unmercifully, and they were not ashamed when they saw him enduring this treatment patiently, and offering himself to it, and even bleeding from wounds. When Antony learned what was going on, he came with haste to his assistance. When the people saw him coming down the Via Sacra, they did not throw stones at him, since he was in favour of a treaty with Pompeius, but they told him to go away. When he refused to do so, they stoned him also. He called in a larger force of troops, who were outside the walls. As the people would not allow him even to pass through, the soldiers divided right and left on either side of the street and the forum, and made their attack from the narrow lane, striking down those whom they met. There was a scene of slaughter and wounds, while shrieks and groans sounded from the house-tops. Antony made his way into the Forum with difficulty, and snatched Octavian from the most manifest danger, in which he then was, and brought him safe to his house. The mob having been dispersed, the corpses were thrown into the river in order to avoid their gruesome appearance. It was a fresh cause of lamentation to see them floating down the stream, and the soldiers stripping them, and certain miscreants, as well as the soldiers, carrying off any particularly elegant item as their own property. This insurrection was suppressed, but with terror and hatred to the triumvirs; the famine grew worse; the people groaned, but did not stir.[29]

THE CONSERVATIVE RESPONSE

The ruling class was split down the middle on the matter of the food supply of Rome. The issue had become thoroughly political; it was a central aspect of the struggle between populist and establishment

[29] Appian, *Bell. civ.* 5.67–8 cf. Cassius Dio 48.31.

politicians, *populares* and *optimates*, the former exploiting the genuine grievances of the plebs to gain their own political ends, and the latter obstructing them as best they could.

The negative stance taken up by conservative senators in the context of food crisis has already been glimpsed. The consul for 138 arrogantly refused even to put a request to the senate for the purchase of supplementary grain. 'Hold your tongues,' he told the citizenry, 'I understand better than you what is in the public interest.' In 100 the senate authorised the purchase of supplementary grain stocks, but also did its utmost to prevent the passage of Saturninus' grain law. The proposal was declared unconstitutional by the senate and vetoed by tribunes. In the end, Caepio the quaestor 'attacked him with the help of some of the aristocrats, destroyed the bridges and threw down the ballot boxes'.[30] It is unknown whether Cotta, the consul of 75, took any more positive action than to remonstrate with the people. 'All except the senate' turned to Pompey in 67, but superior force had to be used to win him the command against the pirates. If conservative senators voted Pompey his grain commission in 57 it was because they judged Clodius the greater menace.

The opposition of the conservatives to Saturninus' initiative is symptomatic of their general antipathy to the distribution system and the laws which established and extended it. Gracchus was accused of introducing largesse on a huge scale, encouraging indolence among the people, draining the treasury and in general acting against the interests of the state. Clodius' measure was condemned as openly demagogic as well as extravagant. Gracchus, Saturninus and Clodius were feared, hated and killed by the 'best men' (*optimates*) and their henchmen (though not solely for their grain laws). Only in the case of Pompey, the beneficiary of two laws addressed to food supply rather than distribution, did they encounter an opponent with whom they could not compete. Their own 'strong man' Sulla swept away the whole system of regular distributions, and its revival was actively resisted for eight years.[31]

Three grain laws were enacted with senatorial support, but they do not represent a fundamental change of attitude among establishment senators. The circumstances and contents of the Lex Octavia (90s?) and the Lex Terentia Cassia (of 73) are unknown or unclear. At best they are attempts by the conservatives to run a distribution system on a reduced scale. A special explanation is required for the Porcian law (of

[30] *Ad Herenn.* 1.12.21.
[31] Sallust, *Hist.* 1.55.11; Licinianus p. 34F (78 BC, attempt at revival by Aemilius Lepidus).

62), a law sponsored by a leading conservative which expanded the distribution scheme.

The Octavian law must have been a conservative measure, because it both replaced the Gracchan grain law and earned a tribute from Cicero, a convinced opponent of regular distributions. Cicero called it 'a moderate measure which the state could bear and which gave the plebs what they needed – therefore injurious neither to the citizens nor to the state'. The law presumably restricted the number of recipients of state grain and raised its price. The Lex Terentia Cassia restored regular distributions. On paper this was a major concession. On the other hand, the return of distributions was inevitable. The vulnerability of the grain supply system had recently been confirmed. Moreover, the campaign to dismantle the Sullan reforms was gathering momentum. The consular law is best regarded as preemptive action by the senate to head off the more radical bill that would surely come once the powers of the tribunate had been restored. It is likely that the consuls modelled their bill on the Octavian rather than the Gracchan law, for a passage of Cicero suggests that only a small fraction of the citizen body were eligible to receive under the law.[32]

In the event, the radical bill that the senate anticipated came from the conservative side around a decade later in circumstances that could hardly have been foreseen in 73. Cato's law of early 62, the Lex Porcia, raised the annual outlay on grain distributions to $7\frac{1}{2}$ million denarii or 30 million sesterces, or it added this sum to the bill.[33] Only fear of revolution in the form of the Catilinarian conspiracy could have persuaded the conservatives to bid for the political support of the plebs so flagrantly. The law in fact destroyed the conservatives' case against state grain. It was only a matter of time before the senate surrendered the initiative again. The credit for abolishing the charge for state grain and for reforming the system of supply went to a demagogue (Clodius) and to a proto-autocrat (Pompey), respectively.

What alternative policy to regular grain distributions might have been acceptable to conservative senators? Some incidents from the 70s already mentioned provide some clues. Cicero as quaestor in Sicily made a special purchase of grain for Rome in the midst of a dire shortage – and was the toast of the city. His arch rival Hortensius, as aedile in the same year (75), won general applause for making grain available to the people. An aedile of the following year, M. Seius, distributed cheap grain in a crisis, 'on account of which he had statues

---

[32] Cicero, *2 Verr.* 5.52. Lex Octavia: Cicero, *Off.* 2.21.72; *Brut.* 62.222; Rickman (1980), 161–5.

[33] Plutarch, *Cato Min.* 26.1; *Caesar* 8.6; with Rickman (1980), 169–72.

erected to him on the Capitol and the Palatine, and he himself at the end of his life was carried to his cremation on the shoulders of the populace'.[34] Finally, a consular law, the same Lex Terentia Cassia, ordered the governor of Sicily to more than double the quantity of grain to be imported from that province.

For a brief period in the 70s, then, the senate directed proceedings. The initiative lay with the leading magistrates acting with the authority of the senate. There was no question of handing over special powers to a Pompey to enable him, as Cassius Dio put it, 'to hold sway over the entire world then under Roman power'.[35] Nor do tribunes play any role in these years. If a minor magistrate was to be permitted to win credit with the people, then it was the quaestor for Ostia (the post held and lost by Saturninus in 104), or the quaestor of a grain-exporting province, or more particularly the aedile. Aediles were traditionally responsible for the grain supply, and in the absence of a regular distribution scheme would sometimes have been in a position to sell surplus state grain at favourable rates with the authority of the senate.

In short, conservative senators would have been happy to turn the clock back to the pre-Gracchan period, before it became a citizen's right to receive regular rations of cheap grain and the obligation of the senate and its magistrates to provide them.

THE ACHIEVEMENT OF THE REFORMERS

How impressive was the system of supply and distribution that evolved in the course of the late Republic? The crucial questions are, how many people were fed, at what cost and how reliably.[36]

Number of recipients

There are no figures until the mid-40s, after the Republic had collapsed. Caesar as dictator whittled down the list from 320,000 to 150,000.[37] Something approaching the former number may have benefited from the handouts in the aftermath of the Clodian law.

The original grain law, the Lex Sempronia of Gaius Gracchus, was a modest proposal. This can be stated even though very little is known

[34] Pliny, *Hist. nat.* 18.16. [35] Cassius Dio 39.8.3.
[36] On the grain laws, see Brunt (1971), 376–82; Schneider (1974), 361ff.; Rickman (1980), 156–72. I do not discuss the law of Drusus of 91 (Livy, *Per.* 71). Nothing is known of it, and it was certainly annulled.
[37] Suetonius, *Iul.* 41.3.

about the law.[38] Appian says that all citizens were eligible, and there is general confirmation that the qualification was citizenship not poverty in the story in Cicero concerning the distinguished senator L. Calpurnius Piso Frugi. Piso had fought the law all the way in the senate but later turned up in the food-queue. When challenged by Gracchus his response was: 'I would prefer that you were not of a mind to divide my property among the citizens individually, but since you are dividing it then I shall ask for my share.' The grain was his property in the sense that it was paid for out of public funds. However, it is not clear whether the sizeable group of freedmen (who were citizens but with certain disabilities) were admitted, whether only citizens who were resident in the city were eligible, and which age and sex restrictions were applied. Nor is the size of the grain ration attested.

The proportion of the population receiving state grain actually fell in the period 123–63. Saturninus' bill, which would have lowered the price of state grain and hence made it more accessible to poor citizens, was rejected. The Octavian law, to have pleased Cicero, must have cut back the numbers of recipients. There were no recipients at all from 81 to 73. A rhetorical passage of Cicero, composed not long after the enactment of the Lex Terentia Cassia in 73, implies that under that law only 40,000 recipients were admitted, at 5 modii per person per month. He says that 33,000 medimnoi, or around 200,000 modii, were more or less sufficient to cover the monthly ration of the Roman plebs.[39] It has already been suggested that this was a conservative measure, closer to the Octavian law of uncertain date which abolished the Sempronian law (the law of Gracchus), than to the Sempronian law itself. If, for example, we take 600,000 as the population of Rome in the late 70s, then under the law of 73 only 6% of the inhabitants of Rome bought state grain, and a maximum of 12% might have been fed by it (since one ration was adequate for two people).[40]

The years 62–58 were a major turning-point in the history of the food distribution system of Rome. The laws of Cato and of Clodius substantially increased the number of recipients. Estimates of the length of Cato's list range from over 100,000 to over 200,000 recipients. As a result of the Clodian law, the list of recipients swelled uncontrollably, so that it numbered 320,000 in 46 when Caesar cut it by more than 50%.

---

[38] The citations are from Appian, *Bell. civ.* 1.21; Cicero, *Tusc. disp.* 3.20.48. See also Livy, *Ep.* 60; Schol. Bobb. p. 135; Cicero, *Off.* 2.21.72; *Sest.* 48.103; etc.; Garnsey and Rathbone (1985).

[39] Cicero, *2 Verr.* 5.52. For Rowland (1965), arguing from *2 Verr.* 3.163, there were 180,000 recipients; but the extra grain ordered was not necessarily destined for the *frumentatio*.

[40] Five modii of wheat per month provided, in round figures, 400 kg. See Pliny, *Hist nat.* 18.66, with Foxhall and Forbes (1982), 43ff.

About a decade earlier, Pompey as superintendent of the grain supply had had it in mind to cut down the list of grain recipients. This is implied in the plan to which Cassius Dio refers, to revise the list of beneficiaries of state grain with a view to identifying recently enfranchised slaves. Pompey was foiled by the destruction of the temple in which the relevant documents were kept, an event which fell between the end of September 57 and March 56, and was attributed by Cicero to Clodius (or his henchman Cloelius). Where Pompey had failed, the dictator Caesar succeeded.[41]

Who were the new beneficiaries under Clodius' law? Non-citizens, free and slave, had never been eligible for state grain, and Clodius did nothing for them. Freedmen were apparently admitted without restriction under the law. Dionysius says that many masters took the opportunity afforded by the introduction of free grain to emancipate slaves, thus passing on to the state part of the burden of their upkeep. Pompey was concerned to weed out such people, as was seen. Before 58 the humbler freedmen and almost all slaves were the responsibility of wealthier individuals who had an interest in keeping them alive. In addition, the age of eligibility among male members of citizen families appears to have been reduced by Clodius to 10 (from 14, presumably).[42]

Finally, Clodius made the distributions somewhat more accessible to poorer citizens. Down to 58, the free poor were excluded *de facto* from the distribution scheme, unless they could meet the cost of the (unmilled) state grain, not to mention milling and baking charges, through payment for casual labour supplemented by the generosity of patrons.[43] Patrons gave or lent their clients cash for grain, and arranged for milling and baking in return for personal services and perhaps a cut of the grain. It was not men of high rank and considerable wealth, but contractors, craftsmen and small businessmen of freed, free-born or even slave status, who kept the poor alive in this way, if anyone did. The rich and powerful patronised the 'respectable' plebs,

---

[41] Cassius Dio 39.24.2–3; Cicero, *Cael.* 78; *Har. resp.* 57; *Mil.* 73; with Nicolet (1976a). For a different view, Rickman (1980), 175. On Cloelius, see Cicero, *Dom.* 25–6, 47–8; *Cael.* 78; with Shackleton-Bailey (1960).

[42] Suetonius, *Aug.* 41, with Brunt (1971), 382. See Dionysius 4.25.5, on the freeing of slaves.

[43] Pliny furnishes a basic price for milled wheat (12 sesterces per modius, *Hist. nat.* 18.90), but no price for unmilled wheat. Duncan-Jones (1982), 345–7 suggests a basic milling price of 6 sesterces per modius, three times that envisaged by Jasny (1944b). On employment opportunities, see Brunt (1980). It was perhaps an aim of the Gracchan building programme to reduce the numbers of citizens excluded from the distributions by poverty; cf. Plutarch, *C. Gracch.* 6 (granaries, roads). On the distributions and the poor, see Rowland (1976); cf. Finley (1985), 198–204. On patronage and the poor, see Garnsey and Woolf (forthcoming).

typically men of some means and prospects, who might have something of value to offer already or in the future in return for patronal services. Clodius made it less expensive for the poor to stay alive, without liberating them altogether from the need to seek out employers and patrons.

Thus, for roughly six decades after its institution, the state distribution system guaranteed only a small fraction of the population of Rome the grain that it needed. Moreover, the number of recipients of state grain relative to the level of population (which rose steadily throughout the period in question) is likely to have been higher under the original law than at any time down to 62. The law of 62, and especially that of 58, for the first time made state grain available to a substantial segment of the population. It remained the case that without employment opportunities (whether provided by the state or private individuals), and without the existence of the institution of patronage, the free poor would not have received their daily bread.

Supply

The recipients of state grain, the *plebs frumentaria*, were a privileged group. But even they, if they had families, had to have recourse to the market. The monthly ration of 5 modii introduced or, more probably, revived by the law of 73, was insufficient to maintain dependants, except where families were represented by more than one recipient. One ration was ample for two people but well below the minimum subsistence requirement for three.[44] Recipients having more than one dependant would ordinarily have had to buy grain at commercial rates. They were exposed to the vagaries of the market.

Price fluctuations were the result of variations in supply, a product of bad harvests in the grain-exporting regions (principally in north Africa, Sicily and Sardinia, but also Italy), difficulties of transport (the consequence of piracy, bad weather and the backwardness of shipping technology) and profiteering. The earmarking of considerable quantities of grain for distribution at a fixed price will have acted as a check on the movement of prices in general, while substantially reducing the vulnerability of privileged consumers in particular.

The Roman authorities did not have the will to eliminate price fluctuations, whether natural or human in origin (or a combination of the two), even if they had had the means. Republican Romans, unlike the Athenians of the fourth century BC, conspicuously failed to produce legislation to protect the consumer. Livy's report under 189 about the

[44] See n. 40.

prosecution of grain-dealers is a unique notice. The first law specifically against manipulation of the grain supply was a Julian law of either the dictator Caesar or the emperor Augustus.[45] Until that time, governments showed little interest in controlling the profits of traders in the market place.

It is even possible that the state authorities speculated in grain. For considerable periods of time between 123 and 62 the state imported in the form of tax far more grain than was needed for the distributions. Thus, for example, in the late 70s the tithe from Sicily alone was around 3 million modii of wheat, or sufficient for 50,000 recipients of state grain, and for 3 years from the passage of the law of 73 (and possibly for longer) enough tax and requisitioned grain was coming in from the same source to distribute to 180,000 people. Yet only 40,000 people received state grain under this law. In these circumstances, rather than risk upsetting the powerful companies of tax-collectors and transporters (whose services were bought by the state) and their friends in the grain-distribution business, the responsible magistrates are likely to have released such grain as was surplus to their requirements at the market rate, whatever it happened to be, not at cost price.

Certain steps were taken from time to time on the supply side to prop up the distribution system and reduce the risks of shortage in the city. These were typically ad hoc measures taken on the spur of the moment, if not actually under duress, and do not add up to a coherent, long-term strategy.

First, Gracchus had state granaries built with the purpose of storing surplus grain against bad seasons and disruptions in supply. However, the granaries attested in the late Republican sources are private, not public.[46] This suggests that the Gracchan measure was not followed up, and that much of the state grain was kept in rented storage-space.

Secondly, special anti-piratical commands were in operation in 102–100, 74–71 and 67, designed to secure (among other things) a safe passage for the grain ships. These ventures resulted in either temporary success or signal failure until Pompey came on the scene. The senate either underestimated the opposition or was simply unwilling to entrust the necessary powers and resources to one man. Pompey's appointment was fiercely contested by the senate.

Thirdly, additional revenues were periodically sought for grain-purchase. The first grain law coincided with the reorganisation of the finances of the new province of Asia under the supervision of Gracchus himself. The finances in question were essentially those of the former kingdom of Pergamum, bequeathed to Rome 10 years previously.

[45] Livy 38.35.5; *Digest* 48.4. [46] Rickman (1980), 138ff.

There cannot be any doubt that money-taxes from Asia helped to meet the cost of the newly established food distributions. Next, Cyrene had been bequeathed to Rome in 96. Its annexation in either 75 or 74 preceded and made possible the restoration of the food distribution system. Finally, and in contrast, the seizure of Cyprus together with the confiscation and sale of king Ptolemy's property followed the passage of Clodius' law, and has the air of an afterthought. The choice of Cato for the mission suggests that its purpose was at least partly political, to silence opposition to the bill. On the other hand, it must have been obvious as soon as the bill of Clodius was passed, if not before, that a major effort was required on the supply side to provide for the regular distributions, let alone to meet future shortages. No less than 18 million modii of wheat had to be on hand in each year for distribution to 300,000 people (or 19,200,000 modii for 320,000). Of this perhaps two-thirds came in as tithe from Sicily, Sardinia and Africa in normal years. The finances of the state had lately benefited from the substantial revenues generated by Pompey in his eastern conquests. But Cyprus' contribution of 168 million sesterces per annum was not negligible.[47]

These several incidents expose the emptiness of the complaints of conservative senators that the distributions were a drain on the treasury.[48] On the contrary, they were a burden on the empire. The Romans fed privileged civilians (and soldiers) on the surplus extracted from subject states.

Fourthly, the Roman senate began belatedly in the aftermath of the passage of Clodius' bill to move towards the establishment of a grain commission to seek supplementary grain and make long-term improvements in the system of supply. Clodius had a candidate for the post, his henchman, the shadowy Cloelius, but was upstaged by Pompey, who was given charge of the grain supply by the consular law of September 57.

Pompey's first task was to secure emergency grain stocks to ease the current shortage. The effort had to be repeated in the following year, and then again in 54 when stored grain was spoiled by flood-water. His long-term strategy for improving the food supply was twofold.

First, Pompey offered small shipowners Roman citizenship as an incentive to serving the food supply of Rome (*annona*) for a number of years. Cicero in the *Pro Balbo* of 56 writes repetitively of the new citizens 'from Africa, Sicily, Sardinia', precisely the main sources of imported grain at this time. Again, in a speech of 54, the *Pro Scauro*, Cicero speaks of 'all those who had the franchise conferred on them by the same

[47] Badian (1968), 46, 76; Oost (1963), 20–1; Badian (1965).
[48] Cicero, *Sest.* 103; *Tusc. disp.* 3.48; *Off.* 2.72.

Gnaeus Pompeius'. This is the first recorded conferral of citizenship for economic rather than military service.[49]

Secondly, Pompey put pressure on richer shipowners to secure their personal participation and that of their clients in the enterprise of bringing in the grain. Pompey was assigned 15 legates, among whom were Cicero and his brother. They were all no doubt men of influence with good contacts among the prosperous businessmen and traders of Rome and Puteoli. One member of this class who surfaces in Cicero's correspondence is C. Avianius Flaccus, a grain trader who had obtained some unspecified concessions from Pompey as grain commissioner. Cicero writes later to a governor of Sicily requesting him to show the same benevolent interest in the affairs of Avianius as Pompey had done.[50]

Pompey's efforts to put the food supply of Rome on a firmer footing, and, for that matter, Caesar's draconian solutions (a drastic reduction of the list of recipients coupled with the dispatch of colonies abroad), had no lasting effect, as civil war overtook the state. Domestic instability was more responsible than any other factor for the chronic insecurity of the food supply and distribution system of Rome in the late Republic.

CONCLUSION

Romans of the late Republic initiated the development of the most imposing system known from antiquity for supplying an urban centre with grain. The system emerged relatively late in the history of Rome, not far short of four centuries after the inauguration of the Republic. Free grain was not part of the scheme, nor were more than a small fraction of the inhabitants of Rome eligible to participate for the first 65 years of its existence. The conservative establishment instinctively distrusted and bitterly opposed the scheme, whether in its initial or its more developed form. Given their attitude, the disturbed political climate of the period, the inadequacies of the system itself and the enormous size of the population of Rome, it is not surprising that the last century of the Republic was anything but a golden era for consumers in the capital.

[49] Plutarch, *Pomp.* 50.1; Cicero, *Balb.* 24, 41; *Scaur.* 43; with Frederiksen (1980–1).
[50] Cicero, *Fam.* 13.75 cf. 79; 35.

14

RULERS OF THE WORLD

After almost two decades of civil war (49–31 BC), the Roman state came under the control of one man. Because of his own experiences as triumvir in Rome, Augustus as emperor could not fail to take a personal interest in the matter of the food supply of the city. If his regime was to be stable and enduring, then repetition of the famine and crowd violence of 43–36 had to be avoided.

Rome under Augustus was a huge metropolis of around one million people. Its vulnerability to food crisis did not miraculously come to an end with the emergence of the Principate. Augustus' personal intervention was required on a number of occasions to alleviate grain shortage. A standard imperial response to food crisis was, simply, largesse. Augustus frequently handed out money or grain (or both), not only in times of shortage. He thus established a tradition of liberality which his successors could hardly ignore. The more responsible emperors also made structural improvements in the system of supply and distribution. Augustus himself introduced several important innovations of this type, most notably the addition of Egypt as a major supplier of the capital, and the inauguration of the office of prefect of the grain supply (*praefectus annonae*). The long-term consequence for Rome of these and other such developments was reduced vulnerability to food crisis.

FOOD CRISES

1. Food shortage is not directly attested but may none the less have occurred in 28 BC.[1] Cassius Dio reports under this year: 'To the populace he distributed a quadruple allowance of grain and to some of the senators he made presents of money.' The case against food shortage is that the gifts of grain do not necessarily imply that grain was short; that in the *History* of Dio this was one of a number of actions taken by Augustus with the aim of winning him support on the eve of the restoration of constitutional government and the legitimising of his

---

[1] Cassius Dio 53.2.1–2; cf. *Res gest.* 18.

position at the beginning of 27 BC; and that the gifts are not included in the list of benefactions in the *Res gestae*, the emperor's public statement of his achievements.

On the other side, one could argue as follows. Dio refers to gifts of money to senators and grain to the people in the same sentence. He claims that the former were necessary as well as expedient: 'For so many of them had become impoverished that none was willing to hold even the office of aedile because of the magnitude of the expenditures involved.' No parallel explanation is offered for the gifts of grain, but the reason may simply be Dio's lack of interest. The grain allowance might be supposed to have also met a present need, precipitated as in 18 BC (see below) by a fall in tax-revenues, that is, by a reduction in the amount of grain coming in as tax in kind. Augustus' silence in the *Res gestae* proves nothing. The only food crisis he mentions is that of 22 BC, which led to his assumption of the administration of the grain supply; the recurring crises of AD 5–9 are passed over completely. That said, Dio's description of the benefaction is suspect. It is scarcely believable that four times the regular dole was handed out to, say, 250,000 people.

2. The first directly attested food crisis of the Principate occurred in 23 BC. Augustus says that in his eleventh consulship (1 January – 1 July 23 BC), he bought grain with his own money and distributed twelve rations to each of at least 250,000 people. This must mean that the grain needed for the monthly dole was not at hand. There is the further implication that market supplies of grain were low.

Tiberius, stepson of Augustus, as Ostian quaestor and under the emperor's orders, helped relieve this crisis by bringing in emergency supplies. According to Velleius Paterculus, Tiberius 'so skilfully regulated the difficulties of the grain supply and relieved the scarcity of grain at Ostia and in the city, that it was apparent from his execution of this commission how great he was destined to become'.

Suetonius, in his biography of Tiberius, talks in general terms of his administration of the grain supply, 'which happened to be deficient'.

As to the causes of the shortage, Cassius Dio supplies some clues. This year and the following 'proved so unhealthy that great numbers perished during them'. Moreover, the epidemic was preceded by a damaging fire and storm and a flood which 'made the city navigable for boats during three days'. To judge from other passages in the historical writers (including a text of Dio shortly to be quoted), it is a safe conjecture that disruption of production in Italy and extensive destruction and spoilage of stored grain contributed to the shortage.[2]

---

[2] *Res gest.* 15. Augustus does not say that his rations (as in AD 6) were in addition to the normal handouts; Velleius 2.94.3 cf. Suetonius, *Tib.* 8; Cassius Dio 53.33.4–5.

3. Under 22 BC Cassius Dio has the following report:

The following year, in which Marcus Marcellus and Lucius Arruntius were consuls, the city was again submerged by the overflowing of the river, and many objects were struck by thunderbolts, especially the statues in the Pantheon, so that the spear even fell from the hand of Augustus. The pestilence raged throughout all Italy so that no one tilled the land, and I suppose that the same was the case in foreign parts. The Romans, therefore, reduced to dire straits by the disease and by the consequent famine, believed that these woes had come upon them for no other reason than that they did not have Augustus for consul at this time also.

Dio goes on to describe how, in scenes reminiscent of 57 BC, the crowd besieged the senate in the senate house, and forced Augustus to take personal responsibility for the grain supply.

Augustus' own version makes no mention of rioting by the people:

I did not decline in the great dearth of grain to undertake the charge of the grain supply, which I so administered that within a few days I delivered the whole city from apprehension and immediate danger at my own cost and by my own efforts.[3]

4. With reference to 18 BC (and other unnamed years), Augustus writes:

From the consulship of Gnaeus and Publius Lentulus onwards, whenever the taxes did not suffice, I made distributions of grain and money from my own granary and patrimony, sometimes to 100,000 persons, sometimes to many more.

A shortfall in grain coming in as taxes-in-kind such as to force the emperor to dip into his own reserves implies a general shortage not only of state grain destined for the dole, but also of grain for sale in the market.[4]

5 to 9. From AD 5–9 food crises were intermittent in Rome, with that of AD 6 the most severe.

In AD 5, according to Cassius Dio:

Violent earthquakes occurred and the Tiber carried away the bridge and made the city navigable for 7 days; there was also a partial eclipse of the sun, and food crisis set in.[5]

Under AD 6, Cassius Dio writes:

There was also a severe food crisis. In consequence of this, the gladiators, and the slaves who were for sale, were banished to a distance of 100 miles, Augustus and the other officials dismissed the greater part of their retinues, a recess of the courts was taken, and senators were permitted to leave the city and to proceed wherever they pleased. And in order that their absence might not prevent decrees from being passed, a ruling was made that all decisions reached by those in attendance at any

---

[3] Cassius Dio 54.1.1–4; *Res gest.* 5.   [4] *Res gest.* 18.   [5] Cassius Dio 55.22.3.

meeting should be valid. Moreover, ex-consuls were appointed to have oversight over the grain and bread supplies, so that only a fixed quantity should be sold to each person. Augustus, to be sure, gave free of cost to those who were receiving doles of grain as much again in every case as they were already getting; but when even that did not suffice for their needs, he forbade even the holding of public banquets on his birthday.

Cassius Dio goes on to say that the food crisis, combined with the new 5% death duty and a serious fire, put the masses in a revolutionary mood, and that the city remained in turmoil until the grain shortage was over and the gladiatorial games were held in honour of Drusus by his sons Germanicus and Claudius – presumably on the birthday of Drusus, which fell in March or April. The crisis therefore began at some point undetermined in AD 6, proceeded through the autumn (Augustus was born on 23 September) and winter, and had terminated by the spring of AD 7, when the sailing season had opened again and Rome could receive imports from abroad.

Suetonius adds to the measures taken by the emperor the expulsion of all foreigners 'with the exception of physicians and teachers', while Eusebius in his *Chronicle* says that the price of grain rose to 5½ denarii, 22 sesterces, per modius.[6]

The food crisis, having subsided by the spring of AD 7, returned in the same year. Dio reports under AD 7:

Inasmuch as the populace was terribly wrought up over both the wars and the food crisis (which had now set in once more), he ... proceeded to do anything that would make the crowd cheerful, regarding such measures as necessary. And in view of the dearth of grain he appointed two ex-consuls commissioners of the grain supply, granting them lictors.[7]

A fragment of Cassius Dio assigned to AD 8 reports games in the Circus in the name of Germanicus and his brother (the future emperor Claudius), 'when at last the food crisis had abated'.[8]

Under AD 9 Cassius Dio connects the sending of Tiberius into Dalmatia with food crisis in Italy:

But since in spite of these reverses the remainder of the Dalmatians rose, and the war kept dragging on, and food crisis occurred in Italy largely because of the war, Augustus sent Tiberius once more into Dalmatia.

In the summer of AD 9 Germanicus brought the news to Rome that the Dalmatians had surrendered. The plans for celebration were disrupted by the almost simultaneous report of the destruction of 3

[6] Cassius Dio 55.26.1; Suetonius, *Aug.* 42.3; Eusebius, *Chron*, ed. Schoene, II pp. 146–7.
[7] Cassius Dio 55.31.3–4.
[8] Cassius Dio 55.33.4 (Xiphilinus). The entry resembles but is not identical with 55.27.3. But the dating is insecure.

legions in Germany. A motley army was sent with Tiberius to Germany in the last months of the year to try to repair the situation. If Dio's explanation of the food crisis is to be accepted, the situation of consumers in Rome remained very vulnerable for as long as important campaigns were in progress in the north (until AD 11). Unfortunately, Dio's continuous narrative breaks down in AD 9, to be resumed mid-way through AD 11. The missing section presumably included the appointment of the prefect of the grain supply, who was certainly in office by AD 14, and the end of the recurring food shortages.[9] Augustus' total silence in the *Res gestae* on the subsistence crises of these years is remarkable.

10. In AD 19 prices rose, the people protested, and Tiberius imposed a maximum price, compensating merchants at the rate of 2 sesterces per modius. Tiberius was offered in gratitude the title of Pater Patriae, which he refused.[10]

11. Under AD 32 Tacitus writes:

Under the same consuls, the excessive price of grain all but ended in rioting; and large demands were for several days made in the theatre with a freedom not usually employed towards the emperor.

Tiberius (from Campania) chided the magistrates and senate, and a consular edict rebuked the people. No other governmental action is recorded.[11]

12. In the winter of 40–41 grain was very short. A rhetorical passage of Seneca suggests that when the emperor Gaius (Caligula) died (on 24 January 41), there were supplies in Rome for only 7 or 8 days. He goes on:

While he was building his bridges of boats and playing with the resources of the empire, we were threatened with the worst evil that can befall men even during a siege – the lack of provisions; his imitation of a mad and foreign and unluckily proud king was very nearly at the cost of the city's destruction and famine and the general revolution that follows famine.

It is a moot point whether Seneca is charging Gaius with anything more specific than scandalous negligence. For Suetonius, writing half a century after Seneca, the building of a bridge between Puteoli and Baiae over which Gaius could drive his chariot was merely extravagant pageantry. The vessels are described as merchant ships, but there is no

[9] Cassius Dio 56.12.1, 18.1, 23; Tacitus, *Ann.* 1.7; D'Escurac (1976), 317–19.
[10] Tacitus, *Ann.* 2.87.1. Tacitus mentions problems with the *annona* under AD 23, but only in the context of a review of the performance of Tiberius as emperor up to that point (*Ann.* 4.6.6). Other general notices in Velleius 2.126.3; Tacitus, *Ann.* 3.54.6.
[11] Tacitus, *Ann.* 6.13.

suggestion that the emperor's bizarre bridge-building was directly responsible for a food crisis in Rome. Suetonius chooses other preposterous actions as illustrations of Gaius' cavalier attitude to the food supply: taking over the animals from the bakeries 'so that bread was often scarce at Rome', shutting up the granaries, thus condemning the people to hunger, and expressing the wish that great disasters would mark his reign, such as famine and plague.

It was Cassius Dio, living a century after Suetonius, who made a clear causal connection between the bridging of the Bay of Naples and food crisis. Under AD 39, he writes:

Of the ships for the bridge, some were brought together there from other stations, but others were built on the spot, since the number that could be assembled there in a very brief space of time was insufficient, even though all the vessels possible were got together – with the result that a very severe food crisis occurred in Italy, and particularly in Rome.

The charge is fantastic, and the emperor's extravaganza dated too early to have affected the food situation in the winter of AD 40–41.

Whatever the verdict on these unsatisfactory sources, a food crisis in the winter of 40–41 can be accepted as genuine. How Claudius reacted to the crisis is not mentioned. Cassius Dio writing under AD 42 says that a 'severe food crisis' stimulated Claudius into planning a new harbour for Rome. He must have resolved the crisis by persuading merchants to put to sea in the winter, as in 51.[12]

13. In AD 51 a bad harvest and resulting food crisis were seen as signs of divine displeasure, according to Tacitus. Claudius escaped a hostile mob in the forum (Suetonius says he was pelted with crusts of bread) with the aid of his praetorian troops. It was found that there were only 15 days' worth of provisions left in the city. Claudius sent for grain in the middle of winter – fortunately mild weather made possible winter sailing – and took steps to attract merchants into the service of the Roman food supply by offering privileges.[13]

14. Under AD 62 Tacitus says that Nero threw dole grain that was old and spoiled into the Tiber to dispel popular anxiety about shortage. He adds that 'the price was not raised', despite the loss of some 200 grain ships in port at Ostia through storm and 100 more at Rome through fire. The passage is obscure. Apparently Rome experienced

---

[12] Seneca, *Brev. vit.* 18.5; Suetonius, *Gaius* 19; cf. 39.1; 26.5; 31; Cassius Dio 59.17.2. See also Josephus, *Ant. Iud.* 19.6; Aurelius Victor, *Caes.* 4.3. Claudius' food supply problems at the beginning of his reign are reflected in the CERES AUGUSTA coinage of AD 41, repeated in 42. See *BMC* I pp. 183–4, 191. Rickman (1980), 257–67, has a useful appendix on 'corn and coins'.

[13] Tacitus, *Ann.* 12.43; Suetonius, *Claud.* 18.2; Orosius 7.6.17.

fear of shortage rather than actual shortage, which was headed off, it may be supposed, by imperial intervention in the market. However, it is difficult to believe that the loss of 300 grain ships with their cargoes had no effect whatever on the availability of grain and its market price.[14]

15. The Great Fire of AD 64 left the city without grain stocks. Nero had essential foodstuffs brought up from Ostia and the nearby cities, and imposed a maximum price of 3 sesterces per modius on grain in the market. The distributions were suspended. It was probably in this year that a governor of Moesia on the Lower Danube became the first to have 'brought relief to the food supply of the Roman people by sending a great quantity of wheat from that province'.[15]

16. AD 68–70. Civil war inevitably endangered the food supply of Rome. In any contest for power at Rome, Africa and Egypt were crucial possessions. After Nero's death the governor of Africa, Clodius Macer, put pressure on the new emperor Galba by holding back grain shipments. At the beginning of AD 70, when bad weather delayed the African ships, it was assumed in Rome that another proconsul of Africa, Piso, had revolted against Vespasian. Meanwhile, Vespasian had moved into Egypt to stop the dispatch of grain, and after his partisans defeated Vitellius at Cremona, prepared to invade Africa. When he eventually released the Egyptian grain ships, they arrived just in time: 10 days' supplies were all that remained in the granaries at Rome.

Even without blockade, prices were bound to rise in Rome as essential supplies were reserved for military consumers. As Tacitus puts it:

But the mob and the mass of the people, whose vast numbers kept them aloof from the cares of state, gradually began to feel the evils of war, for all money was now diverted to the use of the soldiers, and the prices of provisions rose.

He goes on to say that the plebs had been less affected during the revolt of Vindex, which had been acted out in Gaul in AD 68, than in the following year, when the war moved into Italy.

To make matters worse, a terrible flood in the spring of AD 69 reduced the common people to hunger by depriving them of food and the opportunity to earn money to pay for it.[16]

[14] Tacitus, *Ann.* 15.18.
[15] Tacitus, *Ann.* 15.39.3; Cassius Dio 62.16.5 (Xiphilinus); Suetonius, *Nero* 38.1 (granary destroyed); *ILS* 986. The striking Annona–Ceres sestertii of AD 64–6 were intended to advertise the emperor's rehabilitation of the grain supply after the fire, but they indirectly confirm the scale of the disaster. See *BMC* I pp. 127–30, 220–1.
[16] Tacitus, *Hist.* 1.73 cf. Plutarch, *Galba* 13 (Macer); Tacitus, *Hist.* 1.86 (flood); 1.89 (civilians lose out in the competition for grain); *Hist.* 3.8, 48; 4.38, 52; Suetonius, *Vesp.* 6.3. See Bradley (1972); Gallotta (1975).

After the civil war period the extant historical record deteriorates markedly, and the 'famine' notices are fewer and variable in quality.[17]

17. Domitian's unenforced edict forbidding the planting of additional vines in Italy and ordering the destruction of vines in the provinces was issued, according to Suetonius, 'upon the occasion of a plentiful wine crop coinciding with a scarcity of grain'.[18]

18–20. The biographer of Hadrian refers generally to the occurrence of famines, plagues and earthquakes which the emperor alleviated to the best of his ability.

The biographer of Antoninus Pius claims that the emperor 'relieved a scarcity of wine and oil and wheat with loss to his own private treasury, by buying these and distributing them to the people free'.

The biographer of Marcus Aurelius writes:

But now to interrupt the emperor's happiness and repose, there came the first flood of the Tiber – the severest of their time – which ruined many houses in the city, drowned a number of animals and caused a most severe food crisis; all these disasters Marcus and Verus relieved by their own personal care and aid.

Of the three notices, only the third produces a food crisis that is approximately datable. In the biographer's account, it coincides with the beginning of hostilities with the Parthians in 161. That is, it occurred not long after the beginning of the reign of Marcus and Verus.[19]

[17] The coinage frequently refers to the food supply but the precise significance and message is usually unclear. The depiction of ANNONA, the personification of the food supply, and of her superior, the goddess CERES, may merely be designed to advertise an emperor's concern in a general way. This seems to be the implication where the ANNONA coin type is scattered throughout a reign, as in the case of Antoninus Pius. A concentration in particular years might be taken to suggest a recovery, and by inference a breakdown, of the grain supply. Vespasian began to use the ANNONA type only in the last years of his reign. Was there a crisis following the epidemic of AD 77? Domitian's ANNONA series runs from AD 84 to 89 and is more or less coextensive with his German and Dacian wars and Saturninus' rebellion in AD 89. Did he have to purchase additional supplies at a time of a major military effort? Nerva's coin legend of AD 97 'PLEBEI URBANAE FRUMENTO CONSTITUTO S.C.', 'the fixing of the grain supply for the plebs of Rome', picks up a similar legend on Domitian's sestertii of AD 89, and suggests adjustment after a period of dislocation. See *BMC*II pp. 51–2 (Vespasian); pp. 360, 365, 375–6 (Domitian); III p. 21 (Nerva). But again the inference is uncertain. The ANNONA type is encountered at the beginning of the reigns of other emperors such as Titus, Hadrian and Commodus, see *BMC* II pp. 254–5 (Titus), III p. 402 (Hadrian), IV 698ff. (Commodus), and may point to the giving of largesse (cf. the LIBERALITAS coins that become common from the reign of Hadrian, *BMC* III p. 405 etc); or they may merely be designed to foster an atmosphere of security. In general, the numismatic evidence is best used to support the literary sources, where available.
[18] Suetonius, *Dom.* 7.2.
[19] *SHA Hadr.* 21.5 cf. 6 (flood); *Ant. Pius* 8.11 cf. 9.3 (flood); *Marc.* 8.4–5 cf. 12.13–14. The plague which reached the west in 167 is not specifically associated with food crisis by any author, though cultivation ceased in Italy, according to Orosius 7.15.5–6, 27.7. See Gilliam (1961), for references and discussion. The coinage of Marcus depicts Annona (but

21. In 189 Rome experienced a serious food crisis. According to Herodian it coincided with an epidemic, which was particularly serious in Rome. But he attributes the blame to the manipulations of the powerful freedman of Commodus, Cleander:

He amassed a large sum of money and bought up most of the grain supply, but then cut off its distribution, the idea being that, if he first caused a shortage of supplies and then won people over by generous distributions when they were desperately in need, he would gradually gain the loyalty of the people and the soldiers.

In the epitome of Cassius Dio the intrigue has another level. The root cause is given as Cleander's 'thefts', but the prefect of the grain supply deliberately made things worse in order to turn the people against Cleander.

The biographer of Commodus says there was a second phase of scarcity, the unintended consequence of Commodus' interference in the market:

And because he was so careless, moreover, a great shortage arose in Rome, not because the crops were deficient, but merely because those who then ruled the state were plundering the food supply. As for those who plundered on every hand, Commodus afterwards put them to death and confiscated their property; but for the time he pretended that a golden age had come, 'Commodian' by name, and ordered a general reduction of prices, the result of which was an even greater scarcity.

The popular violence which forced a terror-stricken emperor to sacrifice Cleander to the mob is ignored by the biographer, but described graphically by both Cassius Dio and Herodian.[20]

22. The biographer of Septimius Severus says that stocks of grain were very low when the emperor arrived in Rome (in May 193), but that when he died there was a surplus amounting to 7 years' tribute. The plausibility of his story is not undermined by the silence of the two historians (Cassius Dio in epitome, and Herodian). The quality of their coverage of the civil war period is patchy and narrowly focused in comparison with Tacitus' of the civil war years AD 68–70. The biographer also claims that Septimius Severus instituted a distribution of free oil. The emperor's interest in the food supply of Rome is confirmed by the coinage, which figured ANNONA from 194–201 (except for 200) and again in 206–7; CERES FRUGIFERA is also prominent.[21]

without the legend) in December 165 – December 166, and CONG(IARIUM) AUG in the following year. See *BMC* IV pp. 433, 435, 439, 445, 447, 589, 598.

[20] Herodian 1.12.2–4; Cassius Dio 72.13.2; *SHA Comm.* 14.1–3. The coinage of 189 ignores the troubles of that year.

[21] *SHA Sept. Sev.* 7.5 cf. 7.7; 18.3; 23.2. For the coins, see *BMC* V pp. 98, 100, 103, 106, etc.

23. The biographer of Severus Alexander claims that the emperor restored the food supply 'by purchasing grain at his own expense', after the depredations or sheer negligence of Elagabalus. Elsewhere he says that the emperor's response to a request for a reduction of prices, especially those of beef and pork, was to work for cheaper prices by encouraging meat production. The story, if genuine (and this *Life* incorporates a great deal of fiction), suggests that Alexander had a greater understanding of economic behaviour than Commodus.[22]

CAUSES OF FOOD CRISIS

Natural causes

For Suetonius, harvest failure (*sterilitas*) in unspecified locations lay behind the food shortages of AD 6 and 51. There was a low Nile and therefore a poor harvest in an unidentified year between 25 and 21 BC when Strabo's friend Petronius was prefect of Egypt, and Augustus intervened to distribute cash, grain or both in Rome in 24, 23 and 22 BC. The conjunction is not proven, and in any case crop failure in Egypt did not necessarily lead to food shortage in Rome. In AD 99 when the Nile flood failed, the emperor Trajan actually sent stored grain back from Rome to its province of origin.[23]

The biographer of Commodus asserted that the crisis of AD 189 was caused not by an absolute shortage of grain, but by corruption in high places. Even if harvests did not fail, a hold-up in the transport of the grain or shipwreck could cause distress in Rome, depending on the amount of cargo affected. St Paul caught a grain ship on the Alexandria–Puteoli run late in the season, was shipwrecked, and joined another that was wintering in Malta. But these were single ships; the delay or destruction of an entire convoy (as in AD 70 and AD 62, respectively) was a more serious matter.

Epidemic disease formed part of the background of food crisis in 23–22 BC and AD 189. The great plague that hit Rome in 167 doubtless caused difficulties which have gone unrecorded. Cassius Dio, in describing the earliest of these crises, asserts that the onset of disease meant that agriculture was neglected in Italy and perhaps elsewhere.

---

[22] *SHA Sev. Alex.* 21.9 cf. 22.1–3, 7; 39.3. The literary sources for the disturbed mid-third century are thin and often unreliable. They say a lot about plague, much less about food crisis. But see e.g. Cyprian, *Demetr.* 10; *Orac. Sib.* 13.106–8.

[23] Strabo 17.1.3, suggesting, unconvincingly, that the harvest did not suffer. Bonneau (1971), 152n., 155n., 740, has slight evidence for a bad harvest in June 22 BC (too late to have brought on a food crisis in Rome); cf. 148–58 for the reign of Augustus in general; 162

Finally, the spoiling of grain stocks through flooding occurred sporadically in Rome, as in 23–22 BC, AD 5 and 69.

Human error, corruption and irresponsibility

Under this heading come the fires of 23–22 BC, AD 62 and AD 64, the scheming of those close to Commodus in AD 189 and the outlandish behaviour of Gaius and Elagabalus (if the sources can be believed).

Warfare

Civil war caused food crisis in Rome in 68–70, and at the least ran existing stocks dangerously low in 192–193. In such circumstances grain fleets were held up and the needs of soldiers put above those of civilians. But in addition foreign war might worsen the position of the population of Rome. Cassius Dio commented that food crisis in Italy in AD 9 was caused largely by the revolt of the Dalmatians. This war must have diverted supplies on a considerable scale during its three-year course. Dio had stated under AD 6 that 'many wars' were taking place at that time. His list of trouble-spots includes Isauria and Germany, but also two grain-exporting provinces, Sardinia and Africa. Sardinia was overrun by 'pirates', 'so that Sardinia had no senator as governor for some years, but was in charge of soldiers with equestrians as commanders'. His comment on Africa runs as follows:

> The Gaetulians also were discontented with their king, Juba, and, scorning the thought that they too should be ruled over by the Romans, rose against him. They ravaged the neighbouring territory, slew many even of the Romans who made a campaign against them, and, in sum, gained so great headway that Cornelius Cossus, who subjugated them, received triumphal honours and also a title from them.

The success of Cossus Cornelius in AD 6–7 is confirmed by Orosius and also indirectly by Victory coins of Juba. However, Cossus appears to have taken over in Africa from another general, Passienus Rufus, who held a special command in about AD 3–6. In fact, the Roman army became embroiled with the Gaetulians as early as the late 20s BC. Juba II was appointed in about 25 BC king of Mauretania, but with a kingdom extending through 'Gaetulian' territory in pre-desert Algeria and Tunisia to Tripolitania. The appointment may quite quickly have provoked opposition. The Romans were certainly at war shortly after Juba's accession, because two generals celebrated triumphs in 22 BC and 21 BC for successful campaigns in Africa. These events suggest a

n. 795, citing Pliny, *Hist. nat.* 5.9, for a record high Nile in the reign of Claudius, perhaps in AD 45, when unusually high prices are recorded in Egypt; cf. Gapp (1935), 259 n. 7.

correlation between food crisis and disruption in a major grain-producing province (Dio refers to the ravaging of Roman territory, presumably in Proconsularis) in both 23–22 BC and AD 5–7. Parallels are to be found in Tacfarinas' invasion of Proconsularis at the end of AD 18 or early 19 and disturbances involving Musulami and Numidians in AD 40 and the grain shortages of AD 19 and 41 in Rome.[24]

RESPONSE OF GOVERNMENT: SHORT-TERM MEASURES

The emergency measures taken by Augustus in AD 6–7 included the following:

1 Temporary expulsion to a distance of 100 miles of certain classes of extraneous personnel – according to Cassius Dio, gladiators and unsold slaves, according to Suetonius, all foreigners except for doctors and teachers.
2 Dismissal of most of their retinues by the emperor and his high officials.
3 Permission given to members of the senatorial order to leave Rome (presumably with their entourages).
4 Recess of the Courts.
5 Appointment of senior senators to watch over the grain and bread supplies.
6 Grain rationing (under the supervision of the senior senators).
7 A cutback in expensive celebrations.
8 Doubling of the grain dole.

This was drastic action, without parallel in the annals of Rome. It is rivalled only by Nero's suspension of the grain distributions and imposition of a low maximum price at the time of the Great Fire. These crises were self-evidently particularly harsh. The short-term measures taken by Roman governments were usually very limited in scope.

The search for supplementary grain was standard procedure, and details are rarely given in the sources. Augustus claims to have drawn on his own granary to supplement deficient supplies of tax-grain in 18 BC and at other times. To have resolved the crisis of 22 BC so quickly, he must have had spare grain close at hand. Nero, in the aftermath of the Great Fire, had grain brought in from Ostia and other nearby cities. He might have had to go further afield, for example, to Puteoli. Puteoli had been an important centre of trade in Cicero's day and remained so for two further centuries. Under Augustus it was given the additional function of receiving Egyptian grain, reloading much of it into smaller coastal and river vessels and passing it on to Ostia and Rome. Puteolan merchants of the generation after Augustus can be seen at work

---

[24] Cassius Dio 56.12.1; 55.28, with Orosius 6.21.18 and Mazard (1955), 202–3 (victory of AD 6–7); *CIL* VIII 16456; *ILS* 120 (Rufus); *Inscr. It.* XIII 1 569 (Atratinus, Balbus); Tacitus, *Ann.* 3.20 (invasion of Tacfarinas). On Tacfarinas see Lassère (1982); Benabou (1986), 140–1, criticising Shaw (1982).

through the newly discovered tablets, stacking grain from Alexandria in city-owned granaries and using it as security for loans.[25]

Emperors on occasion had to seek additional stocks of grain beyond Italy. Claudius, shaken by his encounter with a hungry mob, was prepared to send out traders in search of grain in the depths of winter, and to offer compensation for damage or losses suffered from storms. In later times, special officials were appointed with responsibility for the purchase of grain for Rome in close-to-hand surplus-producing provinces. The emperor Trajan commissioned one T. Flavius Macer to buy grain in Numidia for the city of Rome. It was more unusual for grain to be sent from the eastern provinces, Egypt apart. A Neronian governor at Moesia in the Danubian basin claimed to be the first to have sent wheat from his province to Rome, perhaps in AD 64.[26]

Price-fixing was occasionally resorted to by emperors, as by Tiberius in AD 19, Nero in AD 64 and Commodus in 189. (Severus Alexander is said to have refused to set maximum prices for food, meat in particular.) On such occasions, the probable consequence that grain would be taken off the market was not always foreseen. Tiberius sought to avoid this by offering compensation to the grain merchants. Commodus' 'general reduction in prices' led to the disappearance of food from the market. Julian fell into the same trap when he tried to resolve the food crisis in Syrian Antioch in AD 362 by bringing in grain and putting it up for sale at a fixed below-market price. Because his cheap grain was not rationed, it was quickly bought up by speculators, and sold at a high price in the countryside or abroad.[27]

Emperors on the whole rejected price-fixing in favour of the grand gesture, the furnishing of grain or cash by special distribution. The liberality of Augustus is better attested than that of any other emperor, but was not necessarily unique in scale and frequency. He made handouts of grain or money (the means to buy grain and other necessities) before he assumed the office of supervisor of the grain supply (*curator annonae*) in 22 BC, and indeed before his position in the state was regularised in 27 BC. In 29, 24 and 11 BC, he gave 400 sesterces to each of 250,000 people; in 5 BC he gave 240 sesterces to 320,000 people, and in 2 BC 240 sesterces to a few more than 200,000. In 28, 23 and 22 BC and in AD 6 he provided grain, while in 18 BC 'and in other

[25] Tacitus, *Ann.* 15.39.3; *Res gest.* 15 (22 BC); *AE* 1972, 86–7, 143; 1973, 167 (Puteoli tablets): the grain appears to have been privately owned. On Puteoli see Frederiksen (1980–1) and (1984), Ch. 14.
[26] Suetonius, *Claud.* 18.2; *ILS* 1435 cf. Pflaum (1960–82) II 229ff., no. 98 (Macer) cf. *ILS* 1432, with D'Escurac (1976), 129–34 (procurator at Arles); *ILS* 986 (Moesia).
[27] See Liebeschuetz (1972), 126ff.; Petit (1955), Ch. 2.

years' he gave grain and money to at least 100,000 'and sometimes many more'.[28]

RESPONSE OF GOVERNMENT: LONG-TERM MEASURES

Imports

The emperors added substantially to the amount of grain-bearing land under direct Roman control, introduced changes in the administration of the food supply system or *annona*, sought to attract additional traders into the service of the *annona*, and improved the port facilities of Rome, first at Puteoli and later at Ostia.

The expansion of the agricultural resources under the control of Rome was principally the work of Augustus. First and foremost, he brought Egypt into the empire. The author of the fourth-century *Epitome* says that 20 million modii (around 133,300 tonnes) of Egyptian wheat were exported annually to Rome under Augustus. This is considerably more than the emperor needed for the free grain distributions (15 million modii or 100,000 tonnes for 250,000 people, 12 million modii or 80,000 tonnes for 200,000), and represents two-thirds of a plausible figure for the actual consumption rate of wheat (30 million modii or 200,000 tonnes among a million people). It was also more than half the total annual assessment of Egypt in the time of Justinian of 8 million artabas or 36 million modii (240,000 tonnes).[29]

No comparable figures are available for north Africa, another area in which Rome under Augustus advanced. At the end of his reign, Rome's African territory encompassed the greater part of the productive area of Tunisia and of eastern Algeria. Josephus, writing in the mid-first century AD, has Agrippa II state that north African grain exports ran currently at twice the level of those of Egypt, and fed Rome for 8 months of the year. The passages from the *Epitome* and Josephus, when taken together, point to a total import of 60 million modii or 400,000 tonnes, or twice my estimated actual wheat consumption in Rome, and from Egypt and Africa alone.[30] It is no wonder that the idea has found favour that under the Principate grain was no longer brought in from Sicily in the form of tax.

Precise figures for wheat imports into Rome are unattainable. It is

---

[28] *Res gest.* 15; 18; Cassius Dio 53.2.1; 54.1.1; 55.10.1; 55.26.2. See also Suetonius, *Aug.* 41.5: he often distributed grain free or for very little charge when food was short.
[29] Epitome, *Caes.* 1.6; Justinian, *Edict* 13.
[30] Josephus, *Bell. Iud.* 2.383, 386; cf. Tacitus, *Ann.* 12.43 (Egypt and Africa); Garnsey (1983), 118–21, with bibliography.

misguided to base any calculations on the texts just presented, considered singly or (even more so) in combination. Once the temptation to settle for an import figure of 60 million modii (and more) is rejected, then a putative tax-reform that substituted a money-tax for tax in kind in Sicily loses its attraction.[31] The evidence for such a reform is in any case very flimsy and it predates the Principate. This means both that a plausible historical context for the reform is difficult to find, and that Augustus can be held responsible at most for not returning to the earlier arrangements.

Augustus neither behaved nor wrote like an emperor faced with an embarrassment of riches. Rather, as he himself indicates in the *Res gestae*, shortfalls in 'taxes' necessitating distributions of grain and money were recurrent events. The Sicilian tithe was not dispensable.

Perhaps Rome did import as much as 60 million modii of grain in some years. But the explanation is not that the inhabitants of Rome needed or normally ate so much grain. Rather, the reservoir of surplus grain that could be drawn upon from year to year was unpredictable because of harvest fluctuations. Only the volume of grain coming from Egypt could be ascertained in advance, because the grain transported to Rome was always the previous year's crop.[32] The emperors made a virtue of necessity: far from setting a ceiling on grain imports, they brought in as much as they could. Tiberius was particularly aggrieved at the popular demonstrations of AD 32, because he knew that he was bringing in record amounts of grain. Claudius' incentive schemes for traders were an attempt to raise the level of imports even further.

Administration

In the area of administration, the important development was the institution of a permanent office of the food supply headed by a prefect of equestrian rank responsible to the emperor. This appointment was foreshadowed by Augustus' assumption of personal control of the food supply in 22 BC, in circumstances described by Cassius Dio:

They took the 24 rods and approached Augustus, begging him to consent to being named dictator and to becoming commissioner of the grain supply, as Pompey had once done. He accepted the latter duty under compulsion, and ordered that two men should be chosen annually from among those who had served as praetors not less than five years previously in every case to attend to the distribution of the grain.

---

[31] Recently restated by Rickman (1980), 64–5 and Gabba (1986), 77–8.
[32] There was too little time for the new grain to ripen, be harvested and processed, spend one to two months at sea and arrive in Puteoli by the first half of June (cf. Seneca, *Ep.* 77).

There was, however, no prefect of the grain supply for a further 30 years or more: the creation of the office was more or less an afterthought of the twilight years of his reign. The appointment was prompted by the food crisis which began in AD 5. Even so, Augustus' first reaction was to appoint ad hoc officials with consular rank to handle the emergency (in both AD 6 and 7).

What the prefect actually did is not known in detail. His responsibilities were worldwide. The prefect was at the head of an organisation which had offices staffed by subordinate officials in all the areas that provided Rome with grain and (by the late second century) olive oil. He might be importuned by states wishing to import grain from Egypt – or by shippers from Gaul complaining about fraud. His contact with shippers who served Rome was particularly important. He issued their contracts, supervised their activities and made arrangements for special purchases of grain when required.[33]

Transport

In the absence of a state-owned merchant fleet, the interest and co-operation of shipowners and traders was absolutely vital.

The improvement of port facilities was a matter of direct interest to both traders and governments. The largest merchant ships could not safely unload at Ostia, essentially a river port. Augustus expanded the dock area at Puteoli, which did have a suitable harbour, extending it toward Lake Avernus and adding the new Porto Giulio. The first attempt to provide harbour facilities near Ostia was a failure. Claudius launched the project, but soon after its completion under Nero 200 ships in AD 62 went down in a storm. It was not until Trajan built a smaller inner harbour (Portus) that the larger ships were able to sail direct to Ostia to unload their grain in relative safety.[34]

Claudius is the first emperor known to have offered inducements to shipbuilders and shipowners, allegedly in direct response to the difficulties he had experienced with the food supply. Anyone who had a ship capable of holding 10,000 modii (around 70 tonnes) of wheat, and was prepared to commit it to supplying the city with grain for 6 years, was offered special benefits. They included exemption from a law which penalised the rich and childless, the Lex Papia Poppaea (in the case of

[33] In general, D'Escurac (1976); briefly, Rickman (1980), 79ff., App. 2 (subordinates); Seneca, *Brev. vit.* 18.3 ('tu quidem orbis terrarum rationes administras'); 19.1 (supervision of traders); Epictetus 1.10.2 (Egypt); *ILS* 6987 (Arles).

[34] Rickman (1980), 17–19; Frederiksen (1984), 324–8, 331–4, on ports.

Roman citizens), citizenship (in the case of Latins), and rewards for those with three children (in the case of women).

Others had offered incentives before Claudius. It was Pompey's innovation to confer citizenship for economic rather than military services. I suspect that Claudius was taking a leaf out of Augustus' rather than Pompey's book. Augustus was in personal charge of the grain supply from 22 BC, and he did not renounce his responsibility when he appointed the prefect in effect as his deputy towards the end of his reign.

What did Augustus do as supervisor of the grain supply? He is credited with having got the grain ships moving between Alexandria and Puteoli. The incident reported in Suetonius (if it is historical), when Alexandrian sailors hailed Augustus as their benefactor, suggests that he gave traders a clear incentive to work this route. In general, Augustus may be assumed to have worked closely with the more influential traders. Rome was an attractive market. Consumer demand was huge, and prices were high. But it was worth an emperor's while to have a good rapport with leading traders. Augustus was an excellent customer, with no financial worries, and had the concerns of traders at heart. Suetonius says that he was at least as alive to the interests of farmers and traders as to those of consumers.[35]

The history of the award of privileges to shippers serving the *annona* is only patchily attested after Claudius. The next emperor known to have concerned himself with these matters is Hadrian. Legal sources for his reign (early second century) show that immunity from public liturgies, the compulsory services imposed by municipal authorities, was now enjoyed by shippers serving the *annona*, and that limits were placed on its availability. Hadrian ruled that only those could enjoy immunity who invested 'the greater part' of their resources in the service of the *annona*. The Antonine emperors that followed condemned 'phantom' shippers who 'built' but did not actually launch ships. Finally Scaevola, a jurist of the Antonine age, refers to a measure similar to that of Claudius, enacting, among other things, that in order to qualify for exemptions it was necessary to own a ship with a capacity of 50,000 modii (about 350 tonnes) or several (perhaps five) ships of 10,000 modii each.[36]

None of this legislation changed the status of the shippers concerned.

---

[35] Claudius' incentives: Suetonius, *Claud.* 18.3–4; 19; Gaius, *Inst.* 1.32c; *Digest* 3.6 (Ulpian), with Pomey and Tchernia (1978), 237–43. For Augustus, see Suetonius, *Aug.* 98.2; 42.3.
[36] *Digest* 50.6.6.5, 6, 8, 9; 50.5.3.

They were still free agents bound only by the terms of their contracts to serve the state. The representatives of the 'five colleges of shippers of Arles', in dispute with the association of grain measurers in AD 201, made precisely this point in their petition to the prefect of the *annona*.[37] There was no abandonment by the government of the strategy of recruitment by incentive, and exemption from civic liturgies offered greater material benefits and had wider appeal than any privilege formerly available. In return, Antonine emperors substantially raised the level of investment that would qualify for privilege, and tried to eradicate abuse of the system.

The biography of Commodus refers to the 'institution' of an 'African fleet' called the 'Commodiana Herculea', which was intended to come to the rescue if the flow of grain from Alexandria dried up. If this vague assertion by a suspect source is to be taken seriously, then some reorganisation of the African shippers took place on the instigation of Commodus. It is unnecessary to believe that the terms of their service were substantively altered.

Some similar development had overtaken the Alexandrian traders more than a century earlier, again without any effect on their status and relationship with the state. It appears that in the reign of Nero, or shortly before, there was formed an 'Alexandrian fleet', in the sense of a single convoy bringing all or most of the grain from Egypt for Rome. Seneca writes to a friend in about AD 64, early in the month of June:

Today, without warning, the Alexandrian *tabellariae* came into view. They are the ships which they always send on ahead to give the news that the fleet is on its way. This is a very welcome sight for the Campanians; the whole population of Puteoli settles down on the quayside and tries to spot the Alexandrian ships by the type of rigging ... Everyone was in such a rush to get down to the sea, and it was a great satisfaction to me to control myself and not to be in a hurry to get the business letters which I was expecting with the fleet ...[38]

In sum, the grain trade under the Principate remained in the hands of private individuals, the more prominent and committed of whom were offered inducements, in the form of privileges and favourable terms. The trade was under increasing surveillance by the government, which strove to increase the number of shippers contracted to perform state service and to supervise their activities, and encouraged their formation into associations (*collegia*). However, the transformation of the transport of grain to Rome into a compulsory public service lay in the future.

[37] *ILS* 6987 (Arles).   [38] *SHA Comm.* 17.7; Seneca, *Ep.*77.

Distribution

Faced with the daunting task of feeding around one million people, emperors followed a two-pronged strategy: to guarantee free grain to a minority of favoured consumers, and to ensure that there was enough grain coming into the city to satisfy the needs of the whole population.[39]

Decisive steps were taken by Augustus, though not at the earliest opportunity. It was he who limited the grain recipients (*plebs frumentaria*) to about 200,000. Some think Augustus reduced the number by an additional 20%, on the supposition that the 150,000 legatees under the will of Augustus in AD 14 and under that of Tiberius in AD 37 were, precisely, the *plebs frumentaria*. Whatever may be thought of that argument, some internal reorganisation of the list of recipients occurred in the period between Augustus and the turn of the second century, without any increase in overall numbers. A passage in Cassius Dio implies that civilian recipients and the praetorian guard together made up 200,000 in AD 202. He does not include other elite groups, mainly soldiers, who are known to have been added to the list, perhaps as early as the reign of Nero. Moreover, at some stage in the first century the age of eligibility was lowered below 10; Trajan is said by Pliny to have introduced 5,000 new infant grain recipients.[40]

The essential point is that Augustus opted for a relatively low figure. He might have adopted the Clodian solution and allowed more or less unrestricted eligibility to resident citizens. Instead he chose to move in the direction of Pompey as *curator annonae* and Caesar as dictator, and rule that not all resident citizens were entitled to the grain dole. One group that he excluded at some point consisted of recently manumitted freedmen. Suetonius writes:

With equal dignity and firmness, when he had announced a distribution of money and found that many had been manumitted and added to the list of citizens, he declared that those to whom no promise had been made should receive nothing, and gave the rest less than he had promised, to make the appointed sum suffice.[41]

The passage relates to a cash handout, not to the regular distributions, but it has implications for the latter. It may be inferred that Augustus succeeded where Pompey had failed in excluding newly manumitted slaves from the dole.

It would be more accurate to say that Augustus moved from a Clodian to a Pompeian position on grain distributions. Between 27 and

---

[39] On the distributions, see Van Berchem (1939); Rickman (1980); Nicolet (1976b).

[40] Pliny, *Pan.* 26–8 (Trajan); Dio 76.1.1 (Severus). On post-Augustan developments, see Rickman (1980), 182–97.

[41] Suetonius, *Aug.* 42.2.

2 BC only minimal criteria of eligibility appear to have been applied. This was the period also in which Augustan liberality was concentrated. At least a quarter of a million people benefited from cash handouts in (at least) 29, 24 and 11 BC. (In addition, a higher and a lower figure are mentioned, 320,000 and 100,000.) The same number were issued 12 rations of grain purchased at the emperor's expense in 23 BC. Did recipients of state grain at the distributions (*frumentatio*) regularly number about 250,000 prior to 2 BC, or did the numbers fluctuate from year to year, as Dio implies in his discussion of the developments of that year? Either way, those who benefited from the dole in 2 BC and thereafter were fewer than previously.

In 2 BC, the year in which Augustus assumed the title Pater Patriae, he felt sufficiently confident of his political position to overhaul the distribution system and make it rather more compatible with his own values.[42] These were deeply conservative. If he had had the nerve, he would have abolished the system altogether. After the grain crisis of AD 6 had eased, he wrote the following memorandum or diary entry:

I was strongly inclined to do away for ever with distributions of grain, because through dependence on them agriculture was neglected; but I did not carry out my purpose, feeling sure that they would one day be renewed through desire for popular favour.[43]

Distributions might be suspended *in extremis*, as apparently they were in AD 64 at the time of the Great Fire, simply because there was no grain to hand out. Abolition was not an option.

Augustus' compromise solution was to produce a list of pre-Clodian dimensions, even if this meant excluding about 20% of those who had been in the habit of receiving the dole. The entry in the *Res gestae* describing his decision is understandably imprecise, making no reference to a revision of the lists or to the imposition of a *numerus clausus*:

In my 13th consulship I gave 60 denarii apiece to the plebs who were at that time in receipt of public grain; they comprised a few more than 200,000 persons.

But there is no good reason for doubting Dio's judgement that the list was closed now for the first time, and that it stood at around 200,000 in 2 BC. It is even possible, as we saw, that Augustus later pared down the list by a further 20%.

Augustus certainly resisted any temptation to expand the list. An obvious opportunity was to hand in AD 6, had he been so minded. In that year he gave out twice as much grain as usual at the distributions.

---

[42] Cassius Dio 55.10.1 cf. *Res gest.* 15; Suetonius, *Aug.* 40.3 (*recensio*).
[43] Suetonius, *Aug.* 42.3.

However, this was done not by doubling the list of recipients, but by issuing double rations to those already eligible to receive. In the same way, whichever emperor lowered the age of eligibility for the dole was choosing to nurture an inner core of already privileged families in preference to spreading the benefits more widely. Finally, the distributions of free oil instituted at the turn of the second century by Septimius Severus, to which Aurelian in the 270s added free pork and cheap wine, benefited only those entitled to the grain dole.[44]

There was more to providing for the *plebs frumentaria* than handing out free grain to their male representatives over the age of 10. If, as seems likely, the ratio had not risen above the late Republican level of 5 modii, then a number of families would have had to buy grain. In issuing a double dole in AD 6, Augustus was recognising that grain was in short supply and expensive in the market.

At the same time, no prudent emperor could neglect the interests of the rest of the lower-class population of Rome, whose dependence on the market was greater. The level of political risk was too high. Emperors accepted the responsibility, exercised through their deputy, the prefect of the grain supply, of ensuring that sufficient grain was for sale and at a reasonable price. Their efforts on the supply side have already been outlined. Much less is known about government policy in relation to distribution.

In particular, it would be interesting to know how often state grain was released in the market, in what quantities and at what price (in relation to market rates). The attitude of the prefect of the grain supply was crucial. According to Tacitus, Faenius Rufus, prefect in AD 55–62, did not profit from the office in the customary way. No details are given.

The prefect was in a position to make money for the state, as well as on his own behalf. He could release surplus stocks at the market rate. Alternatively, he could force up the market price by withholding grain. The latter strategy was followed by Commodus' prefect Papirius Dionysius for political ends, to rouse the mob against Cleander. Faenius Rufus may have won the hearts of the Neronian plebs by selling state grain cheaply.[45]

Under the Principate, manipulation of the grain supply was prohibited by a specific law, a Julian law on the food supply, probably of Augustus. A similar law became a standard feature of municipal constitutions in the west under the early Empire.[46] No one is known to have been prosecuted under the law.

[44] *SHA Sev.* 18.3; *Aurel.* 35.2, 48.1.   [45] Tacitus, *Ann.* 14.51; Dio 72.13.2.
[46] *Digest* 48.4; Gonzales (1986), Ch. 75.

The most effective way for a government to control speculation was to enter the market on the side of the consumer. Tacitus' comment on Faenius Rufus is one indication that behaviour of that sort was unusual. Tiberius' conduct when prices rose enough to anger the populace is also revealing. In AD 19 he fixed a maximum price for grain but paid compensation to traders, while in AD 32 he took no action whatever. If Tiberius is any example, a moderate degree of speculation was tolerated by emperors. After all, it was in their interest to attract traders to the Roman market. It would have been counterproductive systematically to reduce their profit margins.

Two further items are worth brief mention, one relating to storage, the other to food processing. First, large private granaries fell increasingly into imperial ownership through confiscation, legacy and inheritance. Secondly, the emperor Trajan is known to have been exercised over the shortage of bakers in the city. By means of incentives similar to those dangled before traders by Claudius, Trajan encouraged more men of means to go into the baking business and existing bakers to expand their enterprises.[47]

In comparison with these developments, whose effect on the material welfare of the ordinary inhabitants of Rome is hard to measure and may have been marginal, emperors such as Augustus, Nero, Domitian and Trajan conferred tangible benefits on the urban poor by providing them with employment, particularly in the building trade, and therefore with the means to buy food. It is too much to claim that this was a conscious aim of every emperor who launched a building project. A well-known anecdote reveals that Vespasian at least was sensitive to this issue:

To a mechanical engineer, who promised to transport some heavy columns to the Capitol at small expense, he gave no mean reward for his invention, but refused to make use of it, saying: 'You must let me feed my poor commons.'[48]

Emperors did not and could not provide everything that the ordinary Roman needed for his welfare. Tacitus acknowledges the existence of private patronage linking 'part of the populace' with 'the great houses'.[49] His social prejudices prevented him from mentioning, or noticing, the vertical ties that helped the free poor at the bottom of the social hierarchy to survive. Their patrons were drawn from the clients of the rich, not the rich themselves.

[47] Rickman (1971), 164–73 (storage); Gaius, *Inst.* 1.34 cf. *CIL* VI 1002 (dedicated to Antoninus Pius by the College of Bakers).
[48] Suetonius, *Vesp.* 18.   [49] Tacitus, *Hist.* 1.4.

CONCLUSION: PLEBS AND PRINCEPS

If Suetonius has not misrepresented the attitude of Augustus, only political factors, the danger to his own regime of provoking the plebs, prevented him from following the example of Sulla and abolishing the distributions altogether. In general, the risk and reality of pressure from below dictated the short-term and long-term responses of emperors to food crisis.

In extreme cases popular pressure took a violent form. According to Cassius Dio, the people of Rome blamed the epidemic and food crisis of 22 BC on the resignation of Augustus from the consulship. Dio goes on to say that they 'wished to elect him dictator, and shutting the senators up in their meeting place, forced them to vote this measure by threatening to burn down the building over their heads'. The crowd next approached Augustus and tried to persuade him to accept dictatorial office. They failed in this, but did compel him to become commissioner of the grain supply 'as Pompey had once done'.

Dio explicitly evokes the events of 57 BC, and his accounts of the two riots in fact run closely parallel. In both cases the senate in session was besieged by an angry crowd which threatened to burn the building and those within it. Both crises quickly subsided: in 22 BC it was over 'in a few days'. As in 57, the political context helps to explain the scale of the riots. The people were afraid that when he vacated the consulship (on 1 July 23 BC), Augustus was abandoning direct responsibility for the food supply and the welfare of the plebs in general.

This was the last of the 'old-style' riots, which were typically aimed at the senate in session. After 22 BC, when the grain supply officially passed into the emperor's control, there was no longer any point in laying siege to the senate. But rioting was now if anything more threatening to an emperor's position than before.

Under AD 6, Cassius Dio reports Augustus' emergency measures to deal with the food shortage and the formation of the nightwatchmen or *vigiles*, who were seven divisions of freedmen under an equestrian prefect, to combat fires. He goes on:

Now the masses, distressed by the food crisis and the tax and the losses sustained in the fire, were ill at ease, and they not only openly discussed numerous plans for a revolution, but also posted at night even more numerous bulletins.

This opaque notice needs to be interpreted in conjunction with a passage in Suetonius:

Except as a fire-brigade at Rome, and when there was fear of riots in times of scarcity, he employed freedmen as soldiers only twice . . .

In other words, the new force was deployed by Augustus to prevent or counter food riots as soon as it was created and perhaps in subsequent years.[50]

The anxieties of Augustus are understandable in the light of Claudius' experience of AD 51, when he was rescued by his troops from a hungry crowd in the forum, and the terrible fate of Cleander in AD 189. Cassius Dio's version of Cleander's downfall runs as follows:

It was not the soldiers, however, that killed him, as in the case of Perennis, but the populace. A food crisis occurred, sufficiently grievous in itself; but its severity was vastly increased by Papirius Dionysius the grain commissioner, in order that Cleander, whose thefts would seem chiefly responsible for it, might incur the hatred of the Romans and be destroyed by them. And so it came to pass. There was a horse race on, and the horses were about to contend for the seventh time. A crowd of children ran to the Circus, led by a tall maiden of grim aspect, who, because of what happened afterwards, was thought to have been a divinity. The children shouted in concert many bitter words, which the people took up and then began to bawl every conceivable insult; and finally the throng leapt down and set out to find Commodus (who was then in the Quintilian suburb), invoking many blessings on him and many curses upon Cleander. The latter sent some soldiers against them, who wounded and killed a few; but, instead of being deterred by this, the crowd, encouraged by its own numbers and by the strength of the Praetorians, were already drawing near to Commodus, whom no one had kept informed of what was going on, when Marcia, the notorious wife of Quadratus, reported the matter to him. And Commodus was so terrified (he was always the greatest coward) that he at once ordered Cleander to be slain, and likewise his son, who was being reared in the emperor's charge. The boy was dashed to the earth and so perished; and the Romans, taking the body of Cleander, dragged it away and abused it and carried his head all about the city on a pole. They also slew some other men who had enjoyed great power under him.[51]

The impression given by the sources is that public disorder of this kind was a peripheral phenomenon under the Principate as opposed to the late Empire. The plebs of Rome is not often shown to have resorted to violence to remind emperors of their responsibilities. Non-violent protest was a different matter. In AD 32 when prices were high the people raged for several days in the theatre against the emperor Tiberius 'with unusual insolence, almost crossing the border between demonstration and riot'. It was not unusual for theatre and hippodrome crowds to offer vociferous criticisms of government action or inaction.

Mass popular protest in the context of an autocracy is a curious

[50] Dio 55.27.1–2; Suetonius, *Aug.* 25.2.
[51] Dio 73.13 cf. Herodian 1.12.5–13.6. See Whittaker (1964).

phenomenon demanding explanation, especially as emperors did not merely permit it to go on, but regularly witnessed it in person.[52]

Emperors went to shows, first, because they were expected to display the virtue of *civilitas*, mixing with ordinary people and enjoying their pleasures. This was a central plank of the ideology of a regime which was supposed to have 'restored' not displaced the old order after a period of civil war.[53]

Secondly, emperors went to shows because they expected, and normally received, rapturous applause from what was in effect a vital part of their constituency. Even if the modern conception of the plebs of Rome as a pampered mob living off 'bread and circuses' is a fabrication traceable to the poisoned pen of Juvenal the satirist,[54] Augustus and his successors did improve the material conditions of the poor of Rome. They did this basically in the interests of tranquillity and the perpetuation of their rule.

Thirdly, popular demonstration of this kind was tolerated because it was safe. It posed no political threat to the regime, at most reminding the emperor of his obligation to feed his people. It took place in a controlled environment. It rarely spilled over into violence.

It was only in late antiquity that food riots at Rome became dangerous, at any rate in the short run (they did not outlast the arrival of grain), because the departure of emperors for other, preferred capitals had left a vacuum of authority. Romans then, like any other provincials, turned on their municipal government and its key officials when prices rose and starvation threatened. One Tertullus was unfortunate enough to have been urban prefect of Rome in AD 359–61 when the grain-fleet from Africa was held up by bad weather. He was saved from death by a dramatic gesture – he appeased the rioters by offering them his small sons – and by a timely sacrifice to Castor and Pollux, who calmed the winds and let the ships enter harbour.[55]

Thus there was established and maintained over a long period of time a kind of 'right' to protest, as an inescapable complement to the more desirable and presumably more commonly utilised 'right' to applaud. It would be a mistake to take an essentially negative view of the 'prerogatives' of the people, in the light of the quite considerable evidence that the authorities often listened to the crowd and made a positive response. Tiberius in Rome in AD 19 and Julian in Antioch in AD 362 each set prices in response to popular protest. When Symmachus as urban prefect of Rome in AD 397 learned of the people's

[52] See Cameron (1976).   [53] On *civilitas*, see Wallace-Hadrill (1982).
[54] Juvenal, *Sat.* 10.77–81.
[55] Ammianus 19.10; Symmachus, *Ep.* 4.5, 6.61; Sidonius, *Ep.* 1.10.2.

'entreaties for food', he judged it prudent to withdraw from the city. The theatre crowd called for his return – and he came back. Symmachus' reference in this context to 'the votes of the citizens' (*suffragia civium*) conjures up the ghost of the Republican constitution, which guaranteed to every citizen the right to vote in a sovereign assembly (*ius suffragii*). It is tempting to introduce the notion of a judicial authority of the people (*ius iudicandi*), in view of the incident that followed the fall of Gildo and the eventual release of the grain ships that he had held up in Africa. The Africa-based grain officials were paraded in Rome and executed or freed according to their reception by the populace.[56]

[56] Symmachus, *Ep.* 6.66; Claudian, *Cons. Stil.* 3.99–105, with Kohns (1961), 86ff.

15

THE SUBJECTS OF ROME

Rome's massive population of around one million in the age of Augustus, a number unequalled by any European city before the early nineteenth century,[1] was primarily sustained by means of a regular inflow of food and manpower from all over the Roman world. Contributions from Rome's provincial subjects also financed the grandiose building projects, expensive public amenities and lavish entertainments of the capital city. They paid for the court and civil administration, supported the extravagant lifestyle of the Rome-based aristocracy and fed and equipped an army of around 300,000–400,000 men.[2]

In this chapter I ask how these demands affected the livelihood of the populations of Italy and the provinces. My aims are, of necessity, limited. It is not possible to show precisely how living standards were affected all over the Roman world, nor to measure changes in the frequency and intensity of food crises. Without aiming at unrealistically precise estimates, we can assess the impact of taxes and rents, and identify certain long-term developments in provincial society, such as a steady increase of public ownership of land and other economic assets,

[1] Peking had 3 million inhabitants in 1793 according to a contemporary observer. See Elvin (1974), 1–2, quoting Fr. Amiot, *Mémoires* ..., Vol. 8, 217–19; cf. Elvin (1978), 79, on China between AD 900 and 1200: 'four or five were probably not far from a million inhabitants.' Londoners numbered about 900,000 in 1800, see Wrigley (1978), 215.
   This chapter is complementary to, and can be read in conjunction with, Garnsey and Saller (1987), Ch. 5.
[2] There was wealth-creation as well as wealth-consumption in the city of Rome (cf. Garnsey (1976)), but the latter was far more significant, and the empire at large bore the brunt of the expense.
   I have chosen not to present the relation between Rome and the empire in terms of the core–periphery model of Wallerstein (1974), (1980) and (1984). Wallerstein's world-system theory applies to the modern capitalist world economy, the roots of which are traced no further back than the sixteenth century. His interest in pre-capitalist systems is no more systematically worked out than that of Marx, and the problems involved in applying his model to antiquity are commensurate. For a Marxist analysis of Roman imperialism, see Deman (1975), criticised by Thompson (1982).

and a concentration of wealth in the hands of the few. These and other matters, notably, the level of civic patriotism and initiative among leaders of local government, and the manner in which the Romans husbanded the agricultural surplus which was now under their control, have implications for the subsistence and survival of communities and households.

APPROPRIATION OF WEALTH

The Roman state under the Principate exacted tax somewhat more efficiently than preceding governments (Roman and non-Roman) had done, and over a wide area. Augustus may not have introduced a universal and regular provincial census, as has been claimed, but he certainly carried out censuses in newly or recently annexed areas, thus preparing the ground for the systematic taxation of the population concerned. The Romans levied a land tax (*tributum soli*) in all provinces. A poll tax (*tributum capitis*) was also exacted, though its ubiquity is uncertain; it was a regressive tax, levied at the same rate for rich and poor.

The property tax took different forms and was levied at different rates from region to region. Syrians paid *tributum* in the form of a capital levy at the rate of 1% p.a., roughly equivalent to an income tax of 20% at a standard rate of return on rural property of 5%. Egyptian landowners paid roughly half-to-three-quarters as much, but in the form of a quantum of produce, not cash, the rate being fixed usually every five years. The *tributum* might also be paid as a quota of produce. There is record of tenths (in Bithynia, probably also in Sicily and Sardinia), eighths (in north Africa), sevenths and fifths (in areas unspecified). Tax-rates no doubt varied according to, among other things, land use and soil productivity. But local traditions also played a part, and these were by no means swept aside by the Romans. This means in practical terms both that existing taxation systems, where available, were taken over without significant alteration, and that rates of taxation were maintained at a stable, relatively low, level. Vespasian is the only emperor known to have raised taxes.[3]

A high level of direct taxation was unnecessary, given the low level of public expenditure, and would have provoked unrest and rebellion. Revolts attributable in part to taxation did occur, but only among recently conquered peoples for whom subjection to formal taxation was

---

[3] Suetonius, *Vesp.* 16. On tax rates, see Appian, *Syr.* 50; Wallace (1938), 11–19; *CIL* viii 25902 (Hr. Mettich); Hyginus p. 205. On taxation in general, see Jones (1974), 151–86; Neesen (1980), reviewed in Brunt (1981).

a new and humiliating experience. The taking of the census was particularly unpopular, even if the brutality of Roman census officials in AD 306, as dramatised by Lactantius, was untypical:

But now public calamity and common distress came upon them: a census was imposed on all the provinces and cities. Census officials were sent out in every direction and universal confusion followed. It was as if the enemy had broken in and men were suffering the terrors of captivity. The lands were measured field by field, the vines and trees were counted, animals of every kind were registered, the numbers of men were recorded. In the cities the common people of the towns and the country were assembled together; all the public places were packed with troops of families; every one was present with his children and slaves. The air resounded with torments and whips, sons were hung up to make them testify against their fathers, the most loyal slaves were tortured against their masters and wives against their husbands. If all else failed, men were tortured against themselves, and when pain had triumphed, they were credited with possessions they did not have. Age and infirmity gave no exemption. The sick and feeble were entered on the lists, the ages of every person were calculated, years were added to children and subtracted from the old.[4]

Any comprehensive assessment of state-imposed exactions must include additional taxes (they may have doubled the total tax burden in Egypt), and a wide range of irregular impositions, including requisitions of food, animals and equipment, and billeting. It was a sign of the disintegration of the civil administration in the third century AD that such extraordinary demands in effect displaced the regular tax system. However, supplementary burdens, imposed by both civilian officials and the military, had long been the bane of both townspeople and peasants. The second emperor, Tiberius, intervened on behalf of his subjects in the Asian province of Pisidia to curb such practices. His edict was not the first issued with this purpose in the province, and is unlikely to have been the last. A prefect of Egypt referred in an edict of AD 68 to petitions from farmers 'throughout the whole country', who complained 'that they have been condemned to pay many unprecedented charges . . . through payments in kind and money, although it is not open to any who wish to introduce recklessly some general innovation'. A decade earlier, the emperor Nero had outlawed taxes 'invented' by certain tax-collectors (*publicani*).[5]

Such impositions were irregular and unevenly distributed. Some provincials rarely saw a Roman soldier, though many more were caught up in the network of army supply (*annona*), especially when a.

---

[4] Lactantius, *Mort. pers.* 23. The story is of course intended to reflect badly on the persecuting Caesar, Galerius.
[5] Mitchell (1976); Chalon (1964), 27–39 (ll. 47–8); Tacitus, *Ann.* 13.51.

campaign was on foot. Three inscriptions from villages dependent upon Side in eastern Pamphylia praise three different local magnates for, among other things, escorting the *annona* to the imperial armies in Syria, sometimes more than once. The force assembled by Severus Alexander in AD 233 to invade Persia was certainly one of the armies provisioned with the aid of the men of Side (and doubtless other gentry from the region). Billeting could be a problem even in a relatively tranquil province. Cicero, writing to Atticus in the winter of 51–50 BC from Cilicia in south-west Asia Minor, spoke of his enthusiastic reception by the provincials:

> For during the six months of my administration, there had been no requisitions and not a single case of billeting. Before my time this season had been devoted every year to the pursuit of gain. The richest states used to pay large sums to escape from having soldiers billeted on them for the winter. The people of Cyprus used to pay 200 Athenian talents, while under my administration, in literal truth, not a penny will be demanded.[6]

This type of situation recurred in the Principate.

When a whole army or an emperor with his entourage actually descended on a town, a food crisis could follow. The irony of the emperor Julian's tussle with the grain speculators of Antioch in AD 362–3 lay in the fact, appreciated by the historian Socrates, that the presence of his massive army in and around the city had intensified the food shortage. Emperors on tour did sometimes furnish grain to cities. Julian had grain brought to Antioch, first from the Syrian cities of Chalcis and Hierapolis, and later from Egypt. Caracalla and Severus Alexander appear to have remedied deficiencies in Tarsus, and Septimius Severus did likewise in Antioch, Laodicea and Sidon. Hadrian, the tourist emperor, is given credit in a fragment of Cassius Dio's history for his gifts to all and sundry of food, among other things. However, the inscriptional evidence emanating from cities on Hadrian's route suggests that local benefactors were kept busy absorbing the shock caused by the emperor's travels. The language of the inscriptions, naturally, is tactful. An inscription from Lete in Macedonia juxtaposes food shortage and the passage of the army without making an explicit causal link, and the name of the emperor is not given, though it is certainly Hadrian:

> The city celebrates Manius Salarius Sabinus, gymnasiarch and benefactor, who very often in times of shortage sold grain much more cheaply than the current price, and when the emperor's army was passing through, provided for the *annona* 400

---

[6] Bean and Mitford, *Journeys in Rough Cilicia 1964–8* (1970), nos. 19, 20, 21a; Cicero, *Att.* 5.21.

medimnoi of wheat, 100 of barley and 60 of beans, plus 100 metretae of wine at a much cheaper rate than the current price.

An honorific inscription from Epidaurus of the late 70s BC is in contrast quite matter-of-fact about the responsibility of a Roman army for a food shortage, and treats the soldiers quite openly as unwelcome guests:

Euanthes undertook to be market official in the 74th year and conducted himself nobly, maintaining in everything a zeal for justice and a generous spirit. Having sent to our city suitable provisions when Marcus Antonius was governor over the Cretans, Euanthes still went on selling to all in like manner, and was most prudently benevolent to the mass of the soldiers. Thus when there was a general grain shortage in the city because the resident mobs were buying up more than 60 medimnoi of grain everywhere, and a medimnos of wheat was selling at 10 drachmas, he sold it at the lower prices of 5 drachmas and 4 drachmas throughout the year, bearing the cost himself, the soldiers having stayed for that amount of time.

The two inscriptions nicely capture the change in atmosphere between the turbulent late Republic – a time of incessant war, requisitions, sieges and destruction for the communities of old Greece – and the more tranquil but by no means burdenless Principate.[7]

So much for taxes and extraordinary exactions and services of one sort or another. Some provincials in addition paid rents to the state or to upper-class Romans. The expansion of the Roman state in Italy, Sicily and abroad was accompanied by the selective confiscation of land. Some of this property (*ager publicus*) was awarded to permanent immigrants, who were typically ex-soldiers, but much of it fell into the hands of rich absentee landowners. In time, the emperors entered the field, acquiring land (and mines) for themselves through confiscations, gifts, legacies, inheritance and other methods, and assigning some of it to followers and favourites. The elder Pliny claimed that one-half of Africa Proconsularis became imperial property when the emperor Nero sequestered the estates of six Roman senatorial landowners. One-sixth of the province is a more reasonable estimate. Anyway, imperial properties in the province were very substantial, in particular in the fertile Medjerda valley south-west of Carthage. The payments made by the free tenants on such estates amounted to as much as one-third of

---

[7] Socrates, *Hist. Eccl.* 3.7 cf. Julian, *Misop.* 370B. Roger Tomlin advises me that it is possible that a significant proportion of Julian's force was dispersed during the winter of 362–3, and that he picked them up on the way to the Euphrates, cf. Ammianus 23.2.6. See also Downey (1951), De Jonge (1948), Petit (1955), 105–22. For the Severan emperors, see Ziegler (1977) and (1978); on Hadrian, Cassius Dio 69.5.3 (a generalisation); *ABSA* 23 (1918–19), no. 7, pp. 72ff. cf. *ABSA* 27 (1925–6), 227ff. (Sparta); for Epidaurus, see *IG* IV²1 66 cf. *SEG* XI 397.

produce, and presumably represented tax plus rent. In Egypt, tenants on the various categories of public land had to surrender between one-third and two-thirds of their produce.[8]

Peasants often paid more than was due in taxes and rents. Corrupt and oppressive officials were a fact of life, and the only remedy against them, apart from physical violence, was to seek redress from a higher authority. A certain Tiberius Nicephorus, apparently a minor treasury official, was withdrawn from south-west Phrygia after the emperor Claudius received an embassy from the town of Cibyra complaining about systematic inequitable exaction of grain and extortion of cash. The tenants of an imperial estate in north Africa (the *saltus Burunitanus*) secured the intervention of the emperor Commodus, after complaining against the excessive demands for labour and produce of their overseers backed up by an imperial procurator. These incidents give a false impression of the accessibility of emperors and the efficacy of the remedies available to ordinary provincials. Similarly, the main message conveyed by scattered references to tax remissions is that taxation was burdensome, not that relief was customarily at hand. In AD 215–16 Caracalla wrote off 'all the debts owed to the *fiscus*, whether in grain or in cash' by the town of Banasa in Mauretania. Such measures gave temporary relief to a few lucky communities. Tax exemption was a more enduring benefit, for the few cities which secured it.[9]

A minority of Rome's subjects at any time paid both taxes to Rome and rents to Roman emperors and Rome-based aristocrats. Private tenancy where the landlord was resident in the town, region, or province is relevant to any assessment of the burdens of the farming population, though not to the flow of resources towards the imperial capital. The revenues generated through agricultural production on the land of local notables were mostly expended locally, although there was some transfer of funds to foreign traders in return for imported luxuries. If, however, a local magnate advanced into the Rome-based aristocracy, then the bulk of his revenues were likely to be exported abroad and lost to his place of origin. The proportion of provincials in the Roman senate and equestrian administration steadily grew in the course of the Principate. The numbers involved were few, and the average loss to subject communities was tiny. However, in areas where investment by Roman aristocrats, whether of Italian or provincial origin, was substantial, as in the north African provinces, Gallia Narbonensis (essentially, Provence) and south and east Spain, the

[8] Pliny, *Hist, nat.* 18.35 cf. Charles-Picard (1959), 60. On imperial properties, see Crawford (1976); Millar (1977), 133–201.
[9] Magie (1951); *FIRA²* 1 no. 103, p. 496, 11 ll. 10ff.; *AE* 1948, 109; *Digest* 50.15.1, etc.

impact on local economies was considerable. In contrast, Egypt was little affected. There were no senators at all from Egypt before the third century; nor were Roman senators and equestrians permitted to acquire Egyptian property.

A significant development affecting all areas within the empire was the redistribution of resources within the provincial communities. Roman rule not only promoted the acquisition of land abroad by Rome-based proprietors, but also increased social and economic differentiation within the provincial populations. Property was concentrated in the hands of the rich at the expense of smallholders, and the lowering of the legal status of the peasantry and the reduction of their economic independence was set in train or accelerated.[10]

Did the acquisition of property abroad reduce the assets of local communities and so undermine their economies? By no means universally. The Romans inherited or confiscated extensive royal domains in areas such as Egypt, Cyrene, Crete and Asia Minor that were not part of the territories of cities, and vast tracts of provincial territory, for example in north Africa, over which again settled communities had established no claim. A great deal of public and imperial property was marginal, and emperors if they wanted it to be cultivated at all had to offer attractive terms to potential lessees. A law of Hadrian for north Africa, referring back to a Mancian law of unknown origin concerning virgin land or land that had gone out of cultivation, gave anyone who undertook the farming of such land the right to possess it and enjoy its produce, alienate it or transmit it to heirs, and conferred tax exemption for an initial period. The same emperor lowered rents on deserted or damaged property belonging to the state in Egypt.[11]

There is another side to the picture: the expropriation of land from peoples (urban or tribal) who were judged to stand in the way of Rome's imperialistic designs, and a continuing pattern of encroachment which involved the transference of valued resources to the state. The more important mines had passed out of private and civic control by the early second century. The accumulation of rural property proceeded steadily, though sometimes the pace accelerated dramatically. For example, Septimius Severus punished supporters of his defeated civil war rivals with large-scale confiscations in Britain, Gaul, and especially the Iberian peninsula. By these actions he cut into the

---

[10] Increased social differentiation in the provinces is a theme of Garnsey (1978). For the advance of provincials, see Sherwin-White (1973), 279ff., with bibliography; Saller (1982), Ch. 5; Atti Colloquio AIEGL (1982); Pflaum (1960).

[11] See Haywood in Frank (1938), 89ff. cf. Courtois (1952); Westermann (1925).

economic resources of a sizeable number of cities, and reduced their capacity to withstand subsistence crises and other calamities. The most dramatic coup in the history of the Principate, with momentous implications for Rome, Egypt and the eastern provinces, was of course the seizure of Egypt by Augustus. The regular production of a grain surplus by Egypt and north Africa was the crucial enabling factor in the maintenance of the city of Rome at its high population level and the prosperity of its inhabitants.

THE MANAGEMENT OF THE SURPLUS

In AD 322 the emperor Constantine issued the following directive to an official with responsibilities in Africa:

We have learned that provincials suffering from lack of sustenance and the necessities of life are selling or pledging their own children. Therefore, if any such person should be found who is sustained by no substance of family fortune, and who is supporting his children with suffering and difficulty, he shall be assisted through Our fisc before he becomes a prey to calamity. The proconsuls and governors and the fiscal representatives throughout all Africa shall thus have the power, they shall bestow freely the necessary support on all persons whom they observe to be placed in dire need, and from the State storehouses they shall immediately assign adequate sustenance. For it is at variance with Our character that We should allow any person to be destroyed by hunger or to break forth to the commission of a shameful deed.

This rescript was preceded in AD 315 by a communication addressed to an official, perhaps the vicar of Italy (an area which since Diocletian no longer enjoyed privileged non-provincial status), announcing that a law against infanticide would be promulgated and posted in all the cities of Italy, and that any parent too poor to rear a child should be provided with the requisite food and clothing.[12]

These measures, effective or not, have no known counterparts in an earlier period (nor for that matter were they followed up by later emperors). It is still worth asking how the Roman administration dealt with the surplus which it controlled but did not need in the early Principate.

In AD 99 the emperor Trajan ordered that grain be sent from Rome to Egypt, then in the grip of a food crisis. In AD 19 Germanicus, the adopted son of the emperor Tiberius, relieved a food shortage in Alexandria by magnanimously releasing wheat from the granaries. Do

---

[12] *Cod. Theod.* 11.17.1–2.

either of these grand gestures fit into a pattern of redistribution of the surplus by emperors or their agents?[13]

Trajan's action, as far as we can tell, was quite unique. It is the only rescue operation of its kind recorded for Egypt – or anywhere. The city of Rome is better described as a bottomless pit than a grain redistribution centre.

Trajan's poor relief ('alimentary') programme for a number of Italian towns bears some superficial resemblance to his gift of grain to Egypt. The state made over to estate-owners sums amounting to about 8% of the declared value of their land; they in turn paid interest of 5% on these sums towards the nourishment of boys and girls in the town concerned. At Veleia, 263 legitimate boys received 16 sesterces each per month, 35 legitimate girls 12 sesterces each, 1 illegitimate boy 12 sesterces, and 1 illegitimate girl 10 sesterces. The size of the foundation at Veleia, 1,116,000 sesterces, if reproduced in 50 cities, would have represented a very considerable investment. However, if Trajan was refunding the taxpayer in AD 99 (and it must be doubtful whether the grain dispatched to Egypt penetrated beyond Alexandria), he was doing no such thing in Italy. Italians were not taxpayers. Trajan's project was equivalent to a modest extension of the Roman grain dole to another privileged category of subjects.

The state only exceptionally funded poor relief schemes, or, for that matter, grain doles. I know of one of each: Hadrian gave an alimentary scheme to Antinoöpolis, the Egyptian town that he founded in honour of his favourite Antinous, who drowned in the Nile, and a corn dole to Athens, his spiritual home. It was Trajan's policy, as revealed by a letter of Pliny, and presumably that of other emperors who concerned themselves with such matters, to stimulate senators and other wealthy individuals into acts of generosity (in cities other than Rome, of course), rather than burden the central exchequer.[14]

The closest parallels to Trajan's action in favour of the Egyptians are gifts of grain to host cities by emperors on tour or on campaign. As was earlier noted, the shortages that occasioned such gifts would have been

---

[13] Pliny, *Pan.* 30–2; Tacitus, *Ann.* 2.59; Suetonius, *Tib.* 52.2; Josephus, *Ap.* 2. 5. In AD 99 the price paid for requisitioned wheat in Egypt was twice as high as usual (16 drachmas rather than 8); see Duncan-Jones (1976a), 248. The scale (and reality) of the food crisis in AD 19 is doubtful.

[14] Duncan-Jones (1982), Ch. 7 (*alimenta*); H. I. Bell, *Aegyptus* 13 (1933), 518–22 cf. *JRS* 30 (1940) 143 (Antinoöpolis); Cassius Dio 69.16.2 (Athens), a gift of *sitos etesios*. But does this mean an endowment for a grain purchase fund, or an arrangement for shipment from source? See Spawforth and Walker (1985), 90. For a possible alimentary programme at Athens in the 130s, see Miller (1972).

less serious, or non-existent, had the emperors concerned not honoured the cities with their presence.[15]

At first sight, Germanicus' performance in Alexandria falls into the category of interventions by travelling emperors. In fact it was a singular event. Germanicus was not the emperor, but was behaving as one. That is why the incident caught the attention of the sources. For Tacitus, it was one episode in the saga of the deteriorating relationship between an obsessively suspicious emperor and his heroic but naïve adopted son. Moreover, Alexandria was different, for two reasons. First, Alexandria was in Egypt, and Augustus had ordained that Egypt should be out of bounds to high-placed Romans. Germanicus not only went there without authority, but proceeded, again on his own initiative, to an act more appropriate to an ambitious pretender than a loyal prince. He was strongly criticised in his absence by Tiberius in the Roman senate. Secondly, Alexandria was the second largest city in the empire,[16] a heavy grain consumer, with a bad reputation for civil disturbance.

While emperors apparently did not see it as one of their own functions to redistribute surplus grain to those in need, they may nevertheless have held it to be a function of government, to be entrusted to subordinates, for example, the prefect of the grain supply, governors of surplus-producing provinces, or other imperial officials with control over grain stocks.

The business of the prefect of the grain supply was to ensure that Rome was adequately supplied. The only hint that he might have been involved in redistribution comes from a casual remark of Epictetus, who moved in court circles in the late first century AD, and was personally acquainted with a prefect of the grain supply (whom he does not name). The prefect's daily round apparently contained as a standard item the receipt of 'a little petition' running like this: 'I beseech you to allow me to export a small amount of grain.' It is inherently probable that such approaches were made under the Empire – there is a precedent from the middle Republic in the request of Rhodes to the Roman senate for grain from Sicily in 169 BC. Epictetus does not help us decide whether the prefect as the representative of the emperor had to be consulted, and what response he might have been expected to make.[17]

[15] See n. 7 above. I agree with D'Escurac (1976), 129–34, that the equestrian official C. Cominius Aper of *ILS* 1432 was occupied with the food supply of Rome, not with rescuing Narbonensis and Liguria from grain shortage; cf. *ILS* 1347.

[16] On the population of Alexandria, see Diodorus, 17.52.6 (mid-first century, 300,000 free persons); 1.31.6–8 (largest city in the world); cf. Fraser (1972), I 91; II 171–2 (1 million).

[17] Epictetus 1.10.2; Polybius 28.2.5.

The matter can be taken further if the responsibilities of key officials based in the provinces are considered. The evidence for north Africa, such as it is, suggests that the numerous cities (and their rural hinterlands) were expected to look after themselves, in bad years as in good. Food crises were resolved with the aid of men of wealth within the community, whether magistrates or private individuals. At most, the Roman administration is likely to have taken precautions with regard to the food supply of Carthage, the provincial capital and one of the most populous cities in the Roman world.[18]

Similarly, one would expect it to have been a high priority that Alexandria did not starve, for it too had a very substantial population, one that was highly politicised and dangerous if provoked. The feeding of Alexandria (as opposed to the fellahin) was certainly a priority with the Ptolemies. On 27 October 50 BC, no doubt in a lean year, a royal decree pronounced that grain should be shipped to Alexandria and nowhere else, on pain of death. The Ptolemies controlled (among other things) the storage of grain destined for Alexandria. The Romans had no reason to change this arrangement. The granaries were in the custody of Roman officials under the ultimate authority of the prefect. A letter from Trajan to the city of Alexandria in AD 98, introducing the new prefect, confirms his responsibility for the food supply:

Having a personal feeling of benevolence towards you, I have commended you first of all to myself, then in addition to my friend and prefect, Pompeius Planta, so that he can take every care in providing for your undisturbed tranquillity and your food supply and your communal and individual rights.

Nevertheless, the sources do not refer to any regular grant of grain from imperial supplies to the civic authorities of Alexandria for distribution before the turn of the third century AD.[19]

If from the early Principate the prefect of Egypt had the key to the granaries, then the conduct of the incumbent of this office at the time of the visit of Germanicus in AD 19 becomes a matter of some interest. The matter hinges on the state of the food supply in that year. It was not beyond the ingenuity of the Alexandrians to conjure up a food shortage,

---

[18] See *Cod. Theod.* 14.25 (AD 315). But Hymetius, proconsul of Africa, gets into trouble in AD 366 for selling grain intended for the Roman people to the Carthaginians, 'who were by that time worn out from lack of food'; see Ammianus 18.1.17.

[19] *C. Ord. Ptol.* 73, quoted Thompson (1983), 74; *P. Oxy.* 3022 (Trajan); Johnson and West (1949), 71, 237 (Diocletian), referring to Procopius, *Anec.* 26.40 and *Cod. Theod.* 14.26.2. Trajan's promise to maintain Alexandria's *euthenia* may perhaps imply the existence of a civic *annona* in the city. See also *OGIS* 705 (AD 158: a man in charge of the *euthenia* of the B district); cf. *PSI* x 1123 (AD 151–2: the prefect forces villages to sell wine for the supply of Alexandria); *BGU* II 649 = Wilcken, *Chr.* 428 (AD 187/8: pigs kept 'for the *euthenia* of Alexandria').

or exaggerate its dimensions, in order to get free grain from a vain and gullible prince. If, on the other hand, there was a serious food crisis, then the prefect stands guilty of negligence (or worse) for doing nothing while the Alexandrians languished.

An appraisal of the performance of the Romans as custodians of other people's grain should be broadened to take in the needs of states that were not ordinarily surplus-producers. How far and by what procedures did the Romans permit other states to have access to grain stocks under their control but surplus to their requirements? The problem is a recurring one in Roman history. It was raised in a stark form every time the Roman state made a major territorial advance. When Campania, Sicily and north Africa were annexed, communities that had previously had economic links with these regions were forced to turn elsewhere, or approach Rome. The treatment they received on any particular occasion depended upon the Roman perception of their own best interests. In 169 BC Rhodes' request for some 100,000 medimnoi (600,000 modii) of Sicilian grain was granted: Rhodes at this time was still enjoying Rome's friendship. Two years later such a 'deal' would have been impossible. Relations had turned sour. Rome punished Rhodes' equivocal stance in the Third Macedonian War by declaring Delos a free port, thus dealing the Rhodian economy a severe blow.[20]

At the beginning of the Principate it was the turn of Egypt to fall to Rome. Egypt had been an exporter of grain to various city-states for centuries, especially from the Ptolemaic period. Now its surplus was cornered by a conquering power which had had little or no interest in it before.[21] Egypt was a significant but never the main contributor of grain to Rome – that was the role of the north African provinces. Some grain in normal years was available for other states. How did the Romans steward the Egyptian surplus?

Roman policy is to some extent illuminated by a letter sent by an unknown second-century emperor to the Ephesians:

It is clear that you will make prudent use of this agreement, bearing in mind the necessity that first the imperial city should have a bounteous supply of wheat procured and assembled for its market, and then the other cities may also receive provisions in plenty. If, as we pray, the Nile provides us with a flood of the customary level and a bountiful harvest of wheat is produced among the Egyptians, then you will be among the first after the homeland.[22]

---

[20] Polybius 28.2, 5 cf. Schmitt (1957), 151–72.
[21] See Garnsey and Saller (1987), 98–100, against Casson (1954).
[22] Wörrle (1971).

Rome heads the queue, but there is an expectation that there will be plenty of grain to go around in a normal year once Rome's interests have been met. This is confirmation, if it were needed, that the Romans did not want the entire surplus of Egypt, and were ready in principle to release some of it, at a price. There is evidence for the relief of local shortages with Egyptian grain touching a number of states in Greece, Asia Minor and Judaea, and spanning the period from the first decade of Augustus' Principate to the early third century. How did the states concerned secure the grain they needed?

The evidence is confusing and betrays a lack of systematic planning. It involves three Roman officials (including the emperor), and two categories of states, regular and irregular importers.

When Epictetus indicates that the prefect of the grain supply often received requests for the export of grain, he makes no specific reference to Egypt, and it is unbelievable that all requests for Egyptian grain had to go through the prefect's office in Rome.

It is also unlikely that the emperor was always consulted. The Ephesians were seeking a privilege which could only be conferred by him. On another, probably earlier, occasion, they had capitalised on Hadrian's presence in the city in AD 129 to secure his permission to import Egyptian grain. Another Asian town, Tralles in the Maeander valley, appears to have taken advantage of a Hadrianic visit to the home town of a favourite freedman, Phlegon. A grain commissioner of this city is honoured because he 'secured grain for his homeland from Egypt to the amount of 60,000 modii by the favour of the lord Caesar Traianus Hadrianus Augustus'. There is nothing casual about this reference to the emperor; it was a feather in the cap of the official to have secured Hadrian's assistance, and something that the whole city could boast about. If no such special intervention is mentioned, as in other inscriptions from Tralles and Ephesus, in addition to one from Sparta, then it is a reasonable assumption that there was none. This is likely to have been the norm.[23]

It was the prefect of Egypt who received the bulk of the requests for Egyptian grain. This can be confidently stated, even if his involvement is rarely attested. In 24 BC, when a drought in Judaea was in its second year, Herod the Great rehabilitated himself in the sight of his hostile subjects by buying grain from Egypt. As Josephus tells the story, he took advantage of his friendship with the newly arrived prefect, C. Petronius:

[23] *SIG³* 839 (AD 129); *CIG* 2927, 2930; Sterrett, *MDAI* (A) 8 (1883), 328ff. no. 10; *FE* III p. 106 no. 16; *ABSA* 26 (1923–5), 163, A 10.

Being in such straits, Herod considered how to meet the crisis, but this was difficult, both because the neighbouring peoples could not sell grain, having suffered no less themselves, and because he did not have the money, even if it were possible to obtain small quantities at a high price. Thinking it best, however, not to neglect any source of help, he cut up into coinage all the ornaments of gold and silver in his palace, without sparing even objects made with special care or having artistic value. And this money he sent to Egypt, where Petronius had received the office of prefect from Caesar. Petronius, to whom a great many persons had fled because of the same needs, was a friend of Herod and wished to rescue his subjects, and so he gave them priority in the export of grain, and fully assisted them to purchase and transport it by ship, so that the greater part if not the whole of this aid came from him.[24]

The incident suggests that the prefect was able to sell as much grain as he liked to whomsoever he wished, the only restraint on his actions being that he might have to justify his conduct before the emperor at a later stage. Not only did he permit a friend of his to jump the queue, but he also gave him the opportunity to indulge in 'corn diplomacy'. The king was sold much more grain than he needed. He had enough left after he had provided for his subjects to aid the neighbouring cities and provide seed-corn for the Syrians.

Without the imperial letter to Ephesus cited above, there would be no reason to believe that any procedural rules were ever introduced governing the export of Egyptian grain and by implication reducing the prefect's initiative. The Ephesians are told that they would be 'among the first after the fatherland'. This shows that there were states that regularly needed to import grain from Egypt, and that the emperors were under pressure to produce a ranking order, or, if they had done so already, to amend it in the interests of this or that petitioning state. The effect of these manoeuvrings is impossible to gauge, but they must have left the ordinary cities of the eastern Mediterranean at several further removes from the grain they needed in emergencies.

INTERVENTION AND ITS LIMITS

How were food crises resolved under the Principate? In a number of incidents, local authorities are shown to have been weak and ineffectual in the face of shortages, and high-placed private individuals and officials to have been reluctant to act for the common welfare. The local wealthy were in a position to act as either speculators or euergetists.

[24] Josephus, *Ant. Jud.* 15.299ff., esp. 305ff.; cf. 20.51–3, 101 (Helena of Adiabene buys grain for Jerusalem). For the procurator of the granaries of Alexandria, presumably subordinate to the prefect of Egypt. see D'Escurac (1976), 134–9.

There is suspicion that the presence of Roman officials and their readiness to intervene had the paradoxical result of undermining civic patriotism among the wealthy and reducing the capacity of communities to cope with subsistence crises.[25]

In AD 92 or 93 the provincial governor of Cappadocia, Antistius Rusticus, was called in by the local magistrates and councillors of Pisidian Antioch to resolve a food crisis. He issued a decree requiring those with grain stocks to release that which was surplus to their own subsistence needs at below the current market rate. Why were the local authorities unable or unwilling to deal with the crisis themselves?

A second-century decree from the city of Aelium Coela in the Thracian Chersonese honoured the governor of the province because he had 'increased both the city and the province ... and during the severest shortage of foodstuffs looked after the interests of everybody with zeal'. Where were the euergetists of this city in its time of crisis?

Across the straits in Prusa, within the province of Bithynia/Pontus, at the turn of the first century AD, the villa of Dio, the Stoic philosopher and politician, was attacked and almost put to fire in a riot. The hungry crowd was not convinced by his claim that there was no food crisis and that in any case he had no grain in his barns. Perhaps did he not on this occasion. But did he lack cash as well, and was this why he had failed to contribute to the appeal launched by the local authorities at the time?

At Aspendus, Pamphylia, in the reign of Tiberius, wealthy grain-dealers had aggravated a crisis by cornering the market in grain and holding their supplies for export. The leading magistrate would have lost his life at the hands of rioters but for the intervention of the philosopher and wonder-worker Apollonius of Tyana. The people suspected collusion between officials and merchants, who may anyway have overlapped in personnel.

The emperor Hadrian promulgated a law at Athens regulating the export of olive oil. He was acting technically not as Roman emperor but as Athenian law-giver (*nomothetes*), a kind of latter-day Solon (in terms of the content of his measure, a Solon in reverse, since Solon allegedly prohibited export of all agricultural produce except olive oil). Did only a Roman emperor have the necessary authority, or motivation, to prevent traders from causing artificial shortages of oil by sending it abroad?

On 17 March AD 246, a Roman judicial official in Egypt, one Claudius Aurelius Tiberius, issued a proclamation requiring the registration within 24 hours of private grain stocks in the city and nome of

---

[25] *AE* 1925 162b; *FE* III no. 48; Dio Chrys. *Or.* 46; Philostratus, *Vita Ap.* 1.15; *SEG* xv 108 = Oliver (1953), 960ff.; *P. Oxy.* 3048.

Oxyrhynchus; evasion would be punished by confiscation of both the grain and the building where it was stored. On the following day one Calpurnia Heraclia alias Eudamia declared over 5,000 artabas of grain held in five villages in the nome.

Such evidence appears to provide a foretaste of the celebrated conflicts between emperors or their deputies and local speculators in fourth-century Antioch.

It is too easy to blame Roman rule for the inactivity of local governments, and their inability, on occasions, to instil the spirit of civic patriotism into the more influential members of the community.

First, speculation in essential foodstuffs was not a novelty in the Graeco-Roman world; nor is it easily demonstrated that it became more of a problem under the Principate.

Secondly, intervention by Roman governors in food shortages did not begin under the Principate. Cicero as governor of Cilicia (51–50 BC) wrote as follows to Atticus, in a passage which is very revealing of the mentality of members of the Roman governing class:

My tour through Asia was such that even the crowning misery of food crisis, which was rampant in my part of Asia after the total failure of the harvest, gave me a welcome opportunity. Wherever I passed, without force, without legal process, without hard words, by my persuasive influence and exhortation I persuaded both natives and Roman citizens who had hoarded grain to promise large quantities to the public.[26]

Thirdly, despite Cicero, the typical governor was not a mobile problem-solver. There is no reason to believe that governors commonly intervened in food crises outside certain prominent cities, especially the provincial capital that was their place of residence. Aelium Coela was one such city, as were Athens and Syrian Antioch. Ephesus comes into the same category. A second-century proconsul of Asia could hardly ignore the 'disorder and riots' into which Ephesus was plunged as a result of a bakers' strike. He 'brought them to their senses' with an edict, which ran, in part:

Wherefore, I forbid the bakers to assemble in association and their officers to make inflammatory speeches, and I order them to give complete obedience to those in charge of the community's welfare, and to provide the city fully with the necessary production of bread.[27]

Fourthly, Roman officials were not averse to feathering their own nests by speculation and extortion, or by conniving at such actions by

[26] Cicero, *Att.* 5.21. On the other hand, in Cicero, *Flacc.* 17, a man of Cyme in Asia Minor is punished by the local courts for exporting grain in a food crisis.
[27] *SEG* IV 512 = Abbott and Johnson no. 124.

others. Most escaped prosecution because such offences were routine, and the offending officials took trouble to win over or neutralise key local figures. Even the malpractices of Verres as governor of Sicily, as exposed (and exaggerated) by Cicero, were not in all respects novel or unexpected. For example, it was customary at the time (late 70s BC) to supplement the tithe on Sicilian farmers with no fewer than three compulsory purchases, the last of which was for the governor's personal use and could be commuted for cash. Verres took over this system from his predecessors together with the exorbitantly high rate of commutation that they had exacted. In another notorious case, the Caesar Gallus' confrontation with governor and local authorities of Antioch in AD 354, it was the conduct of Gallus rather than that of his opponents that was singular. Gallus ordered the death of the leaders of the local council of Antioch (they were saved by a high official), refused to alleviate the crisis by bringing in supplies from neighbouring provinces 'after the manner of emperors whose widely extended power sometimes cured local troubles', and in effect roused the mob to violence against both the governor and council leaders:

To the multitude, which was in fear of the direst necessity, he delivered up Theophilus, *consularis* of Syria, who was standing by, constantly repeating the statement that no one could lack food if the governor did not wish it. These words increased the audacity of the lower classes, and when the lack of provisions became more acute, driven by hunger and rage, they set fire to the pretentious house of a certain Eubulus, a man of distinction among his own people; then, as if the governor had been delivered into their hands by an imperial edict, they assailed him with kicks and blows, and trampling him under foot when he was half dead, with awful mutilation tore him to pieces.

Ammianus, while presenting a very hostile picture of Gallus, does not pretend that his victims were innocent.[28]

Finally, the epigraphic evidence for food crisis from all over the empire suggests that the cities by and large looked after themselves. The relevant inscriptions from north Africa almost uniformly show local benefactors alleviating shortages. The exception is an inscription of AD 144 from Sala (Chella) in Morocco, where a garrison commander of equestrian rank and Roman origin, 'liberator and patron' of the city, is thanked for, among other things, 'warding off pressing food-supply problems by drawing on the supplies of his troops, acting very often for our benefit and never to the detriment of his soldiers'. The case is exceptional: without the presence of the garrison the town would have

[28] Cicero, *2 Verr.* 2.3.214–5; Ammianus 14.7.2 and 5.

been helpless in the face of the 'raids and razzias to which we had grown accustomed'.[29] The far more copious evidence from the eastern provinces conveys a similar impression. There are thousands of inscriptions celebrating the generosity of local benefactors who gave grain, oil and wine or sold it cheap, contributed to funds for the purchase of extra stocks, and served as grain commissioners. The spirit of patriotic munificence was contagious, and it touched people of modest wealth, not just the highest ranking notables.

Even where benefactors were in short supply, as in Boeotian Acraephia during the reign of Claudius, there is no sign of imperial intervention. This city, situated on the east of Lake Copaïs, appears to have suffered flooding in addition to the food shortage which affected numerous states in Greece and elsewhere in the 40s and early 50s. For three years its inhabitants went without eponymous magistrates and were unable to carry out traditional feasts in honour of Apollo Ptoös and Augustus. In the end three citizens came forward to hold a plurality of offices and pump some life back into the stricken city. The danger signals can be read in an earlier inscription from Claudius' reign celebrating the spectacular generosity of one Epaminondas to Acraephia and the Boeotian League as a whole. Epaminondas saw to the repair and plastering of 'the very great dike which protects our land', revived the games (the Ptoïa) that had suffered three decades of neglect, and made copious distributions of food to all with a stake in the community. The inscription exposes the city's unhealthy overdependence on one extremely wealthy man, who no doubt held in his possession a disproportionate share of local agricultural resources.[30]

The experience of Acraephia provides a useful contrast to the picture sketched later in the century by Plutarch of declining local initiative among Greek cities in the face of government interference, but it also raises doubts about the ability of the cities of the empire to help themselves.[31] In the remaining part of this chapter, I ask whether Rome's subject cities made any significant improvements in their food supply systems in the course of the Principate. This has a direct bearing on the matter of local initiative, but will also bring us back to the question with which I began, whether the demands made by the Romans undermined the economic well-being of their subjects.

[29] *AE* 1931, 36–8 (Sala) cf. Gsell and Carcopino, *MEFR* 48 (1931), 1–39. Other crises: *ILAlg.* I 2145; *CIL* VIII 1648; 25703–4; 26121; *ILS* 5553, 6879; *AE* 1913, 159; 1928, 23.

[30] Robert, *BCH* 59 (1935), 438–52; cf. Oliver, *GRBS* 12 (1971), 221–37. For the 'universal famine' under Claudius, see Gapp (1935).

[31] Plutarch, *Mor.* 798–825; Jones (1971), 110ff.

SELF-HELP AND ITS LIMITS

Hellenistic cities had developed wide-ranging contacts with traders and other communities, a system of liturgies designed to procure food in emergencies, and sometimes grain reserves and grain funds. These mechanisms remained and were perhaps more widely dispersed in the Roman period. Can any additional institutional developments be identified which improved the food-supply system? Were, for example, 'alimentary' projects, or schemes for poor relief, and grain doles introduced? As was seen, central government funds were only exceptionally forthcoming for such institutions outside Italy, but the emperors gave general encouragement to the propertied classes to indulge in euergetism. Meanwhile, the alimentary programme in Italy and the grain dole in Rome provided models for provincial cities to follow.

The response was meagre. In the first place, privately funded alimentary projects were rare. I give three instances from a small sample. The younger Pliny spent more than half a million sesterces on an alimentary project for his home town of Como, and made other expensive benefactions. At Sicca Veneria in Africa Proconsularis in the late 170s, a private benefactor left 1,300,000 sesterces to provide support for 300 boys aged 3–15 at 10 sesterces per month and for 300 girls aged 3–13 at 8 sesterces per month. A generation earlier, at Xanthus in Lycia, the 'millionaire' Opramoas had launched a scheme which also recalls, and was presumably influenced by, the imperial alimentary programme in Italy. After listing benefactions to a number of cities, the inscription goes on:

He educates and supports all the children of the citizens, having accepted their charge in person for 16 years, and having for this purpose made over to the city properties and moneys together with initial capital for a year, so that from the interest his charity is preserved for ever. He gives a funeral fund for the dead and provides for the dowries of needy daughters, and he nourishes the poor.[32]

The evidence for corn doles is also sparse, being largely confined to the provinces of Lycia in the second century and Egypt in the third. At the consecration of the buildings that he presented to Xanthus, Opramoas gave 1,000 drachmas to each of three groups, the city council, the council of the elderly, and those who received distributed grain (*sitometroumenoi andres*), and in addition 10 drachmas apiece to the

---

[32] Balland, *Fouilles de Xanthos* 7 (1981), 185ff.; Pliny, *Ep.* 7.18.2–4 (Como); *ILS* 6818 (Sicca). Otherwise in the east only *IGR* III 800–2 (Sillyon, Pamphylia) and in the western provinces *CIL* II 1174 (Hispalis) are certain. Both at Xanthus and Sillyon all the children of citizens benefit; this is unusual in the west. See Duncan-Jones (1982), 136, 171–3 (Italy), 288–319 (in general).

rest of the citizens and resident aliens. This shows that there was a list of adult males in Xanthus who received grain when it was distributed. Not every adult male citizen was on the list and nothing is indicated about the frequency of distributions, whether of grain or cash.

The list of grain recipients appears to have been a Lycian feature. There were 1,100 people on the list at the town of Tlos. They appear in an inscription as beneficiaries of a certain Lalla:

Having promised for her tenure of the gymnasiarchy of the young the sum of 12,500 denarii, which have been put down by her on contract to bear interest, so that in this also the city may draw profit, from not having to select persons to invest the capital or to recover it, she having pledged herself to pay each year as interest to each of the 1,100 grain recipients 1 denarius per head on 15 June, the first day of the magisterial elections. In return, the city in the electoral assembly urged the priest of the Augusti by acclamation to propose that Lalla bear the title Mother of the City and be honoured ...

The sum would have enabled each recipient to buy perhaps two weeks' supply of newly harvested grain (or considerably less if the new crop was unavailable).[33]

At another city, Oenoanda, the number of grain recipients was fixed at 500. An inscription of the same period indicates that city councillors, that is, the local aristocracy, were included on the list, and that some citizens were not.

In a second inscription from Oenoanda, a benefactor claims to have been the first to perform the Sitometreia or grain distribution, and the first to do so twice; in a third inscription, a woman called Ammias is said to have given 10,000 drachmas to the city 'for the grain distribution'.

A text from Bubon refers to the grain distribution in company with a number of liturgies performed by the ancestors of the honorand.

The Lycian system can be tentatively reconstructed along the following lines. First, those on the list were a privileged group of citizens including city councillors, the curial class. They may well have included poor people, but it is unlikely that poverty was a formal criterion for inclusion. Euergetism was not charity: it was not directed towards the poorest members of the community as such. When Opramoas singled out the 'poor' and 'needy' as recipients of 'education and nourishment',

---

[33] At 2.25 sesterces per modius (the normal rate at Pisidian Antioch in the late first century) and *c.* 6.75 kg per modius. For the Lalla decree, see Chr. Naour, *ZPE* 24 (1977), 265ff. no. 1. See also, from Tlos, *TAM* II. 2, 578. The inscriptions that follow are unpublished. I am very much in debt to the late Dr Alan Hall and Professor M. Wörrle for allowing me to refer to them. A *sitometrion* is also recorded at Patara (ll. 14–15 of the Opramoas inscription from Xanthus), Corydalla (*TAM* II. 3, 905, XIXA, ll. 7–8) and Balboura (*LBW* 1228).

funeral funds and dowries, he had in mind ordinary citizens, not the unemployed, beggars and down-and-outs. Nevertheless, this benefaction was unusual in its exclusion of the better-off members of the community. In addition, Opramoas broke new ground in the way he divided his largesse on the day of dedication: he gave less per head to citizens in the three privileged categories than to the residue of citizens and to metics. Usually in multiple distributions those people who needed least received most.[34]

Secondly, the Sitometreia was privately funded.[35] It has in fact all the hallmarks of (yet another) liturgy undertaken by the wealthy and public-spirited. Like other liturgies, it typically involved a single donation, which could be repeated.

Alternatively, a donor might choose to set up a foundation to fund a distribution on a given day in each year. This is perhaps what Ammias was doing when she gave 10,000 drachmas for the Sitometreia; unfortunately the inscription is uninformative on this point. Foundations to provide cash for grain-purchase and distributions of food or cash are common in other parts of the empire. The imperial freedman Publius Aelius Onesimus left to his home-town Nacolea in Asia the sum of 200,000 sesterces (50,000 denarii or 50,000 drachmas), on condition that 'this sum be let out at interest and the interest produced in the next three years be allocated to a grain fund, so that grain may be bought with it annually'. The terms of the will laid down that after the expiry of the three-year period,

the interest on this entire sum be divided annually among my fellow citizens, after a census is taken, on the most fortunate birthday of our lord Traianus Hadrianus. I desire moreover that one half of this interest be allocated for gifts in such a way that one half is distributed on the holiday called ... [*here the text breaks off*]

If Ammias was setting up a foundation at Oenoanda (and the inscription says nothing of this), then Lalla's slightly larger gift for nearby Tlos might appear to provide a model. However, Lalla's gift was made in connection with the tenure of a gymnasiarchy rather than specifically for the Sitometreia (unlike Ammias' gift), and issued in annual handouts of cash, not grain. It should be seen as a perquisite additional to the grain distribution. The Grain Receivers, once they

---

[34] Duncan-Jones (1982), 184–6 (a collection of western evidence). On euergetism and the poor, see Bolkestein (1939), 181–5; Hands (1968), 62ff.

[35] There is just a hint in an unpublished inscription from Oenoanda that a local tax fed the grain fund. I quote a letter from Alan Hall referring to 'parts of two letters, one Imperial, most of the contents dealing with failure to observe regulations and payments for water supplies. An Emperor – Marcus I think, but it could be Commodus or even Caracalla – tells his curator that it was reasonable to take thought for the *seitonikon* (line 12). I'm led to wonder whether the money from the water-rates was used to buy corn.'

were established as a special category, attracted largesse outside the framework of the grain distributions, either by themselves or alongside other categories of receivers. In this respect they resemble a class of citizens at Lete in Macedonia who came together for banquets, but also qualified for special distributions alongside councillors and ex-politarchs.[36]

There is much that remains mysterious about the Lycian distributions. They are not seen in action in time of shortage. However, the class of Grain Receivers must have been created precisely for such circumstances, to guarantee a designated group of people, a Lycian equivalent of the Roman *plebs frumentaria*, privileged access to grain when it was short. In principle, it is possible that in Lycian cities, as in Rome, distributions were regular and continuous, but this seems unlikely, given the way they were funded. It was beyond the resources of the communities to distribute grain in good times as in bad. The mere presence of a class of Grain Receivers does not entail the existence of distributions on this scale, but it does suggest an unusual degree of commitment among the wealthy to the welfare of a substantial number of ordinary citizens.

I turn finally to the Egyptian evidence.[37] Papyri published in 1972 demonstrate that the Egyptian town of Oxyrhynchus really did have a corn dole, at least between 268 and 272. Alexandria and Hermopolis appear to have had distribution systems in about the same period, but few details survive. Some aspects of the system at Oxyrhynchus – for example, the machinery for filling vacancies and identifying recipients – are modelled on Roman Imperial practice.

There is one very significant difference between Oxyrhynchus and Rome. This is obscured by the editor of the corn dole archive, when he writes that 'the doles were not a provision for the very poor, but a perquisite of the already privileged middle classes of the cities, as in Rome'. Poverty was not a formal criterion for membership of the *plebs frumentaria* at Rome. On the other hand, given the numbers involved (from 150,000 to 320,000) it is obvious that the bulk of participants were in practice ordinary, poor citizens. In contrast, the class of recipients at Oxyrhynchus was socially select, being formed from three categories of residents, all distinguished by birth and/or wealth. Three-quarters of the 4,000 were made up of an exclusive social group,

---

[36] *ILS* 7196 (Nacolea); cf. Buckler, *JHS* 57 (1937), 1–10 (Orcistus). See the list of Italian foundations in Duncan-Jones (1982), 171–84.

[37] Rea (1972); *P. Lond*, III 955 (= Wilcken, *Chr.* 425; a *siteresion* at Hermopolis Magna, application dated 15 February 261); Eusebius, *Hist. Eccl.* 7.21 (Alexandria); Kraut, *ZPE* 55 (1984), 167ff. (Hermopolis Magna, AD 62). On the Roman dole and the poor, see Veyne (1976), 446–58, Carrié (1975), 1030ff.; Rowlands (1976); Finley (1985), 198–204.

consisting of those who had undergone scrutiny (*epikrisis*) to establish that they were eligible for the metropolite class by virtue of having parents who were both metropolites. (Alexandrian and Roman citizens were also eligible and were listed with those who had passed the scrutiny, *epikrithentes*.) Since the city council was formed from this class, it cannot be excluded that councillors qualified for the corn dole. A second group of 900 (called *rhemboi*) was made up of people who had served in liturgies. They were men of means but not necessarily good birth, for there were freedmen among them. Finally, a small group of 100 (*homologoi*) are thought to have been or included people with one metropolite parent.

The accessibility of Egyptian corn doles to those of high social status is confirmed by three recently published papyri from Hermopolis datable around AD 62. The documents are applications for registration on a list for a handout of wheat. All three applications came from the gymnasial class; that is to say, they were descended from those on the original list of members of the gymnasial class drawn up by order of Augustus in AD 4–5 from those with Greek ancestry on both paternal and maternal sides.

Generalising about the presence or absence of grain doles in Egypt under the Empire is a hazardous business, when the publication of single documents can completely alter the picture. If there were other doles thus far unattested, they need not have followed the Oxyrhynchite (and Roman) model and operated in all seasons.[38] The applicants for the corn dole in Hermopolis all stated that they had no grain. This suggests that grain was distributed there only in times of shortage. Such a system was much cheaper to run, it operated (I believe) in Lycia, and I suggest that Egyptian grain doles, in so far as they existed, were usually of this kind, at least until the 260s.[39]

CONCLUSION

The period of the Principate witnessed little significant innovation in the methods by which food shortage was averted or alleviated in the

[38] For a civic *annona* at Alexandria, see n. 19, above. The evidence for eutheniarchs at Oxyrhynchus begins in AD 199, before a council was introduced by Septimius Severus; see *P. Oxy.* 908 = Wilcken, *Chr.* 426 (a board of 6 involved in bread supply). A systematic study of the Egyptian evidence is called for.

[39] How it was that doles sprang up in the 260s is a matter for conjecture. Was more wheat available in Egypt because Roman emperors were distracted by civil war (the revolt of Macrianus and Quietus falls between September 260 and November 261, invasion by the Palmyrenes between autumn 270 and late spring 272)? But such disruption may be supposed to have reduced production. It is just possible that the doles were financed by the emperors who apparently sanctioned them. See *P. Oxy.* 2898 col. ii, ll. 9–11; *P. Lond.* iii 955; Carrié (1975), 1033–4.

localities. Alimentary schemes were extremely rare, whether designed
for all citizen children as in the east, or for children of poor citizens as in
the west. Regular and continuous grain doles are known only from
Egypt, their duration is uncertain, and they were meant to benefit a
privileged section of the citizen population rather than all citizens or the
poor. The Lycians in the mid-second century also isolated a *plebs
frumentaria* within the larger citizen body, with the aim of preserving in
adverse times those citizens regarded by the governing class (not
themselves excluded) as most valuable to the community.

Euergetism continued to prop up the communities of the Graeco-
Roman world, while defining the limits within which any particular
community was able to cope with uncertainty and crisis. The converse
of private affluence was public poverty, the inability of civic treasuries
to finance effective responses to risk and crisis. But in addition, there is
the suspicion that the wealthy were more prepared to distribute their
surplus for the public welfare in good seasons than in bad. In the
autumn of AD 248, two decades before the earliest document in the corn
archive, Oxyrhynchus had difficulty finding eutheniarchs (food supply
officials); gymnasiarchs were pressed to take on that office as well, and
sometimes refused to do so. In the spring of AD 246, in the same city, a
Roman official ordered the registration and compulsory sale of grain in
private hands; one wealthy landowner, as has been seen, declared over
5,000 artabas of wheat.[40]

Was euergetism a more fragile defence against food crisis than
previously in the cities of the Roman world, and if so, was this a
consequence of Roman rule? Given the character of the evidence, this
question cannot be answered by a numerical calculation of the frequency with which food crises were resolved by external as opposed to
internal agencies. However, it is clear that the period of the Principate
witnessed increased interference in local affairs and a gradual decline in
the civic spirit, which served as a shield against hunger and starvation.
There was, for example, intervention in local finances through legislation checking local taxation and expenditures, and through the activities of city 'curators'. Among their other responsibilities, such officials
were charged with preventing the diversion or embezzlement of funds
set aside for emergency grain-purchase.[41]

The argument for the erosion of local initiative and patriotism might
take in also the regulation and modification of the system of compulsory
services or liturgies, the mounting burden of such services and other
demands of the central government on local communities, and the

[40] *P. Erl.* 18; *P. Oxy.* 2854, 3048.
[41] *Digest* 50.8.12.2 (*curator* and grain fund); Garnsey and Saller (1987), 34–40 (interference).

absolute reduction of local resources through expropriation by Roman emperors and aristocrats. The impact of Roman rule was of course felt unequally. Egypt suffered most. Before the Roman annexation there was little flow of wealth out of the country. Under Rome, Egypt paid more taxes and lost more productive land to its imperial overlord than any other part of the empire, while supporting a permanent garrison of two legions plus as many or more auxiliary troops. The fellahin must have been worse off under the Romans than under the Ptolemies. The lightest load was borne by Italians, who paid no direct tax apart from the death duty. Yet, unless the alimentary programme was mere theatrical display, rural poverty was endemic in the Italian countryside. Elsewhere, the economic pressures exerted by central administration, local administration, large landowners and moneylenders ensured that the position of the mass of the inhabitants of the empire would be marginal.

The surplus extracted from the provinces was consumed by the city of Rome, the court, the bureaucracy and the military. Systematic redistribution among the taxpayers themselves at the expense of the imperial treasury was out of the question. Roman emperors, who operated in Rome a food supply and distribution system that they would have preferred to do without, were not interested in foisting it on the cities of the empire in order to produce a fairer balance between the interests of rich and poor in urban society, any more than they were likely to try to reduce the social and economic gap between city and countryside. If there had been ubiquitous grain doles in the cities, the peasants would have paid for them.

The Romans controlled more grain than they needed, and were prepared to part with it at a price. Their performance as custodians of other people's grain is likely to have been erratic, varying with the quality of their officials. In general, it may be suspected that the mass of ordinary cities of the empire frequently lost out in the competition for grain to states which were favoured by prefects or emperors for political or personal reasons. The Romans were openly discriminatory in serving out the grain. Has any imperial power with its hands on scarce resources conducted itself otherwise?

CONCLUSION

CONCLUSION

I

Food crisis was endemic in the Mediterranean in classical antiquity. Its origins lay in nature and in man, often operating together. Harvest failure was an underlying cause of food shortage. However, food crisis was the consequence of a sharp reduction not in the absolute level of food supply, but in food availability. The causes of famine are to be sought not only in the physical environment and conditions of production, but also in distribution mechanisms, their limitations, and their disruption through human intervention.

Not every food crisis was catastrophic, on the scale of famine. Food crises ranged from mild, transient shortage to protracted, devastating famine. Shortage was common, but famine rare, the outcome of abnormal conditions. Every food crisis was a specific event; it can be classed in terms of its whereabouts on the shortage/famine spectrum, supposing adequate information exists about causes, context and impact. The most serious food crises were a consequence of a succession of harvest failures, wars of long duration or the conjunction of harvest shortfall and epidemic disease. Severe inflation in the prices of foods (as opposed to non-food items), drastic reactions by both ordinary consumers and governments, and above all a sharp rise in mortality among all classes other than the rich (who were vulnerable to disease but not starvation), are other indications that a given food crisis belongs towards the famine end of the spectrum.

II

The unique urban civilisations of antiquity were supported, when all is told, by the common labour of peasants. The survival of the peasantry hinged on the nature of their response to environmental constraints and to the demands of those wielding political and economic power.

271

Peasants followed a production strategy designed to minimise risk, endeavouring to reduce their vulnerability by dispersing their land-holdings, diversifying their crops and storing their surplus. It was also essential for them to cultivate reciprocal relationships with their social equals, kin, friends and neighbours, and superiors, who could act as patrons. In addition, peasants sought to maintain a balance between the size and economic resources of the family by following various adaptive strategies, including the adjustment of age at marriage and the interval between births, the practice of contraception and abortion, and in particular, infant exposure.

City governments devised very little in the way of permanent institutions for maintaining a regular food supply system and coping with food crisis. Networks of supply were loose. There were neither state merchant fleets nor traders in the permanent employ of particular cities. Largely informal contacts were made with independent traders and between neighbouring states or those bound together by traditional links such as those between mother city and colony. Governments likewise did not interfere with domestic production, which remained fundamental to the livelihood of all cities. The distribution of local produce was also left in the hands of the landowners and whatever agents they employed. The most governments did in times of crisis was to issue temporary prohibitions on the export of grain and order the release and sale of private grain stocks. But outside Athens and Rome there is no sign that the profits of traders, millers or bakers were regulated. Finally, although some cities possessed grain reserves and grain-purchase funds, regular distributions of free grain were very rare in the cities of the Graeco-Roman world.

The weakness of the official response to subsistence crisis reflects the social, economic and political power of the local aristocracies. The crucial role in the resolution of food crises was played by members of the elite, whether as magistrates, liturgists or private benefactors. As grain commissioners they raised grain-purchase funds and sought emergency food stocks, as private individuals (or officials) they themselves put up money or cut-price grain. However, euergetism, the public generosity of the wealthy, was an institution devised by the rich in their own interests. As the grain stocks of the community were in their barns, they could time their release to suit themselves; that is why the same class produced euergetists and profiteers. But in addition, through euergetism and the performance of unpaid public services, the few competed with one another for office, prestige and honour – and avoided the less attractive alternative of financing necessary expenditures through regular tax-payments to the civic treasury. By opting for contributions that were irregular, semi-voluntary and enhanced their reputations, rather than regular and obligatory transfers which would bring no credit on the giver, the rich effectively pre-empted the possibilities for instituting a regular state-funded supply or distribution scheme.

Oligarchies characterised by these practices were the standard form of government in the cities of the Graeco-Roman world. Democracies also drew on the resources of the wealthier citizens; even Athens looked to the propertied class for liturgical contributions, while avoiding recourse to euergetism and private patronage by the rich.

III

Imperial and democratic Athens could not survive on home-grown produce alone. However, the productive capacity of Attica has been persistently underrated and its dependence on foreign imports exaggerated. Athens became dependent upon imported grain not in the archaic period, but in the course of the fifth century in consequence of rapid population growth which coincided with the emergence of the Athenian empire. Food supply was not a problem in the inter-war period (480–431), and food shortages were rare. Athens had little difficulty in securing the grain that it needed, thanks to its control of the sea, the attractiveness of its market and of the return cargo of silver that it could offer. The Athenians did not have to substitute a tax in grain for the money-tax that they exacted from their allies, and they were able to persist in distributing cash to their citizens (through payment for office, jury-service, employment in the fleet and on the docks, and so on) rather than grain. To some extent Athens spread the burden of feeding its population by settling citizens abroad for shorter or longer periods. Such strategies eased the pressure at home, but are not to be accounted for only or primarily with reference to economic motives. The outbreak of the Peloponnesian War in 431 was a crucial turning-point; the Athenians became more heavily dependent on imports and also had to take active steps to secure these, effectively for the first time.

In the fourth century, the Athenians had the ambition but lacked the resources, naval and financial, to run an old-style empire and dominate the trade routes of the Aegean. Their main asset was the large and stable market which they offered to suppliers and distributors. The Athenians exploited this advantage in two ways: first, they were active diplomatically in securing advantages for the traders who served them – most notably, from the rulers of the Bosporan kingdom in the northern Black Sea; secondly, they enacted tough laws which forced traders based in Attica or backed by Athenian finance to transport grain to their ports and nowhere else – on pain of death. The crucial issue, however, was whether the Athenians could secure safe passage for the merchant fleet. Their ability to do so varied with the changing fortunes of Athens in the wider arena. At their strongest, in the two decades of the so-called Second Athenian Confederacy, the Athenians were usually able to defend the grain ships or gain their release if captured by quick action. But for most of the century, their food supply, in so far as it depended on imports, was chronically insecure. The last decade and a half of democracy and independence was a time of struggle for survival against the dominant Macedonians, ubiquitous pirates, and rogue traders. Athens was already betraying the anxieties and incapacities of a typical Greek state of the Hellenistic period. Food crises were common.

IV

The expanding Roman state of the period of the Republic developed the capacity to feed a growing population with the fruits of conquest, but only slowly and reluctantly produced the armoury of institutions without which a secure food supply was unattainable.

For the first century and a quarter of its history, Republican Rome competed on more or less equal terms with neighbouring cities and tribal groups, and was particularly vulnerable to food crisis arising from warfare and civil strife. In the period that followed, down to the Hannibalic War of the late third century, the Romans' susceptibility to food crisis decreased with the development of their ability to control their own resources and draw on those of others.

The Hannibalic War played a similar role in Roman history to the Persian Wars in the history of Athens. The Romans had discovered what could be achieved with a large, semi-professional army, and they soon acquired ambitions to match their new strike-power. There were scores to settle with former friends and allies who had changed sides, and memories of hunger and hardship to eradicate. Campania and the Syracusan kingdom (now incorporated in the province of Sicily), Sardinia, and from 146 BC the new province of Africa were put to work to produce food as tax- and rent-in-kind for Rome and its armies. The foundations of a comprehensive network of supply for the city of Rome were laid.

The inhabitants of Rome drew limited benefit from the improved system of supply in the second century. The food supply of Rome was far from stable. Rome's population was rising fast. Yet, successive

274

governments, on the one hand, committed large Roman armies to almost continuous warfare and gave priority to the military rather than civilian consumer, and on the other, persisted with the traditional strategy of dealing with each food shortage as it came. The existing system gave individual politicians, usually market officials and generals, the chance of winning popular favour. The same was not true of private citizens, because euergetism was frowned upon in Rome. The monopoly over patronage exercised by aristocratic houses was left unchallenged. This was a system that offered too little protection to the mass of ordinary people of Rome against price fluctuations, hunger and starvation.

The tribune Gaius Gracchus introduced in 123 BC the most imposing system the Mediterranean world had thus far seen for supplying an urban centre with grain and distributing it to the population. The system was late in emerging; from 123 to 58 BC the grain was not free nor were all resident citizens eligible to receive or able to buy it; and the distributions, which supplied those eligible with more than enough grain for one man but insufficient for a family, were an inadequate safeguard against food crisis in the disturbed political climate of the first century BC. The aims of the reformers other than Clodius in 58 BC were too moderate, the opposition of the conservatives too intransigent, and the strains put on the system by piracy, foreign war, and above all, civil war and disturbance, too great.

Foreign wars, especially under Augustus, occasional civil wars and the practical difficulties involved in organising regular food imports for around a million people ensured that food crises would not disappear under the monarchy. The emperors, sensitive to pressure from below, gave handouts of money and grain and introduced improvements into the system of supply. The range of suppliers was extended, notably to include Egypt, the office of the prefect of the grain supply was introduced, efforts were made to attract more traders and shippers into the service of the grain supply, and port facilities in Puteoli and then Ostia were improved. In the matter of distribution, it was the policy of the emperors to guarantee free grain to a privileged minority of around 200,000 consumers (120,000 fewer than under Clodius' law and about one-fifth of the total population), while encouraging traders to import enough grain to satisfy the needs of all residents.

How did the material situation of Rome's subjects change under the Principate? There were no important innovations in the mechanisms for coping with food crisis. Imperial governments did not, for example, fund grain doles or schemes of poor relief outside Italy. In general, they did not practise a policy of transferring imperial revenues among their subjects. At most there was selective redistribution on behalf of a few specially favoured communities. Similarly, where the Romans commanded food resources superfluous to their needs, as was often the case with Egyptian grain, they disposed of them profitably and in such a way as to favour the more powerful and diplomatically aggressive states, or others with which special connections had been forged. Such states were also more likely to be able in a food crisis to secure the backing or direct intervention of a Roman governor. Regular outside interference could be counterproductive within such communities, if it undermined the willingness or capacity of local elites to apply the traditional remedies to food crisis.

However, the extent of the intervention of the imperial state in civil society can be exaggerated. Provincials were expected to help themselves, and they did so in time-honoured ways. Hungry peasants combined belt-tightening with drawing on their own stores, looking to kin, friends and neighbours, and where necessary to patrons or moneylenders. In the cities euergetism continued to be the main shield of the common people against adversity.

If the traditional mechanisms continued to operate under the Principate, did increased burdens from outside undermine their effectiveness? At the very least, the taxes and irregular payments and services imposed by the central government, coupled with local government demands, and the increased burden of rent that accompanied the progressive conversion of smallholders into tenants, ensured that the standard of living of the mass of the rural population would not rise above the level of subsistence. Again, the expropriation of valued resources (mines, land) by emperors and the Rome-based aristocracy, who increasingly included men of provincial origin, tended to undermine local economies.

Against this have to be set the benefits associated with the imposition of the *pax Romana* by the emperors on a world that had been in turmoil, and would again at the end of our period subside into chronic insecurity. Under the Principate, Italy and the core provinces were on the whole spared the scourges of war and civil strife, which upset the precarious balance between ancient peoples and their environment. The Principate was a period of prolonged tranquillity in comparison with the mid-third century, when chronic instability of government and repeated foreign invasions removed for many of Rome's subjects, in Italy, Greece, Asia Minor and north Africa as well as the outer provinces, the security and protection that were the main benefits of Roman rule. Almost three centuries earlier, the victory at Actium of Octavian (the later Augustus) put an end to the best part of two centuries of warfare and suffering inflicted on the Greek world by the Romans. Let the last word be with Plutarch, as he tells of the experiences of Greeks on the eve of the decisive battle:

In consequence of this, Caesar [*sc.* Octavian] sailed to Athens, and after making a settlement with the Greeks, he distributed the grain which remained over after the war among their cities; these were in a wretched plight, and had been stripped of money, slaves and beasts of burden. At any rate, my great-grandfather Nicarchus used to tell how all his fellow-citizens were compelled to carry on their shoulders a stipulated measure of wheat down to the sea at Anticyra, and how their pace was quickened by the whip; they had carried one load in this way, he said, the second was already measured out, and they were just about to set forth, when word was brought that Antony had been defeated. This was the salvation of the city, for immediately the stewards and soldiers of Antony took to flight, and the citizens divided up the grain among themselves.[1]

[1] Plutarch, *Ant.* 68.6–8.

BIBLIOGRAPHY

Abrams, Ph. and Wrigley, E. A., eds. (1978) *Towns in Societies: Essays in Economic History and Historical Sociology*, Cambridge.

Abulafia, D. (1981) 'Southern Italy and the Florentine economy, 1265–1370', *Econ. Hist. Rev.* 33: 377–88.

Allan, W. (1965) *The African Husbandman*, Edinburgh.

Amouretti, M.-C. (1986) *Le Pain et l'huile dans la Grèce antique*, Besançon.

Andrewes, A. (1978) 'Spartan imperialism?' in Garnsey and Whittaker (1978), 91–102.

Andreyev, V. N. (1974) 'Some aspects of agrarian conditions in Attica in the fifth to third centuries BC', *Eirene* 12: 5–46.

Angel, J. L. (1945) 'Skeletal material from Attica', *Hesperia* 14: 279–363.

Applebaum, S. (1979) *Jews and Greeks in Ancient Cyrenaica*, London.

Appleby, A. B. (1979) 'Grain prices and subsistence crises in England and France, 1590–1740', *Jl Econ. Hist.* 39: 865–87.

Arnon, I. (1972) *Crop Production in Dry Regions*, 2 vols., London.

Atti Colloquio AIEGL (1982) *Atti del Colloquio Internationale AIEGL, Roma 14–20 maggio 1981, su Epigrafia e ordine senatorio*, 2 vols., Rome.

Austin, M. (1970) *Greece and Egypt in the Archaic Age*, Cambridge.

Austin, M. and Vidal-Naquet, P. (1977) *Economic and Social History of Ancient Greece*, London.

Badian, E. (1965) 'M. Porcius Cato and the annexation and early administration of Cyprus', *JRS* 55: 110–21.

 (1968) *Roman Imperialism in the Late Republic*, 2nd edn, Oxford.

Banfield, E. C. (1958) *The Moral Basis of a Backward Society*, Chicago.

Barbagallo, C. (1904) 'La produzione – media relativa dei cereali e della vite nella Grecia, nella Sicilia e nell'Italia antica', *Riv. Stor. Ant.* 8: 477–504.

Beloch, J. (1886) *Die Bevölkerung der Griechisch-Römischen Welt*, Leipzig.

Benabou, M. (1986) 'L'Afrique', in Crawford (1986), 127–41.

Bennett, H. (1922–3) 'The exposure of infants in ancient Rome', *CJ* 18: 341–51.

Bennett, M. K. (1968) 'Famine', *Int. Encycl. Soc. Sc.* Vol. 5: 322–6.

Berchem, D. van (1939) *Les Distributions de blé et d'argent à la plèbe romaine sous l'empire*, Geneva.

Berve, H. (1937) *Miltiades, Studien zur Geschichte des Männer und seiner Zeit*, Hermes, Einzelschriften 2.

Bibliography

Bintliff, J. (1982) 'Climatic change, archaeology and quaternary science in the eastern Mediterranean region', in Harding, A. F., ed., *Climatic Change in Later Prehistory*, Edinburgh, 143–62.

Bintliff, J. L. and Snodgrass, A. M. (1985) 'The Cambridge/Bradford Boeotian Expedition: the first four years', *Jl Field Arch.* 12: 123–61.

Birot, P. and Gabert, P. (1964) *La Méditerranée et le Moyen-Orient* Vol. 1, Paris.

Bloch, M. (1954) *The Historian's Craft*, New York.

Bloedow, E. F. (1975) 'Corn supply and Athenian imperialism', *Ant. Cl.* 44: 20–9.

Boardman, J. (1980) *The Greeks Overseas: Their Early Colonies and Trade*, new enlarged edn, London.

Bolkestein, H. (1939) *Wohltätigkeit und Armenpflege im vorchristlichen Altertum*, Utrecht.

Bonneau, H. C. (1971) *Le Fisc et le Nil. Incidences des irrégularités de la crue du Nil sur la fiscalité foncière dans l'Egypte grecque et romaine*, Paris.

Boren, H. C. (1957–8) 'The urban side of the Gracchan economic crisis', *AHR* 63: 890–902.

Boswell, J. E. (1984) '*Expositio* and *oblatio*: the abandonment of children and the ancient and medieval family', *AHR* 89: 10–33.

Bowman, A. K. (1986) *Egypt after the Pharaohs: 332 B.C. – A.D. 642; from Alexander to the Arab Conquest*, London.

Bradford, J. (1957) *Ancient Landscapes: Studies in Field Archaeology*, London.

Bradley, K. R. (1972) 'A *publica fames* in AD 68', *AJP* 93: 451–8.

Braudel, F. (1973–5) *The Mediterranean and the Mediterranean World in the Age of Philip II*, tr. S. Reynolds, 2 vols., London.

(1981) *The Structures of Everyday Life. The Limits of the Possible*, rev. S. Reynolds, London.

Braund, D. (1984) *Rome and the Friendly King*, London.

Bravo, B. (1977) 'Remarques sur les assises sociales, les formes d'organisation et la terminologie du commerce maritime grec à l'époque archaïque', *DHA* 3: 1–59.

(1983) 'Le commerce des céréales chez les Grecs de l'époque archaïque', in Garnsey and Whittaker (1983), 17–29.

Bremmer, J. (1983) 'Scapegoat rituals in ancient Greece', *HSCP* 87: 299–320.

Brichambaut, G. P. de and Wallen, C. C. (1963) *A Study of Agroclimatology in Semi-arid and Arid Zones of the Near East*, Geneva.

Broughton, T. R. S. (1946) 'Notes on Roman Magistrates', *TAPA* 77: 35–43.

(1952) *The Magistrates of the Roman Republic*, 2 vols., New York.

Brown, P. (1971) 'The rise and function of the Holy Man in late Antiquity', *JRS* 61: 80–101.

Brunt, P. A. (1966a) 'Athenian settlements abroad in the fifth century B.C.', in *Ancient Society and Institutions: Studies Ehrenberg*, Oxford, 71–91.

(1966b) 'The Roman mob', *Past and Present* 35: 3–27 (repr. in Finley, M. I., ed., *Studies in ancient Society*, London, 1974).

(1971) *Italian Manpower, 225 B.C.–A.D. 14*, Oxford.

(1972) Review discussion of White (1970), *JRS* 62: 153–8.

(1980) 'Free labour and public works at Rome', *JRS* 80: 81–100.

(1981) 'The revenues of Rome', review discussion of Neesen (1980), *JRS* 71: 161–72.

Bryson, R. A. and Padoch, C. (1980) 'On the climates of history', *Jl Interdisc. Hist.* 10: 583–7.

Burford Cooper, A. (1977–8) 'The family farm in Greece', *CJ* 73: 162–75.

Burstein, S. M. (1978a) '*IG* ii² 1485a and Athenian relations with Lysimachus', *ZPE* 31: 181–5.

(1978b) '*IG* ii² 653, Demosthenes and Athenian relations with Bosporus in the fourth century B.C.', *Historia* 27: 428–36.

Bury, J. B. and Meiggs, R. (1975) *A History of Greece. To the Death of Alexander the Great*, 4th edn, London.

Buttrey, T. V. (1979) 'The Athenian currency law of 375/4 BC', in Mørkholm, O. and Waggoner, N. M., eds., *Greek Numismatics and Archaeology: Essays in Honour of Margaret Thompson*, 33–45, Wetteren.

(1981) 'More on the Athenian coinage law of 375/4 BC', *Riv. Quad. Tic. di Num. e Ant. Class. Lugano* 10: 71–94.

Cagnat, M. R. (1916) 'L'annone d'Afrique', *Mém. Inst. Nat. de Fr., Acad. Inscr.* 40: 253–77.

Cameron, A. (1974) *Bread and Circuses: The Roman Emperor and his People*, inaugural lecture, London.

(1976) *Circus Factions: Blues and Greens at Rome and Byzantium*, Oxford.

Camp, J. McK. (1979) 'A drought in the late eighth century B.C.', *Hesperia* 48: 397–411.

(1982) 'Drought and famine in the fourth century B.C.', in *Studies H. A. Thompson*, *Hesperia* Suppl. 20: 9–17.

Carandini, A. (1981) 'Sviluppo e crisi delle manifatture rurali e urbane', in Giardina, A. and Schiavone, A., eds., *Società romana e produzione schiavistica*, 3 vols., 2: 249–60, Rome.

Carcopino, J. (1906) 'La Sicile agricole au dernier siècle de la République romaine', *Vierteljahresschrift für Sozial- und Wirtschaftsgeschichte* 4: 128–85.

Carey, C. and Reid, R. A. (1985) *Demosthenes: Selected Private Speeches*, Cambridge.

Cargill, J. (1981) *The Second Athenian League: Empire or Free Alliance?*, Berkeley.

Carrié, J.-M. (1975) 'Les distributions alimentaires dans les cités de l'empire romain tardif', *MEFR* 87: 995–1101.

Cartledge, P. A. (1979) *Sparta and Lakonia: A Regional History 1300–362 B.C.*, London.

(1983) '"Trade and politics revisited": archaic Greece', in Garnsey, Hopkins and Whittaker (1983), 1–15.

(1987) *Agesilaos and the Crisis of Sparta*, London.

Cary, M. (1949) *The Geographic Background of Greek and Roman History*, Oxford.

Casson, L. (1954) 'The grain trade of the Hellenistic world', *TAPA* 85: 168–87.

(1980) 'The role of the state in Rome's grain trade', in D'Arms and Kopff (1980), 21–33.

Cawkwell, G. L. (1961) 'A note on Ps.Dem. 17.20', *Phoenix* 15: 74–8.

Chalon, G. (1964) *L'Edit de Tibérius Julius Alexander*, Olten.

Charles-Picard, G. (1959) *La Civilisation de l'Afrique romaine*, Paris.

Bibliography

Chase, C. (1983) 'Symbolism of food shortage in current Polish politics', *Anthr. Qu.* 56: 76–82.

Chayanov, A. V. (1923) *The Theory of Peasant Economy*, 1986 edn, Wisconsin.

Clark, C. and Haswell, M. (1970) *The Economics of Subsistence Agriculture*, 4th edn, London.

Clinton, K. (1971) 'Inscriptions from Eleusis', *EA*: 81–136.

Coarelli, F. (1977) 'Public building in Rome between the second Punic war and Sulla', *PBSR* 45: 1–23.

Cohen, E. E. (1973) *Ancient Athenian Maritime Courts*, Princeton.

Coldstream, J. N. (1968) *Greek Geometric Pottery: A Survey of Ten Local Styles and Their Chronology*, London.

Coleman-Norton, P. R., Bourne, F. C. and Fine, J. V. A., eds. (1951) *Studies in Roman Economic and Social History in Honor of Allan Chester Johnson*, Princeton.

Cook, R. M. (1972) *Greek Painted Pottery*, 2nd edn, London.

Corbier, M. (1986) 'Le système palatial en Orient, en Grèce et à Rome', in Levy, E., ed., *Actes du Colloque de Strasbourg 19-22 juin 1985*, 411–43.

Coster, Ch. H. (1951) 'The economic position of Cyrenaica in classical times', in Coleman-Norton, Bourne and Fine (1951), 3–26.

Courtois, C. (1952) *Tablettes Albertini*, Paris.

Crawford, D. J. (1976) 'Imperial estates', in Finley (1976b), 57–70.

Crawford, M. H. (1974) *Roman Republican Coinage*, 2 vols., Cambridge.

(1982) *La monetà in Grecia e a Roma*, Bari.

(1986) *L'Impero Romano e le strutture economiche e sociali delle province*, Como.

Dando, W. A. (1980) *The Geography of Famine*, London.

D'Arms, J. H. and Kopff, E. C., eds. (1980) *The Seaborne Commerce of Ancient Rome*, *MAAR* 36, Rome.

Davies, J. K. (1971) *Athenian Propertied Families, 600–300 B.C.*, Oxford.

Day, J. (1942) *An Economic History of Athens under Roman Domination*, New York.

De Jonge, P. (1948) 'Scarcity of corn and corn prices in Ammianus Marcellinus', *Mnem.* 1: 238–45.

Deman, A. (1975) 'Matériaux et réflexions pour servir à une étude du développement et du sous-développement dans les provinces de l'empire romain', *ANRW* II. 3: 3–97.

De Neeve, P. W. (1984) *Colonus: Private Farm-tenancy in Roman Italy during the Republic and Early Principate*, Amsterdam.

Denton, G. H. and Karlen, W. (1973) 'Holocene climatic variations', *Quaternary Res.* 3: 155–205.

De Ste Croix, G. E. M. (1972) *The Origins of the Peloponnesian War*, London.

(1981) *The Class Struggle in the Ancient Greek World, from the Archaic Age to the Arab Conquests*, London.

D'Escurac, H. Pavis (1967) 'Notes sur le phénomène associatif dans le monde paysan à l'époque du Haut-empire', *Ant. Afr.* 1: 59–71.

(1976) *La Préfecture de l'Annone: service administratif impérial d'Auguste à Constantin*, Paris.

De Vries, J. (1980) 'Measuring the impact of climate on history: the search for appropriate methodologies', *Jl Interdisc. Hist.* 10: 599–630.

Dontas, G. S. (1983) 'The true Aglaurion', *Hesperia* 52: 48–63.

Downey, G. (1951) 'The economic crisis at Antioch under Julian the Apostate', in Coleman-Norton, Bourne and Fine (1951), 312–21.

Duncan-Jones, R. P. (1964) 'The purposes and organisation of the alimenta', *PBSR* 32: 123–46.

(1976a) 'The price of wheat in Egypt under the Principate', *Chiron* 6: 241–62.

(1976b) 'The choenix, the artaba and the modius', *ZPE* 21: 43–52.

(1976c) 'The size of the modius castrensis', *ZPE* 21: 53–62.

(1982) *Economy of the Roman Empire. Quantitative Studies*, 2nd edn, Cambridge.

Eckstein, A. M. (1980) '*Unicum subsidium populi Romani*: Hiero II and Rome, 263 B.C.–215 B.C.', *Chiron* 10: 183–203.

Ehrenberg, V. (1969) *The Greek State*, Oxford.

Elvin, M. (1974) 'Introduction', in Elvin, M. and Skinner, G. W., eds., *The Chinese City between Two Worlds*, 1–15.

(1978) 'Chinese cities since the Sung dynasty', in Abrams and Wrigley (1978), 79–89.

Engels, D. (1980) 'The problem of female infanticide in the Greco-Roman world', *CPh* 75: 112–29.

Epstein, J., ed. (1938) *The Babylonian Talmud: Seder Mo'ed in Four Volumes*, Vol. 4, London.

Evans, J. K. (1980) 'Plebs rustica. The peasantry of classical Italy, II', *AJAH* 2: 134–73.

Eyben, E. (1980–1) 'Family planning in Graeco-Roman antiquity', *Anc. Soc.* 11–12: 5–82.

Fei, H.-t. (1939) *Peasant Life in China: A Field Study of Country Life in the Yangtze Valley*, London.

Finley, M. I. (1965) 'Classical Greece', *Second International Conference of Economic History, Aix-en-Provence 1962, I, Trade and Politics in the Ancient World*, 11–35.

(1976a) 'Private farm tenancy in Italy before Diocletian', in Finley (1976b).

ed. (1976b) *Studies in Roman Property*, Cambridge.

(1979) *Ancient Sicily*, rev. edn, London.

(1983) *Politics in the Ancient World*, Cambridge.

(1985) *The Ancient Economy*, rev. edn, London.

Flambard, J.-M. (1977) Clodius, les collèges, la plèbe et les esclaves', *MEFR* 89: 115–56.

Fontenrose, J. (1978) *The Delphic Oracle*, California.

Forbes, H. A. (1976) '"We have a little of everything": The ecological basis of some agricultural practices in Methana, Trizinia', *Annals N. Y. Acad. Sc.*, 268: 236–50.

(1982) 'Strategy and soils: technology, production and environment in the peninsula of Methana, Greece', dissertation, University of Pennsylvania.

Foxhall, L. (1986) 'Greece ancient and modern – subsistence and survival', *History Today*, 36 (July 1986): 35–43.

Foxhall, L. and Forbes, H. A. (1982) 'Sitometreia: The role of grain as a staple food in classical antiquity', *Chiron* 12: 41–90.

Bibliography

Francotte, H. (1905) 'Le pain à bon marché et le pain gratuit dans les cités grecques', in *Mélanges Nicole*, Geneva, 135–57.

Frank, T., ed. (1938) *Economic Survey of Ancient Rome*, Vol. 4, Baltimore.

Fraser, P. M. (1972) *Ptolemaic Alexandria*, 2 vols., Oxford.

Frayn, J. (1979) *Subsistence Farming in Roman Italy*, London.

Frederiksen, M. W. (1976) 'Changes in patterns of settlement' in Zanker, P., ed., *Hellenismus in Mittelitalien. Abh. Akad. Wiss. Gött*, Phil.-Hist. Kl. Dr. Folge 97: 341–55.

  (1980–81) 'Puteoli e il commercio di grano in epoca romana', *Puteoli* 4–5: 5–27.

  (1981) "I cambiamenti delle strutture agrarie nella tarda repubblica: la Campania' in Giardina and Schiavone (1981): 265–88.

  (1984) *Campania*, ed. N. Purcell, British School at Rome.

French, A. L. (1956) 'The economic background to Solon's reforms', *CQ* 6: 11–25.

  (1964) *The Growth of the Athenian Economy*, Cambridge.

Frier, B. W. (1982) 'Roman life expectancy: Ulpian's evidence', *HSCP* 86: 213–51.

  (1983) 'Roman life expectancy: the Pannonian evidence', *Phoenix* 37: 328–44.

Frost, F. J. (1984) 'The Athenian Military before Cleisthenes', *Historia* 33: 283–94.

Gabba, E. (1972) 'Urbanizzazione e rinnovamenti urbanistici nell'Italia centro-meridionale del I sec. a. C.', *SCO* 21: 73–111.

  (1977) 'Considerazioni sulla decadenza della piccola proprietà contadina nell'-Italia centro-meridionale del II sec. A.C.', *Ktema* 2: 269–84.

  (1986) 'La Sicilia Romana', in Crawford (1986), 77–85.

Gagé, J. (1966) 'Le dieu "Inventor" et les Minucii', *MEFR* 78: 79–122.

Gajdukevic, V. J. (1971) *Das Bosphoranische Reich*, Berlin.

Gallant, T. W. (1982a) 'An examination of two island polities in antiquity: the Lefkas–Pronnoi survey', Ph.D. thesis, Cambridge.

  (1982b) 'Agricultural systems, land tenure, and the reforms of Solon', *BSA* 77: 111–24.

  (1985) *A Fisherman's Tale: An Analysis of the Potential Productivity of Fishing in the Ancient World*, Miscellanea Graeca 7, Gent.

Gallo, L. (1983) 'Alimentazione e classi sociali: una nota su orzo e frumento in Grecia', *Opus* 2: 449–72.

  (1984) *Alimentazione e demografia della grecia antica*, Salerno.

Gallotta, B. (1975) 'L'Africa e i rifornimenti di cereali all'Italia durante il principato di Nerone', *RIL* 109: 28–46.

Gapp, K. S. (1934) 'Famine in the Roman world: from the founding of Rome to the time of Trajan', Ph.D. dissertation, Princeton.

  (1935) 'The universal famine under Claudius', *Harv. Theol. Rev.* 28: 258–65.

Garnsey, P. (1976) 'Urban property investment', in Finley (1976b), 123–36.

  (1978) 'Rome's African empire under the Principate', in Garnsey and Whittaker (1978), 223–54.

  (1979) 'Where did Italian peasants live?', *PCPhS* 25: 1–25.

  (1980) 'Non-slave labour in ancient Rome', in Garnsey, P., ed., *Non-slave Labour in the Graeco-Roman World*, Cambridge.

Bibliography

(1983) 'Grain for Rome', in Garnsey, Hopkins and Whittaker (1983): 118–30.

(1985) 'Grain for Athens', in Cartledge, P. A. and Harvey, F. D., eds., *Crux: Essays Presented to G. E. M. de Ste Croix on his 75th Birthday*, 62–75.

(1986) 'Mountain economies in southern Europe: thoughts on the early history, continuity and individuality of Mediterranean upland pastoralism', in Matmüller, M., ed., *Wirtschaft und Gesellschaft in Berggebieten, Itinera* 5/6, 1–25.

Garnsey, P. (1992) 'Famine in history', in Bourriau, J. ed. *Understanding Catastrophe*, Cambridge, 145–78.

Garnsey, P., Gallant, T. and Rathbone, D. (1984) 'Thessaly and the grain supply of Rome during the second century B.C.', *JRS* 74: 30–44.

Garnsey, P., Hopkins, K. and Whittaker, C. R., eds. (1983) *Trade in the Ancient Economy*, London.

Garnsey, P. and Morris, I. (1989) 'Risk and the polis: The evolution of institutionalised responses to food supply problems in the early Greek state', in Halstead, P. and O'Shea, J., eds., *Bad Year Economics*, Cambridge.

Garnsey, P. and Rathbone, D. (1985) 'The background to the grain law of Gaius Gracchus', *JRS* 75: 20–5.

Garnsey, P. and Saller, R. (1987) *The Roman Empire: Economy, Society and Culture*, London.

Garnsey, P. and Whittaker, C. R., eds. (1978) *Imperialism in the Ancient World*, Cambridge.

eds. (1983) *Trade and Famine in Classical Antiquity*, Cambridge.

Garnsey, P. and Woolf, G. (1989) 'Patronage and the rural poor in the Roman world', in Wallace-Hadrill, A., ed., *Patronage in Ancient Society*, London, 153–70.

Gauthier, Ph. (1966) 'Les clérouques de Lesbos et la colonisation athénienne au vᵉ siècle', *REG* 79: 64–88.

(1973) 'A propos des clérouques athéniennes du vᵉ siècle' in Finley, M. I., ed., *Problèmes de la terre en Grèce ancienne*, Paris and The Hague, 163–86.

(1981) 'De Lysias à Aristote (Ath. Pol. 51.4): le commerce du grain à Athènes et les fonctions des sitophylaques', *RHDFE* 59: 5–28.

(1985) *Les Cités grecques et leurs bienfaiteurs*, *BCH* Suppl. 12.

Gellner, E. and Waterbury, J., eds. (1977) *Patrons and Clients in Mediterranean Societies*, London.

Gérard, J. (1976) *Juvénal et la réalité contemporaine*, Paris.

Gernet, L. (1909) *L'Approvisionnement d'Athènes en blé au Vᵉ et au IVᵉ siècle*, Université de Paris, Bibl. Fac. Lett. 25, *Mélanges d'histoire ancienne*, Paris.

(1938) 'Sur les actions commerciales en droit Athénien', *REG* 51: 1–44.

Giardina, A. and Schiavone, A., eds. (1981) *Società romana e produzione schiavistica*, 3 vols., Bari.

Gilliam, J. F. (1961) 'The plague under Marcus Aurelius', *AJP* 82: 225–51.

Golden, M. (1981) 'Demography and the exposure of girls at Athens', *Phoenix* 35: 316–31.

Gomme, A. W. (1933) *The Population of Athens in the Fifth and Fourth Centuries BC*, Oxford.

Gonzales, J. (1986) 'The Lex Irnitana: a new copy of the Flavian municipal law', *JRS* 76: 147–243.

Bibliography

Goubert, P. (1986) *The French Peasantry in the Seventeenth Century*, tr. I. Patterson, Cambridge.

Graham, A. J. (1964) *Colony and Mother City in Ancient Greece*, Manchester.

Green, P. (1970) *Armada from Athens*, London.

Greig, J. R. A. and Turner, J. (1974) 'Some pollen diagrams from Greece and their archaeological significance', *Jl Arch. Science* 1: 177–94.

Griffith, G. T. (1935) *The Mercenaries of the Hellenistic World*, Cambridge.

(1978) 'Athens in the fourth century', in Garnsey and Whittaker (1978), 127–44.

Gruen, E. S. (1984) *The Hellenistic World and the Coming of Rome*, 2 vols., Berkeley.

Grundy, G. B. (1948) *Thucydides and the History of his Age*, 2 vols., Oxford.

Guillet, D. (1983) 'Toward a cultural ecology of mountains: the central Andes and the Himalayas compared', *Current Anthropology* 24: 561–74.

Gummerus, H. (1906) *Der römische Gutsbetrieb*, *Klio* Beiheft 5.

Hajnal, J. (1965) 'European marriage patterns in perspective', in Glass, D. V. and Eversley, D. E. C., eds., *Population in History*, London, 101–43.

(1983) 'Two kinds of pre-industrial household formation system', in Wall *et al.*, eds., *Family Forms in Historic Europe*, Cambridge.

Halstead, P. (1981) 'Counting sheep in neolithic and bronze age Greece', in Hodder, I., Isaac, G., and Hammond, N., eds., *Pattern of the Past: Studies in Honour of David Clarke*, Cambridge.

(1984) 'Strategies for survival: an ecological approach to social and economic change in the early farming communities of Thessaly, N. Greece', Ph.D. dissertation, Cambridge.

(1988) 'The economy has a normal surplus: economic stability and social change among early farming communities of Thessaly, Greece', in Halstead, P. and O'Shea, J., eds., *Cultural Responses to Uncertainty*, Cambridge.

Hammond, N. G. L. (1967) *A History of Greece*, 2nd edn, Oxford.

Hands, A. R. (1968) *Charities and Social Aid in Greece and Rome*, London.

Hansen, M. H. (1981) 'The number of Athenian hoplites in 431 B.C.', *Symb. Osl.* 56: 19–32.

(1982 publ. 1985) 'Demographic reflections on the number of Athenian citizens 451–309', *AJAH* 7: 172–89.

(1986) *Demography and Democracy: The Number of Athenian Citizens in the Fourth Century B.C.*, Vojens, Denmark.

Hanson, V. D. (1983) *Warfare and Agriculture in Ancient Greece*, Pisa.

Harris, W. V. (1979) *War and Imperialism in Republican Rome*, Oxford.

(1982) 'The theoretical possibility of extensive infanticide in the Graeco-Roman world', *CQ* 32: 114–16.

Hart, J. (1982) *Herodotus and Greek History*, London.

Hassall, M., Crawford, M. and Reynolds, J. (1984) 'Rome and the eastern provinces at the end of the second century B.C.: the so-called "Piracy Law" and a new inscription from Cnidos', *JRS* 64: 195–220.

Heichelheim, F. M. (1930) *Wirtschaftliche Schwankungen der Zeit von Alexander bis Augustus*, Jena.

(1935) 'Sitos', in Pauly-Wissowa, *RE* Suppl. 6: 819–92.

Bibliography

Heurgon, J. (1950) 'La lettre de Cicéron à P. Sittius, Ad Fam. v, 17', *Latomus* 9: 375ff.

Hodkinson, S. J. (1983) 'Social order and the conflict of values in classical Sparta', *Chiron* 13: 239–81.

(1986) 'Animal husbandry in the Greek polis', *Papers of the Ancient History (Greece and Rome) Section of the 9th International Economic History Congress*, Bern, August 1986

Hopkins, K. (1965) 'The age of Roman girls at marriage', *Pop. St.* 18: 309–27.

(1966) 'On the probable age structure of the Roman population', *Pop. St.* 20: 245–64.

(1978) 'Economic growth and towns in classical antiquity', in Abrams and Wrigley (1978), 35–77.

(1983a) 'Models, ships and staples', in Garnsey and Whittaker (1983), 84–109.

(1983b) *Death and Renewal*, Cambridge.

Hornblower, S. (1983) *The Greek World, 479–323 B.C.*, London and New York.

Humbert, M. (1978) *Municipium et civitas sine suffragio. L'organisation de la conquête jusqu'à la guerre sociale*, Rome.

Huxley, G. L. (1971) 'Crete in Aristotle's *Politics*', *GRBS* 12: 505–15.

Isager, S. and Hansen, M. H. (1975) *Aspects of Athenian Society in the Fourth Century B.C.*, Odense.

Isager, S. and Skydsgaard, J. E. (1992) *Ancient Greek Agriculture: an Introduction*, London and New York.

Jameson, M. H. (1977–8) 'Agriculture and slavery in classical Athens', *CJ* 73: 122–45.

(1983) 'Famine in the Greek world', in Garnsey and Whittaker (1983).

Janushevich, Z. V. (1981) 'Die Kulturpflanzen Skythiens', *Zeitschrift für Archäologie* 15: 87–96.

Janushevich, Z. V. and Nikolaenko, G. M. (1979) 'Fossil remains of cultivated plants in the ancient Tauric Chersonese', in Körber-Grohne, *Festschrift Maria Hopf, Archaeo-physika* 8: 115–34.

Jardé, A. (1925) *Les Céréales dans l'antiquité grecque*, Paris.

Jasny, N. (1941–2) 'Competition among grains in classical antiquity', *AHR* 47: 747–64.

(1944a) *The Wheats of Classical Antiquity*, Baltimore.

(1944b) 'Wheat prices and milling costs in classical Rome', *Wheat Studies of the Food Research Institute* 20: 137–70.

Johne, K.-P., Köhn, J. and Weber, V. (1983) *Die Kolonen in Italien und den westlichen Provinzen des römischen Reiches*, Berlin.

Johnson, A. C. and West, L. C. (1949) *Byzantine Egypt, Economic Studies*, Princeton.

Johnston, A. W. (1979) *Trademarks on Greek Vases*, Guildford.

Jones, A. H. M. (1940) *The Greek City from Alexander to Justinian*, Oxford.

(1957) *Athenian Democracy*, Oxford.

(1964) *The Later Roman Empire*, 2 vols., Oxford.

(1974a) 'The Roman colonate', in Finley, M. I., ed., *Studies in Ancient Society*, London.

(1974b) *The Roman Economy: Studies in Ancient Economic and Administrative History*, ed. P. A. Brunt, Oxford.

Jones, C. P. (1971) *Plutarch and Rome*, Oxford.

(1978) *The Roman World of Dio Chrysostom*, Harvard.

Jordan, B. (1972) *The Athenian Navy in the Classical Period*, Berkeley.

Jutikkala, E. (1955) 'The Great Finnish Famine in 1696–97', *Scand. Econ. Hist. Rev.* 3: 47–63.

Kayser, B. and Thompson, F. (1964) *Economic and Social Atlas of Greece*, Athens.

Keller, D. R. and Rupp, D. W. (1983) *Archaeological Survey in the Mediterranean*, BAR Int. Ser. 155, Oxford.

Kingsley, B. M. (1986) 'Harpalos in the Megarid (333–331 B.C.) and the grain shipments from Cyrene (*S.E.G.* IX 2+ = Tod, *Greek Hist. Inscr.* II no. 196)', *ZPE* 66: 165–77.

Kohns, H. P. (1961) *Versorgungskrisen und Hungerrevolten im spätantiken Rom*, Bonn.

(1964) 'Die staatliche Lenkung des Getreidehandels in Athen (zu Lysias, Or. 22)', in *Studien zur Papyrologie und antiken Wirtschaftsgeschichte, F. Oertel zum achtzigsten Geburtstag gewidmet*: 146–66, Bonn.

Kraay, C. M. (1964) 'Hoards, small change and the origin of coinage', *JHS* 84: 76–91.

Kuenzi, A. (1923) *Epidosis*, Bern.

Kuniholm, P. and Striker, C. (1983) 'Dendrochronological investigations in the Aegean and neighbouring regions, 1977–1982', *Jl Field Arch.* 10: 411–20.

Labarbe, J. (1961) 'La distribution de blé de 445/4 à Athènes et ses incidences démographiques', *Sozialökonomische Verhältnisse im Alten Orient und im klassischen Altertum*, 191–207.

Lanciani, R. (1888) *Ancient Rome in the Light of Recent Discoveries*, London.

Larsen, J. A. O. (1938) 'Roman Greece', in Frank (1938) *Economic Survey of Ancient Rome*, Vol 4, Baltimore.

Lassère, J. M. (1982) 'Un conflit routier: observations sur les causes de la guerre de Tacfarinas', *Ant. Afr.* 18: 11–27.

Latte, K. (1948) 'Kollektivbesitz und Staatsschatz in Griechenland', *Nachr. Akad. Wiss. Gött. 1945/1948*, Phil.-hist. Kl. 1946/47: 64–75 = *Kleine Schriften zu Religion, Recht, Literatur und Sprach der Griechen und Römer*, 294–312, Munich.

Lauffer, S. (1956) *Die Bergwerkssklaven von Laureion*, 2 vols., Berlin.

Le Bonniec, H. (1958) *Le Culte de Cérès à Rome: des origines à la fin de la République*, Paris.

Legon, R. P. (1981) *Megara: The Political History of a Greek City-state to 336 B.C.*, Ithaca.

Lehmann, D., ed. (1982) *Ecology and Exchange in the Andes*, Cambridge.

(1986) 'Two paths of agrarian capitalism, or a critique of Chayanovian marxism', *CSSH* 28: 601–27.

Le Houérou, H. N. (1977) 'Plant sociology and ecology applied to grazing lands research, survey and management in the Mediterranean basin', in Krause, W., ed., *Handbook of Vegetation Science*, 13: *Application of Vegetation Science to Grassland Husbandry*, 211–74. The Hague.

Le Roy Ladurie, E. (1966) *Les Paysans de Languedoc*, Paris.

Le Roy Ladurie, E. and Baulant, M. (1980) 'Grape harvests from the 11th to the 19th century', *Jl Interdisc. Hist.* 10: 839–49.

Levick, B. M. (1985) *The Government of the Roman Empire: A Source Book*, London.

Lewis, D. M. (1973) 'The Athenian Rationes Centesimarum', in Finley, M. I., ed., *Problèmes de la terre en Grèce ancienne*, 187–212.

(1977) *Sparta and Persia*, Leiden.

Liebenam, S. (1939–44) 'The martyrs of Caesarea', *Ann. Inst. Phil. Hist. Or. Sl.* 7: 395–446.

Liebeschuetz, J. H. W. G. (1972) *Antioch: City and Imperial Administration in the Later Roman Empire*, Oxford.

Lintott, A. W. (1968) *Violence in Republican Rome*, Oxford.

(1970) 'The tradition of violence in the Annals of the early Roman Republic', *Historia* 19: 12–29.

McKechnie, P. (1985) 'Greeks outside the polis in the fourth century B.C.', D.Phil. thesis, Oxford.

MacMullen, R. (1966) *Enemies of the Roman Order*, Cambridge, Mass.

(1974) *Roman Social Relations*, New Haven and London.

Magie, D. (1951) 'A reform in the exaction of grain at Cibyra under Claudius', in Coleman-Norton, Bourne and Fine (1951), 152–4.

Malthus, T. (1798) *An Essay on the Principle of Population*, repr. 1970, London.

Mariolopoulos, E. G. (1962) 'Fluctuation of rainfall in Attica during the years of the erection of the Parthenon', *Geofisica pura e applicata* 51: 243–50.

Markle, M. M. (1985) 'Jury pay and assembly pay at Athens', in Cartledge, P. A. and Harvey, F. D., eds., *Crux: Essays presented to G. E. M. De Ste Croix on his 75th Birthday*, 265–97.

Martin, R. (1971) *Recherches sur les agronomes latins et leurs conceptions économiques et sociales*, Paris.

Mattingly, H. B. (1961) 'Athens and Euboea', *JHS* 81: 124–32.

Maurizio, A. (1932) *Histoire de l'alimentation végétale*, Paris.

Mazard, J. (1955) *Corpus Nummorum Numidiae Mauretaniaeque*, Paris.

Meiggs, R. (1972) *The Athenian Empire*, Oxford.

Migeotte, L. (1983) 'Souscriptions athéniennes de la période classique', *Historia* 32: 129–48.

(1984) *L'Emprunt public dans les cités grecques: recueil des documents et analyse critique*, Paris.

Millar, F. (1977) *The Emperor in the Roman World*, London.

Miller, S. M. (1972) 'A Roman monument in the Athenian agora', *Hesperia* 41: 50–95.

Millett, P. (1984) 'Hesiod and his world', *PCPhS* 30: 84–115.

(1989) 'Patronage and its avoidance in Classical Athens', in Wallace-Hadrill, A., ed., *Patronage in Ancient Society*, London and New York, 15–48.

Missiou-Ladi, A. (1986) 'Deliberative oratory, politics and ideology: Andokides' "On the Peace with the Lakedaemonians"', Ph.D. thesis, Cambridge.

Mitchell, S. (1976) 'Requisitioned transport in the Roman empire: a new inscription from Pisidia', *JRS* 66: 106–31.

Mohler, S. L. (1931) 'The *cliens* in the time of Martial', in Hadzsits, G. D., ed., *Classical Studies in Honor of John C. Rolfe*, Philadelphia.

Momigliano, A. (1936) 'Due punti di storia romana arcaica', *SDHI* 2: 373–98 = *Quarto Contributo*: 329–61.

Mommsen, Th. (1854–6) *Römische Geschichte*, 3 vols., Leipzig.

Montanari, M. (1979) *L'alimentazione contadina nell'alto Medioevo*, Napoli.

(1984) *Campagne medievali: strutture produttive, rapporti di lavoro, sistemi alimentari*, Turin.

Moritz, L. (1958) *Grain Mills and Flour in Classical Antiquity*, Oxford.

Morris, I. (1987) *Burial and Ancient Society: The Rise of the Greek City-State*, Cambridge.

(1991) 'The early polis as city and state', in Rich, J. W. and Wallace-Hadrill, A., eds., *City and Country in the Ancient World*, London and New York, 25–58.

Morrow, G. R. (1960) *Plato's Cretan City: A Historical Interpretation of The Laws*, Princeton.

Murra, J. V. (1975) *Formaciones economicas y politicas andinas*, Lima.

Murray, O. (1980) *Early Greece*, London.

Neesen, L. (1980) *Untersuchungen zu den direkten Staatsabgaben der römischen Kaiserzeit (27 v. Chr. - 284 n. Chr.)*, Bonn.

Nenci, G. (1964) 'Una ignorata revisione delle liste dei cittadini Ateniesi nel 424/23 A.C.', *RFIC* 92: 173–80.

Nesselhauf, H. (1933) *Untersuchungen zur Geschichte der Delisch-Attischen Symmachie*, *Klio* Beiheft 30.

Netting, R. McC. (1972) 'Of men and meadows: strategies of alpine land use', *Anthr. Quart.* 45: 132–44.

(1981) *Balancing on an Alp: Ecological Change and Continuity in a Swiss Mountain Community*, Cambridge.

Nicolet, Cl. (1965) 'L'inspiration de Tibérius Gracchus', *REA* 67: 142ff.

(1976a) 'Le temple des Nymphes et les distributions frumentaires à Rome d'après les découvertes récentes', *CRAI*: 39–46.

(1976b) 'Tessères frumentaires et tessères de vote', *Mélanges J. Heurgon*, Rome, 695ff.

(1976c) *Le Métier de citoyen dans la Rome Républicaine*, Paris.

Noonan, T. S. (1973) 'The grain trade of the northern Black Sea in antiquity', *AJP* 94: 231–42.

North, J. (1976) 'Conservatism and change in Roman religion', *PBSR* 44: 1–12.

Ogilvie, R. M. (1965) *A Commentary on Livy Books I–V*, Oxford.

Oliver, J. H. (1953) *The Ruling Power. A Study of the Roman Empire in the second century after Christ through the Roman Oration of Aelius Aristides*, Philadelphia.

(1965) 'Athens and Roman problems around Moesia', *GRBS* 6: 51–5.

Oliverio, G. (1933) *Cirenaica 2.1: La stela dei nuovi commandamenti e dei cereali*, Bergamo.

Oost, S. I. (1963) 'Cyrene, 96–74 B.C.', *CPh* 58: 11–25.

Oppenheim, A. L. (1955) 'Siege-documents from Nippur', *Iraq* 17: 69–89.

Orlove, B. S. (1980) 'Ecological anthropology', *Ann. Rev. Anthr.* 9: 235–73.

Ormerod, H. A. (1924) *Piracy in the Ancient World: An Essay in Mediterranean History*, Liverpool.

Osborne, M. J. (1981–2) *Naturalization in Athens*, 2 vols. in 1, Brussels.

Osborne, R. (1985a) *Demos: The Discovery of Classical Attika*, Cambridge.

(1985b) 'Buildings and residence on the land in classical and hellenistic Greece: the contribution of epigraphy', *BSA* 80: 119–28.

Parke, H. W. (1933) *Greek Mercenary Soldiers from the Earliest Times to the Battle of Ipsus*, Oxford.

Patai, R. (1939) 'The "control of rain" in ancient Palestine', *Hebrew Union College Annual* 14: 251–86.

Patlagean, E. (1977) *Pauvreté économique et pauvreté sociale à Byzance 4ᵉ–7ᵉ siècle*, Paris.

Patterson, C. (1981) *Pericles' Citizenship Law of 451–50*, New York.

Pečirka, J. (1966) *The Formula for the Grant of Enktesis in Attic Inscriptions*, Prague.

Perreault, J. (1986) 'Céramiques et échanges: les importations attiques au Proche-orient du viᵉ au milieu de vᵉ siècle av. J.-C.', *BCH* 110: 145–75.

Petit, P. (1955) *Libanius et la vie municipale à Antioche au IVᵉ siècle après J.C.*, Paris.

Pfister, Chr. (1980) 'The Little Ice Age: thermal and wetness indices for central Europe', *Jl Interdisc. Hist.* 10: 665–96.

Pflaum, H.-G. (1960–82) *Les Carrières procuratoriennes équestres sous le Haut-Empire romain*, 3 vols. + suppl. vol., Paris.

Philippson, A. (1952) *Die griechischen Landschaften* 1.3, Frankfurt.

Picard, G. Ch. (1956) 'Néron et le blé d'Afrique', *CRAI*: 68–72.

Pollera, A. (1979) 'La carestia del 439 a. C. e l'uccisione di Spurio Melio', *BIDR*: 141–68.

Pomeroy, S. B. (1983) 'Infanticide in Hellenistic Greece', in Cameron, A. and Kuhrt, A., eds, *Images of Women in Antiquity*, 207–22, London.

Pomey, P. and Tchernia, A. (1978) 'Le tonnage maximum des navires de commerce romains', *Archaeonautica* 2: 233–51.

Popkin, S. L. (1979) *The Rational Peasant: The Political Economy of Rural Society in Vietnam*, Berkeley.

Potter, D. S. (1984) '*IG* ii² 399: Evidence for Athenian involvement in the war of Agis III', *BSA* 79: 229–36.

Préaux, C. (1978) *Le Monde hellénistique. La Grèce et l'Orient de la mort d'Alexandre à la conquête romaine de la Grèce (323–146 av. J.-C.)*, 2 vols., Paris.

Pritchett, W. K. (1971–4) *The Greek State at War*, 4 vols., Berkeley.

Raepsaet, G. (1974) 'A propos de l'utilisation de statistiques en démographie grecque: le nombre d'enfants par familie', *Ant. Class.* 42: 536–42.

Rathbone, D. W. (1981) 'The development of agriculture in the "Ager Cosanus" during the Roman Republic: problems of evidence and interpretation', *JRS* 71: 10–23.

Rea, J. R. (1972) 'Public documents: the corn dole in Oxyrhynchus, and kindred documents', *P. Oxy.* 40: 1–26.

Redfield, R. (1956) *Peasant Society and its Culture*, Chicago.

Renfrew, C. and Wagstaff, M., eds (1982) *An Island Polity: The Archaeology of Exploitation in Melos*, Cambridge.

Reynolds, J. M. (1978) 'Hadrian, Antoninus Pius and the Cyrenaican cities', *JRS* 68: 111–21.

Rhoades, R. E. and Thompson, S. I. (1975) 'Adaptive strategies in alpine environments: beyond ecological particularism', *American Ethnologist* 2: 535–51.

Rhodes, P. J. (1981) *Commentary on the Aristotelian Athenaion Politeia*, Oxford.

Richardson, J. S. (1986) *Hispaniae: Spain and the Development of Roman Imperialism 218–82 B.C.*, Cambridge.

Rickman, G. (1971) *Roman Granaries and Store Buildings*, Cambridge.

(1980) *The Corn Supply of Ancient Rome*, Oxford.

Robert, L. (1974) 'Des Carpathes à la Propontide', *Stud. Clas.* 16: 53–86.

Robertson, N. (1986) 'Solon's axones and kyrbeis and the sixth-century background', *Historia* 35: 147–76.

Roesch, P. (1965) *Thespies et la Confédération Béotienne*, Paris.

Romilly, J. de (1963) *Thucydides and Athenian Imperialism*, Oxford.

Rostovtzeff, M. (1912) 'Frumentum', in Pauly-Wissowa, *RE* 7: 126–87.

(1941) *The Social and Economic History of the Hellenistic World*, 3 vols., Oxford

(1957) *Social and Economic History of the Roman Empire*, 2nd edn, rev. P. M. Fraser, Oxford.

Rotberg, R. I. and Rabb, Th. K., eds. (1983) *Hunger and History: The Impact of Changing Food Production and Consumption Patterns on Society*, Cambridge.

Rowland, R. J., Jr (1965) 'The number of grain recipients in the late Republic', *Acta Antiqua Academiae Scientiarum Hungaricae* 13: 81–3.

(1974) 'The case of the missing Sardinian grain', *The Ancient World: Early Trade and Traders in the Mediterranean* 10: 45–8.

(1976) 'The "Very Poor" and the grain dole at Rome and Oxyrhynchus', *ZPE* 21: 69–72.

Rudé, G. (1964) *The Crowd in History: A Study of Popular Disturbances in France and England 1730–1848*, New York.

Runnels, C. and Van Andel, Tj. H. (1987) 'The evolution of settlement in the southern Argolid, Greece: an economic explanation', *Hesperia* 56.

Russell, D. A. (1983) *Greek Declamation*, Cambridge.

Sallares, J. R. (1986) 'Towards a New Approach to Ancient History. The Interaction of Biological Phenomena, the Economy, and Social Structure', Ph.D. thesis, Cambridge.

Sallares, R. (1991) *The Ecology of the Ancient Greek World*, London.

Saller, R. P. (1982) *Personal Patronage under the Early Empire*, Cambridge.

(1987) 'Men's age at marriage and the consequences in the Roman family', *CP* 82: 21–39.

Salmon, E. T. (1969) *Roman Colonisation under the Republic*, London.

Salmon, P. (1965) *La Politique égyptienne d'Athènes (VIᵉ et Vᵉ siècles avant J.-C.)*, Brussels.

Sanders, G. D. R. (1984) 'Reassessing ancient populations', *BSA* 79: 251–62.

Schmitt, H. H. (1957) *Rom und Rhodos*, Munich.

Schneider, H. (1974) *Wirtschaft und Politik: Untersuchungen zur Geschichte der späten römischen Republik*, Erlanden.

(1983) 'Die Getreideversorgung der Stadt Antiochia im 4. Jh. n. Chr.', *Münstersche Beiträge zur Antiken Handelsgeschichte* 2: 59–72.

Schofield, R. (1983) 'The impact of scarcity and plenty on population change in England, 1541–1871', in Rotberg and Rabb (1983), 67–93.

Scott, J. C. (1976) *The Moral Economy of the Peasant: Rebellion and Subsistence in Southeast Asia*, New Haven and London.

Seager, R. (1966) 'Lysias against the corndealers', *Historia* 15: 172–84.

Bibliography

Semple, E. C. (1932) *The Geography of the Mediterranean Region. Its Relation to Ancient History*, London.

Sen, A. (1981) *Poverty and Famines: An Essay on Entitlement and Deprivation*, Oxford.

Shackleton-Bailey, D. R. (1960) 'Sex. Clodius – Sex. Cloelius', *CQ* 10: 41–2.

Shanin, T. (1971) *The Awkward Class: Political Sociology of Peasantry in a Developing Society: Russia, 1910–25*, Oxford.

Shaw, B. D. (1982) 'Fear and loathing: the nomad menace and Roman Africa', *Rev. de l'Univ. d'Ottawa* 52: 25–46.

Shear, T. L. (1978) *Kallias of Sphettos and the Revolt of Athens in 286 B.C.*, *Hesperia* Suppl. 17.

(1987) 'Tax tangle, ancient style', *ASCS Newsletter*, Spring 1987, 8.

Sherwin-White, A. N. (1973) *The Roman Citizenship*, 2nd edn, Oxford.

Sherwin-White, S. M. (1978) *Ancient Cos*, Göttingen.

Shipley, G. (1987) *A History of Samos, 800–188 BC*, Oxford.

Silverman, S. F. (1968) 'Agricultural organization, social structure, and values in Italy: amoral familism reconsidered', *American Anthropologist* 70: 1–20.

Small, A. M. (1981) 'The environment of San Giovanni in the Roman period', in Barker, G. and Hodges, R., eds., *BAR* Int. Ser. 102.

Smith, C. Delano (1979) *Western Mediterranean Europe: A Historical Geography of Italy, Spain and Southern France since the Neolithic*, London.

Snodgrass, A. M. (1977) *Archaeology and the Rise of the Greek State*, inaugural lecture, Cambridge.

(1980) *Archaic Greece: The Age of Experiment*, London.

(1983) 'Two demographic notes', in Hagg, R., ed., *The Greek Renaissance of the 8th century B.C.: Tradition and Innovation*, 167–71.

Spawforth, A. J. and Walker, S. (1985) 'The world of the Panhellenion: 1. Athens and Eleusis', *JRS* 75: 78–104.

Sperber, D. (1974) 'Drought, famine and pestilence in Amoraic Palestine', *Jl Ec. Soc. Hist. Or.* 17: 272–98.

Spurr, M. S. (1986) *Arable Cultivation in Roman Italy c. 200 B.C. – c. A.D. 100*, London.

Staerman, E. M. and Trofima, M. K. (1975) *La schiavitù nell' Italia imperiale*, Rome.

Starr, C. G. (1977) *The Economic and Social Growth of Early Greece, 800–500 B.C.*, New York.

Stefan, A. (1974) 'Die Getreidekrisen in den Städten an den westlichen und nordlichen Küsten des Pontos Euxeines in der hellenistischen Zeit', *Hellenische Poleis Krise-Wandlung-Wirkung*, Welskopf, L., ed., Vol. 2, 548ff., Berlin.

Stroud, R. S. (1974) 'An Athenian law on silver coinage', *Hesperia* 43: 158–88.

Sutherland, H. (1943) 'Corn and coin: a note on Greek commercial monopolies', *AJP* 64: 143–7.

Talbert, R. J. A. (1974) *Timoleon and the Revival of Greek Sicily, 344–317 B.C.*, Cambridge.

Tarn, W. W. and Griffith, G. T. (1952) *Hellenistic Civilization*, 3rd edn, London.

Taylor, L. R. (1960) *The Voting Districts of the Roman Republic*, *MAAR* 20, Rome.

Tchernia, A. (1986) *Le Vin de L'Italie romaine*, Rome.

Tengstrom, E. (1974) *Bread for the People. Studies of the Corn-supply of Rome during the Later Empire*, Stockholm.

Bibliography

Thompson, D. J. (1983) 'Nile grain transport under the Ptolemies', in Garnsey, Hopkins and Whittaker (1983), 64–75.

Thompson, E. P. (1971) 'The moral economy of the English crowd in the eighteenth century', *Past and Present* 50: 73–136.

Thompson, L. A. (1982) 'On "Development" and "Underdevelopment" in the early Roman empire', *Klio* 64: 383–402.

Thomsen, R. (1972) *The Origins of Ostracism: A Synthesis*, Copenhagen.

Tilly, L. (1971) 'The food riot as a form of political conflict in France', *Jl Interdisc. Hist.* 2: 23–57.

Toynbee, A. (1965) *Hannibal's Legacy*, 2 vols., London.

Travlos, J. (1960) *The Development of the City of Athens and its Buildings*, Athens.

Travlos, J. and Tsimbides-Pendazos, E. (1973) *Athens Centre of Ekistics* 21: *Attiki*, Athens.

Tucker, W. F. (1981) 'Natural disasters and the peasantry in Mamluk Egypt', *Jl Ec. Soc. Hist. Or.* 24: 215–24.

Vallet, G. (1962) 'L'introduction de l'olivier en Italie centrale d'après les données de la céramique', in *Hommages à Albert Grenier*, III, 1554–63.

Van Andel, Tj. H., Runnels, C. N. and Pope, K. O. (1986) 'Five thousand years of land use and abuse in the southern Argolid, Greece', *Hesperia* 55: 103–28.

Van Dam, R. (1985) *Leadership and Community in Late Antique Gaul*, Berkeley.

Vandier, J. (1936) *La Famine dans l'Egypte ancienne*, Cairo.

Van Zeist, M. and Casparie, W., eds. (1984) *Plants and Ancient Man*, Rotterdam.

Vergote, J. (1959) *Joseph in Egypt: Orientalia et Biblica Lovaniensia*, Louvain.

Veyne, P. (1976) *Le Pain et le cirque*, Paris.

Vial, Cl. (1984) *Délos Indépendante, BCH* Suppl. vol. 10.

Virlouvet, C. (1985) *Famines et émeutes à Rome des origines de la République à la mort de Néron*, Rome.

Vita-Finzi, C. (1969) *The Mediterranean Valleys*, Cambridge.

Wagstaff, J. M. (1981) 'Buried assumptions: some problems in the interpretation of the Younger Fill raised by recent data from Greece', *Jl Arch. Science* 8: 247–64.

Walbank, M. B. (1985) 'Athens, Carthage and Tyre (*IG* II² 342+)', *ZPE* 59: 107–11.

(1987) 'Athens grants citizenship to a benefactor: *IG* II² 398a + 438', *The Ancient History Bulletin* 1: 10–12.

Walker, D. S. (1962) *The Mediterranean Lands*, 2nd edn, London.

Wallace, S. L. (1938) *Taxation in Egypt from Augustus to Diocletian*, Princeton.

Wallace-Hadrill, A. (1982) 'Civilis Princeps: between citizen and king', *JRS* 72: 32–48.

Wallerstein, I. (1974) *The Modern World-system*, I, New York.

(1980) *The Modern World-system*, II, New York.

(1984) 'The quality of life in different social systems: the model and the reality', in Wallerstein, I., ed., *The Politics of the World-economy*, Cambridge, 147–58.

Weitz, D. (1972) 'Famine and plague as factors in the collapse of the Roman Empire in the third century', Ph.D. thesis, Fordham University.

Westermann, W. L. (1925) 'Hadrian's decree on renting state domains in Egypt', *JEA* 11: 165ff.

Westlake, H. D. (1948) 'Athenian food supplies from Euboea', *CR* 62: 2–5.
(1969) *Essays on the Greek Historians and Greek History*, Manchester.
White, K. D. (1970) *Roman Farming*, London.
Whittaker, C. R. (1964) 'The revolt of Papirius Dionysius, A.D. 190', *Historia* 13: 348–69.
(1980) 'Rural labour in three Roman provinces', in Garnsey, P., ed., *Non-slave Labour in the Graeco-Roman World*, Cambridge.
Wightman, E. M. (1978) 'Peasants and potentates: an investigation of social structure and land tenure in Roman Gaul', *AJAH* 3: 43–63.
Wigley, T. M. L. and Farmer, G. (1982) 'Climate of the eastern Mediterranean and the Near East', in Bintliff, J. and Van Zeist, M., eds., *Palaeoclimates, Palaeoenvironments and Human Communities in the Eastern Mediterranean Region in Later Prehistory, BAR* Int. Ser. 133: 3–37.
Wilhelm, Ad. (1932) 'Sitometria', in *Mélanges Glotz*, 899ff., Paris.
Williams, D. A. (1976) 'Were "hunger" rioters really hungry? Some demographic evidence', *Past and Present* 61: 70–5.
Wolf, E. R. (1966) *Peasants*, New Jersey.
Wrigley, E. A. (1969) *Population and History*, London.
(1978) 'A simple model of London's importance in changing English society and economy 1650–1750', in Abrams and Wrigley (1978), 215–43.
Wrigley, E. A. and Schofield, R. (1981) *The Population History of England, 1541–1871: A Reconstruction*, Cambridge, Mass.
Yavetz, Z. (1969) *Plebs and Princeps*, Oxford.
Yeo, C. (1946) 'Land and sea transportation in Imperial Italy', *TAPA* 77: 221–44.
(1952) 'The economics of Roman and American slavery', *Finanzarchiv* 13: 445–85.
Ziebarth, E. (1929) *Beiträge zur Geschichte des Seeraubs und Seehandels im alten Griechenland*, Hamburg.
Ziegler, R. (1977) 'Münzen Kilikiens als Zeugnis kaiserlicher Getreidespenden', *Jahrbuch für Numismatik und Geldgeschichte* 27: 29–67.
(1978) 'Antiochia, Laodicea und Sidon in der Politik der Severer', *Chiron* 8: 493–514.

INDEX

Printed in the United Kingdom
by Lightning Source UK Ltd.
9620600001B